Buying Nature

American and Comparative Environmental Policy
Sheldon Kamieniecki and Michael E. Kraft, series editors

Russell J. Dalton, Paula Garb, Nicholas P. Lovrich, John C. Pierce, and John M. Whiteley, *Critical Masses: Citizens, Nuclear Weapons Production, and Environmental Destruction in the United States and Russia*

Daniel A. Mazmanian and Michael E. Kraft, editors, *Toward Sustainable Communities: Transition and Transformations in Environmental Policy*

Elizabeth R. DeSombre, *Domestic Sources of International Environmental Policy: Industry, Environmentalists, and U.S. Power*

Kate O'Neill, *Waste Trading among Rich Nations: Building a New Theory of Environmental Regulation*

Joachim Blatter and Helen Ingram, editors, *Reflections on Water: New Approaches to Transboundary Conflicts and Cooperation*

Paul F. Steinberg, *Environmental Leadership in Developing Countries: Transnational Relations and Biodiversity Policy in Costa Rica and Bolivia*

Uday Desai, editor, *Environmental Politics and Policy in Industrialized Countries*

Kent Portney, *Taking Sustainable Cities Seriously: Economic Development, the Environment, and Quality of Life in American Cities*

Edward P. Weber, *Bringing Society Back In: Grassroots Ecosystem Management, Accountability, and Sustainable Communities*

Norman J. Vig and Michael G. Faure, eds., *Green Giants? Environmental Policies of the United States and the European Union*

Robert F. Durant, Daniel J. Fiorino, and Rosemary O'Leary, eds., *Environmental Governance Reconsidered: Challenges, Choices, and Opportunities*

Paul A. Sabatier, Will Focht, Mark Lubell, Zev Trachtenberg, Arnold Vedlitz, and Marty Matlock, eds., *Swimming Upstream: Collaborative Approaches to Watershed Management*

Sally K. Fairfax, Lauren Gwin, Mary Ann King, Leigh Raymond, and Laura A. Watt, *Buying Nature: The Limits of Land Acquisition as a Conservation Strategy, 1780–2004*

Buying Nature
The Limits of Land Acquisition as a Conservation Strategy, 1780–2004

Sally K. Fairfax, Lauren Gwin, Mary Ann King, Leigh Raymond, and Laura A. Watt

with assistance from Sarah Connick, James Behan, and Jennifer Wong

The MIT Press
Cambridge, Massachusetts
London, England

MIT Press books may be purchased at special quantity discounts for business or sales promotional use. For information, please email special_sales@mitpress .mit.edu or write to Special Sales Department, The MIT Press, 5 Cambridge Center, Cambridge, MA 02142.

This book was set in Sabon on 3B2 by Asco Typesetters, Hong Kong.
Printed and bound in the United States of America.

Library of Congress Cataloging-in-Publication Data

Buying nature : the limits of land acquisition as a conservation strategy, 1780–2004 / by Sally K. Fairfax ... [et al.].
    p.   cm. — (American and comparative environmental policy)
    ISBN 0-262-06248-8 (alk. paper) — ISBN 0-262-56210-3 (pbk. : alk. paper)
    1. Public lands—United States. 2. Land use—Government policy—United States. 3. Natural areas—Government policy—United States. 4. Land trusts—United States. 5. Nature conservation—United States. I. Fairfax, Sally K. II. Series.
HD216.B89   2005
333.73′16′0973—dc22   2004063261

Printed on recycled paper.

10 9 8 7 6 5 4 3 2 1

This book is dedicated to the memory of Ellen and Bill Straus

Their work has inspired thousands of people to think deeply about combining the gentle management of working landscapes and the production of safe, healthy food. Their lives have taught us what can be done when people work with their neighbors to protect the land they live and depend on. We are so very grateful to both of them.

Contents

Series Foreword

The acquisition of land for conservation purposes is much in vogue of late and has proven to be popular with citizens. At the state and local level, ballot measures for land conservation have been successful even when other environmental policy proposals are mired in controversy. Among leading environmental organizations, no group in recent years has rivaled The Nature Conservancy in membership growth, operating budgets, or financial assets. The conservancy's devotion to land acquisition doubtless has facilitated its success. Even private individuals, such as Ted Turner, have garnered praise from nearly all quarters for their dedication to buying large expanses of land in the United States and abroad and setting aside the acreage for conservation.

The grand scale of land acquisition for conservation, within government and outside of it, inspires both praise and concern. As the authors of this volume make clear, it is not enough to focus only on how much money is spent and how much land has been protected from development. At one level this criticism is profound and correct. As ecologists and astute policymakers have long recognized, money spent and acreage set aside are poor indicators of whether conservation goals can be met. This is especially true for the preservation of critical ecosystem functions that may correlate only weakly with the physical dimensions of land preserves.

In this book, Sally Fairfax, Lauren Gwin, Mary Ann King, Leigh Raymond, and Laura Watt offer a comprehensive and intriguing history of U.S. land acquisition for conservation from 1780 to the present. The wealth of information and historical detail are enough to make it a standard reference in the field of conservation history. Equally important is the authors' thesis about the limits of land acquisition as a conservation strategy. The limitations include its high cost, emphasis on the interests of land sellers, a tendency to obscure public accountability (for example, in the lack of transparency in acquisitions), and uncertainty over who controls the land's uses. Moreover, they say, the current emphasis on private acquisitions of land may lead to diminished interest in or support for public efforts to preserve land.

In short, they argue that private acquisition of land for conservation by land trusts or other means, much like public ownership of land, is not without problems. Both must be understood within the larger context of conservation history and the mosaic of agents, targets, and tools that have shaped conservation policy over time. In particular, the authors challenge the common assumption that buying land for conservation purposes is new, simple, or necessarily the most effective strategy.

The picture they draw of land acquisition reminds us of the complexity that is increasingly recognized in most other areas of environmental policy. Analysts and policymakers have learned to ask pointed questions about what goals are worth pursuing, what the role of government is vis-à-vis the private sector, what capabilities or weaknesses government agencies bring to the table, what policy tools are available, and if used, which of these tools are likely to prove the most effective, efficient, and equitable. As Fairfax and her colleagues note, for land conservation, acquisition may be less important than other tools that can encourage, limit, condition, or prohibit particular land uses without transferring title. Yet even if ownership is not a magic bullet, one still needs to think about when, where, and how acquisition may help to achieve conservation goals, and which policy instruments will work best.

The authors' sweeping and compelling appraisal of the myths, realities, and limits of land acquisition as a policy strategy is an important contribution to knowledge. Among other things, it adds to the budding literature on new governance by describing at length the various ways in which public and private actions to conserve land have come together in often unpredictable ways, shaped by a confluence of internal and external variables. These include the motives of individuals and private groups involved in conservation leadership, the dominant ideas at any time about property rights and land conservation goals, views of the proper roles of federal and state governments, and prevailing economic conditions, among others. The unusual mix of scholarship one finds here, from legal, constitutional, and economic history to rich case studies of land conservation and quantitative analysis of public and private land ownership patterns over time, substantially raises the bar for conservation history.

For all these reasons, the book should appeal to a diverse audience. Those concerned with conserving historic and natural resources will find the authors' analyses provocative and instructive, as will environmentalists and individuals associated with a variety of nongovernmental organizations. Along with public officials involved with conservation of natural resources, they will learn much from this account and will appreciate the well-told stories that are unburdened by academic jargon. Academics in history, political science, law, public administration, environmental studies, and natural resources management will also find much to pique their interest.

The analyses presented in this book illustrate well our purpose in The MIT Press series in American and Comparative Environmental Policy. We encourage work that examines a broad range of environmental policy issues. We are particularly interested in volumes that incorporate interdisciplinary research and focus on the linkages between public policy and environmental problems and issues both within the United States and in cross-national settings. We welcome contributions that analyze the policy dimensions of relationships between humans and the environment from either a theoretical or empirical perspective. At a time when environmental policies are increasingly seen as controversial and new approaches are being implemented widely, we especially encourage studies that assess policy successes and failures, evaluate new institutional arrangements and policy tools, and clarify new directions for environmental politics and policy. The books in this series are written for a wide audience that includes academics, policymakers, environmental scientists and professionals, business and labor leaders, environmental activists, and students concerned with environmental issues. We hope these books contribute to public understanding of environmental problems, issues, and policies of concern today and suggest promising actions for the future.

Sheldon Kamieniecki, University of Southern California Michael Kraft, University of Wisconsin-Green Bay American and Comparative Environmental Policy Series Editors.

Preface

Our colleagues in the land acquisition business frequently discuss their programs in terms of the bucks they have spent and the acres they have acquired. The twenty-first century will require moving beyond those relatively easily assessed metrics and figuring out where acquisition fits among diverse communities and tools for land conservation.

This conclusion will not, most likely, surprise those working on land acquisition because they have been thinking about these issues for some time. In fact, one of the things that has made this study both fun and interesting is the number of deeply reflective practitioners we have encountered. The people we have met are the most important resource in land acquisition, and their dedication, professionalism, and enthusiasm bode well for the future.

We would violate the publisher's page limits if we told readers here all about those who helped us and how much their guidance and friendship have meant. We have harassed many of them, sometimes over a period of a decade or more, to inquire about their organizations, their goals, their work, how they do it, with whom, with what tools and constraints, and with what results. Our gratitude to those who shared their experience is genuine and substantial. We acknowledge many of you in the endnotes, and we thank you all for your knowledge and your generosity. We have made the best use we can of the help you gave us. We believe that in your names readers will find convincing authority for the analysis that follows.

The lengthy list of authors and assistants on the title page also requires some explanation. This project has been no one's dissertation, but a large number of both graduate and undergraduate students have dedicated time and ideas to it during their time in our lab. Sarah Connick and Leigh Raymond worked on different pieces early in their days at Berkeley, and both played an important role in framing the initial analysis. Leigh now teaches his own students at Purdue University but has remained involved to help frame the final conclusions and the volume as a whole. Lauren Gwin joined later, did much of the fieldwork and early editing, and obtained almost all of the numbers. Mary Ann King worked on the Redwoods history, the maps, and the numbers, while Laura Watt worked particularly on National Park Service (NPS) issues. Numerous other students and former students (they never quite leave, which is the best part of teaching) have also helped. Jennifer Wong worked on early wildlife refuges and highlighted equity concerns at the start of our process. Matt Gerhart worked on the Conservation and Reinvestment Act and the Land and Water Conservation Fund. Kata Bartoloni worked with us on the Washington, D.C., material and Gerri Unger did the fieldwork on Cuyahoga Valley National Park.

We are also grateful to the folks who have helped Mary Ann with maps and charts—most notably Ruskin Hartley of the Save-the-Redwoods League; Aida Parkinson, Redwood National and State Parks; Henry Savarie and Sunita Halasz of the Adirondack Park Agency; Tammy Stidham, NPS National Capital Region; John Creaser of the University of California-Berkeley (UCB) Earth Science and Map Library; Kathy Harrison of the NPS at Gettysburg; Ken Crevier of the White Mountain National Forest; and Cindi Wolff, UCB federal documents librarian. Mike Garon took all the documents we collected and made them into printable maps, sometimes creating them out of almost thin air. Because maps and mosaics are so important to our thinking, we have been happy to have so much help.

Finally, we pay special tribute to those who read our large first draft and many thereafter. Helen Ingram (University of California-Irvine), has read and made enormous improvements in almost everything I have ever written. She plowed through this manuscript several times in its entirety, and for some parts many more times than that. Jim Snow (Office of General Counsel, U.S. Department of Agriculture) has also read and corrected many versions. Peter Berck, Jen Sokolove, and Betty Deakin (University of California-Berkeley); Susan Schrepfer (Rutgers University);

Craig Thomas (University of Massachusetts, Amherst); Randal O'Toole (The Thoreau Institute); Barton Thompson (Stanford Law); Bruce Yandall (Clemson University); and Samuel P. Hays (emeritus, University of Pittsburgh) have also read and commented generously, as did three anonymous reviewers for MIT Press.

Jean Hocker (president-emeritus, Land Trust Alliance), Russ Shay (Land Trust Alliance policy director), Karen Marchetti (Maine Coastal Heritage Trust), Gil Livingston (Vermont Land Trust), Jane Difley and Paul Doscher (Society for the Protection of New Hampshire Forests), Peter Kareiva (The Nature Conservancy), Wesley Ward and Peg Wheeler (The Trustees), Mike Clark (Yellowstone Heritage Trust), and Michael Blaney (NPS, Acadia National Park) have also read and commented, read and commented, and read and commented.

It is not easy to give an author, let alone five of them, useful guidance. Critics have to read closely, think hard, and write very carefully. We thank those who worked so diligently on this project. We have listed five authors, but we could easily have added many more who have helped and encouraged us along the way.

List of Acronyms

AAA	Agricultural Adjustment Act
ADK	Adirondack Mountain Club
AFT	American Farmland Trust
AMC	Appalachian Mountain Club
ANC	Adirondack Nature Conservancy
AON	Assessment of Need
APA	Adirondack Park Agency
BLFT	Black Family Land Trust
BBS	Bureau of Biological Survey
BLM	Bureau of Land Management
BRP	Blue Ridge Parkway
CARA	Conservation and Reinvestment Act
CCC	Civilian Conservation Corps
CLT	Community Land Trust
CRP	Conservation Reserve Program
CTNC	Conservation Trust for North Carolina
CVCC	Cuyahoga Valley Countryside Conservancy
CVNP	Cuyahoga Valley National Park
DOI	Department of the Interior
DU	Ducks Unlimited
EIS	Environmental Impact Statement
ESA	Endangered Species Act
FACA	Federal Advisory Committee Act

FLEFA	Federal Land Exchange Facilitation Act
FLP	Forest Legacy Program
FLPMA	Federal Land Policy and Management Act
FLTFA	Federal Land Transaction Facilitation Act
FNPG	Friends of The National Park at Gettysburg
FSA	Farm Services Agency
FTA	Fort Ticonderoga Association
FWS	Fish and Wildlife Service
GAO	General Accounting Office
GATT	General Agreement on Tariffs and Trade
GBPA	Gettysburg Battlefield Preservation Association
GLO	General Land Office
GSA	General Services Administration
HCP	Habitat Conservation Plan
IRS	Internal Revenue Service
JNEM	Jefferson National Expansion Memorial
League	Save-the-Redwoods League
LTA	Land Trust Alliance
LTE	Land Trust Exchange
LPP	Land Protection Plan (NPS)
LWCF	Land and Water Conservation Fund
MACLT	Madison Area Community Land Trust
MBCA	Migratory Bird Conservation Act/Norbeck-Andersen Act (1929)
MBCC	Migratory Bird Conservation Commission
MBTA	Migratory Bird Treaty Act (1918)
MDFWP	Montana Department of Fish, Wildlife and Parks
MLR	Montana Land Reliance
MVLA	Mount Vernon Ladies' Association
NAFTA	North American Free Trade Agreement
NCCUSL	National Conference of Commissioners on Uniform State Laws

NEFF	New England Forestry Foundation
NEPA	National Environmental Policy Act
NFA	Northern Forest Alliance
NFLC	Northern Forest Land Council
NFRC	National Forest Reservation Commission
NIRA	National Industrial Recovery Act
NPCA	National Parks and Conservation Association
NPS	National Park Service
NRDC	Natural Resources Defense Council
NWR	National Wildlife Refuge
OMB	Office of Management and Budget
ORRRC	Outdoor Recreation Resources Review Commission
PILTs	Payments in Lieu of Taxes
PWA	Public Works Administration
PFW	Partners for Wildlife (now Partners for Fish and Wildlife)
SCORP	Statewide Comprehensive Outdoor Recreation Plan
SCS	Soil Conservation Service
SNPLMA	Southern Nevada Public Land Management Act
SPNHF	Society for the Protection of New Hampshire Forests
TCF	The Conservation Fund
TFG	The Forestland Group
TGA	Taylor Grazing Act
TLCT	The Land Conservation Trust
TNC	The Nature Conservancy
TPL	Trust for Public Land
TTOR/The Trustees	The Trustees of (Public) Reservations
TU	Trout Unlimited
UCEA	Uniform Conservation Easement Act
USDA	United States Department of Agriculture

USFS	United States Forest Service
VANR	Vermont Agency of Natural Resources
VLT	Vermont Land Trust
VOF	Virginia Outdoors Foundation
WMNF	White Mountain National Forest
WMA	Wildlife Management Area
WPA	Waterfowl Production Area
WRP	Wetlands Reserve Program
WSSC	Washington Suburban Sanitary Commission
WTO	World Trade Organization
WVLT	Western Virginia Land Trust

While we could still say nothing but "Please" to private forest owners, on the national Forest Reserves we could say, and we did say, "Do this," and "Don't do that." We had the power . . .

—Gifford Pinchot, *Breaking New Ground*

When the private landowner is asked to perform some unprofitable act for the good of the community, he today only assents with outstretched palm.

—Aldo Leopold, *A Sand County Almanac*

1
Acquisition Myths and Realities

Conserving Mount Vernon and the Myths of Land Acquisition

Since before the Civil War, George Washington's estate at Mount Vernon has been conserved by a group of well-connected women. With the purchase of Mount Vernon, they started the first private national conservation organization in the United States. How could this be? How could a government that acquires a parking lot full of old Canadian trains and the Eugene O'Neill National Historic Site (O'Toole 1995) not be responsible for the home of its founding father?

The answer is not simple—indeed, this book has been inspired by this apparent oddity of American conservation history. The more one looks at the history of land acquisition for conservation in the United States, the more one realizes that the story of Mount Vernon's preservation is not an exception; it is in many ways a microcosm of what has happened in acquisition of land for conservation over the past 150 years. Thus, we see no better way to introduce this volume than with an account of our first president's estate.

When George Washington's heir fell on hard times, he tried to sell Mount Vernon to the state of Virginia or the federal government as a memorial to the former president. Both turned him down. It was not clear in the 1840s that the federal government was authorized to acquire land to conserve it, and the state legislators did not want to buy the estate without assurances that Congress would reimburse them. So, Ann Pamela Cunningham, a well-to-do South Carolinian, created the Mount Vernon Ladies' Association of the Union (MVLA). The state played a key role; the MVLA borrowed money from Virginia to buy the property in 1856. The organization charged visitors a small fee to repay the loan and continues to do so to maintain and restore the property.

Over time the story became far more complex. By World War I, assumptions about what the federal government could and should do about land and conservation had expanded, and many came to believe that the federal government ought to own the nationally important site. Proposals for a federal takeover of Mount Vernon were almost constantly before Congress. Then in the 1930s the National Park Service (NPS) completed the George Washington Parkway, which ended almost literally at Mount Vernon's doorsill. Why should one drive for free over a $4.5 million federal parkway, many then asked, and have to pay to enter the first president's home? The MVLA successfully deployed its powerful allies and held its ground, noting that 25 cents was a small price to pay to support the upkeep of the site.

Having staved off a federal takeover, the MVLA was soon faced with the new challenge of urban development. After World War II, oil tanks, a golf course, and then a sewage treatment plant were all proposed for construction directly across the river from Mount Vernon's veranda. Preserving the view as well as the house and grounds had become an important goal, and the MVLA transformed itself into the core of a still-growing mosaic of organizations and tools to achieve new conservation priorities.

The Mount Vernon story raises some large issues. It suggests a wide range of public and private actors involved in acquisition policy as well as continuous jostling for influence between and among them. It also allows us to recognize the expanding objectives of acquisition policy over time and the expanding toolkit for accomplishing those acquisitions. Even a brief overview reveals a central theme of this book: the growing complexity of land acquisition for conservation efforts.

Finally, the account of the MVLA and Mount Vernon helps us see not only the successes but also the limits of acquisition as a conservation strategy. Describing these limits in more detail, as well as exploring ways to move beyond them, is another major goal of this volume.

It is important to realize that many of these issues challenge the conventional wisdom regarding acquisition of land as a conservation option.

The story of the MVLA questions what we have found to be ubiquitous assumptions: that buying land for conservation is a new, simple, or particularly effective approach to protecting resources. It is certainly not new; the MVLA began operations in 1853. Nor is it simple. After paying off its initial loan, the MVLA had to protect itself and the property from both sides during the Civil War, and from an intensifying array of threats thereafter. Thus acquisition by itself was not effective in securing the future of Washington's home and its setting.

In fact, the history of acquisition policy is a complicated, important, and lengthy one, and the purpose of this book is to present it with the care and detail it deserves. Unfortunately, many specifics of that history, and many reasonable and important policy issues, are obscured by nearly theological debates over the pros and cons of private as opposed to public ownership of land. Those distinctions are further clouded by two narratives that shape conservation history: a "shift to retention" on public lands in the 1890s and a "shift to privatization" in the late twentieth century. Both are problematic.

The "Shift to Retention"

Most histories of public land policy are presented as three-act plays: acquisition of the public domain by the federal government, disposition to private owners, and finally retention for federal management (Clawson and Held 1957: 16–35). In this drama, the turning point came when the federal government sagely decided to retain the remaining public domain in federal ownership. In fact, the three-part story of early public land policy is deeply misleading, especially regarding the wide range of federal control that remains over nominally retained public land (Raymond and Fairfax 1999).

Many of the histories embracing this view concentrate on the glorious saga of a single agency and are shaped to meet its political needs. Consequently, they are not always reliable.[1] Most familiarly, when we repeatedly encounter an uplifting tale about the national park "idea" springing to life around a campfire in Yellowstone, we tend to believe it; yet the story is mostly a fabrication.[2]

By accepting the "shift to retention" story, we lose the ability to see the gradual emergence of new ideas about government, property rights, and publicly owned land, or to grasp the slow evolution of distinctions among national parks, memorials, forests, and grazing districts (Muir 1909: 39). We also muddy a second vital point: public acquisition of private land began in 1790 and continues to the present day. While sagas of the battle to save this or that particular site abound (Campbell 1960; Righter 1982; Pollock 1960), we find no analysis that comprehensively addresses acquisition of land for conservation.

Approximately 9 percent of the land at present owned by the federal government for conservation purposes has been acquired from private owners, as figure 1.1 illustrates. Moreover, state, local, and private acquisitions for conservation are literally too numerous and dispersed to be counted accurately. The "shift to retention" version of events is seriously flawed. Our understanding of conservation policy needs to include a serious discussion of land acquisition.

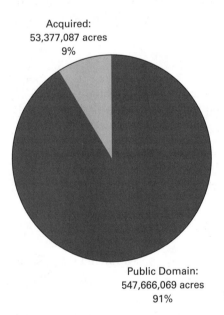

Acquired:
53,377,087 acres
9%

Public Domain:
547,666,069 acres
91%

Figure 1.1
Percent of acquired and public domain land: U.S. Forest Service, National Park Service, Fish and Wildlife Service, and Bureau of Land Management combined. Source: U.S. GSA (2002).

The "Shift to Privatization"

The more recently evolved idea about a "shift to privatization," i.e., that land trusts and other private acquisition efforts are a dominating, late twentieth-century innovation (Brewer 2003), is a parallel myth—less embedded in the literature but an important part of the current narrative nonetheless (Raymond and Fairfax 2002). Private efforts at land acquisition and conservation are neither new nor are they consistently private. Private actors have played a vital role in acquisition and conservation efforts for more than 180 years. Over that time, their influence relative to the public sector has waxed and waned. While it is true that market-based instruments are an important part of early twenty-first century policy (Raymond 2003), the magnitude and clarity of this trend is often overstated (Raymond and Fairfax 2002).

Both shift ideas allow a kernel of truth to obscure critical aspects of land acquisition policy. The current debate over private versus public ownership of land, the changing configuration of acquisition institutions, and the current enthusiasm for land trusts and easements all suggest a need to explore how public, private, and partnered acquisition efforts have coexisted over time. More than 200 years into the process, we believe an assessment of land acquisition as a conservation strategy is overdue.

Our Story: Evolving Mosaics on the Land

The account of the MVLA's efforts suggests that the evolution of acquiring land for conservation is a tale of growing complexity rather than simple shifts. In this book we will talk about mosaics of conserved land: combinations of different agents, targets, and tools of acquisition. Partnerships of public and private actors are revealed early on as a constant element of land conservation. Mosaics are a sign of further complexity—different types of land purchased by different acquirers, under varying terms and conditions, and managed to meet very different goals. The accounts we give are accompanied by maps at different scales. These mosaics illustrate the complexity of both the acquisition and the management of conserved land.

Mosaics have been becoming more and more intricate over time. The first mosaics consisted simply of mixed ownerships and began in the late 1820s when Congress started granting alternating sections of land to states and corporations to encourage the construction of roads, canals, and railroads. Congress retained the intervening sections to sell at double the minimum price. The first mosaics of public and private land, called checkerboards, occurred where both the government and the grantees held onto their parcels (Gates 1968: 343).

We focus on policies reflecting a durable notion in the United States: to truly protect land, you need to own it. By "acquisition for conservation," we mean the purchase of real estate, or partial title to real estate, such as easements, for conservation purposes. We are not concerned with acquisition of land for amusement parks, highways, urban renewal, or similar purposes, nor do we focus, except in passing, on regulation or conservation strategies other than acquisition. We will of necessity spend some time discussing reservation of public domain lands that the federal government already owned. While they were not acquisitions, public domain reservations both reflected and shaped the expectations and the government authority over land that are central to this analysis.

The primary *agents of acquisition* have changed steadily over time, as the MVLA story makes evident. In answering the question of "who acquires?" we describe an intricate dance among diverse private and public actors. We treat federal, state, and local governments as public actors, and philanthropists, for-profit corporations, and nonprofits—including foundations, conservation organizations, and land trusts—as private actors. The variety matters: acquisition of land for conservation has always been a mixture of both public and private efforts. However, the relative influence of various parties waxes and wanes, with the federal role peaking in the early twentieth century and the private sector gaining greater influence of late. Throughout these general trends, the partners continue to argue and change positions in terms of who leads and who follows.

Targets of acquisition, or answers to the question of what land is acquired, have also evolved as our sense of which resources are important, threatened, or scarce has changed. Early acquisition programs, both public and private, emphasized nation building and civic pride in historic and spectacular natural sites (Runte 1984: 19). A few decades later, concerns about fire, floods, and destructive logging practices led to state and federal purchases of extensive timberlands in the eastern United States. The Depression emphasized federal acquisition for economic recovery through the purchase of submarginal lands. The post-World War II economic boom, suburban expansion, and civil unrest in the cities aroused some quite ancient and elite private groups from their slumber and focused attention on eastern and urban properties for outdoor recreation. In the 1980s, growing concern for wetlands, species habitat, and other ecologically important areas directed conservation efforts toward larger landscapes, including mixes of public and private lands that contained those resources.

Finally, as land conservation goals and institutions have grown more complex, the *tools of acquisition* have followed suit. At first the states, rather than the federal government, were viewed as having general authority to conserve land. States undertook many of the first large-scale conservation acquisitions, including the Adirondacks and the Pacific Coast redwoods, with support and encouragement from private conservation interests. The federal government initially relied upon the Constitution's war powers and the enclave clause for limited acquisitions of oak forests for naval purposes. Over time, however, federal authority expanded to include a broader range of acquisition powers and tools, including eminent domain, for a wide variety of conservation purposes that included watershed protection, wildlife management, and even public recreation.

Easements and other partial interests in land also gradually gained acceptance. Municipalities first used easements as early as the 1890s. Partial interests in real property became more familiar during the Depression. Many national wildlife refuges were acquired entirely by easements, while split estates became a common way to divide control over mineral versus surface rights on many ostensibly private parcels (Williams 1962). However, common law support for an open market in property confounded the ability of private organizations to acquire and hold such partial interests for conservation purposes. Making easements available as a tool of private conservation was a major political project of the early land trust movement, coming to fruition in Internal Revenue

Service (IRS) decisions of the 1980s that provided confidence that donated easements were tax-deductible charitable contributions.

Of course, these tools remain unevenly distributed and utilized. States continue to exercise unique and important influence over acquisitions within their borders. Meanwhile, private acquirers still lack certain acquisition options held by government institutions, most notably the power of eminent domain. Moreover, the federal agencies approach the same acquisition tasks very differently. The U.S. Forest Service (USFS), for instance, has always been more tolerant of inholdings, private property within the established boundaries of units, than the NPS, which early on viewed human habitation as a threat to scenic values that should be removed.[3] These ideas and the corresponding use of various tools have also evolved, with more recent NPS efforts to protect cultural landscapes frequently including local residents as essential partners.

We will conclude that acquisition is not a simple solution to conservation issues. It has become ever more complex. Multiple agents now own partial interests in a single parcel of land for a wide variety of purposes that are often in conflict. The result, at Mount Vernon and in many other settings, is an interlocking network of policies and actors that defies easy categorization. Neither regulatory nor market based, neither public nor private, the result is best described as an emerging mosaic of claims on the land.

The term *mosaic* is not entirely new in the literature on public policy. The idea appears occasionally in the new governance literature, for instance, which studies the devolution of political authority from federal to state, local, and private actors (Kettl 1988; Milward and Provan 2000; Salamon 1989, 2002). Occasionally authors speak of mosaics of policy tools to describe a diversifying array of approaches, typically to social policy since World War II (Salamon 2002: 3). We go a step further, however, by discussing not only mosaics and diversity of tools but also the resulting mosaics of control that are inscribed on the ground, giving the language of new governance a specifically spatial expression. The coalition of actors and tools protecting an expanding range of resources around Mount Vernon is a mosaic of conservation authorities and efforts that would likely astound Ann Pamela Cunningham.

Why Mosaics? Forces of Change on the Land

Why this paradoxical result? Why have efforts to simplify conservation through acquisition actually increased complexity on the land and in the courthouse? We begin with the standard postmodern disclaimer that in one sense every case is unique—the mosaic that has emerged at Mount Vernon is a product of different forces than those operating in the equally complex landscape of Cuyahoga Valley National Park (CVNP). We have identified four factors that explain many, if not all, of the mosaics we see emerging.

The first is a *changing philosophy of governance* and the proper locus of political power. Initially, a weak central government left room for state and private actors to play a leading role in acquisition policy. The emergence in the late nineteenth and early twentieth centuries of a Progressive era belief in strong federal government and bureaucracy was therefore crucial. A gradual expansion of federal acquisition programs began in the late nineteenth century and peaked during the Depression. The subsequent devolution of political authority back to state, local, and private institutions in the late twentieth century is reflected in the federal agencies' current dependence on private land acquisition groups. Evolving ideologies about the proper distribution of political power have an important role in shaping the mosaics we describe.

The story is more complex, however, than the rise and fall of the federal government as the primary acquirer of conservation land. At no time, we emphasize, have these changing views of governance allowed federal agencies to "crowd out" private acquisition efforts; even many Depression-era acquisitions relied heavily on private donations. Instead, we see a growing integration and blurring of boundaries between the traditional roles of public and private actors in this field.

Second, mosaics are created in part by *changing conservation goals*. The late nineteenth-century development of two clear strands in conservation philosophy—one oriented toward use and the other toward preservation—made previously unimaginable acquisitions plausible. In addition to the retention of public lands for tourism, resource management, and protection as scenic wonders, pressure from conservationists expanded this agenda to include acquiring private lands for similar goals. First the Depression and later the concerns of the modern environmental movement further reshaped the acquisition agenda to serve new recreation and ecological goals. Ann Pamela Cunningham aimed to save a portion of Washington's home and estate as he experienced them. It did not occur to her that the viewshed and surrounding environment would need protection as well. A hundred years later, new environmental values and the threat of economic development made such protection seem vital.

These changes in environmental values are less important in driving acquisition policy than our third factor: *changing economic conditions.* A standard hypothesis in environmental policy studies suggests that conservation efforts increase with economic development; poor families or countries are less interested in resource conservation than more developed or prosperous ones (Raymond 2004; Grossman and Krueger 1995). Hence, one might think that more land would be acquired for conservation at times when government and private donors have more money. Our analysis suggests that the relationship between wealth and acquisition of land for conservation frequently runs in the other direction. Although most acquisition stories emphasize conservation goals and "victories" for the buyers, our research suggests that the sellers' priorities are more often controlling. When landowners need to unload property in bad economic times, government-subsidized acquisition becomes the solution to an impressive array of problems. In more prosperous times, by contrast, owners unwilling to part with their land have supported other tools that lower the costs of ownership while restricting development.

Finally, *changing ideas about property* are vital to the mosaic of tools for land acquisition. A continuous reinterpretation of property has resulted in complex ownership ideas and in increasingly fragmented and intricate arrangements among public and private actors in conservation acquisition. For example, the weakening of private property rights after the Civil War enabled greater participation by public institutions in acquiring land for conservation. At the same time, growing complexity in the form and function of ownership—symbolized by the new metaphor of property as a "bundle of sticks"—was crucial to the emergence of the easement as an acquisition tool. The metaphor also undermined the traditional identity between ownership and control over land, thereby making mosaics of competing and connected claims increasingly the norm on both public and private property. More recently, a resurgence of traditional views of ownership has helped support the modern land trust movement and the opposing private property rights movement, while further increasing the complexity of the ownership tools and resulting mosaics we see on the ground.

Why Mosaics Matter: The Limits of Acquisition

The fragmenting and multiplying agents, targets, and tools of acquisition are not just of theoretical interest; they hold important implications for land acquisition as a conservation strategy. In particular, the mosaics we described earlier are crucial to another major task of this volume: describing and outlining *the limits of acquisition* as a conservation strategy.

We do not want to be misinterpreted; we are not opposed to acquisition of land for conservation. We focus here on the limits of acquisition, primarily because the topic is so little considered. While many authors have described acquisition as a dramatic improvement on other conservation options (Brewer 2003), few have ruminated at length on the limits and shortcomings of the approach. Given the growing popularity of the idea, we think it high time to think seriously, not only about when acquisition seems to be effective, but also about when it does not. Four specific problems with acquisition as a conservation strategy are revealed in our discussion of emerging mosaics.

Acquisition Is Costly
Acquisition is not cheap. Acquisitions like the Headwaters Forest in California emphatically demonstrate that we will never be able to afford to buy all the land we want to conserve. While we have moved beyond the "not one cent for scenery" attitude of the early twentieth-century Congress (Pratt 1936: 1029), funds for conservation acquisitions remain scarce compared with the lands identified as acquisition priorities (Newburn 2002: 146).

The high cost of conservation acquisitions also raises some important equity concerns. Some deals are rightly criticized for overcompensating sellers for low-value land, or for reducing the ownership burdens for wealthy owners of large, scenic parcels while failing to provide adequate public benefits. This is a particular concern when conservation easements on private land do not include recreation access that has long accompanied most public acquisitions.

More generally, we fear that we are sometimes paying private owners too high a price to do what they should do (and might already be planning to do anyway) with their land. This is a well-hidden cost of acquisition as a conservation strategy because it strengthens a view of private property that grants owners rights to develop their land so intensely that they damage their own property and the surrounding parcels. While this view of ownership has never been controlling, every time we buy land to protect it, we reinforce those expectations of private owners and make regulation that much harder the next time around.

Acquisition Emphasizes the Needs of Sellers

Not only is acquisition of land expensive, it is also historically controlled by the priorities of sellers rather than those of buyers. Very little acquisition for conservation is conducted via eminent domain or other forms of involuntary purchase. Rather, the basic pattern has been that sellers determine what land gets acquired, when it gets acquired, and under what terms. This has critical implications for acquisition as a conservation strategy.

Most obviously, reliance on willing sellers creates a potential mismatch between conservation priorities and actual transactions. The parcels most desirable for conservation are frequently those that landowners are least willing to part with. A "willing seller" approach restricts our ability to allocate scarce conservation dollars to the most desirable ends.

Furthermore, although we are skeptical that federal ownership is always the preferred conservation option, we are struck by the way in which public acquisitions are hogtied in the very contexts where they would be most useful. A reliance on willing sellers can create a monopoly power for certain landowners, such as those with inholdings in wilderness areas, which makes a voluntary transaction difficult and costly for the public. In the extreme, such situations create the potential for "green-mail" in which the private owner threatens to develop his or her property to the hilt (ruining the surrounding wilderness) unless paid an outlandish sum by the government to give up the parcel (Simon et al. 1998). Yet involuntary purchases through condemnation and eminent domain are frequently banned either in law or practice in just these settings. Through its deference to willing sellers, the federal government disarms its unique ability to play a more strategic and constructive role in the acquisition for conservation process.

Nevertheless, we do observe an important qualification to the limits imposed by a reliance on willing sellers. The various beat-up, cut-over, and submarginal lands that were acquired with almost no thought to their resource values during the Depression, for example, are now cherished elements of both the nation's ecological heritage and its sense of identity. Perhaps we were lucky in our earlier purchases and stumbled on parcels with critical environmental values. Or perhaps *any* land acquired today for conservation will be seen as important in another 50 to 100 years.

Acquisition Obscures Public Accountability

Never sharp to begin with, the line between public and private has been blurred considerably in modern conservation transactions. Current government agencies rely heavily on private actors such as land trusts as go-betweens and intermediaries in many acquisitions. Meanwhile, ostensibly private transactions between nongovernmental actors rely on critical public subsidies in the form of tax breaks and other policy incentives. The mosaics of ownership, management, and control that we see on the land reflect similar mixtures of public and private actors participating in conservation transactions.

As constructed at present, this intermingling of public and private authority in land acquisition threatens standard mechanisms of public accountability. Although they are supported by public funds and work closely with public agencies, land trusts frequently promote their activities as private, voluntary transactions. Economists sometimes discuss land trusts in terms of reducing the transaction costs of private acquisitions, making it easier for private citizens to organize and protect views and resources, on their neighbors' land. These "private" transactions, however, usually rely on public financial support and often occur at the specific request of public agencies.

Thus the issue of public accountability is important even in the context of land trust actions. While they lower transaction costs, nominally private transactions may be raising the cost of information too high. Modern land acquisitions are only loosely embedded in traditional electoral mechanisms. We are taught in high school civics that in some remote way, if you do not like a public policy, you can change it by voting for somebody else, or you can "sue the bastards" that are violating the law. This specific accountability to the public has always been indirect (Key 1968). However, encouraging hundreds of private organizations to use public money and authority to acquire and manage land, thereby lengthening the "implementation chain" (Posner 2002), complicates accountability enormously.

In addition, sharing government funds and authority with proliferating nonprofits risks further excluding those who most need greater access to both environmental amenities and political involvement. Here the problem is more one of willing buyers than willing sellers. If we rely on private groups to buy land for conservation, then, not surprisingly, those purchases will reflect the desires of those with wealth to spare. In practice, this factor has substantially limited the range of landscapes protected by land trusts, to the detriment of less wealthy citizens who are often concentrated in urban and minority communities.

The problem is not whether the transaction is public or private per se, but rather, the current lack of transparency in land acquisitions of all stripes. Whatever the ailments of federal land management, at least you can find out what resource agencies are up to by reading the *Federal Register* over your morning coffee. Even something as minimal as a notice and comment period, however, is not standard for private acquisitions. Indeed, the relative secrecy of the transaction may be a key point of appeal for the seller. The transparency issue extends beyond the process of acquisition as well. In a world of mosaics, it is no simple task for an outside observer to find basic information about existing easements in a community (Guenzler and Douthit 2002). Nor is it easy to track down the multiple and diverse private groups playing a key role in land management today. Thus, our accountability questions concern the ease of public access and involvement, regardless of whether the transaction is presented as public or private.

It is of some comfort to realize that these issues are not peculiar to land acquisition—the dispersion and devolution of government programs (Fairfax and Guenzler 2001, chap. 1) imply a need to broaden our understanding of public accountability in general (Feldman and Khademian 2001, 2002). When long implementation chains involve diverse public and private actors, it is even more important to be clear about who is accountable to whom, and for what.

Ironically, while political scientists are discussing these devolved and dispersed tools of third-party government, free-market economists are looking at land acquisition trends through the other end of the telescope. They argue that public acquisition efforts are so pervasive that they threaten to discourage private initiatives (Thompson 2002–2003: 251).

Our data squarely address this issue and do not support the assertion. In fact, we raise the opposite concern: that private acquisitions may be crowding out important public efforts at protecting land by deluding us in too many cases into thinking that private, market-driven approaches to the problem will do the job effectively. While they are important, private efforts have serious limitations in terms of acquisition tools and targets that are sometimes overlooked.

Acquisition Is No Guarantee of Control

It is easy to assume that in the United States, ownership of property conveys effective control over a parcel, but this is frequently not the case. Accordingly, we emphasize that contrary to expectations, ownership may not produce sufficient control over a parcel to protect or conserve it.

The disjuncture between ownership and control can be attributed partially to the legal fragmentation of ownership rights in the nineteenth century, when property evolved from a unilateral and exclusive power over a material item to a more malleable and divisible set of specific rights. Prior to the Civil War, property in the United States was generally viewed in terms discussed by John Locke. In Locke's work, labor provides the justification for these powers of ownership, creating a "natural" right that must be respected by legitimate government actions at all costs (Locke 1689/1960). In its first century, the U.S. government attempted (often with little success) to create an agrarian democracy of small, self-sufficient property owners in this Lockean tradition (Scott 1977; Opie 1987). Control over private property was concentrated in the owner; government regulation of private property, while not unheard of, remained relatively limited (Treanor 1995).

After the Civil War, America's strong commitment to the Lockean view of ownership weakened, and our concept of property fragmented. The familiar "bundle of sticks" metaphor emerged, allowing society to treat rights of ownership as easily severable. The right to develop one's property was one stick, while the rights to transfer or to exclude were distinct and separable. This metaphor facilitated exchange and transfer of various rights of ownership among different actors. Where owners had previously exercised near total dominion over their property, now one might hold the right to revenue, say, but not to control day-to-day use of the property.

This legal separation of specific ownership rights is critical to our analysis. The idea of conservation easements would be impossible under the older, more unified theory of property. Under the new vision, an easement represents the acquisition of just another stick in the bundle: the right to develop one's property.

Since the Progressive era, in terms of separating ownership from control, increasingly savvy states, local communities, and private actors have relied implicitly on the new vision of property to obtain the various sticks they desired (privileged access and use, revenue via taxation, limits on transfer, etc.) while frequently leaving the federal government with formal title but little else.

More generally, the legal separation of ownership from control relies on a vision of property as a socially constructed institution. Property rules require near-universal support to work effectively. In other words, a widespread reluctance to accept certain duties imposed by a property claim puts that right of ownership at serious risk. Property rights also impose significant burdens on others, thus presenting a substantial social cost.

Legal scholar Carol Rose has noted the need for persuasion in asserting successful ownership claims:

It is not enough, then, for the property claimant to say simply, "It's mine," through some act or gesture; in order for the statement to have any force, some relevant world must understand the claim it makes and take that claim seriously. (Rose 1994: 18)

What makes a claim persuasive varies. In the United States, evidence of productive use is often a convincing claim to resource ownership. In other settings, simple possession is adequate. However, sometimes asserted ownership claims, including those formally backed by the law, remain unconvincing to many. If such property claims are not persuasive, the legal owner's control over her property is weakened. Thus, ownership is a poor method for gaining control over a parcel of land in the absence of general community recognition of the legitimacy of the property claim.

In our story, unpersuasive land ownership claims are common. The federal government has frequently failed to protect its timber from trespassers who do not view themselves as such. More recently, land trusts face a similar problem regarding the persuasiveness of conservation easements. As parcels under easement change hands, subsequent owners may not feel a commitment to restrictions on the development of land sold or donated by a previous owner. What is essential in either context, according to Rose, is that the easement holder speak and "*keep on speaking*," communicating her property claim to the surrounding world (Rose 1994: 14). What such speech looks like can vary tremendously; fences are a persuasive reminder in some cases, while in others, clear indications of continued use or monitoring of easement compliance may be adequate.

The need to be persuasive in making ownership claims raises the related issue of audience; to whom must the claim be convincing? In most instances, local residents and communities are vital. When neighbors and local residents are not persuaded, enforcement of any sort of ownership claim becomes difficult.

This has an important implication for land trusts. While trusts may work hard to monitor and enforce their rights, they can only do so successfully with community support. Without it, the land trust is stuck trying to enforce unpopular or unacknowledged easements and ownership claims in a hostile or indifferent environment. The result may not be immediate losses, but it will surely diminish the effectiveness of the land trust and its tools. With community support, land trust easements will be more persuasive and far easier to enforce over long periods of time as required. In this book, we will repeatedly point out the importance of persuasiveness in property claims, noting the separation of legal ownership and effective control of land that unpersuasive claims imply.

In sum, ownership no longer represents the ultimate mechanism for control over the use or protection of a parcel of land. To view it as such, as some advocates on all sides of the acquisition debate tend to do, is a serious mistake that ignores one of the key limits of acquisition as a conservation strategy.

A Road Map to Our Analysis

We discuss land acquisition using macro, micro, qualitative, and quantitative evidence. A broad sweep of constitutional, economic, administrative, and to some extent philosophical history provides the macro-scale backbone of our narrative. The first two chapters (including this one) are introductory. Chapter 2 describes the era up to the Civil War, a period when government and private institutions engaged in limited conservation acquisitions for limited purposes, yet established important patterns that have carried through to the present day.

Chapters 3 through 5 describe pivotal early state and private acquisition programs while tracing the gradual emergence of federal authority to acquire and manage land. Chapter 3 documents changes in governance, property, and conservation goals through the Progressive era. New York State's protection of the Adirondacks set the pattern, but the chapter culminates with the passage of the first major federal acquisition statute for conservation, the Weeks Act in 1911. Chapter 4 explores the years between the Weeks Act and the Depression, when federal agencies solidified and became powerful actors in land acquisition. Thus, statutory and administrative arrangements became the focus of debate, and state and private programs were increasingly shaped by federal initiatives. Finally, chapter 5 examines the Depression, a boom time for federal acquisition of land (although many transactions were funded by states and private philanthropists). Submarginal lands devastated by drought were the focus of this era, as financially strapped landowners dumped cut-over and beat-up land on the federal government in the name of conservation.

Chapters 6 through 8 document a gradual and inconsistent weakening of federal acquisition efforts and a reemergence of state and private leadership. Chapter 6 opens with the economic boom of the 1950s, which brought an enormous emphasis on outdoor recreation, natural beauty, and eventually urban and eastern "parks for the people." Ironically, even as federal acquisition peaked with the passage of the Land and Water Conservation Fund (LWCF) Act in 1964, the Progressive era approach began to falter. By the 1980s, discussed in chapter 7, environmental advocacy shifted more to private lands, focusing on ecosystems, wildlife habitat, and working landscapes. President Reagan's first secretary of the interior, James Watt, tried unsuccessfully to halt federal acquisition of land just as the IRS began to experiment with tax deductions for donations of partial interests in land for conservation, and land trusts flourished in the altered political environment. Chapter 8 then moves to the present day by describing how the Farm Bill has replaced the LWCF as a primary source of acquisition funds. When the federal government shut down in 1996 owing to an ostensible lack of funds, land trusts brokered larger and ever more complex transactions. Finally, chapter 9 concludes by revisiting our major arguments and findings in light of the many details presented.

Our micro perspective illustrates this larger history throughout by revisiting case studies of public and private acquisitions. In particular, we return frequently to six sites: Mount Vernon in Virginia, Fort Ticonderoga in New York, Gettysburg Battlefield in Pennsylvania, the Blue Ridge Parkway in Virginia and North Carolina, Redwood National and State Parks in California, and Cuyahoga Valley National Park in Ohio. All are important examples of acquisition for conservation, and each provides unique and distinctive insights into the themes of this book.

We have already introduced the MVLA as a synecdoche of our larger project. Fort Ticonderoga is an old and venerable private conservation effort that ultimately fits into another conservation mosaic that grew within the Northern Forests in the 1990s. The battlefields around Gettysburg testify to the intense conflicts that can arise between local and national expectations in acquisition settings. Similarly, the Blue Ridge Parkway is a classic Depression-era acquisition that allows us to chart the uneven process of federal agencies learning to work with a growing array of local land trusts. In the redwoods of northern California, an early twentieth-century private conservation effort forms the core of what has become the most expensive suite of public land acquisitions in history, forcing us to ask how much land is enough, and how much money is too much. Finally, at Cuyahoga Valley National Park we see the difficulties in acquiring and managing yet another mosaic-like rural landscape intended as an urban park for the people.

Of course, our analysis would be incomplete without some numbers. Along the way, readers will encounter numerous tables and graphs trying to quantify land acquisition efforts at various times and places. We are acutely aware that the numbers do not always add up and are frequently inconsistent over time or among agencies. In this sense, our problems collecting these data were not so different from those encountered half a century ago:

Data on federal land ownership are notoriously difficult to obtain on an accurate, comparable, inclusive, and non-double-counting basis. This is largely because, until recently, no single inventory or other record of all federal land holdings existed. Moreover, since some tracts of lands are under the jurisdiction of two or more agencies for different purposes, and since some lands are withdrawn for special uses or purposes, a compilation of federal land may or may not include them, depending on definitions used. (Clawson and Held 1957: 403)

The situation has not improved (National Research Council 1993: 207). We have chased the numbers around and in some cases have caught them. In general, they support the pictures we draw and at times provide a useful point of reference, but the numbers do not explain the emergence of mosaics or their importance. It is the stories, both large and small, that paint the picture.

2

From the Confederated Congress Through the Civil War, 1780–1865

The first century of U.S. experience with acquiring land for conservation purposes, before it was a clearly defined public or government priority, can be seen as the status quo ante of this history. Federal programs were limited, and much of the activity was undertaken by state and private organizations. States exercised most of the authority over land we now presume the federal government has (for example, eminent domain). Federal authority for acquiring land was either limited or absent, and federal institutions for holding and managing conservation land did not exist.

Nevertheless, two key patterns are apparent. First, a hierarchy of roles became visible. State and private action was appropriate for local tourism and individual monuments whereas federal attention centered on protecting resources needed for defense and on national grandeur. Second, long before national parks and forests were on the horizon, a hierarchy distinguished different types of resources as well. The federal government paid little effective attention to monuments or scenic wonders. This may be because federal conservation acquisitions relied upon the war powers. Occasional congressional reservations to exclude land from homesteading, for example, Hot Springs in Arkansas, were not challenged on constitutional grounds. Forests were different. In 1817, Congress granted the president general authority to reserve forests for naval purposes. Congress approached forests as a storehouse of commodities necessary for federal purposes, but was and continues to be less clear about its authority to protect areas with scenic or tourism values. Almost a century before national parks and forests became familiar, a pattern of treating economic resources differently from scenic or commemorative sites was clearly discernable.

We address this initial, experimental period by describing three different kinds of land protection: federal acquisitions, private conservation efforts, and public domain reservations. Early federal acquisitions are discussed first; these are the Capital District and conservation of timber for the navy. They illustrate how constitutional provisions for federal acquisition of land were understood by the people who wrote them, and how the enclave clause provisions worked in practice.

We follow with examples of four privately protected sites: the Washington Monument, the Bunker Hill Monument, Fort Ticonderoga, and Mount Vernon. The federal government was less involved than one might predict in memorializing battles and heroes. For example, in 1781 the Continental Congress authorized a memorial at Yorktown that was not built until after the Civil War. In the 1820s a private group incorporated in Boston to build the Bunker Hill Monument and protect the battlefield. In the 1840s Congress donated land on what is now the Mall to another private group to build the Washington Monument (also not finished until the late nineteenth century). In 1823 the Pell family purchased another revolutionary war landmark, Fort Ticonderoga, for tourism and a family estate. George Washington's home at Mount Vernon was protected after the MVLA began a national movement in the early 1850s to raise money to buy the property. These early acquisitions were all relatively simple fee acquisitions, but early public-private partnerships were already very much in evidence.

The chapter concludes with a brief discussion of reservations from the public domain. It is important to distinguish federal acquisition of privately held property, as for the nation's capital, from reservation of land that the federal government already owned. Nevertheless, policies adopted in one sphere were rapidly folded into the other. Most obviously, agencies formed to manage western reservations—the USFS, NPS, and Fish and Wildlife Service (FWS)—also managed the eastern acquisitions. Indeed their earliest supporters were instrumental in justifying federal acquisitions. An understanding of the ad hoc process of early federal reservations will help to clarify the development of federal acquisitions later on.

Early Federal Acquisitions of Land

The District of Columbia

Acquisition of the land in the Capital District and the laying out of the capital city faithfully followed the requirements of the Constitution's enclave clause. It teaches us much about early constitutional tools for federal acquisition of land, which were surprisingly narrow, and about early enthusiasm for attracting federal facilities. It provides a clear example of the "givings" that frequently balanced loss of land in early assessments of just compensation. Finally, the transaction tells us about early concepts of parks. Although the primary goal was to establish a seat of government, the creation of dignified public spaces that combined natural features with formal statuary to create a sense of national grandeur, weight, and stability was a central part of that undertaking.

Competition among the mid-Atlantic states for the Capital District was intense; each sought the advantages of having the nation's capital within its boundaries. Maryland, New Jersey, Pennsylvania, and Delaware offered land for the capital before the Constitution was even ratified, and both Virginia and Maryland offered loans and grants for construction (Tindall 1909: 8, 82–83). Congress ultimately accepted these last two, locating the capital on the Potomac River.

The 1790 "Residence Act" (Tindall 1909: 81–82) identified an approximate location for the capital and authorized President Washington to appoint three commissioners to survey and approve plans for the District. This is the first of many instances of private citizens overseeing and managing a public acquisition process, much as land trusts do today. The actual acquisition process was defined by the enclave clause in Article I of the Constitution. Although it is now regarded as somewhat archaic, the enclave clause limited federal authority to buy land in states until the Civil War. Moreover, vestiges of the enclave clause shaped acquisitions, particularly for national parks, until the 1960s.

The enclave clause allows Congress

To exercise *exclusive Legislation*[1] in all Cases whatsoever, over such District (not exceeding ten Miles square) as may, by *Cession* of particular States, and the *Acceptance* of Congress, become the Seat of the Government of the United States, and to exercise like authority over all Places purchased by the *Consent of the Legislature* of the State in which the Same shall be, for the Erection of Forts,

Magazines, Arsenals, dock-Yards, and other needful Buildings. (Article I, § 8, cl. 17)

There are four key elements to this passage: (1) federal acquisitions require state consent; (2) the federal government exercises exclusive jurisdiction over lands acquired within a state; (3) the state must cede both the land and the jurisdiction over it; and (4) the federal government must accept both (U.S. Interdepartmental Comm. for the Study of Jurisdiction Over Federal Areas 1956–57, vol. I: 7).

Two points are particularly important. First, the Constitution gave states control over federal land acquisitions. Most responded by enacting blanket cessions that permitted all federal acquisition and ceded all related authority to the federal government. Such general cessions are the first, and perhaps the most convincing, counter to a general presumption that states or localities have felt burdened by or been coerced into accepting federal land acquisitions (U.S. Interdepartmental Comm. for Study of Jurisdiction Over Federal Areas 1956–57, vol. I: 8, 232; vol. II: 29–40).

Second, the constitutional preference for exclusive federal jurisdiction over federal enclaves faded soon after the Civil War, leaving as residue a ritual of cessions and acceptance of authority. Early in the twentieth century, states learned to impose conditions on cessions, manipulating the continuing ritual to retain authority that would benefit them—such as the power to tax—while saddling the federal government with the costs of ownership and management. This trend is fundamental to the mosaics of control that became a part of twentieth-century land acquisition programs.

The acquisition of the District of Columbia was the first major transaction under the enclave clause, and it followed the prescribed process closely. When the District was specifically located, the federal government was deemed to have accepted the land cessions from Virginia and Maryland. The federal government did not assume exclusive jurisdiction under the enclave clause until the government relocated to the District in 1800.[2] From that moment forward, however, it held both the powers of the federal sovereign *and* the powers reserved in the Constitution to the states. As a result, federal authority to acquire land from citizens within the District has never been seriously questioned. (The same exclusive federal jurisdiction operated in western territories.) Outside the Dis-

Table 2.1
Land Purchased and Donated for the Capital

Land acquired for the capital	
Total number of acres acquired for the city	6110.94
Donated to the United States for avenues, streets, and alleys	3,606
Purchased by the United States, 10,136 building lots	982
Purchased by the United States for public buildings and use	541
Total acres acquired by the United States	5,129
10,136 lots given back to former owners	981.94

Source: Tindall (1909: 22).

trict, the opposite is true. The federal government's authority to acquire and hold land, and the purposes for which it can do so, have been the subject of continuing controversy. When an acquisition is for conservation purposes, the debate is particularly intense. Those issues did not arise within the District of Columbia. Accordingly, many federal powers, most notably the power to condemn land, were accepted first in the nation's capital.[3]

President Washington personally negotiated the acquisition with the owners of bog, farm, and forestland in the area. Apparently his much-discussed acumen in land transactions served him well. Private owners donated much of the land for the eventual district, while other purchases were funded by the subsequent sale of the donated lots.[4] The final result was that of the 6,111 acres initially in the District, 5,129 were given to the government, and the rest were acquired without cost (Tindall 1909: 22). The transactions are summarized in table 2.1. Landowners retained control over their property until the land was converted to government use, as well as the right to sell timber from their lands to the government at a set price.

Landowners were willing to donate acreage to the government because they were allowed to retain ownership of a small number of parcels in the new District. The value of those parcels was vastly enhanced by the presence of the capital. Thus, landowners saw the deal as a government "giving" of value to them rather than a federal "taking" of their private property. Uncompensated public acquisitions based on givings were common early in American history. When donating a strip of property for a road, for example, a farmer might benefit enormously from public investment in improved access to markets. "Just" compensation was provided by the benefit of the road alone (Horwitz 1977, chap. 3).

Such arguments have all but disappeared in the modern era. In practice, private owners of land surrounded by conservation easements often see a similar increase in the value of their remaining private lots, but such transactions no longer reflect that increase in assessments of compensation for private owners. Thus, the District of Columbia transaction illustrates that the high purchase costs that constrain acquisitions today were not always such a dominant factor.

Early governance of the District is also of interest. The initial National Capital Commission—three appointed citizens—was authorized to engage in real estate transactions, and then to protect and care for all the federal lands in the District. Similar commissions will appear repeatedly throughout this volume to exercise what today seems like extraordinary authority. A superintendent of public buildings eventually replaced the commission and served until 1867, when the chief engineer of the U.S. Army took over (Tindall 1909: 23ff). From then until the 1930s, the War Department had primary responsibility for the federal lands within the District of Columbia. Indeed, the War Department played a key role in land conservation until the Depression, and variants on the commission format are still relied upon today.

Finally, the District offers an early, cautionary note regarding the building envelope and the limits of acquisition in an era of strong property rights. President Washington hired, as is well known, Pierre (Charles) L'Enfant to design the federal district. L'Enfant did not lay out the streets fast enough to please one aspiring homeowner, who built ahead of the survey. The location turned out to be in the middle of a broad avenue. Impulsively, L'Enfant had the house removed in what could be described as an early, unauthorized expression of federal powers of condemnation. He was fired for his transgression (Osborne 1901: 173–198).

Early Forest Acquisitions for the Navy

The War Department played an unexpectedly large role in early conservation acquisitions beyond the nation's capital. In fact, the enclave clause notwithstanding, the war powers provided the earliest and most consistent constitutional authorization for federal purchase of private land.[5]

Federal protection of forests in the early eighteenth century relied on congressional authority to provide and maintain a navy.[6] Live oak timber was required for constructing battleships, and interest in protecting the oaks waxed and waned as the young nation felt more or less threatened by outside forces. The program was started when Algerian pirates beset American merchant ships. In 1799 Congress appropriated $200,000 for purchasing growing timber, lumber, or lands on which appropriate timber was growing. Two privately owned islands in Georgia were the first purchases (Hough 1878: 10): Grover's Island (350 acres for $7,500) and Blackbeard's Island (1,600 acres for $1,500).

Purchases slowed when the nation signed a treaty with the pirates but sprang back to life when the treaty was abrogated. The program gained momentum after the War of 1812 (Wood 1981: 29–34), when British forces burned the White House and most of the ships of the U.S. Navy. In 1817, Congress granted the president general authority to select and reserve from the public domain timber suitable for the navy. When Florida was added as a territory in 1821, the program refocused on the superior oaks found in that state. Preexisting Spanish title confused ownership and precluded reservations, but purchases continued. By 1825 they formed the core of what is now Pensacola Navy Yard. By 1868, oak lands in Louisiana, Mississippi, Alabama, and Florida totaled 268,000 acres (Hough 1878: 10).

Ownership did not ensure control; many American settlers believed that the trees "belonged to nobody, and therefore to anybody who cared to take them" (Cameron, J. 1928: 21), and the remote American government fared no better than had the British in protecting distant resources. Unpersuaded by the federal government's claims, and unconcerned about penalties, local settlers continued to clear timber on many naval reserves, either to sell it or simply to make way for farms. No questions were raised about the government's formal authority to purchase or reserve the timber; protecting the oaks was an accepted exercise of Congress' war powers. Clearly, however, federal ownership was not a reliable route to protection.

Nor were the oak reserves and acquisitions the start of permanent federal forest management (Snell 1983). The goal was never to retain parcels as a renewable source of timber, as was the case subsequently during the Progressive era. Rather, the navy wanted to protect existing timber at minimum cost; land could be purchased or reserved, the timber harvested, and then the land resold or opened to entry.[7] By 1843, settlement pressure in the Southeast forced Congress to return the reservations in Alabama and Louisiana to the public domain for settlement (Cameron, J. 1928: 88–89).

The *coup de grace* for the naval reserves was the famous Civil War battle between the *Monitor* and the *Merrimack*. Attention shifted to iron ships, rendering the live oak requirements of the navy obsolete.[8] Between 1879 and 1894, all remaining naval reservations were returned to the public domain and opened to settlement (Cameron, J. 1928: 92–93; Raymond and Fairfax 1999: 718–725). For reasons that are not clear, acquired lands were treated differently. The initial purchase, Grover's Island, was sold, but not until 1920, to luxury resort developers in Sea Island, Georgia. Blackbeard Island was converted into a wildlife refuge in 1940. The other acquired tracts were added to the Pensacola navy base (Cameron, J. 1928: 92–93), which now includes a small park managed by the NPS to commemorate the naval oak program. Ironically, the last oak reservations were opened to settlement in the Southeast at the same general time that Congress granted the president authority to reserve land for forest protection in the western states and territories.

State and Private Efforts for Memorials and Historic Preservation

It would be misleading to leave the impression that the federal government was the leader in early land conservation efforts. No single institution or agency of government was a dominant player in the nineteenth century; conservation activities were limited, sporadic, and scattered, but a rough division of labor was taking shape. While the federal government focused on lands primarily related to national grandeur, security, and other utilitarian objectives, diverse private groups organized to preserve historic battlegrounds, memorialize victories, and protect noteworthy buildings.

During the American Revolution, the Continental Congress attempted to establish monuments at the sites of great military victories, particularly Yorktown,[9] and to honor prominent heroes, notably George Washington (Allen 2000: 25). The deaths of key figures of the American Revolution—Washington in 1799, and Thomas Jefferson and John Adams on July 4, 1826—intensified public interest in such memorials. An emerging sense of national pride and identity, enhanced throughout the nineteenth century by the major anniversaries of various Revolutionary War and Civil War battles as well as the national centennial in 1876, increased awareness of the relics of our nation's brief history. In light of relatively weak federal authority, most of the ensuing conservation efforts were privately initiated, although several involved local or state governments as well.

The Washington Monument
In 1783 the Confederated Congress directed that an equestrian statue of General Washington be erected in the District of Columbia. Washington himself approved a location for the statue in L'Enfant's plan (Olszewski 1971). However, as president he could not justify the expense, and the idea languished. His death in 1799 set off decades of wrangling about an appropriate memorial. In 1833, with the hundredth anniversary of Washington's birth approaching, Congress tried again and produced a statue so unpopular that it was banished from the Capitol Building to the Smithsonian (Freidel and Aikman 1988: 32). Local luminaries formed a private organization, the Washington National Monument Society, the same year (Olszewski 1971: 2) to overcome the inertia. The project quickly became a public-private partnership when the District's mayor gave the group office space in a spare room in the basement of the City Hall. By 1836 the society had raised sufficient funds to justify holding a design competition. Congress reentered the scene, giving the society 37 acres of land on what is now the Mall.

Construction of the now famous obelisk began in 1854 but was halted when the society ran out of funds. At that point, Congress contributed $200,000 to complete the project. That the federal government would donate money and federal land to a private group rather than develop the memorial itself, even within the District of Columbia, is telling evidence of the different expectations and roles for public and private conservation groups of the time.

Problems continued to plague the project. The society had encouraged states and territories to donate stones for the interior walls of the building. A stone donated by the Pope was stolen by the Know-Nothings, an anti-Catholic, anti-immigrant political party. Subsequently, the Know-Nothings took over the society (in what some claim was a rigged board election) in order "to assure that the Monument fit their definition of 'American'."[10] Although the old and new boards both claimed control, the anti-Papists retained the upper hand and continued to build the monument (Torres 1985: 26). Appalled at the new management, Congress withdrew its $200,000 donation. When the new board subsequently ran out of funds, they acquiesced and returned control and all project records to the original society, but the project remained stalled until after the Civil War. This early experience suggests one kind of public accountability problem that can hinder private acquisition and conservation efforts: It can be fairly easy for a group of motivated citizens to take over a small organization and bend it to their own peculiar ends.[11]

Bunker Hill

As every schoolchild knows, the battle of Bunker Hill actually took place on Breed's Hill (Lee 1972: 28; Mackintosh 1990: 33–34).[12] This was the first full-scale encounter between American and British troops during the Revolution. Fifteen hundred raw recruits of the "New England Army" held off 2,400 British soldiers, giving an early boost to the American side. Stung by their defeat, the British limited their military operations for the rest of the year, thereby giving the colonists critical months to build and train the new Continental army.[13]

Modern visitors to Boston's Freedom Trail—which is mapped, publicized, and interpreted by the NPS—can be forgiven for thinking that the federal government built the monument to the battle. However, it was a private project that became an early partnership with the state. The fiftieth anniversary of the battle was preceded by a number of major publications concerning the encounter, and soldiers who had fought there returned to visit the site for the first time since 1775 (Evans and Snell 1982: 18–20). When a nearby newspaper noted that the site, including a memorial to local hero General Warren, and many of the breastworks of the battle were advertised to be sold at auction, action to protect the historic property began.

A private purchaser led the way. Young Daniel Webster was among those who persuaded General Warren's son to buy the land to protect it. Warren "preacquired" the site,[14] we might now say, and held it until the state legislature chartered the Bunker Hill Monument Association (Evans and Snell 1982: 21). In May 1823, local luminaries called a public meeting in Boston to develop an act of incorporation. The act empowered them, "as trustees, to collect and hold subscriptions for the purpose of erecting an enduring monument 'to the memory of those statesmen and soldiers who led the way in the American Revolution.' ... Each man present subscribed $5, and signed the agreement" (Evans and Snell 1982: 21).

When the association encountered significant difficulty in making crucial additional purchases at affordable prices, the state joined the project. The Massachusetts legislature granted the private organization the right of eminent domain—the right "to take and appropriate to the legal uses of said association any land on Breed's Hill ... necessary in the design of erecting a monument and laying out the surrounding ground in the appropriate manner" (Evans and Snell 1982: 27). It was—and remains—common for states to authorize private entities to exercise eminent domain authority to construct projects in the public interest. By April 1825, the association had acquired approximately 15 acres of the battlefield (Evans and Snell 1982: 27, quoting Sheldon 1865: 136).[15]

The state aided the association in two other ways. First, it enlisted inmates at the state prison in Charleston to construct, hammer, and prepare the stone to be used in the monument. Second, it donated two historic cannons owned by the governor and the state to be used at the memorial. Subsequent research demonstrated that the prison labor actually would have cost more than hired stonemasons, so it was not used (Evans and Snell 1982: 59). Despite the state's support, the cost of building the monument was a continuing problem. By 1834, the association was $25,000 in debt and undertook a fascinating real estate transaction as a fund raiser. It sold 10 of its 15 acres to "friends of the enterprise" at double their market value. Each sale was accompanied by an agreement that the association could repurchase the land if it could raise adequate funds.

Unlike the acquisition at Mount Vernon, the real estate transactions at Bunker Hill failed to save the day. Four years later, the association informed the purchasers that it was unable to repurchase the lands. While the acres still protected have become a lively part of Boston's civic culture (now owned and administered by the NPS), the majority of the battlefield was developed into housing.[16] In an era in which fee purchase was the primary option for acquisition (conservation easements remained many decades in the future), the costs proved too high.

Fort Ticonderoga

Early conservation of Fort Ticonderoga, another major revolutionary war site, also began as a private effort,[17] but it was very different from Bunker Hill and the Washington Monument. It was an explicitly commercial undertaking, instituted during a tourist boom that hit upper New York state in the late eighteenth century. Located at the southern end of Lake Champlain, the site had been known as the "key to the continent" (Hamilton 1964: 5, 88) for all the time that the Huron and Iroquois nations contended for control. When the British, French, and their Indian allies fought for the region, the French constructed a fort. The British then dislodged the French in 1759 and renamed the site Fort Ticonderoga. During the Revolution, in a famous predawn 1775 raid, Benedict Arnold and Ethan Allen's Green Mountain Boys surprised a small British contingent and took the fort, allegedly "in the name of the Great Jehovah and the Continental Congress" (Millard 1997).

The peace treaty with Great Britain signed in September 1783 passed title to the fort to the American government. However, under the Articles of Confederation, the central government had only limited authority to hold land (Abernethy 1937). Abandoned military posts were routinely granted to the states in which they were located. Fort Ticonderoga was transferred to the State of New York, which vested title in the regents of the anticipated University of the State of New York. Because no state university yet existed, the regents donated the land to the only colleges that did, Columbia University in New York (established 1754) and Union College in Schenectady (established 1795). However, public ownership again failed to ensure effective control, and the fort fell into ruins; sheep grazed among its fallen battlements, and settlers moving into the area took its stones for more useful buildings. The fort was, nevertheless, a much-romanticized place for tourists in the North Country. After the War of 1812, the universities sought some financial return on the property (Brockway 2001: 27), and William Pell leased and then purchased the ruin and 546 acres of garrison grounds in 1820. The standard story is that he intended to create a country retreat, and the fort was ideal for that purpose—it came complete with a "genuine" ruin at a time when the English aristocracy was constructing faux ruins to add romance to their rural estates (Brockway 2001: 32). More recent analysis suggests, however, that Pell also anticipated considerable revenues from the fort's status as a major tourist destination (Westbrook 2002).[18] He constructed The Pavilion, which was used as a hotel for many decades (Brockway 2001: 32). James Madison and Thomas Jefferson had followed a well-trod path when they visited the fort in 1791 (Maguire 1995). When the Champlain Canal opened riverboat transportation all the way to Albany in 1823, travel was simplified, and the tourist trade boomed (Westbrook, V. 2001).

The Pells also became the fort's first peacetime defender. Although significant restoration of the ruins was a century away, the first private owner of the property accommodated visitors and prevented further destruction of the fort (Brockway 2001: 37–39). Economists and market advocates might contrast the relative success of the Fort Ticonderoga experience, based on tourism and commercial benefits, with the more philanthropic misadventures of the Washington Monument debacle.

Mount Vernon

In 1846, descendants of George Washington offered his estate to the federal government for $100,000. Even though Congress was in the throes of its protracted debate on how to honor the first president, it declined to buy his home. Five years later, an army board proposed to acquire the property, not as a memorial to Washington, but in order to convert it into an asylum for the relief and support of disabled soldiers. Washington's insulted descendants doubled the asking price, which the board could not justify paying (Johnson 1991). Persistent rumors that private businessmen wanted to develop a hotel on the property prompted public pleas to preserve it. In 1853, the governor of Virginia requested that the state legislature develop a plan to protect Mount Vernon, suggesting that the estate might be used for a number of purposes, including an agricultural school or a literary institution. However, developers were unwilling to pay John Washington's asking price, which remained $200,000.

In response, as indicated in chapter 1, an organization of prominent southern women built a national movement to acquire the property. Responding to a call from Ann Pamela Cunningham of South Carolina, they created a network of state-based organizations to raise funds, and the Virginia state legislature chartered the Mount Vernon Ladies' Association of the Union in 1856.[19] The legislature still wanted to hold title, but provided no funding for the effort. Peeved at having been spurned, John Washington rejected any arrangement that allowed the State of Virginia to own his family's home (Johnson 1991).[20] In 1858, the MVLA won a charter change that allowed the state to issue $200,000 worth of bonds to be repaid by the MVLA. The property would be owned and maintained by the association.

The deal was closed in April 1858, but shortly thereafter, the Civil War broke out. For almost five years, Mount Vernon was in a "no man's land in which cavalry patrols were constantly battling and across which armies occasionally surged ... and bushwhackers ... little better than robber bands" plied their trade (Johnson 1991: 33).

MVLA secretary Sara Tracey took up residence at the site and charged admission from visitors who continued to arrive. With intelligence, courage, and what must have been an incredible amount of grace and luck, Tracey protected the estate throughout the war.[21] After the fighting stopped, the MVLA funded restoration of the building with private contributions, admission fees, and the sale of produce and flowers raised on the grounds. Through dire times, it was a self-supporting conservation effort.

Anyone trying to build an organization to protect and manage a cherished resource can take inspiration and direction from the MVLA. Cunningham succeeded in organizing a national fund-raising effort when the far more eminent men trying to raise money to build the Washington Monument failed consistently. The pattern she established in 1856 has been maintained, both at Mount Vernon and within the growing mosaic of conservation efforts.

Early Parklike Reservations from the Western Public Domain

Reservations from the public domain are probably a digression from our focus on acquisitions of private land for conservation purposes. However, it is important to review them briefly for three reasons: First, if we want to dispel the standard myth of the "shift to retention" by focusing on acquisitions, we need to introduce this version of events. Second, many of the federal programs, agencies, and powers that ultimately play a central role in land acquisition emerged in the process of— harmoniously or in contrast to—congressional efforts to deal with the reserved public domain. Finally, we want to sharpen some legal distinctions, keeping acquired public lands separate from those in the original public domain in order to keep the relevant constitutional authorities for acquisition straight. Thus, an account of acquisition for conservation provides a chance to recapitulate briefly another of our favorite stories: public domain history.

A Brief Introduction to the Public Domain

The term *public domain* includes all lands west of the Appalachians that the federal government acquired by discovery, cession, treaty, conquest, purchase, or occupation—displacing Native Americans as it went. It is standard practice (Raymond and Fairfax 1999) to discuss public domain history in terms of three eras: first acquisition, then disposition, and finally retention. It is important to understand that Congress did indeed take three broad approaches to the public domain, but the three-era model is misleading because Congress has acquired, disposed of, and reserved land simultaneously for most of our history.

Nineteenth-century Americans waxed increasingly rhapsodic about their "manifest destiny," but the Constitution gave little guidance regarding what to do with the new western territories. Congress was not accustomed to considering such extensive federal ownership of land and, with very few exceptions, attempted to dispose of the land to private owners as quickly as it accumulated. Congress sold, granted, donated, and acquiesced in trespass on federal lands, thereby ensuring the rapid if not orderly settlement of the western territories.

Along the way, however, Congress or the president also reserved some lands for specific public purposes, starting with the naval reserves. Such reservations prevented private entrepreneurs from entering those parcels for purposes of taking title to, or patenting, the land. Thus the reservations were an important early counter to the disposition policy. Congressional experience with reserving land—in a fairly comprehensive way for forest conservation, less systematically for what are now parks—gradually expanded beyond its beginnings in the war powers. National parks and forests are the most familiar conservation reservations that eventually resulted, although lands have also been reserved for Indian settlement, irrigation, and many other government uses.

Pre-Civil War conservation reservations were quite different from later Progressive era actions that created national forests and parks. The 1832 Hot Springs reservation in Arkansas, for example, was perhaps the first reservation for parklike purposes. Because Arkansas was not yet a state, Congress apparently intended to hold onto this four-square-mile area that Indians and early settlers believed had medicinal value until it could decide how the area should best be utilized. Although the NPS now manages the site, some national park mavens typically reject it as the "first" national park.[22] Indeed, in the 1830s almost nobody had thought about the concept.[23] Congress "more or less" forgot about the reservation (Miller 1973: 271), which remained under the jurisdiction of the Department of the Interior, and Interior officials only began calling it a park in the 1880s (O'Toole 1995: 5).[24] Nevertheless, it appears to be among the first federal reservations that did not rely upon the war powers; it in fact made no explicit connection to constitutional authority.

Yosemite is a more typical starting place of "real" conservation reservations beyond the war powers, but its provenance is also confused.[25] In 1864, Congress reserved the valley and the nearby Mariposa grove of giant sequoias for "public use, resort, and recreation."[26] Unlike Arkansas in 1832, California was a state in 1864. Accordingly, Congress granted the land to California for management on behalf of the nation. For that reason, Yosemite is not generally regarded as the "first" national park. The federal government accepted the re-cession of the valley in 1906.

Before the Civil War, however, these reservations were quite rare. It is fair to conclude that pre-Civil War conservation reservations mainly relied on the war powers and left other conservation purposes to states and the private sector. The lands that were neither reserved nor passed into state or private ownership—the unreserved, unentered public domain—remained under the nominal control of the General Land Office (GLO). The result of this history is that government-owned lands are not evenly distributed throughout the nation. Acquired lands are a far more important element of the landscape in the eastern and southern states than in the West, where the public domain remained in government ownership.

Federal land ownership in Alaska is so extensive that many datasets are distorted by it. We will occasionally exclude Alaska from our discussions in order to focus on data for the lower 48 states in which land acquisition appears as more than a blip. For example, table 2.2 shows current agency holdings with and without Alaska.

It is common to say that today the federal government owns "one third of the nation's land" (U.S. Public Land Law Review Commission 1970). For some purposes that is correct, but that figure includes everything—post offices, hospitals, offices, highways, Army Corps of Engineers and Bureau of Reclamation dams, and prisons—and we are not including any of those in our discussion. When we say public lands we are referring to reserved and acquired land managed by the USFS, the NPS, the BLM, and the FWS. Occasionally we will use the term *federal lands* synonymously with public lands, that is, the areas managed by the four federal agencies of concern. We do not include state or local government lands in the term *public lands*, because doing so would confuse both the discussion and the already sketchy available data.

Summary

In the first century of land conservation, efforts were sparse, involved few institutions, and in most cases focused on nation building and national shrines. Beyond the enclave clause, which provided for the acquisition of the nation's capital, the federal government relied primarily upon the war powers but employed them sparingly—mainly to procure timber for

Table 2.2
Public Domain Acreage and Acquired Land Owned by Federal Agencies (Current Acres)

Agency	Units	Public domain	Alaska total acres	Alaska as % of total	Acres acquired	% Acquired	Alaska acquired	Total
U.S. Forest Service	155	148,190,915	21,989,781	12	29,359,328	17	8,492	177,550,243
National Park Service	388	63,336,751	50,823,100	67	12,741,921	17	255,526	76,078,672
U.S. Fish and Wildlife Service	618	82,049,131	76,580,911	87	6,255,067	7	274,532	88,304,198
Bureau of Land Management	NA	259,177,395	85,953,625	33	2,279,930	1	NA	261,457,325

Note: NA = not applicable.
Sources: USFS, NPS: U.S. GSA (2000); FWS: U.S. FWS (2002a). Acquired acres = purchased by the FWS plus acres acquired by another federal agency but on which the FWS is sole or primary manager. BLM: U.S. BLM (2002, table 1-4) (assumes lands acquired under the Depression era Land Utilization Act are the only acquired lands). Alaska data sources: NPS: U.S. NPS (2002c); USFS: U.S. FS (2000b); FWS: U.S. FWS (2002a); BLM: U.S. BLM (2002, table 1-4).

the navy. These initial forest reservations and acquisitions for the practical purpose of national defense proceeded by general authority, whereas the few federal reservations for what are now parks were the result of ad hoc, site-by-site decisions.

The small role of the federal government is explained in part by constitutional authorities, and in part by the low profile of the federal government and the nation's identity in general. Federal authority to condemn land directly was still decades away, and the nation remained largely in the grasp of a Lockean concept of property that emphasized private rights. Nevertheless, the notion of a "givings" was an important exception. When landowners anticipated great benefits from proposed federal facilities, they willingly donated the necessary land. Until well after World War II, states and localities ardently sought federal facilities and regarded them as an economic boon.

In a climate of strong property rights and weak federal authority, private citizens formed groups and protected various historic sites—Bunker Hill, the Washington Monument, Fort Ticonderoga, and Mount Vernon—that would clearly be viewed as federal responsibilities at the beginning of the twenty-first century. Transactions were simple, always in full fee title, and there was little in the way of mosaics in these early acquisition efforts.

While complex mosaics had yet to appear, the line between public and private efforts was already blurred. Congress donated land and money to the private Washington National Monument Society, while private individuals donated land for the capital. Outside of Washington, Bunker Hill provides an especially interesting example of a public-private partnership in which public authority for eminent domain was delegated to a private group for conservation purposes. Mount Vernon is privately conserved, and although it charges entrance fees, it has always presented itself as a public charity acting on behalf of the nation. Fort Ticonderoga was also privately protected, but as a more commercial effort, oriented toward tourism.

In sum, the blending and mixing of public and private conservation efforts currently viewed as a post-World War II phenomenon actually began much earlier. Issues of public accountability for nominally private conservation efforts are vividly underscored by the Washington Monument Know-Nothings fiasco, but are evident in all of these examples.

Overall, most fee simple acquisitions during the nation's first seventy-five years worked well to achieve limited goals on small sites like Fort Ticonderoga and Mount Vernon. Sara Tracey almost single-handedly protected Mount Vernon from the ravages of the Civil War. However, the approach was only a qualified success elsewhere; Bunker Hill was reduced to one-third of its original size by financial constraints, and the Washington Monument project dissolved into chaos amid conflicting agendas and interests. Nor were federal reservations clearly more successful at protecting resources. Entrepreneurial types with a different idea of property wreaked havoc on government-owned naval reserves. Understanding when and why acquisition has promise as a conservation tool and where it may not is at the heart of our story.

3

Changing Expectations: From the Civil War to the Weeks Act, 1865–1911

The emergence of a continental nation and corporate economy following the Civil War radically changed American life. Industrialization and its consequences put new and diverse conservation goals onto the national agenda. The idea of limited government eroded, and growing numbers of interest groups, including those interested in conservation, organized to direct expanding federal programs to their own benefit. In fact, the growing scale of conservation activity was not a federal intrusion, but an expansion of the scope of both public and private activities. Land acquisition efforts began to create complexity on the landscape, relying on new acquisition tools and ownerships embodying new rights, rules, and consequences for the land and surrounding communities.

A new set of private conservation groups continued to concentrate on protecting historic homes and local open spaces but also supported the expansion of public acquisition efforts by states and the federal government. For example, in the 1880s, New York began to conserve Adirondack forests, with substantial support from interests concerned about water supplies. Acquisition advocates also focused on natural wonders and archeological resources, with an explicit eye on tourism. With the exception of ecosystem conservation, which did not become a specific goal until the late 1900s, by the late nineteenth century advocates were pursuing virtually every other modern justification for protecting land.

Protection of Civil War battlefields provides a clear view of shifting state and federal roles. Private acquisition of important sites, assisted by states, was the earliest incubator of federal acquisition authority. The 1911 Weeks Act provided closure on the basic constitutional debate that had historically limited federal participation; the act relied on the expanding commerce clause rather than the more focused war powers as the source of federal authority to acquire private forest land for conservation purposes. However, as noted in chapter 2, forest advocates seem to have had an easier task than did park and wildlife advocates because the economic value of watersheds and timber provided a solid argument for protection. Federal acquisition authority for wildlife habitat was so limited that programs relied on international treaties protecting migratory birds, while park advocates could find no acquisition authority at all.

Perhaps surprisingly, most modern acquisition tools, including those regarded as innovative in the 1980s and 1990s, were extensively deployed in the post-Civil War era. Conservation easements as we now know them were rare, but in acquiring land for Civil War memorials, Congress presumed that farming would remain the dominant land use and allowed and encouraged farmers to continue working the landscape as they had before the war. At Gettysburg, for example, acquisition efforts initially focused on paths and roads to give visitors access to memorials and battle sites.

We will explore these major transitions—in who acquires what lands and under what terms and conditions—under four headings. First, we address the emergence of new ideas about property, federal authority, and conservation goals in the post-Civil War era. Then we address major state and private innovations, focusing on the Adirondack forest of New York and The Trustees of Public Reservations in Massachusetts. Next, we follow the emergence of federal acquisition authority, initially defined by the Civil War battlefields.

After that, we digress once again to discuss the western public domain and reserved lands. Here we observe the erosion of the presumption that the federal government would completely dispose of the public domain. As a result, reservations of western land presented important issues of jurisdiction, policy toward inholders, and management authority that quickly shaped acquisition efforts as well. Both the USFS and later the NPS were organized initially to manage reserved western lands, yet both became major advocates of federal acquisition of land. We also consider the complex situation surrounding wildlife protection. Ironically, just as the federal government assumed a growing role in conservation, a

Supreme Court decision located most authority over wildlife with the states.

However, federal acquisition rather than reservation is the center of this account. Thus in the final section we turn to the 1911 Weeks Act, the first general acquisition authority at the national level for conservation purposes, and a model for many federal acquisition programs that followed. Although the Weeks Act is often presented as a great conservation victory, it forcefully introduces one of the limits of acquisition: the dominance of willing sellers.

Changing Views of Ownership, Government, and Land

During and after the Civil War, an increasingly confident and powerful national identity and economy underwrote and required an increasingly assertive federal government. Progressives defined the basis for an activist state. Despite populist rhetoric (Pinchot 1911), Progressives viewed themselves as scientists using their expertise to prevent waste of public resources (Hays 1959). Nevertheless, "client-serving" bureaucracies had formal relationships with their constituencies (Wilson 1975: 95), working together to expand the agencies and their budgets, and hence the services available to "clients" (Selznik 1966; Noll 1971).

New Ideas of Property

By the 1870s, the private corporation had become the dominant form of business organization. Corporate charters were no longer special contracts between a legislature and an enterprise, and corporations were no longer subject to monitoring and significant threat of charter revocation. American jurisprudence strengthened the legal protection for these economic creations, giving corporations the legal status of "persons" in 1886.[1]

That breathtaking rise of the "modern business enterprise" (Chandler 1977) put traditional ideas about property under great pressure to adapt. Starting with railroads and telegraph companies, corporations displaced smaller entrepreneurs as the dominant property owners in the United States. This weakened the Lockean justification of ownership; corporate owners do not labor directly on their property or sweat in the Lockean sense. The change was even more dramatic in terms of what was subject to ownership. Property rights evolved from a focus on the physical thing—the land itself—to its market value (Horwitz 1977: 149; Lustig 1982: 96; Freyfogle 1995: 97–98). Even the corporate charter, although granted by government, was eventually considered private property (Lustig 1982: 92–93).

This shift made room for the development of the now familiar bundle of sticks metaphor as a tool for understanding property (Horwitz 1977: 149; Freyfogle 1995: 99). As indicated earlier, in this metaphor property is portrayed, not as a single right, but rather as a collection of specific powers (or "sticks") such as exclusion, use, alienation, and bequest. In this new way of thinking, property rights could be more easily divided, with different individuals holding different sticks in the bundle.

It is particularly important to note that after the Civil War the link between ownership and control began to weaken. New corporate structures disconnected owners (the company's shareholders) from those controlling day-to-day operations (the salaried managers). At the same time, the abolition of slavery weakened the connection between ownership and control from another direction. Lockean principles suggest that both freed slaves and wage laborers would own their own labor. Nevertheless, employers in the late nineteenth century did not have to own their workers to exercise substantial control over them. Coercive labor practices and competition for jobs spurred by liberal immigration policies oppressed wage workers, and once again ownership and control parted ways.

At the same time, a more socially oriented view of property developed that required claims of individual ownership to adjust to larger social goals. Advocates of a laissez faire approach to regulation, which strongly supported the sanctity of individual private property rights, fought this trend with relatively little success (Friedman 1973: 359–362; Selvin 1987: 285). The Supreme Court was a more effective opponent, frequently rejecting regulation of working conditions and similar types of state legislation. Nevertheless, the mere contemplation of such regulations in the late nineteenth and early twentieth centuries attests to an expanding social view of property and ownership: The government can take what is needed by society. By the Depression, social regulation that created significant costs for private property owners was widely accepted.

Changing Government Ownership: The Property Clause

So clearly important to the growth of corporations, these changes in property law were also vital for defining government land ownership and, ironically, government conservation. The development of a federal power of eminent domain evinces a social notion of property since it requires that owners give up their private holdings to meet some public purpose. And, no less than corporations, the government is an abstraction owning land; as the agencies developed, they were not owners but hired managers.[2]

New federal conservation programs presented basic questions about constitutional authorities to reserve, acquire, and manage land. Because the current understanding assumes that the federal government has always had the authority to do those things, it is interesting to watch basic questions arise historically. Could the federal government permanently own land—not just post offices and arsenals but millions of acres? Could it acquire private land without a military justification, and if so, for what purposes? What kind of management authority is conferred by the Constitution? For example, could an executive agency charge fees and impose regulations? In dealing with Civil War battlefields and memorials in the East and with the public domain in the West, Congress and the executive branch began to define federal participation in land acquisition and management. The Supreme Court gradually put its imprimatur on expansive federal acquisition programs as well. As Progressive ideas about property and government gained traction, their political advocates developed a strong, centralized federal government that frequently relied on science to resolve public disputes.

Nevertheless, the process was gradual and involves questions about the property clause as distinct from the enclave clause emphasized in chapters. Article IV, section 3 of the Constitution addresses the public domain and provides that:

The Congress shall have Power to dispose of and make all needful Rules and Regulations respecting the Territory or other Property belonging to the United States.

The current presumption, controversial in many quarters, is that federal authority to manage its land is without limit. That idea did not fully flower until the 1970s, when it was clearly articulated in the case of

Kleppe v. New Mexico [426 U.S. 529 (1976)].[3] It arises from the "all needful rules" phrase in Article IV. The decision is still debated (Cowart and Fairfax 1988), but in the era between the Civil War and the Weeks Act, it would have been unimaginable.

Changing Ideas About Land and Conservation Goals

Finally, ideas about land also began to shift after the Civil War. The township and range survey, instituted in 1785, laid out 160-acre squares of public domain and treated them as if they were interchangeable. The survey system worked fairly well for the relatively consistent and mesic lands of the midwestern grain belt. By the time settlers reached the famed hundredth meridian, however, the inadequacies of the standardized system of disposition became unavoidable.

John Wesley Powell brought problems in the arid West to the attention of Congress in his famous 1878 *Report on the Lands of the Arid Region* (Stegner 1954). He suggested a system of land classification that defined policy for land in accordance with its specific characteristics. Powell's proposals were not popular in Congress, but similar ideas of targeting land management to particular resources were soon advocated by diverse economic interests. They pushed Congress for policies that met the special needs of marketing timber as different from minerals, coal as distinct from gold, and scenic wonders as distinguished from watersheds. Each subset of advocates wanted an agency to cater to its own priorities. It is not clear today that dividing responsibilities for the land among frequently hostile agencies was a good one.

These changing ideas about government, property ownership, and land radically altered conservation priorities and policies. By the end of this chapter we will see an embryonic sorting of the Progressive Era conservation movement's handiwork, as forests, parks, and wildlife were separated by Congress and on the landscape.

State and Private Conservation Leadership

The typical account of conservation puts the federal government and the shift to retention at the center of growing public attention to land conservation in the late nineteenth and early twentieth centuries. Thus, many stories do not address either privately held lands in the West or issues in the East, where industrialization had altered many formerly rural or natural areas and increased the pressure for conserving what remained. State and private innovations shaped subsequent federal programs.

In 1900, following a tour of the Big Basin redwoods, a group of central California coast citizens organized the Sempervirens Club to protect the area as a laboratory for the forestry school proposed for the University of California, Berkeley (Schrepfer 1983: 11). A year later, in Concord, New Hampshire, citizens concerned about forest destruction organized the Society for the Protection of New Hampshire Forests (SPNHF) (Fairfax and Guenzler 2001). The discussion that follows emphasizes state efforts in the Adirondacks, the founding of The Trustees of Reservations in Boston, and—suggesting that the increasingly assertive federal government was capable of crushing small private groups as well as depending on them—the fate of the Washington National Monument Society.

The Adirondack Forest Preserve

Conservation of the Adirondack forest, which all but surrounds Fort Ticonderoga in northern New York state, preceded the federal forest reservations and followed a similar path. As such, it provided a model for the protection of large forested landscapes.

The state owned considerable acreage in the region. The first step toward conservation, therefore, was to convince the state to hold onto the land it already owned. Step two was to establish a system for acquiring more land. Step three was to establish a process for managing the area. In this third aspect the Adirondacks model differs from the later Forest Service trajectory. Land owned by the state within the forest reserve was to be maintained as "forever wild." All three steps occurred in a series of significant battles over the region's fate beginning in 1883.

The early history of private ownership in the Adirondacks established an unsettling pattern of exploitation (Wuerthner 1988: 54–68; Adirondack Museum and Adirondack History Network 2000). Throughout the eighteenth and nineteenth centuries, downstate speculators acquired enormous parcels of land, logged them, and, rather than pay taxes, allowed the land to revert to state ownership. When the state allocated more than 600,000 acres to pay Revolutionary War soldiers, title to land in the area was already so confused that very few smallholders took advantage of the program. The region enjoyed a brief period of notoriety as a source of iron during the Civil War, then quickly relapsed into remote poverty.

Repeated destructive harvests and subsequent fires precipitated action. Steps toward land conservation reinforced outside control and semifeudal ownership patterns. In 1883, the state legislature halted further sale of state land. In 1885, six years before Congress authorized forest reservations from the federal public domain, state legislation declared the 681,000 acres of state-owned lands in the region to be a forest preserve. The decisive element in the decision was water—the Adirondacks were viewed as a "hanging sponge" that held and gradually released water, preventing floods and siltation of rivers and providing a clean water supply (Graham 1978: 90).

It was not clear at first what the preserve meant for management. Preservationists thought it precluded any timber cutting, while conservationists thought it mandated scientific management and timber harvest. State constitutional provisions adopted in 1895 expressed the priorities of the preservationists,[4] declaring that:

the lands of the state, now owned or hereafter acquired, constituting the forest preserve as now fixed by law, shall be forever kept as wild forest lands. They shall not be leased, sold or exchanged, or be taken by any corporation, public or private, nor shall the timber thereon be sold, removed, or destroyed. (N.Y. Const. art 7, § 7 1895)

Even before the "forever wild" constitutional provision, the state began to acquire land to enlarge the preserve, exercising unquestioned purchase authority of a sort that the federal government was forced to improvise twenty years later to sustain the Weeks Act.

In 1892, the legislature approved an Adirondack park that indicated a boundary, a "blue line" within which public purchases would be focused. The blue line, shown in figure 3.1, initially enclosed 2.8 million acres of private land in addition to the less extensive state holdings. Within the blue line, the plutocrats of the Gilded Age established Great Camps, and repaired to the pseudorustic splendor of palatial estates and hotels. Vanderbilts, Morgans, and Whitneys all located in the area; the

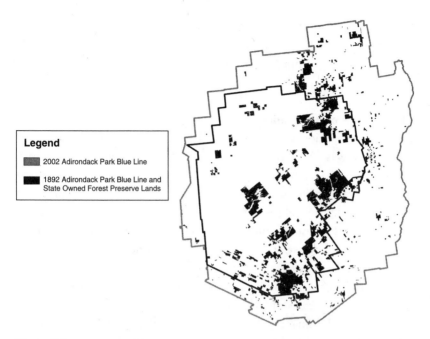

Legend

2002 Adirondack Park Blue Line

1892 Adirondack Park Blue Line and
State Owned Forest Preserve Lands

Figure 3.1
Original state and private land within the 1892 blue line (2002 blue line indicated in light gray). Source: Base maps courtesy of the New York State Adirondack Park Agency. Reproduced with permission.

Rockefeller family owned 84,000 acres, and the Vanderbilt/Webbs held a 42,848-acre tract (Terrie 1977: 71). Although many locals made their living guiding tourists, they were not included in the debate about the future of the area; the decisions were made in Albany and New York City.

The state legislature continued to appropriate significant funds to buy land, but surprisingly, timber harvesting continued. The Forest Preserve Board, established in 1897, exercised the authority not only to condemn land but also to put land to use. The legislature established a forestry school at Cornell University that immediately contracted with commercial interests to purchase Adirondack timber (Rodgers 1951: 259ff). A series of bad fire seasons gave the preservationists the upper hand, however, and allowed them to use the forever-wild principle to stop the logging, but the protection reduced economic opportunities for local residents. One of the unmistakable lessons of early Adirondacks legislation is that the initial terms of an acquisition have repercussions for future opportunities. Resentments born in the region's early history continue to limit management of what is now the Adirondack Park.

The Trustees of Reservations

Private conservation groups organized to meet regional needs. One of the earliest was The Trustees of [Public] Reservations (The Trustees), founded in 1891 in Boston.[5] Private conservation of locally important sites appears to have begun where rural America first disappeared—in New England.[6] As industrialization and urbanization transformed the area's pastoral landscape, numerous groups organized to acquire threatened resources and encourage municipalities to do the same. Many of these groups have persisted to the present day, and it is particularly instructive to observe The Trustees' long history as it has adapted to different styles and priorities of land conservation.

Discussions leading to creation of The Trustees began within the council of that Boston Brahmin outdoor organization, the Appalachian Mountain Club (AMC) (Ashburne et al. 2001). Charles Eliot, son of the renowned Harvard University president of the same name, invited influential persons throughout the Commonwealth to form an organization to preserve scenic and historic properties. Those who gathered in May 1890 resolved to seek special legislation to establish a corporation to acquire and hold "for the benefit of the public, beautiful and historic places in Massachusetts" (Abbott 1993: 10–12). Less than a year later, in May 1891, those words were incorporated into the founding legislation for The Trustees (Abbott 1993: 10–12). The organization attracted the Massachusetts elite and worked closely with eminent landscape architect Frederick Law Olmsted.

Reflecting the rhetoric of the 1890s, Eliot and Olmsted rejected the term *park* for the properties to be protected by the group. To them, a park still connoted statuary, carriage trails, and similar accoutrements of the memorial and national capital tradition (Abbott 1993: 16). The Trustees were impressed with the early public domain reservations, which implied that land was withheld from development and left in its natural state. Hence, they became The Trustees of Reservations.

At the end of its first decade of activity, the organization had acquired four reservations by donation, the largest of which was 87 acres. Most of the early properties were estates of prominent Boston-area citizens. Like the MVLA before it, The Trustees worked effectively in partnership with state and city governments. For example, in December 1891 The Trustees convened a meeting of municipal officials and advocates to focus attention on the inadequacy of Boston-area parks. It did so, as had been done in the Adirondacks, by emphasizing the role of open space in protecting water supplies. Within three months, the city government had appointed a joint special committee on public reservations (with Charles Francis Adams, grandson of President John Quincy Adams, as chair). The joint committee began acquiring parks and beaches throughout the Boston region in 1893.

The Trustees' model was replicated throughout New England and elsewhere. In England, housing reform advocate Octavia Hill turned her attention to the industrialization of Wordsworth's cherished Lake District and adapted The Trustees' approach for protecting land in the area (Gwin and Fairfax 2004; Abbott 1993: 22).[7] Hill was one of three well-placed advocates who successfully launched the National Trust in Great Britain (Waterson 1994).[8]

The Demise of the Washington National Monument Society
The Trustees and MVLA notwithstanding, private organizations did not always prosper as partners of government. During the nation's centennial in 1876, interest in completing the Washington Monument was rekindled. Congress reinstated its pre-Civil War $200,000 appropriation, but it did so on the condition that title to the site be returned to the federal government.[9] Simultaneously, Congress decreed that construction of the monument would henceforth be under the direction of the president of the United States. The Washington Monument Society was reduced to providing a single member of a new commission advising the president on this project.

Construction proceeded under these new auspices, and all of the donated stones (minus the Pope's controversial contribution) found a place in the interior of the monument. However, the shakeup led to sniping and ill will between the society, which had shepherded the monument project for forty years, and the take-charge attitude of the Army Corps of Engineers' Lieutenant Colonel Thomas Casey.[10] In the end, the corps was responsible for the completed monument—another major conservation role for the War Department. The society lobbied unsuccessfully for a plaque at the top of the monument honoring its members' efforts. Casey refused. He wrote the chief of engineers that the proposed inscription was "misleading and unjust, ... largely an aggregation of names ... many of whom had nothing to do with the construction of the obelisk" (Allen 2000: 70).

Further improvement of the monument grounds accompanied the 1890 centennial of moving the capital. Many obstructions that had marred the area—an unsightly clutter of railroad tracks, buildings, and marshes—were removed (Freidel and Aikman 1988: 58–59). Then in 1902, another government commission, headed by Senator James McMillan, planned to revitalize what became known as the Mall. The McMillan Commission returned to L'Enfant's original in a master plan for the area, but the society had been permanently pushed aside.

Fort Ticonderoga

Meanwhile, the Pells were scrambling to protect Fort Ticonderoga from encroaching railroads. In 1870 and 1874, James K. Pell reluctantly sold rights-of-way, first to the Whitehall & Plattsburgh Railroad and then to the New York & Canada Railroad. To avoid forcing a condemnation, he negotiated for sales that required the railroads to tunnel under the garrison grounds rather than cut through them. The two roads met just below the fort in what became known as Addison Junction (Westbrook 2004). Conflict with railroads is a recurring theme in this chapter. In an era in which railroads were becoming a dominant feature of the American economy, it was difficult for any landowner to defend effectively against them.

Early Federal Acquisitions: Civil War Battlefields

Although the Washington Monument Society contested its diminished status for decades, public support for expanded federal authority to acquire land grew rapidly. The strongest context for this change was the preservation of Civil War battlefields, where federal acquisition quickly became a necessity rather than an option.[11] In 1867 Congress identified military cemeteries and memorials as a federal responsibility (Platt 2001: 3), and major Supreme Court decisions put a firm foundation under federal acquisition of land. These powers evolved to create a significant federal role in protecting natural curiosities, scenic wonders, watersheds, and wildlife habitat from the ravages of late nineteenth-century industrial capitalism.

Beginning at Gettysburg

Citizens began protecting Civil War battlefields while the war was still in progress. The battle of Gettysburg took place on July 1–3, 1863. Visitors began arriving at the site literally before the smoke had cleared. Within three weeks, Gettysburg attorney David McConaughy had purchased several major sites from local farmers to secure a cemetery and "the most interesting portions of the illustrious Battlefield that we may retain them in the actual form & condition they were in during the battle" (Platt 2001: 3).[12] Four months later, President Lincoln dedicated the privately owned cemetery.

In 1864, the Pennsylvania legislature chartered a private corporation, the Soldiers' National Cemetery, to work with the state. It focused initially on the cemetery but soon expanded to include the acquisition of nearby farms and fields where the battle had been fought. Little had been done to preserve Confederate Army positions, and the complete task of preserving the battlefield seemed too large for the existing state-private partnership. In 1870, President Grant signed legislation authorizing the War Department to accept title to both Gettysburg and Antietam cemeteries. In 1880, President Garfield signed a bill authorizing appropriation of $50,000 for a survey of the Gettysburg battlefield. In 1887, the northern states started appropriating funds for purchases of additional land (Lee 1973: 22–24).

Chickamauga and Chattanooga

These actions were part of a deliberate reframing of the Civil War to convey a message of national unity.[13] Civil War veterans from both sides began returning to battle sites for reunions that lasted weeks.

Early proposals for conservation of battlefields at Chickamauga and Chattanooga in Tennessee equally encompassed the lines of both armies, and Confederate and Union veterans alike joined with a local committee to establish the Chickamauga Memorial Association.

In August 1890, President Benjamin Harrison signed a law establishing the Chickamauga and Chattanooga battle sites as the first national military park (Lee 1973: 29). The law established an administrative commission similar to the one that helped to establish Washington, D.C. Three commissioners who had participated in the battles administered the area, supervised by the secretary of war. The same approach was followed in future battlefield conservation programs.

Under the new 1890 law, the secretary was authorized to acquire 7,600 acres of land, including the battlefield of Chickamauga itself, and to enter into an early form of a conservation easement on the surrounding parcels. Landowners in the area were allowed to occupy and farm their land, provided they also preserved the buildings, roads, and outlines of fields and forests (Lee 1973: 31). Specifically, the act provides that:

> The Secretary of the Interior is authorized to enter into agreements upon such nominal terms as he may prescribe, with such persons, who were owners of the land on August 19, 1890, as may desire to remain upon it, to occupy and cultivate their then holdings, upon condition that they will preserve the then buildings and roads, and the then outlines of field and forest, and that they will only cut trees or underbrush under such regulations as the Secretary may prescribe, and that they will assist in caring for and protecting all tablets, monuments, or such other artificial works as may from time to time be erected by proper authority. [*U.S. Code*, vol. 16 § 424 (2004)]

The new idea of property as a separable bundle of sticks was being utilized for the first time in acquisition policy. Also new was the idea that control of land was possible without acquiring full fee title or displacing landowners. Protection of land and traditional private uses could be compatible, with conservation accommodating existing private owners rather than excluding them.

Federal Condemnation Authority Confirmed

Although Congress moved expeditiously on the Chickamauga and Chattanooga proposal, it dawdled at Gettysburg. As it became clear that state and private actors lacked the resources for this particular task, conservation advocates argued that protecting Union and Confederate army positions was not the role of the state and was beyond the capacity of the private memorial association. The necessity of federal involvement seemed clear: "It must be done by the National Government or remain undone" (Lee 1973: 25).

Finally, in 1893, the threat of commercial development expedited matters. Congress noted that the battlefield was in imminent danger of being "irreparably defaced by the construction of a railway" (Unrau 1991: 75). Although it agreed to halt construction, the railroad refused to sell the land. In 1894 Congress directed the secretary of war to acquire the land by purchase or condemnation. Two days later the U.S. attorney initiated condemnation proceedings against the company (Lee 1973: 14–15).

This was a significant departure from previous practice. Condemnation had long been viewed as a state prerogative. Prior to the Civil War, the federal government generally obtained needed properties by cooperating with state governments. States condemned parcels and then ceded them to the federal government.[14]

In the 1896 case *United States v. Gettysburg Electric Railway Company* [160 U.S. 668 (1896)], the Supreme Court considered the legality of the federal condemnation. In the process it addressed two questions that remain basic today: (1) whether the federal government has authority to condemn property and (2) whether the action is in pursuit of an authorized public purpose (Meidinger 1980: 19–20). In the Gettysburg case, authority and purpose blended into a single question: Did the federal government have authority to condemn private land for a public park?

The railroad company conceded that the authority of the United States to take private property for public uses was by then "firmly fixed." An 1888 statute had granted all federal agencies the authority to acquire land, including the power to condemn, under which all federal agencies were authorized to rely on eminent domain whenever "necessary or advantageous" to the government.[15] However, the railroad insisted that any condemnation had to be related to a specific constitutional authority. "It is by no means clear," the company argued, "that the United States may condemn land in a State for the purpose of a national park."[16] The Supreme Court disagreed, finding the public purpose in a familiar source:

Any act of Congress which plainly and directly tends to enhance the respect and love of the citizen for the institutions of his country and to quicken and strengthen his motives to defend them ... must be valid. [*United States v. Gettysburg Electric Railway Company*, 160 U.S. 668, 681 (1896)]

In Gettysburg, the park's purpose was to enhance the general welfare by encouraging support of the military. Although the federal government's authority to condemn for some purposes was thereby established, the decision did not include (and in fact appeared to reject) condemnation for aesthetic or land conservation purposes (Meidinger 1980: 19). That would be much longer in coming.

Meanwhile, in 1895, Congress approved Gettysburg National Military Park. It authorized the secretary of war to open additional roads, mark lines of battle, establish penalties for defacing or mutilating property in the park, and acquire additional land, using condemnation if needed (Lee 1973: 27). The park had no formal boundary, but priority acquisitions were identified on a map made by Daniel Sickles, who had interrupted his long service in Congress to fight at Gettysburg. Figure 3.2, what is known as the Sickles map, shows the original purchase boundary for the park. The idea was that the federal government would acquire a linear tract to allow access to a system of avenues leading to the battle sites. The encircled land could be acquired with the presumption that it would remain in farming as it had been during the battles.

Unfortunately, the specific park boundaries remained unclear and the authorization was amended the following year to allow the purchase of "other adjacent lands." The park thus went forward with no official borders (Unrau 1991: 83–84) but with the assumption that the land within the encircling tract would be acquired. This ambiguity stoked conflict between the NPS and local townspeople that continues to this day. At the time, however, there was little dissent. Conserving the hallowed ground was appropriate, federal leadership was necessary, and if private landowners had different priorities, the government would condemn the land.

Reserved Federal Lands: Constitutional Issues of Ownership, Jurisdiction, and Management

The Civil War battlefield experience cemented both public expectations and basic authorities regarding an expanded federal role in conservation.

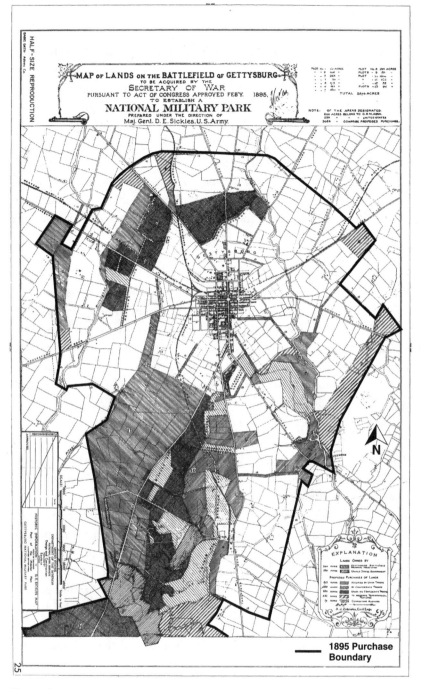

Figure 3.2
Sickles map of the Gettysburg Battlefield. Source: National Park Service Technical Information Center Collection.

Other fundamental questions about federal acquisition were raised and answered in the context of land the government already owned—the public domain in the western states and territories. Growing nationalism and jealous comparisons with European treasures,[17] the growing industrial capitalist economy, the rise of cities and accompanying urge to return to and protect the countryside, and the ostensible closing of the frontier (Limerick 1987) all figured significantly in the broadening of conservation goals. Important questions of management and jurisdiction arose from these changes. We look, therefore, to the public domain to understand emerging ideas about federal authority to own and manage a broader array of landscapes.

Expanding Reservations for Conservation Purposes

Pressure in Congress for additional public domain reservations increased as the nineteenth century drew to a close. Three major reservation statutes—Yellowstone in 1872, the Forest Reserve Act of 1891, and the Antiquities Act of 1906—suggest intense public attention to conservation as well as a growing preference for the federal government as protector. Sweetening the deal were assurances by conservation advocates that the reservations would be self-supporting, imposing no new costs on the treasury (Buck 1946: 11).[18]

The Yellowstone Reservation   Unlike the Yosemite reservation, Yellowstone was reserved before the establishment of the states in which it is now located—Idaho, Montana, and Wyoming. Consequently, the reserved area was retained in federal ownership. Although the reservation is frequently cited as the first expression of the idea of a national park, it was pushed through Congress, not by preservationists, but by Northern Pacific Railroad officials who sought a new tourist trade (O'Toole 1995: 9). As with the naval oak reserves, continued federal ownership did not lead to effective control over the area. The reservation precluded further homesteading in the area but it attracted the diverse predations of hunters, hucksters, and visitors. The destruction was so bad that eventually the U.S. Army was summoned in 1886 to manage the site (Hampton 1971).

The 1891 Forest Reserve Act   Although parklike reservations continued on an ad hoc basis, by 1897 three presidents had used *general* authority to set aside and reserve more than 33 million acres, "wholly or in part covered with timber or undergrowth" [*U.S. Statutes at Large* 26 (1891): 1103 § 24], largely upon petition by interests that believed the tree cover would protect water for irrigation. The reserves originally remained under the authority of the General Land Office (GLO) in the Department of the Interior. They were the beginning of a federal system for forest conservation—that is, an identifiable set of public lands with a definable purpose in common. However, in the absence of congressional direction regarding management or use of the forest reserves, they were closed to entry and use. John Muir was among those who recommended that the army protect the forest reserves as well (Bowers et al. 1895).

The Antiquities Act   The Antiquities Act passed in 1906, the same year that Congress opened the forest reserves to homestead entry and a few months before it rescinded the president's authority to establish new forest reservations. The act granted the president general reservation authority to protect "historic landmarks, historic and prehistoric structures, and other objects of historic or scientific interest" [U.S. Code, vol. 16 § 431 (2004)]. The president was also authorized to accept donations of land (Rothman 1989). Although the act had aimed primarily at protection of southwestern archeological sites, the first fully donated parklike unit was Muir Woods outside San Francisco, given in 1908 by congressman and philanthropist William Kent. Again, important differences between national parks and forests were emerging. Charity has never been a significant element of national forest acquisition. Moreover, until the 1964 passage of the Land and Water Conservation Fund Act, the Antiquities Act was the only general authority under which the NPS could add units.[19]

Reservations Challenged   The scale and frequency of reservations signaled a gradual retreat from disposition of the public domain and invited legal challenge. In the 1897 *Camfield* case [167 U.S. 518 (1897)], the Supreme Court simply presumed that the federal government was authorized to reserve its lands. "A different rule," the Court observed, "would place the public domain of the United States completely at the mercy of state legislation" [167 U.S. 518, 526 (1897)]. But the decision was also narrow; it contained no ringing reference to the Article IV property clause or "all needful rules." The Court treated the federal government as it would any other proprietor (Cowart and Fairfax 1988). *Camfield* is thus a limited but significant recognition that the federal government was authorized to retain the public domain, and that as a legal owner it retained at least theoretical authority to manage and control use of its holdings.

Jurisdiction over New Federal Reserves

In the wake of *Camfield*, it became important to decide whether the state or the federal government had ultimate legal jurisdiction in the new reserves. The outcome was deeply colored by the enclave clause, even though the issue concerned reserved public land that was not obviously subject to the terms of Article I.

Shared Jurisdiction Approved   The first shoe dropped in yet another case concerning a railroad: *Fort Leavenworth R. Company v. Lowe* [114 U.S. 525 (1885)]. Because the railroad was located in a federal enclave within a state, the owner argued that, following the enclave clause, the area was subject to exclusive federal jurisdiction. Therefore, he claimed he did not have to pay state taxes.

The Supreme Court rejected the argument. In doing so, it abandoned the exclusive jurisdiction element of the enclave clause and concluded that the state could attach any conditions to its land and jurisdiction cessions that were not inconsistent with federal use of the land for the stated purpose. Ever since, states have carefully negotiated the terms of federal acquisitions, retaining useful sticks in the bundle, such as the right to tax associated economic activity, while leaving the federal government with many of the costs of ownership.

Exclusive Jurisdiction in Parks   When Wyoming became a state in 1890, Congress reserved exclusive jurisdiction over Yellowstone (Buck 1946: 26–27). Thereafter, until the 1970s, in both reserved and subsequently acquired park units, the NPS norm was to seek exclusive federal jurisdiction for its properties. In forest reserves—where less restrictive land use regulations made total control seem less important—a pattern of shared federal and state jurisdiction prevailed.

This attention to issues of jurisdiction may seem arcane, but it is vital in defining the relationship—then and today—between federal units and local communities. Exclusive jurisdiction allows the NPS to prohibit hunting in parks, for example, while on national forests, state law typically controls. This pattern arose long before either the USFS or the NPS was established and today constitutes an important element of the mosaic of ownerships discernible on the landscape.

Defining Federal Authority over Conservation Reservations
Following the assurances of conservation advocates that reservations would be self-supporting, Congress generally refused to appropriate funds for protection of the reserves (Buck 1946; Hampton 1971). Private use and abuse of what were legally federal lands was the predictable result, and federal control of government property remained weak. After relying on the army for basic protection of the public domain for more than twenty years, Congress at last began to establish management policies and agencies. Because a bureaucracy is mentioned nowhere in the Constitution, the federal courts were called upon to fit the new agencies into the federal scheme.

Founding the First Progressive Era Land Management Agency   In 1905, Congress transferred the forest reserves from the Department of the Interior to the Department of Agriculture (renaming them national forests) and established the USFS to manage them. Congress authorized salaries for forest managers and established a fund to make receipts from timber and grazing permits available, without further appropriation, for national forest administration (Ise 1924). However, the issue of whether the reserves were supposed to make money, simply break even, or enjoy a federal subsidy was not resolved. By 1907, Chief Forester Gifford Pinchot had so angered western congressional representatives that they stripped the agency of its dedicated funds. All Forest Service expenses were thereafter subject to annual appropriations, and Congress has remained reluctant to authorize dedicated funding mechanisms, such as trust funds or user fees.

Congress also granted the states a generous share of agency receipts to compensate them for alleged burdens created by federal land ownership.

The federal government does not pay state or local taxes on land that it owns. Hence, members of Congress frequently insist that federal land units are a financial burden. The arguments intensify regarding land acquisition, which removes private land from local tax rolls, as opposed to reservations, where the land was never privately owned. Starting with the early national forests, the pattern of federal revenue sharing with states and localities grew throughout the century to include payments in lieu of taxes (PILTs) and other goodies. In contrast to the interstate competition to host the nation's capital gratis, subsequent congressmen learned to advocate for PILTs and other compensations (Fairfax 1987; Tribe 1976) even while seeking the economic benefits of federal holdings in their districts.

Challenging Management Authorities   Soon after the USFS was established, long-time users of the reserves challenged agency regulations and fees. In *Light v. United States*, the plaintiffs argued that neither the enclave clause nor the property clause gave Congress the authority to reserve public domain lands from settlement without the consent of the state. The Supreme Court simply disagreed.[20] Sticking to the logic of its *Camfield* decision, the Court argued that Congress had at least the same rights as any other proprietor. The Court also hinted that the federal government was more than a "mere proprietor" and might exercise authority as a sovereign that outstripped the rights of an ordinary landowner:

The courts cannot ... interfere when, in the exercise of its discretion, Congress establishes a forest reserve for what it decides to be national and public purposes. In the same way and in the exercise of the same trust it may disestablish a reserve, and devote the property to some other national and public purpose. These are rights incident to proprietorship, to say nothing of the power of the United States as a sovereign over the property belonging to it. [*Light v. United States*, 220 U.S. 523, 538 (1911)]

A second case, *United States v. Grimaud* [220 U.S. 506 (1911)], addressed one of several standard turn-of-the-century challenges to the growing administrative state. Regulated individuals frequently argued that whatever rule aggrieved them was an illegal delegation of legislative authority. Perhaps because of the agency's heavy emphasis on science,

Forest Service regulations passed muster. In *Grimaud*, the Court upheld Forest Service regulations and fees, thus affirming constitutional authority for federal management of government-owned lands, whether reserved or acquired.

Acquisitions and Reservations: Inholders and Exchanges

Although a majority of western public lands were reserved from the public domain, many key parcels were also acquired. Acquisition was necessary both to remove private inholders from within federal reservations, and, on some occasions, to acquire large expanses of private land.

Dealing with Existing Residents and Inholders   Unlike forest advocates, who were initially as unconcerned about inholders as they were about exclusive jurisdiction, advocates of "park purity" saw the parks as sacrosanct "nature as it is," nominally unsullied. Private land within park boundaries was considered a threat to park protection. In the absence of a clear federal authority to purchase private land for conservation purposes, removing the inhabitants was frequently hard on both Indians and settlers. Generally, the Indians were simply removed,[21] while the claims of white settlers were dealt with in other ways.

Federal treatment of settlers in the Yosemite and Sequoia-Kings Canyon was not atypical. Only three claims had been staked in Yosemite Valley before the area was granted to the state. Two claimants left quietly, but James Hutchins battled the state commission established to administer the park for over a decade before his claim was officially invalidated (Runte 1990: 17–35).[22] The Cooperative Land and Colonization Association in Sequoia-Kings Canyon faced harsher treatment. In 1885, the association entered the area and filed claims with the intention of developing a utopian community. Their efforts to build a railroad into the region failed, but they were able to construct a road to their claim. When the area was reserved in 1890, however, they became a problem. To get rid of them, a special land agent of the Department of the Interior who had initially certified their claim shifted directions and found it invalid. The government acquired the land by asserting it had never been claimed and denied compensation for the road as well (Dilsaver and Strong 1993: 16–17; Hampton 1971: 153–154).

That strategy did not always work. Adding to our discussion of early confusion between parks and forests, two 1890 statutes added a ring of federal park land, called forest reservations, around the valley that had been granted to California. However, adding land to Yosemite also added inholdings—claims that had been staked under a variety of disposition statutes as transportation into the region improved. In 1898, the House Committee on Public Lands calculated that there were 53,931 acres of privately owned lands within the federal reservations surrounding Yosemite Valley. Several proposals were introduced in Congress to establish an in lieu scrip program, to allow the enterprising settlers who had been turned into inholders by the 1890 statutes to select public domain lands elsewhere in lieu of their holdings. Earlier land exchanges had occasioned significant fraud, however, and Congress did not approve the proposals.

An advisory commission established in 1903 considered the problem. In addition to the inholders, the commission noted that the federal boundaries had been drawn on section lines. With no natural boundaries to indicate when a person was in or not in the reservation, the cavalry had difficulty patrolling and protecting the area. In an early sign that ownership does not necessarily convey control, the commission recommended removing more than 500 square miles from the reservation to address both problems. Although 113 square miles were added (Ise 1961: 65–70), the 1905 Yosemite boundary adjustment is the largest removal of land from a national park. Lest one believe that controversial acquisitions are confined to the eastern United States, we will follow controversial NPS efforts to acquire inholdings that continue to be a problem in Yosemite National Park.

Acquisitions by Exchange   Although land exchanges were not used to save the east side of Yosemite, they were the key to acquiring land owned by the Northern Pacific Railway on Mount Rainier. In 1899, Congress authorized an exchange to form part of a new national park in the area. The "generous consideration" afforded the railroad was an embarrassment to the park's supporters. By relinquishing its holdings, Northern Pacific was allowed to select "lieu lands" from the public domain in any state where the railroad ran. The company's selection of

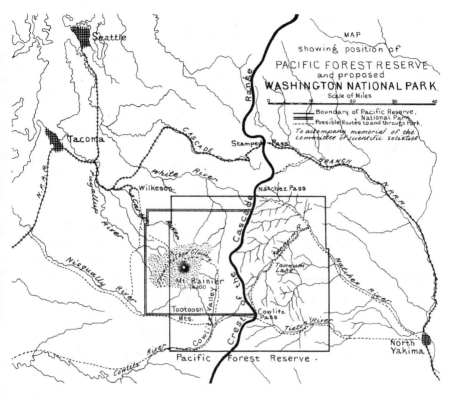

Figure 3.3
Mount Rainier as a part of the Pacific Forest Reserve. Source: U.S. Congress.
Senate (1884).

prime timberland in Oregon did not please Oregonians. Park supporters
were probably more concerned that the deal eliminated 300 square miles
of forested land from the park (Catton 1996, part II). The terms were
controversial, and the transaction was still being investigated and
criticized in the mid-1920s (Ise 1924: 121–122; Donnelly 1924).[23] However, this story does suggest why a corporate exploiter might turn "good
guy" and support a national park.

Mount Rainier and Yosemite were also two of the first parks to include land that had previously been designated as forest reserves. Figure
3.3 shows the Pacific Forest Reserve reductions necessary to create
Rainier. The USFS was not yet established to defend its turf, but park

advocates had to deflect the objection that the park designation was redundant. In so doing, park supporters convinced Congress that even after the 1891 Forest Reserve Act, there was still a need for greater federal control based on the Yellowstone reservation concept. Mount Rainier made it clear that the federal government would develop more than one approach to protecting land (Catton 1996, part II).

Wildlife Refuges: Early Mosaics

Conservation of wildlife occupies a vexed position in this growing set of federal programs and authorities. The enterprise was confused by the peculiar 1896 Supreme Court decision, *Geer v. Connecticut* [161 U.S. 519 (1896)]. The Court upheld state regulations barring interstate trade in wildlife irrespective of their obvious burden on interstate commerce. Establishing what is now known as the state ownership doctrine, the Court avoided normal application of the commerce clause, reasoning that the state owned the wildlife on behalf of its citizens.[24] This decision put federal conservation of wildlife and habitat on a difficult footing compared with growing forest and park programs, and it left wildlife advocates in considerable organizational and intellectual disarray. As a result, wildlife did not become a part of mainstream conservation advocacy until the mid-1920s (Swain 1963: 32).

However, wildlife advocates, generally an elite group of hunters associated with organizations such as the Boone and Crockett Club, viewed federal refuges as essential to wildlife protection. In spite of constitutional constraints, they sought their "own" agency and land dedicated specifically to wildlife. Hampered by *Geer*, they improvised— piggybacking wildlife onto established reservations, squeezing refuge authorizations into appropriations bills, taking advantage of the Antiquities Act, drawing on the 1891 forest reserve authority, or using whatever else might work.

The first dedicated wildlife refuge actually predated the *Geer* decision. President Grant reserved the Pribilof Islands in the Bering Sea in 1868. The islands had just been purchased from Russia and were extremely valuable for their fur seals. A year later Congress authorized the Treasury Department to lease sealing rights on the islands to commercial entities, and the seals did not fare well.[25] President Harrison subsequently used the 1891 forest reservation authority to create the Afognak Forest and Fish-Culture Reserve in Alaska in 1892, to protect salmon fisheries, sea animals, and other animals and birds.[26]

The refuge idea solidified under Theodore Roosevelt. In spite of *Geer*, the president established fifty-three federal refuges while in office (Langston 2003: 67–68). The first was Pelican Island, created on the east coast of Florida in 1903 as an inviolate sanctuary for plumed seabirds, which had been overhunted for making ladies' hats (Fink 1994: 10–11; Environmental Law Institute 1977: 127). The State of Florida had previously outlawed killing all birds other than game, but advocates viewed the protection as inadequate. Nevertheless, Congress made no arrangement for managing the refuge. Affluent wildlife enthusiasts established public-private partnerships when they were unable to persuade Roosevelt to sell the island to the Audubon Society (Langston 2003: 68). They worked through the Ornithologists' Union to pay the Pelican Island warden (Cameron, J. 1929: 85–86).

By 1906, five additional bird refuges were reserved from the public domain—still with limited management provisions—and relied on similar partnerships; the National Association of Audubon Societies paid the wardens' salaries at those sites as well (Trefethen 1975: 141).[27]

Although federal acquisitions for wildlife protection continued to be constitutionally suspect, no opposition was raised to the purchase of 12,000 acres for a National Bison Range in Montana in 1908. The land was part of the Flathead Indian Reservation and became available for sale under the 1887 Dawes Act's infamous reservation allotment process.[28] The American Bison Society agreed to furnish the buffalo (Gabrielson 1943: 11). Congress expanded the authorized acquisition to 20,000 acres in 1909. The 1909 agriculture appropriations act also ended the dependence of the managing agency, the Bureau of Biological Survey (BBS), on private donors for wardens' salaries (Gabrielson 1943: 11–12) and appropriated $7,000 to maintain the Bison Range and other reservations for mammals and birds.[29] The idea of a refuge system was beginning to take shape.

Despite these successes, authority for managing refuges remained scattered. A Division of Economic Ornithology and Mammalogy was established in the Department of Agriculture in 1886, with responsibility for research on birds, plants, and mammals. It had grown by 1906 into the BBS, which managed some early refuges. A Bureau of Fisheries, established in 1871, was incorporated into the Department of Commerce after many renamings and reorganizations.[30] Other federal agencies also played a part. Big game refuges were under the Forest Service; elk protection resided in the Department of Interior; and several bird and small game refuges were under the War Department, the Navy Department, and even the Lighthouse Service (Yard 1928: 313–314). These diverse roots make it difficult to identify a tidy trail to refuge acquisition authority, but they ultimately gave federal wildlife agencies a broad array of authorities and tools for acquiring land.

The Eastern National Forests as the Cornerstone for Future Acquisition Programs

Federal land acquisition for conservation gained full political, if not constitutional, acceptance in 1911 with the Weeks Act.[31] This act is the cornerstone of federal land acquisition programs still familiar almost a century later. It provided general authority for the acquisition of private lands to create the eastern national forests and continues to be the principal authority under which the Forest Service purchases land.[32]

Justifying Federal Land Acquisition for Conservation

By the late nineteenth century, industrialization had severely altered the eastern landscape, with forests having been particularly devastated. Conservation advocates responded by lobbying for federal action, primarily for an eastern national park (Ogden 1980; Smith, C. 1956). But land in the east had largely passed into private ownership at this point. Parks, or forests as it turned out, would have to be purchased.

Advocates focused initially on acquiring recreation and scenic land (Smith, C. 1960a,b; Pratt 1936). While Congress was willing by this time to support land reservations for extraordinarily scenic areas of the public domain, many members would not support the purchase of land for those same purposes. The powerful speaker of the house, Joseph Cannon, summarized the position succinctly: "not one cent for scenery!" (Pratt 1936: 1029).

Accepting that reality, advocates shifted emphasis from parks to forests (Smith, C. 1956: 71–111) and then yet again to protecting stream flow when acquisition for forest conservation proved constitutionally problematic. Advocates thus followed the pattern established in the Adirondacks: justifying acquisition of forests for watershed protection. From there they found a constitutional hook in the commerce clause, arguing that to protect commercial waterways, the prevention of siltation (by protecting upstream forests) was more effective than dredging (Ogden 1980: 214–215; Smith, C. 1956: 281–282). Opponents argued that the federal government had no authority to acquire land for conservation purposes and that doing so would require a constitutional amendment (Smith, C. 1956: 280).

Congress turned to the House Committee on the Judiciary for a legal assessment (Ogden 1980: 193; Smith, C. 1956: 278). The committee concluded that the federal government did not have the authority to acquire land for the sole purpose of forest conservation, which was nowhere enumerated as a power of the federal government. However, because the federal government has the power to regulate interstate commerce, it could purchase land to protect instream flow for navigation purposes (Smith, C. 1956: 286; Ogden 1980: 218–219). Debate then shifted to the empirical question of whether there was any connection between stream flow and forest conditions in the eastern watersheds. Continued scientific dispute on this point led to provisions in the final act that required that the U.S. Geological Survey certify that proposed acquisitions would indeed protect stream flow (Dana, S. 1956: 186).

Enclave clause requirements regarding state permissions and cessions also appear in the bill. Few states waited for the act to pass to get in line for the potential windfall. Again putting the lie to the picture of reluctant states and localities forced to accept federal land ownership within their boundaries, Georgia passed the requisite legislation in 1901 (Smith, C. 1956: 78). North Carolina was so enthusiastic that it moved the same year to obtain options on 494,200 acres of forest for ultimate sale to the federal government (Pratt 1936: 1030). New York and Massachusetts were the only eastern states to refuse permission for Weeks Act acquisitions, although some states put upper limits on the amount of land that could be acquired (Greeley 1953: 166). Maryland originally consented to federal acquisitions but later recanted (Ogden 1980: 189).

Weeks Act advocates were careful not to incur the wrath of state wildlife organizations; the acquisition of national forests would not displace state hunting and fishing laws on the acquired lands (U.S. FS 1914: 4). Other bargains were necessary. Western states, for example, harbored animosity toward Gifford Pinchot and the Forest Service (Smith, C. 1956: 310, 339; Ogden 1980: 173–174) and opposed any new authority for the agency. Ultimately, their support was obtained by adding cooperative forestry and fire conservation provisions to the bill, items of considerable interest to western congressmen as wildfires swept their states in 1910 and 1911 (Greeley 1951). However, as we will see, the big winners were the private sellers.

Weeks Act Provisions
The Weeks Act made two major innovations in public forestry. First, it granted the Forest Service general authority to acquire privately owned lands "on the headwaters of navigable streams or those which are being or which may be developed for navigable purposes." Lands so acquired were to be "permanently reserved, held, and administered as national forest lands."[33] Second, the Weeks Act formalized a policy of including subsidies to local industries and localities as an element of extending federal control. It funded Forest Service programs to assist states in fighting fires.

The act also continued the practice of sharing receipts from federal lands with the states. However, on acquired lands, only 5 percent of the gross receipts were allocated to the state in which the revenue was produced. These sweeteners soon became almost a prerequisite for moving federal land projects through Congress.[34]

The process Congress established to acquire lands was similar to those operating in the District of Columbia and the Civil War monuments. The act established the National Forest Reservation Commission (NFRC), which consisted of government officials, to identify purchase areas known as purchase units for acquisition (Swain 1963: 3). Specific purchase boundaries were then delineated by the Forest Service and approved by the secretary of agriculture (U.S. FS 1961: 7). When sufficient land had been acquired as a purchase unit, that unit would then be designated a national forest and administered as such by the USFS. Although the Forest Service made the actual purchases,[35] the existence of the NFRC suggests that Congress did not trust agency employees to identify the land they would acquire. And although the commission did not actually buy land, it strikes us as having had many functions that land trusts perform today, particularly regarding preacquisitions.

In contrast to advocates of parks, the NFRC did not believe that conservation required the acquisition of all land within a purchase boundary. Indeed, the Weeks Act authorized the secretary of agriculture to sell any lands acquired "of necessity or by inadvertence" that were suited for agriculture and not needed for the purposes of the act. These private lands were not insubstantial; indeed the average eastern national forest today is about 50 percent public land—another form of the simple early mosaic of landowners that we have seen on checkerboard lands and some wildlife refuges.

Although the Weeks Act did not mention it, the attorney general ruled that the secretary of agriculture could also condemn land for Weeks Act purposes.[36] However, condemnation was as politically unpopular then as it is now, and the Forest Service used it only sparingly to clear title or prevent landowners from exacting exorbitant prices (U.S. FS 1914: 5). In a few cases, purchase units were abandoned when it became clear that the agency could not acquire sufficient land to administer it effectively (Shands 1992: 34). In this way, sellers determined which proposed eastern national forests would exist and which would not.

Indeed, although most of the literature portrays it as a conservation "victory," the Weeks Act also forcefully reminds us that for every buyer, there is a seller whose needs must be met. In fact, the law carefully attends to nearly every desire of a potential seller. Extending the bundle of sticks conception of ownership, section 7 of the act allowed sellers to reserve rights to minerals or merchantable timber. In 1913 that authority was broadened to permit purchase of lands subject to privately held rights-of-way, easements, or any other reservations, that, in the judgment of the NFRC and the secretary of agriculture, would not interfere with achieving the purposes of the act (Dana, S. 1956: 184–185). Incredibly, many landowners were able to sell their land while retaining the right to cut timber, leaving the Forest Service to reforest it later (Shands 1992: 35).[37] Many others sold cut-over, badly managed land that they would have abandoned anyway.

Given the generous terms for sellers, it is not surprising that funding soon became an issue. Congress appropriated $1 million for Weeks Act purchases for the fiscal year of 1910, which had already passed, and $2 million for each subsequent fiscal year through 1915, after which the money ran out. Thereafter, purchases were limited chiefly to cut-over areas available at reasonable prices. By 1920, 1.4 million acres had been acquired for $7.6 million, at an average cost of $5.30 per acre (U.S. NFRC 1920: 9; 1933: 8). Weeks Act acquisitions by that date made up about 0.9 percent of total national forest holdings (156 million acres in all in 1920) (U.S. FS 2001). The pace was slower than some had hoped, and dissatisfaction led to another round of legislation in the 1920s (Dana, S. 1956: 186). Nevertheless, the basic constitutional hurdles had been cleared, and both statutory authority and an administrative agency were in place to acquire private forestland for conservation.

Summary

After the Civil War, land acquisition became an important tool of an increasingly coherent land conservation movement. A broadening of conservation goals was precipitated in part by the rapid transformation of the familiar rural landscape, and states and private groups across the nation responded. Their emphasis on purchasing land, rather than regulating private use to achieve conservation goals, is consistent with the Lockean foundations of the nation's political economy and reflects the fact that with some notable exceptions, regulation of land use was still relatively rare. Furthermore, both the federal government and the states, such as New York, still owned considerable acreage. Working politically to ensure government conservation of public lands seemed a reasonable first step. Whether to keep a railroad off a sacred battlefield, or to protect clean drinking water and navigable streams, fee ownership seemed essential.

In an important change, however, much of this conservation and acquisition activity began to occur at the national level. As the federal government moved more to the center of American political and economic life, Congress responded to requests from increasingly well-organized interest groups to protect watersheds, scenic and archeological resources, and wildlife. More and more, those requests required not only reservations but also acquisition of private lands. At first such acquisitions were limited to battlefields under the war powers, but soon the range of acceptable deals expanded considerably. By 1911, the constitutional and statutory arrangements remained incomplete, but the basic model for a federal land management and acquisition program for conservation was in place. This was a major innovation from the days of the MVLA.

At the same time, the federal estate was being divided by statutes and interest groups, and on the ground into scenic and cultural wonders, trees, historic houses, archeological ruins, water, and wildlife. Meanwhile, forest acquisitions and reservations created a proliferation of inholders, particularly under the seller-friendly terms of the Weeks Act. The result was the beginning of institutional fragmentation leading to the mosaics we see today.

Public land ownership was not any more likely to convey effective control than it had before. Once the federal government acquired or reserved land, decision making shifted from the market to the political arena. There the notion of federal lands as burdens created space for manipulation of the enclave clause by state and local governments.[38] This allowed states to procure the advantages of federal investment, such as economic development and shares of federal revenues, while shifting the burdens of management onto the federal government. Private landowners soon caught on and politically designed acquisition programs to meet their needs as well, most clearly through the solicitous terms of the Weeks Act. Reluctant to exercise its condemnation authority, the federal government was largely dependent on willing sellers. The outcome was predictable: mosaics of private and public lands and ownership rights that lacked many elements of effective control.

4

Between the Roosevelts, 1912–1932

Conservation narratives frequently peter out after the presidency of Theodore Roosevelt and do not perk up again until the Depression and FDR's tenure at the White House (Swain 1963: 6). From the perspective of land acquisition, this is a major oversight. Passage of the Weeks Act in 1911 signaled both that key constitutional issues had been resolved and that Americans had accepted the idea that the federal government could and would acquire land for certain conservation purposes. The 1910s and 1920s were a period of growth and consolidation in the federal resource agencies rather than a time of major innovation. That might justify giving the era a light treatment. However, the elaboration of federal programs was affected by major changes in economic conditions, continuing struggles over competing visions of property, and changing conservation goals. The result was new relationships between public and private actors in acquisition efforts, as well as new targets for acquisition.

Changing economic conditions are vital to understanding the era between the Roosevelts. The Depression came early to the natural resource industries. During World War I, federal spending increased rapidly. When Congress subsequently cut back to balance the budget, a severe recession hit. An average of 600 banks failed each year during the 1920s, and the value of farmland fell between 30 and 40 percent. The Ku Klux Klan reached the height of its influence, and the richest 1 percent of the nation held 40 percent of the nation's wealth (Kangas 1997). Economic conditions colored the debate about land protection and strengthened the hand of politically powerful but financially embarrassed landowners.

Second, regulation—and its potential as a tool of land conservation—also became a major theme. Congress considered a series of proposals that would have established a federal forestry commission to regulate cutting on private forest lands. The bill would have reduced the pressure to acquire land to protect it and was tied, like the 1911 Weeks Act, to the federal authority over interstate commerce (Dana, S. 1956: 208–229).

However, Progressive era ideas about the social nature of property had not consistently taken root. A 1920 Supreme Court decision threatened regulations that "went too far,"[1] and Congress ultimately rejected the idea of regulating private forest management. Instead, the Society of American Foresters and the timber industry developed proposals for major federal land acquisitions and for federal "cooperation" with (i.e., subsidies to) the timber industry. Congress accepted both, expanding USFS Weeks Act acquisition authorities. New subsidies and federal-state partnerships were added to the conservation toolkit, but these programs strengthened the agency's commitment to serving the needs of willing sellers, with important limitations as a result.

However, the expansion of federal acquisition authority was inconsistent. Founded in 1916, the NPS quickly captured the heart of American land conservation, yet Congress continued to reject categorically the idea that parks were a constitutional "purpose" justifying expenditure of federal funds. As a result, the NPS was left to repeat the Mount Rainier model throughout the West, nibbling pieces out of national forests. Park Service competition with the USFS became a durable feature of federal land conservation efforts. Wildlife advocates continued to struggle to obtain acquisition authority as well, but took a different tack regarding funding, relying on user fees supported by affluent hunters.

Necessity breeds innovation, and the plight of the NPS and the wildlife agencies led to new approaches to acquisition. Wildlife supporters used any means and authorities possible to secure refuge lands, including partial interests and leases as well as occasional fee purchases. Meanwhile, state and private actors began to assist in acquisitions for parks in new ways, becoming major acquirers of land for the NPS. States in particular were keen to enjoy the benefits of a visible national park unit without experiencing the high costs of managing it.

Private land protection organizations shifted much of their effort to supporting, some might say directing, NPS acquisitions. We see in these early programs the start of what land trusts now call preacquisitions and flip transactions. We also see early warnings about the limits of acquisition in terms of public accountability.

We will cover this critical period in two sections. The next section begins with innovations in state and private acquisitions. The story at the federal level, treated in the second section, is more complex but less innovative. By the 1920s, federal land management and acquisition was proceeding on three different tracks: the formation of the NPS, expansion of the Weeks Act and new general exchange powers for the USFS, and early acquisitions of wildlife refuges. Even the barely there predecessor to the Bureau of Land Management (BLM) merits a brief discussion because it emerged as a marketbasket for the then three other federal agencies.

State and Private Programs

Even as the federal government consolidated and expanded its new acquisition authorities, private and state efforts remained important. The politically savvy women of the MVLA successfully resisted continual efforts at a federal takeover, while private and state groups were fundamental to the expansion of the newly created NPS system. Meanwhile, the Supreme Court's reluctance to sanction land use regulations strengthened the hand of private landowners and tipped the scales further in favor of willing-seller transactions.

Contesting Private Conservation at Mount Vernon

Between 1914[2] and 1934, proposals that the federal government purchase Mount Vernon were almost constantly before Congress.[3] Although actual transfer of the site was never a serious possibility, the debate does testify to the changes that aggressive federal participation brought to the field of land acquisition for conservation.

The main theme of the political discussion was that many people now simply thought it "right" that Washington's home be national property. "The trend of the times," observed Congressman Allen T. Treadway of

Massachusetts, a tireless supporter of the transfer, "is for everything having to do with Washington's memory to be controlled by the federal Government."[4] In a mere eighty years, the federal government had gone from being constitutionally excluded to being morally necessary. Nevertheless, the MVLA called upon its own politically powerful allies and prevailed. Not until the association required assistance from the NPS to fend off urban encroachments in the 1960s did the two organizations establish a working relationship.

A secondary issue was that the MVLA charged an entrance fee. This was considered a questionable practice, even among the association's supporters. A 1921 bill proposed federal purchase of both Mount Vernon and Jefferson's Monticello estate, "to abolish forever the un-American system of tolls or admission charges extracted from the American public for the privilege of being admitted to the tombs of the great American presidents."[5] By extension, the idea initially used by park advocates to justify reservations—that the NPS would become self-supporting by charging admission to its units—was clearly out of favor.

Private Acquisition and the Limits of Regulation

Private lands were drawn more fully into the conservation debate as Progressive era ideas about property gained strength. State and federal regulation of private timber harvesting, for example, was seriously debated and could have reduced the pressure to acquire land for conservation. However, in the early twentieth century, regulation of land use remained both uncommon and controversial, forcing conservationists to pause before embracing new regulatory approaches.

Two 1920s Supreme Court cases suggest the reasons for this ambivalence. In *Pennsylvania Coal Company v. Mahon* [260 U.S. 393 (1922)], an infamous dispute tested the limits of regulation. Passed in 1921, Pennsylvania's Kohler Act addressed the problems presented by severed mineral title. The land overlying coal deposits was owned by ordinary citizens and resembled any town, with houses, businesses, streets, and civic buildings. The subsurface was owned by coal companies, however, who were busily extracting these mineral reserves. The act was intended to prevent coal owners from removing so much coal that the overlying towns literally collapsed.

Challenging the law, the coal company argued that such regulation was a constitutional "taking" of its property right in the coal. While previous legal doctrine had made it clear that public physical invasion or seizure of private property required just compensation under the Fifth Amendment, the idea that a regulation could necessitate the same kind of payment for lost value was new. In a landmark decision, the Supreme Court agreed with the coal company, dealing a blow to land use regulation as a conservation tool. Chief Justice Holmes noted that "government hardly could go on if to some extent values incident to property could not be diminished without paying for every such change in the general law" [260 U.S. 393 (1922): 413]. However, when the regulation "reaches a certain magnitude" there "must be compensation to sustain the act" [260 U.S. 393 (1922): 413]. The Court did not define "certain magnitude," and one way to understand takings law ever since is that we are still trying to do so.

But if *Pennsylvania Coal* weakened regulation of land use and the Progressive view of property, another case soon strengthened both. Four years later, in *Village of Euclid v. Ambler Realty Co.*, the Court established land use zoning as a legitimate use of the state's police power. Zoning was just emerging as a tool in cities and towns to keep industrial areas separate from residential ones. When Ambler Realty was confronted with local zoning that diminished the value of property it planned to develop, it challenged the law as a taking. Surprisingly, after the Pennsylvania case, the Supreme Court rejected the takings argument and supported zoning as a legitimate tool for keeping the proverbial pig out of the parlor:

Until recent years, urban life was comparatively simple; but with the great increase and concentration of population, problems have developed ... which require, and will continue to require, additional restrictions in respect to the use and occupation of private lands in urban communities. [*Euclid v. Ambler Realty Co.*, 272 U.S. 365 (1926): 386–387]

Privately Acquired State and National Parks

Regulation remains a contested conservation tool, but in the wake of *Euclid* it became more viable as an alternative to acquisition. In the interim, however, private conservationists sought to protect private lands in the time-honored fashion of acquiring them. Such acquisitions were

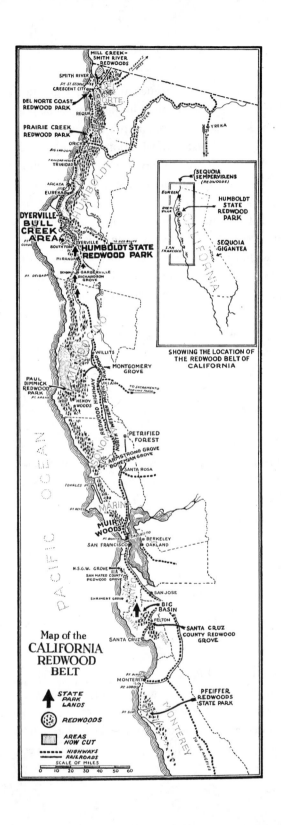

Map of the
CALIFORNIA
REDWOOD
BELT

▲ STATE
PARK
LANDS

◉ REDWOODS

▦ AREAS
NOW CUT

▬▬▬ HIGHWAYS
┅┅┅ RAILROADS

SCALE OF MILES
0 10 20 30 40 50 60

SHOWING THE LOCATION OF
THE REDWOOD BELT OF
CALIFORNIA

SEQUOIA
SEMPERVIRENS
(REDWOODS)

HUMBOLDT
STATE
REDWOOD
PARK

SEQUOIA
GIGANTEA

MILL CREEK-
SMITH RIVER
REDWOODS

SMITH RIVER
PT. ST. GEORGE
CRESCENT CITY

DEL NORTE COAST
REDWOOD PARK

REQUA

PRAIRIE CREEK
REDWOOD PARK

ORICK
BIG LAGOON
TRINIDAD HEAD
TRINIDAD

ARCATA
EUREKA

DYERVILLE-
BULL
CREEK
AREA

PT. GORDA
SOUTH FORK
DYERVILLE

HUMBOLDT STATE
REDWOOD PARK
TO RED BLUFF

MIRANDA

PT. DELGADA
BENBOW
GARBERVILLE
RICHARDSON
GROVE

YREKA

WILLITS

MONTGOMERY
GROVE

PAUL
DIMMICK
REDWOOD
PARK
PT. ARENA

UKIAH
TO SACRAMENTO
AND LAKE TAHOE

HENDY
WOODS

PETRIFIED
FOREST

ARMSTRONG GROVE
BOHEMIAN GROVE

SANTA ROSA

TOMALES PT.

PT. REYES

MARIN

MUIR
WOODS

PT. BONITA
SAUSALITO
SAN FRANCISCO
BERKELEY
OAKLAND

N.S.G.W. GROVE

SAN MATEO COUNTY
REDWOOD GROVE

SAN JOSE

SHRINERS GROVE

BIG
BASIN
FELTON

SANTA CRUZ
COUNTY REDWOOD
GROVE

SANTA CRUZ

PT. PINOS
MONTEREY
PT. LOBOS

PFEIFFER
REDWOODS
STATE PARK

PT. SUR

PACIFIC OCEAN

SONOMA

MENDOCINO

HUMBOLDT

REDWOOD HIGHWAY

NORTH WESTERN PACIFIC R.R.

MONTEREY

TO LOS ANGELES

especially important to expansion of the new national parks system, and raised questions of accountability and transparency long before the first modern land trust was born.

Private Acquisitions: The Redwoods and Acadia   Protection of the coastal redwoods in California gave rise to critical tools used in subsequent conservation acquisitions.[6] Because the redwoods were almost entirely in large industrial holdings by the mid-1880s, it was not possible to reserve redwood stands from the public domain. Protection began with county and state programs spurred and coordinated by private philanthropists and social reformers (Schrepfer 1983). As in the Adirondacks, the state's authority to acquire land for conservation was not challenged.

Following World War I, Californians approved the construction of a highway from San Diego to the Oregon border (figure 4.1). The new highway opened the north coast redwoods both to increased harvesting and to the attention of tourists and conservationists. In 1919, civic leaders concerned about the devastating logging of the redwoods (including such luminaries as NPS Director Stephen Mather and William Kent of Muir Woods fame) organized the Save-the-Redwoods League. The League encouraged Congress to authorize an evaluation of a national park in the redwood groves. In 1920, with park acquisition still not viewed as a legitimate federal purpose, the secretary of the interior's report recommended a park at the site but could "only express the hope that 'public-spirited' individuals might donate the purchase price" (Schrepfer 1983: 12–18).

Undaunted, the Save-the-Redwoods League organized donations. Mather announced that he and Kent would each contribute $15,000 to establish a park. Attracting attention with promises of tourism, Mather persuaded the Humboldt County Board of Supervisors to match the gift (Schrepfer 1983: 20). In 1921, a state representative from Humboldt County successfully sponsored a bill that authorized the California

Figure 4.1
Protected coast Redwoods about 1934 and the Redwood Highway. Source: Merriam (1934: back cover). Reproduced with permission courtesy of the Save-the-Redwoods League. © Permission required for reprint, sale, or commercial use. Contact Save-the-Redwoods League.

Board of Forestry to accept gifts of land and money for the park and moved the authority to exercise eminent domain in connection with highway rights-of-way from the county to the state. This allowed the state to coordinate the acquisition of land for conservation with highway construction.

The League's initial plan had been to purchase superior redwood groves and "present them to Uncle Sam" (Schrepfer 1983: 22). However, under pressure to spread their efforts beyond the north coast, the League gradually became involved in founding a state park system instead. In 1928 it successfully lobbied for a bond measure that would authorize $6 million for the purchase of parks throughout the state.

This measure developed the idea that the state would match private donations to fund acquisitions. The sale of bonds proceeded only as matching funds were provided by private funding (Schrepfer 1983: 32). "Memorial groves" were a successful gambit. Donors could drive through the redwoods, select an attractive grove, buy it, and name it. The groves accounted for a third of the funds raised by the League in the 1920s (Schrepfer 1983: 21–36).[7] By 1928 the League had raised more than half a million dollars to acquire redwoods, and every private dollar was matched with public funds. By 1934, the areas shown in figure 4.1 had been protected. However, there was no mixture of public and private land holdings for conservation. No matter who named the grove, the acquired lands were donated to the state for management.

In addition to providing an early example of matching funds and preacquisitions, the League's activities also signal the importance of planning. The League's support for the establishment of a state park commission and the authorization of a long-range acquisition schedule to ensure the protection of the most scenic and scientifically important areas (Schrepfer 1983: 29) preceded its advocacy for the 1928 state bond measure. When the measure was approved (and strongly supported in the counties anticipating parks, even without PILTs), the League focused its acquisitions in the areas set out in a plan authorized by the state and completed by Olmstead in 1927. In fact, it continues to work within that plan today.

Meanwhile, the Save-the-Redwoods League became less and less comfortable with the NPS emphasis on tourist facilities (Sellars 1997). The

League concluded that the NPS was "degrading the inspirational value of the national parks and destroying their primitive character" (Schrepfer 1983: 52–53). Thus, the group continued to focus on state and private efforts and, in the ultimate insult to the NPS, eventually supported formation of a USFS purchase unit in the area. Ironically, the key elements of the League's land acquisition campaign—blending government ownership, management, and matching funds with private donations—soon found its way into federal park acquisition policy.

Not all private donors soured on the NPS, however. Private donation of whole national parks was not common, but it was the earliest tool of NPS expansion in the eastern United States. Sieur de Monts (now Acadia National Park) in Maine was acquired by a group of wealthy Bostonians who summered on the coast of Maine. In 1901 they established the Hancock County Trustees of Public Reservations—styled after The Trustees of Reservations—and began acquiring land on Mt. Desert Island. When the NPS was established, they passed the land and management costs onto the new agency as a national monument. Legislation establishing the park in 1929[8] allowed expansion of the unit, but only by donation. Again, while the NPS was not inclined to complain about its new unit, the idea of wealthy property owners deciding which local properties would constitute a national park and retaining private parcels included in the protected area raises significant concerns about equity and public accountability.

State Acquisitions: Hawaii and Appalachia   Hawaii National Park, established in 1916, initiated an alternative state donation model of NPS land acquisition. Congress would not buy a park in the islands. Instead, it authorized the governor of the territory to acquire privately owned lands and rights-of-way within a park area Congress had designated. Land acquisition was to be done "at the expense of the Territory of Hawaii ... by exchange or otherwise."[9] The territorial government rapidly assembled and donated the park to the NPS. Most of the lands were seized from Native Hawaiian claimants and the park was dedicated in 1921.[10]

The state-donation approach peaked in the southern Appalachians. As the NPS gained both ambition and public support, it sought, as had the

USFS, to become a more clearly national agency. The creation of a series of parks in the Appalachian Mountains close to Washington, D.C., was therefore a strong political priority, but lack of acquisition authority and funds led Director Mather to acknowledge in 1923 that donations would be required for any eastern units. Secretary of the Interior Hubert Work soon established a commission of distinguished citizens and boosters to investigate possible sites. Mather, John D. Rockefeller, Jr., and other private donors paid the first year's expenses for the commission (U.S. Southern Appalachian Nat. Park Comm. 1931: 2).

Modifying the western "purity" model to fit eastern conditions, the commission established standards for "preserving outstanding features of the southern Appalachians as they appeared in the early pioneer days" (U.S. Southern Appalachian Nat. Park Comm. 1931: 7). Anxious to attract federal investment and tourist development, chambers of commerce, boards of trade, counties, and local boosters put on the ritz to impress the visiting commission with local wonders (U.S. Southern Appalachian Nat. Park Comm. 1931: 2–6). In 1925, the commission recommended two parks: one in Shenandoah, Virginia, and the other in the Smoky Mountains,[11] straddling North Carolina and Tennessee. The Forest Service had already begun to acquire land in the Smokies by that time and tried unsuccessfully to derail the NPS proposal (U.S. NFRC 1933: 11). The Kentucky congressional delegation also forced the NPS to embrace a third unit in Mammoth Caves (Campbell 1960: 44–45).

In April 1926, Congress established criteria under which it would accept donated land in the Appalachians. When each unit reached a minimum acreage, NPS administration would commence. After the acreage reached 521,000 acres in Shenandoah and 704,000 acres in the Smokies, official parks would be established. Although Virginia, North Carolina, and Tennessee worked assiduously, donations of money (as opposed to donations of or offers to sell land) slowed during the Depression, and Congress reduced the acreage necessary for park status several times.[12] Ironically, today Shenandoah National Park is still 56,000 acres below the minimum size originally set for preliminary administration. Short of funds, park advocates sought the support of John D. Rockefeller, Jr., who had already participated in the Acadia and Redwood efforts. Rockefeller donated $5 million to complete the acquisitions in the Smoky Mountains (Campbell 1960: 61).[13]

Much of the area had been farmed for subsistence agriculture for several centuries. Thus, unlike the large industrial tracts acquired under the Weeks Act, most of the parcels the NPS acquired were small, averaging less than 180 acres. But since the proposed parks were discussed as "primeval wilderness," the 15,000 residents who were to be displaced by the commission's proposals were not discussed in Congress (Lambert 1989: 200–203; Brown 2000: chap. 3). The smallholders were generally reluctant to sell, at least on the terms offered. Moreover, the confusion of title in the Appalachians was extreme because tenants, squatters, and historic users asserted a complex of informally established claims to the region.

Again unlike the Weeks Act experience, many of these smallholders lost their land through condemnation. Although Tennessee raised money to buy the land in a fairly straightforward manner, Virginia and North Carolina treated private residents roughly. In 1928, Virginia passed a statute authorizing acquisition through blanket condemnations in each of the eight Shenandoah park counties. The state condemned 1,088 tracts in 1934, involving over 1,300 owners (Lambert 1989: 216, 225). Similarly, at Cades Cove in the Great Smokies, residents were repeatedly promised that their land would not be condemned, but it was taken anyway in 1929 (Dunn 1988: 245).

The states extracted land from among those least able to defend their claims. Thus, although Shenandoah and the Great Smokies were donated by the states to the federal government, most smallholders were not enthusiastic participants in the transactions. Moreover, unlike the landowners involved in the givings that procured our nation's capital, the Appalachian smallholders and occupants were not in a position to benefit from the units established. Local boosters were strongly in favor of establishing the parks, but the smallholders were not. Thus even the first park acquisitions—in which the NPS played an admittedly secondary role to that of the states—exposed the agency to conflict with local landowners in a pattern to be repeated in the future.

We do, however, see in the Appalachian acquisitions the beginning of more tolerant NPS attitudes toward inholders. The hostility of early park advocates to local residents is clear in 1926 in the park commission's decisions. It considered and rejected proposals to allow "desirable" park occupants to continue to occupy their land only for the short term, subject to removal if "they became undesirable for any reason" (U.S. Southern Appalachian Nat. Park Comm. 1931: 23). Congress relented and allowed the secretary of interior to lease acquired properties back to individuals, churches, and schools in areas acquired for the park. However, only forty-three people on a list approved by Ickes in 1934 were allowed to stay at Shenandoah, and by 1937 only seventeen of them remained in the park (Lambert 1989: 241–254).

By the time the southern Appalachian states had to deal with the Department of the Interior on parks, they had already gained significant experience in ceding land to the USFS under the Weeks Act. This approach allowed the states to avoid park management costs by exploiting the skeleton of the enclave clause to retain valuable elements of sovereignty. Virginia kept the right to tax persons and corporations, their franchises, and property on parklands, and also the right to tax gasoline sales in the park. The states also tried to oblige the NPS to maintain local roads, but President Franklin Roosevelt vetoed the proposal.[14] Surprisingly, payments in lieu of taxes were not discussed in the southern Appalachian parks, and, in contrast to the eastern forests, the parks of the era did not share revenues with states or localities.

Clearly, the parks themselves were a sufficiently golden goose to motivate strenuous state and local efforts to procure them. However, the agency's dependence on charity has not been without cost. Why Congress remained so reluctant to give the NPS acquisition authority or funds even as it promoted the parks idea is a bit of a puzzle. One possibility reflects the Constitution. Forests were a legitimate federal "purpose," but Congress could not fit recreation and scenic beauty into any available clause or phrase until after World War II. Of course, such constitutional niceties failed to stop the dramatic expansion of the USFS acquisition authority in the 1920s. One could also argue that the NPS lacked the scientific credibility that legitimated the USFS during the Progressive era.[15] Similarly, parks may have been a harder sell in Congress because they were not consistently viewed as a job-creating industry, nor were the acquisitions tied to bailouts for large and powerful landowners.

More interesting, a reversal of the "crowding out" idea could be relevant here. Perhaps Congress did not invest in parks because others—specifically states, philanthropists, and private groups—were so clearly willing to do so. Some economists might view this as the market responding appropriately, but it could also be viewed as a type of government failure. By refusing to fund park acquisitions, Congress allowed Rockefeller types to control the agenda and put the less powerful at a disadvantage regarding both their own land and access to the benefits of conservation. This abdication of federal control in the pursuit of federal park units has clear implications for public accountability and equity that reappear in our discussion of land trusts and other private actors in the modern era.

Consolidating and Expanding Federal Acquisition Authority

In the wake of the Weeks Act and the *Light* and *Grimaud* decisions ratifying the delegated authority of the conservation agencies, federal acquisition and management for conservation purposes achieved solid legal footing. Political action to expand and consolidate that authority soon followed. The Forest Service remained the leading agency, and its acquisition programs increased in scope and scale in the 1920s as a preferred alternative to regulation of private land. Federal wildlife acquisitions also expanded, albeit in a more fragmentary and halting manner. Even the NPS, lacking acquisition authority, worked closely with private and state actors to expand the national park system. Through this consolidation process, the federal agencies began to dominate land acquisition policy even as the range of valid conservation goals and acquisition tools expanded.

Expanded Acquisition of Forest Lands

While the NPS struggled with its mendicant status, national forest acquisitions under the Weeks Act became mired in a debate over regulation. The forestry community urged some form of control over private forests to address both a "timber famine"[16] predicted for the eastern United States and the "abandoned lands" problem associated with cut-and-run harvesting (Boyd 2002). Federal and state regulations, reform of timber tax laws, and a significant increase in the amount of forestland held in public ownership were all considered as options. Land

acquisition advocates argued that the risks of long-term timber production were too great for private interests to bear.[17] Private forestry
interests vigorously opposed regulation of their practices but had few
complaints about selling land, particularly if they were allowed to reserve the right to harvest the standing timber.

When William Greeley became chief forester in 1920, he took a cooperative stance, advocating federal subsidies for improved forest practices
and state rather than federal regulation (Dana, S. 1956: 213–214). Ultimately a series of 1920s laws—the General Exchange Act of 1922,[18] the
Clarke-McNary Act of 1924,[19] and the McNary-Woodruff Act of 1928
—blended subsidies with an expanded acquisition program.[20]

The General Exchange Act   In 1920, private holdings still constituted
89 percent of the land within the boundaries of Weeks Act purchases
(Steen 1976: 147). Similar mosaics of public and private ownership in
the western reserved forests also caused difficulties. Although it remained
relatively unconcerned about most inholders, the USFS was anxious to
use exchanges to solve specific problems where they arose (Steen 1976:
147). However, nineteenth-century exchange programs had permitted
grand fraud and chicanery (Puter 1908). Congress was still investigating
the Mount Rainier land swap that had so enriched the Northern Pacific
Railroad and as a result was leery of granting the USFS general authority
for land exchanges.

When Congress finally relented, it set stringent limits (Wheatley 1970:
208) that shaped exchange programs for the next seventy years. The
General Exchange Act of 1922 authorized the Forest Service to trade
nonmineral public land for private land within a national forest in the
same state and on the basis of equal value (Cameron, J. 1928: 366).
The same-state requirement was designed to minimize impacts on state
tax revenues. Some congressmen unsuccessfully sought to compensate
counties that lost their tax base as land shifted from private tax rolls to
federal holdings. However, the lands acquired by the USFS were generally cut over and not generating much tax revenue, and the idea of in
lieu tax payments was dropped.[21] Limited this way, exchanges became
a small but important management tool but were not a major element
of land acquisition until new scandals broke out in the 1990s.

The Clarke-McNary Act Congress addressed the debate about cooperation, regulation, and acquisition in the Clarke-McNary Act of 1924.[22] The act expanded the USFS acquisition program and state subsidies for cooperative insect control and reforestation and allowed the federal government to match state and private expenditures for fire control (Dana, S. 1956: 221–222). It rejected federal regulation as a tool for improving private harvest and reforestation practices. Instead, Congress supported willing sellers, mostly financially pressed timber landowners, by extending the generous terms of the Weeks Act to regions that had been excluded because they lacked mountainous headwater areas.

Under the new law, the range of valid goals for conservation acquisitions continued to grow. The act extended both the areas in which forests could be established and the types of land that the federal government could acquire. The Weeks Act phrase "headwaters of any navigable stream" was broadened to "lands within the watersheds of navigable streams" (Wheatley 1970: 237). Because all land lies within the watershed of some navigable stream, Forest Service acquisitions were authorized "practically anywhere at all" (Cameron, J. 1928: 428).[23] Moreover, the act authorized acquisition of land for timber production.[24] In spite of these significant alterations of the Weeks Act authority, constitutional issues were scarcely raised.[25] As the Depression hit the natural resource sectors of the economy, economic factors overshadowed constitutional concerns, and national forests proved to be a popular conduit of economic benefits to rural areas. The link between hard economic times and expanded public acquisition programs continued.

McNary-Woodruff Act Massive flooding on the Mississippi River in 1927 was blamed on denuded forest lands and became another crisis for which USFS land acquisition was the preferred solution. The Forest Service developed a proposal for an eight-year, $40 million land acquisition program to purchase those cut-over lands (Swain 1963: 20), and the National Forest Reservation Commission approved a 9.6 million-acre purchase program (U.S. NFRC 1933: 14). Congress stepped up acquisition appropriations accordingly (Swain 1963: 20); the McNary-Woodruff Act of 1928 authorized an expenditure of $8 million between

1928 and 1931 to purchase land under the Weeks and the Clarke-McNary acts. It also capped the amount of land that could be purchased primarily for timber production in any one state at 1 million acres (Dana, S. 1956: 403). Although appropriations were smaller than the amounts authorized, they supported a growing program (Dana, S. 1956: 225; Swain 1963: 20). By 1931, the Forest Service had acquired more than 4.6 million acres under the Weeks and Clarke-McNary acts—largely from sellers who had already cut their timber and sought a bailout.

Land Acquisition and Wildlife Conservation
Federal wildlife refuges were less readily acquired. The "state ownership of wildlife" doctrine remained a substantial barrier to federal involvement. In 1914, for example, a federal statute protecting migratory game birds[26] was struck down when the Supreme Court concluded that the federal government lacked such authority over wildlife.[27] Undeterred by such setbacks, both preservationists and hunters continued to lobby for federal acquisition of wildlife refuges. Preservationists, in particular, argued that existing state regulation of wildlife had failed; bag limits, closed seasons, and gear restrictions had not discernibly slowed the decline of key populations (Trefethen 1961: 251; Cameron, J. 1929: 106). Federal action was required.

Congress gradually complied, but the international treaties that provided the only constitutional basis for federal acquisitions were a constraint. It appeared that Congress could protect only the migratory birds referenced in the treaties and not other species. Powerful landowners wanting to dump unproductive land found ways to skirt that restriction. By the end of the Depression, the acquisition authorities of the BBS were actually better formed than its tools for refuge management.

Early Expansions of Federal Authority over Wildlife   Federal wildlife management authority began to accrete in 1916 when the United States and Great Britain (acting for Canada) signed a treaty to protect migratory birds (Cameron, J. 1928: 99). The 1918 Migratory Bird Treaty Act (MBTA) implemented the treaty,[28] and in 1920 the Supreme Court relied upon the treaty power to uphold the federal regulations.[29] The act established federal regulations for hunting seasons and forbade the shipment or export of migratory birds or their eggs during the closed season.[30] Again, however, the treaty, and hence the regulatory authority, extended only to migratory birds.

Even before that small breach in the state ownership doctrine, wildlife refuges were created in fits and starts. Each had its own peculiarities and purposes, usually to protect a single species, and frequently originated as part of a congressional appropriations bill. The 1912 Agriculture Appropriations Act,[31] for example, authorized the acquisition of two game refuges and purchase of enough land to ensure adequate water for reestablishing a buffalo range in Wind Cave National Park near Hot Springs, South Dakota. Only a year after the Weeks Act, these actions raised no constitutional issues.

Another refuge had its roots in state action. In 1909, Wyoming began feeding displaced elk whose winter range had been usurped by ranches near Jackson Hole. The state soon sought financial support from the federal government. Congress initially appropriated $20,000 for feed but feared that without adequate habitat, the elk would remain on welfare forever. In 1912 and 1913, Congress provided funding to acquire 2,000 acres for a refuge and $5,000 for maintenance. By 1916, 1,760 acres of private land had been purchased for the elk refuge, and another 1,000 reserved from the public domain (Trefethen 1975: 206–209). Elk are not migratory birds, of course, and therefore the state should have been responsible for the acquisitions. However, protection was expensive, and the state was willing to allow Congress to fund, if not control, the elk program.

The fragmentary state of federal wildlife management at the time raised other important questions. Which federal agency should manage the new reserve: the BBS, the USFS, or the NPS? The answer was related to the heated issue of whether the animals should be fed, harvested, or managed "naturally." And how many elk were there anyway? These things were not known. Despite such unresolved questions, experts recommended further expansion of the Jackson Hole Elk Refuge, and President Coolidge complied in July 1927. The management issues persisted (Righter 1982: 53–54).[32] Instead of resolving the questions of jurisdiction or priorities, the parties just agreed to buy more land. Finally, further refuge acquisitions were sidelined by intense debate over whether refuges should be shooting grounds or inviolate sanctuaries (Trefethen 1961: 251).

Congressional authorization of the Upper Mississippi Wildlife and Fish Refuge in 1924[33] was a major step toward a more structured approach to refuge acquisition. The act authorized the BBS to acquire regularly flooded land in Illinois and Minnesota that was not used for agriculture. The authority contained no Weeks Act-like commission but did reflect the format of the enclave clause, allowing the state legislature to veto proposed acquisitions. The bill also limited the average amount that could be spent per acre to $5, which as land prices rose, required a series of amendments (Cameron, J. 1929: 109).[34] Management of the refuge still reflected some of the chaos that reigned among the federal wildlife agencies, requiring the BBS in the Department of Agriculture to share management responsibility with the Bureau of Fisheries in the Department of Commerce. It also divided the pie on the preserve versus hunting grounds issue, allocating portions of the refuge to each. This arrangement remained a substantial organizational advance on the earlier experience with the elk refuge. It was the first time Congress had appropriated funds to acquire a general wildlife refuge (Gabrielson 1943: 14).

The Upper Mississippi Act authorized $1.5 million for land acquisition, but Congress appropriated only $375,000 for the first year of the program (U.S. BBS 1925: 23). By June 1929, the BBS had acquired 87,900 acres of private land through purchase, lease, donation, or transfer from other federal agencies,[35] and an additional 9,770 acres of state- and city-owned land were included in the refuge area.

General Acquisition Authority: The Migratory Bird Conservation Act
Bills that would have provided the BBS general authority to acquire land continued to flounder on the contentious issue of whether the refuges should be sanctuaries or shooting grounds. Moreover, funding remained an issue. A $1 fee or "duck stamp" proposal, based on the World War I savings stamp program, would have provided money for acquisitions, but the idea ran into logistical and political roadblocks. Not all hunters were sufficiently affluent to want to support refuge man-

agement with user fees, and in 1922 only fourteen states even required a hunting license. Thus selling federal stamps as an adjunct to state license programs presented difficulties. Finally, many states viewed the federal stamp as a usurpation of state authority, and shooting clubs feared that the federal government would expropriate their private hunting grounds.

In 1929, a stripped-down general acquisition bill passed Congress. The Migratory Bird Conservation Act (MBCA or Norbeck-Andersen Act, not to be confused with the 1918 Migratory Bird *Treaty* Act)[36] authorized appropriations from the general treasury to acquire migratory bird habitat to be managed as "inviolate" bird sanctuaries.[37] Sportsmen and conservationists supported a bill without federal licensing, stamp, or public shooting ground provisions (Trefethen 1961: 259). Congress authorized $1 million a year for ten years, anticipating, perhaps somewhat naively, that at the end of a decade, "sufficient areas will have been procured to care for the more pressing and essential needs of the birds" (U.S. BBS 1929: 21).[38]

The MBCA follows the Weeks Act model. It includes a commission (the Migratory Bird Conservation Commission, MBCC) responsible for approving acquisitions. However, a member of the state game commission in any affected state was added as a voting member (U.S. BBS 1929: 21) to prevent excessive loss of taxable property in the county where acquisition was to occur.[39] This is not the same as revenue sharing or PILTs, but does indicate that the "burdens" argument was becoming a standard element of land acquisition.

The treaty power trumped the enclave clause in this context: Where the purchase or lease was intended to effectuate the migratory bird treaty between the United States and Great Britain, state consent was not constitutionally required (Wheatley 1970: 147).[40] Nevertheless, like the Weeks Act, the MBCA statute again required the approval of state legislatures for federal acquisition of land specifically for migratory bird refuges. Further, the act leaves state civil and criminal jurisdiction untouched. Thus while the NPS was insisting on exclusive jurisdiction primarily to protect wildlife, refuge advocates moved in the opposite direction, sharing federal authority with state governments. By 1931, all but eight states had passed laws allowing federal acquisition of refuge lands (U.S. BBS 1931: 35). In this circuitous manner, the BBS gained considerable flexibility to acquire land, if only for a limited conservation purpose.

Unlike the Weeks Act, there were no limits on where refuge acquisitions might occur. The congressional goal was to establish large areas throughout the entire country where migratory birds and other varieties of wildlife could enjoy complete protection (U.S. BBS 1929: 21). The MBCA was extremely flexible, authorizing acquisition of interests in land or full fee purchase, lease, option, or donation. Although the MBCA did not explicitly include a provision for the exercise of eminent domain, a series of cases established that authority as well (Wheatley 1970: 150).[41] Amendments in 1935 also authorized the secretary to exchange lands or resources of equal value, including unreserved, non-mineral, public domain lands, for refuge lands.[42]

Following passage of the MBCA, the BBS mounted an extensive program to identify lands for acquisition. By 1930, studies had been conducted in twenty-four states; federal lands had been withdrawn by executive order to create two new refuges; and two other refuges had been approved by the MBCC for acquisition. Negotiations were under way at eight additional sites (U.S. BBS 1930: 34–35), and it appeared that the agency was on a roll. However, as the Depression gathered force, Congress withheld appropriations, and refuge acquisitions languished (Trefethen 1961: 259; Swain 1963: 41). The rescue of desperate farmers took precedence over the protection of migratory birds.

Acquisition in the National Parks—With No Authority

National parks grew in importance in the lives of Americans as World War I curtailed touring in Europe. Efforts during and after the conflict to divert park resources to ostensibly war-related ranching, mining, and logging were largely unsuccessful, and park supporters easily defeated postwar water development proposals in both Yellowstone and Yosemite.[43]

Nevertheless, the fledgling NPS remained weak in the face of multiple threats. Lacking acquisition authority and funds, it relied on the kindness of others to expand its system.[44] Problems in Yosemite are emblematic. The passage of the Raker Act in 1913 permitted construction of a dam in Hetch Hetchy Valley to provide water for San Francisco. The NPS act three years later looks like a consolation prize (Spence 1999: 115). Yet expanded visitation and pressure to create parks in all parts of the nation led to harsh conflict between the NPS and both its supporters and large and small landowners.

The NPS "Organic" Act   In 1916, park advocates, including the newly formed American Automobile Association and *National Geographic* and *Sunset* magazines, succeeded in gaining passage of a statute authorizing creation of the NPS in the Department of the Interior. The War Department was an enthusiastic supporter because it simply wanted to get out of the parks management business. The Forest Service was less enthusiastic, but by the time the bill passed, it had acquiesced in what had by then become inevitable.

The NPS organic act accomplished three things. First, it provided a consistent administrative structure for the myriad parklike areas managed by the Department of the Interior. Second, Congress finally clarified the distinction between a park and a forest. National parks involve "the preservation of nature as it exists, and the ... development of adequate and moderately priced transportation and hotel facilities" (U.S. Congress. House 1916: 3). The national forests were for "the utilitarian use of land, of water, and of timber, as contributing to the wealth of all the people" (U.S. Congress. House 1916: 3). The Forest Service endorsed this differentiation, largely in the hope of protecting its own turf.

From the perspective of land acquisition, the third element is most important. As implemented by the first NPS director, Steven Mather, the organic act provided a powerful vision for an expanding park system. The apparent commitment to nature "as it exists," or park "purity," suffered from this expansion imperative and was compromised by the rapid addition of transportation infrastructure and hotel facilities. Yet, in the lead up to the NPS act, a major congressional goal was to encourage tourism in the United States. The House Committee on Public Lands underscored this concern:

This economic value of the parks is only recently coming to be realized. ... With equal scenery we are lagging far behind the European countries, notably Switzerland, and are outclassed by the development of park travel and park use in Canada.[45] (U.S. Congress. House 1916: 2)

It is surprising, given the powerful constituency interested in creating the agency, that Congress was stingy in authorizing the NPS to hire personnel and in providing for administrative expenditures (Ise 1961: 190). Congress held park advocates to their oft-repeated promise that the parks would be self-supporting, posing no drain on the treasury (U.S. Congress. House 1916: 5; Ise 1961: 619). It did initially allow the NPS to retain park fees without appropriation for management, including revenue from hotel operators and other entrepreneurs who provided visitor services in parks. However, until 1926 the NPS received no general appropriations. For individual parks, a pattern soon evolved in which Congress was tight-fisted with funds when a park was first authorized, but after it was established, appropriations were gradually increased (personal communication from Jim Snyder, NPS historian, May 19, 2004).

Nevertheless, although Mather asked Congress for funds for roads and improvements at specific parks, frequently with considerable success (Mather 1916), the NPS initially depended on private facilities and concessionaires to accommodate visitors. Mather's tale of a new bridge in Glacier National Park is typical of the early reliance of the NPS on charity for acquisition and development. Mather himself purchased a tract of 160 acres and donated it to the park, using that gift as leverage to persuade an adjoining owner to donate an additional 160 acres and a perpetual easement to preserve the timber on both sides of the road. Flathead County, Montana, donated $10,000 toward the construction, and citizens donated an additional $5,000. With that in place, the parks director was able to convince the interior secretary to allocate $85,000 to complete the bridge and to provide new administrative buildings and a park gate on the same site (Mather 1916: 14).

Early NPS Strategy   The NPS organic act did not convey general or specific authority to acquire land. In the absence of general acquisition or reservation authority, each addition to the system has its own story. It is not possible to speak generically, as we can of the Weeks Act and the Forest Service. Instead, an accretion of tales is necessary to focus the NPS picture.

Significantly, potential sellers were not prominent among the supporters of the new agency. Whereas forests would grow again on marginal land that owners had stripped of timber and were about to abandon, disturbed areas were initially unacceptable to park advocates. Parks were more restrictive on local and private uses and therefore more difficult to fit into many communities than forests or even wildlife refuges.

Yosemite ran into difficulties in the early 1900s. As transportation improved, settlers' scattered claims were consolidated into corporate holdings—timber operators, miners, and hoteliers serving Yosemite tourists. Even after the NPS was formed in 1916, it had no authority to acquire land by purchase. Moreover, exchanges to clear inholdings aroused protest from park mavens who did not want to trade away park land even to get other park land. Soon after the NPS was established, the secretary of the interior arranged a complex set of three-way land swaps that involved both the USFS and private timber owners in consolidating private harvesting in the Alder Creek drainage of Yosemite. In the late 1920s, another rash of inholder logging was resolved by a timely Rockefeller donation of $1.7 million (Roosevelt 1970: 49). The NPS was destined to rely on donations for the next half-century.

Where park designations succeeded, as in the Yellowstone and Mount Rainier cases (one a reservation, the other an exchange), it was most likely because of three factors. First, there were no opposing landowners who either feared loss of control or perhaps hoped for potential gain. Second, park boosters wanted the benefits of a unit without having to pay the management costs; states and localities anticipated economic development and were willing to tolerate a nominal no-hunting regime (Runte 1979). Third, states used the enclave clause to cede to the federal government burdensome aspects of ownership, such as the obligation to build and maintain roads, while retaining lucrative sticks in the bundle, such as the right to tax businesses within the ceded areas.

Moreover, in order to build a national constituency, the NPS had to encourage tourism and create new units. To this end, railroad companies disappointed by the initial level of business generated by the western parks began an enthusiastic advertising campaign to increase visitation (Johns 1996, chap. 2) and, it was hoped, thereby gain political support. These concessions to tourism were not without political or ecological costs. Cars were first allowed in national parks in 1908 and thereafter traffic increased rapidly (Dilsaver 1994: 42–45), creating enormous impacts and inciting the opposition of park "purists" such as members of the Save-the-Redwoods League.

Besides encouraging tourism, the NPS was obliged to compromise its commitment to "nature as it is." Park Service policy encouraged state and local park systems to accept less than "nationally significant" or "pure" sites. Although park purity became a major aspect of NPS debate, the agency nevertheless acquired numerous properties of dubious merit in an effort to attract and maintain congressional support (Ise 1961, chap. 6). Many additions that looked questionable at the time are, however, welcomed in today's altered environment. Some might wish, indeed, that Director Mather had been a little less discriminating. Among the proposals he tried to kill were parks at Lake Tahoe, Mount St. Helens, the Olympics, the Sawtooth Mountains, Indiana Dunes, and Cliff Cities (Shankland 1970: 184–185).[46]

In the decade following the establishment of the NPS, competition between the Park Service and the USFS over land and appropriations reached epic proportions. In the case of appropriations, it was an unbalanced battle. While the NPS received an occasional $50,000 or even $800,000 from Congress, the Weeks Act acquisitions became a $14 million project. The battle over land was intense, particularly in the Yellowstone and Grand Teton area. After his first visit there in 1915, Mather sought to add the Tetons to Yellowstone.[47] A compromise left the greatest part of the land sought by the NPS under USFS jurisdiction (Swain 1963: 137).

NPS ally John D. Rockefeller stepped in, concealed as the Snake River Land Company, and began purchasing land for a "nebulous purpose" (Righter 1982: 66–67). When it was finally discovered in 1930 that an eastern millionaire was acquiring land for a national park, local anger erupted: "Through necessity they had learned to live with the multiple-use policies of the Forest Service, but the 'no-use' philosophy of the NPS was an anathema to all that they understood about individualism and opportunity in America" (Righter 1982: 66–67). A bill establishing Grand Teton National Park in 1929 did not end advocacy for expanding the park southward. Nor did it end Rockefeller's purchase program in the Jackson Hole area. The continuing dispute in the Tetons suggests that even with a sugar daddy, NPS land acquisitions were not easy (Ise 1961: 361ff).

Land Acquisition and the Remaining Public Domain

Competition between the USFS and the Department of the Interior extended to vying for management authority over the remaining unreserved public domain. That authority still rested with the General Land Office (GLO), an older federal agency that was not included in the solidification of conservation authorities during this period. The fate of the remaining public domain lands was therefore undecided and deeply contested; donating the land to the states, or to the ranchers then using it, or establishing a leasing system based on continued federal ownership were options seriously advocated and hotly debated through the 1920s.

What was not seriously on the table was the idea that the GLO would manage these lands for conservation. Instead, the agency served as a supplier of lands to be conserved and managed by other agencies. The Recreation Act of 1926,[48] for instance, authorized the GLO to transfer public domain properties to states, territories, or local governments for recreation. The pattern persisted well after the GLO was transformed into the BLM in the late 1940s. Often the best way the new agency could protect resources was to transfer title to the property to a state or locality (Muhn et al. 1988: 8). Frequently these transfers were significant. One early transfer under the 1926 act formed the core of Anza Borrego Desert State Park east of San Diego, California, then the largest state park in the nation (Peterson 1996: 18). These early transfers largely defined the BLM's role in conservation policy until the late 1980s as a "breadbasket" of lands to be provided to other agencies as required.

Summary

Federal land conservation programs and acquisition authorities that emerged in the wake of post-Civil War industrialization continued to solidify in the decades following the Weeks Act. Resolution of most of the basic constitutional questions allowed the federal agencies to focus on expanding and consolidating their statutory powers and their funding.

The tools for regulating private land use had not yet passed Supreme Court or popular muster. Subsidies for states and landowners were an important element of many land protection programs in the 1920s, and conservation advocates increased pressure on federal and state governments to acquire land to protect it. As the Progressive vision of an activist government took shape, states, the USFS, and later the FWS had little trouble identifying public support and statutory authority to acquire land. Thus, the ascendance of the federal government in land acquisition continued throughout the period.

That said, private and state interests continued to play a vital role. The USFS and the USFWS frequently targeted depleted private lands for acquisition. Deteriorating economic conditions promoted such programs as a form of economic relief for willing sellers. That strategy maintained public support for the federal acquisitions to protect forests and wildlife. It also continued to generate visible mosaics of public and private land within national forests and refuges.

As these expanded acquisition programs won out over regulation of those same owners, the maturity of government acquisition programs became discernible in terms of acres. Between 1909 and 1933, the FWS acquired 172,000 acres, and in a similar period (1911–1929) the USFS acquired just under 3 million acres. While these numbers would pale before the buying frenzy to come during the 1930s, they represented a significant addition to the system of federally protected lands.

The NPS enjoyed enormous public support as well, but recreation and scenic preservation did not fit within the expanding federal remit. To expand, the NPS, therefore, depended on states seeking the economic benefits of tourist development and parks without management fees, and on the generosity of private donors. Moveover, because the NPS aimed at acquiring higher-quality land that sellers sometimes wanted to retain, many of the new park lands were condemned by states. This gave future NPS management in the region and the condemnation tool itself a bad start in conservation.

Undaunted, a plethora of private organizations and donors turned to supporting NPS efforts. Private groups sometimes formed to protect what the NPS could not or would not protect—most notably the redwoods. The innovative partnership between California and the Save-the-Redwoods League allowed the purchase of even more valuable red-wood lands for state parks. Wealthy philanthropists also expanded the system in places like Acadia National Park, enhancing their own private holdings within and around the new park at the same time. Issues of public accountability regarding private acquisition efforts can be seen in these early NPS transactions.

In short, despite its secondary standing in many conservation histories, the period between the Roosevelts was a critical one for land acquisition. When the Depression became the nation's major public policy concern, the various players in the land acquisition field were well prepared to use the disaster to achieve their own goals.

5

Conservation Land Acquisition During the Depression and World War II, 1933–1953

The economic crisis that began in the natural resources industries soon engulfed the nation. Between 1929 and 1932, the stock market lost 90 percent of its value, wages fell 66 percent, and housing starts collapsed. By the time President Franklin D. Roosevelt took office in 1933, a quarter of U.S. workers were unemployed and one-third of American farmers had lost their land (Public Broadcasting Service n.d.).

The economic emergency overwhelmed political opposition to Progressive ideas about centralized scientific management, and the collapse of state and local institutions spurred aggressive federal action. The Depression was an era of national plans and experts marked by a growing acceptance of social and economic regulation. However, the Depression was not, perhaps surprisingly, a period in which land use regulation gained significant acceptance. Particularly in the context of forest and wildlife management, advocates viewed regulatory approaches as inferior to acquisition. Terrible economic times increased the pressure to bail out struggling landowners in a confluence of conservation policy and economic relief. Desperate landowners were happy to go along, beating a path to various federal agencies to sell their land and move on.

The Depression accordingly proved to be a boon for land acquisition for conservation, especially by federal agencies. As figure 5.1 demonstrates, almost 50 percent of all lands acquired by the federal government were bought between 1929 and 1945. Table 5.1 makes a similar point, showing acquisitions and reservations in 1945 disaggregated by agency without Alaska (which would overbalance the percentages in the direction of the public domain).

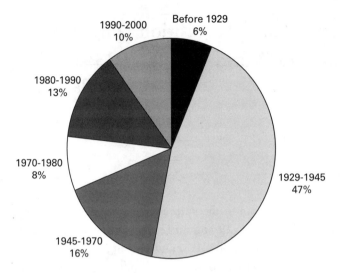

Figure 5.1
Federal agency acquisitions by period and the dominance of the Depression era.
Sources: 1945–1955, Clawson (1951); pre-1955–1955, Clawson and Held
(1957); 1955 to present, U.S. GSA (1957–2000).

Table 5.1
Extent and Percentage of Public Domain and Acquired Lands by Agency, 1945
(Excluding Alaska)

Agency	Public domain		Acquired		Total	
	Million acres	Percent	Million acres	Percent	Million acres	Percent
U.S. Forest Service	134.1	41	23.8	84	157.9	44
National Park Service	11.6	4	2	7	13.6	4
U.S. Fish and Wildlife Service	2.2	1	2.5	9	4.7	1
Bureau of Land Management	180.4	55	0	0	180.4	51
Total	328.3	100	28.3	100	356.6	100

Source: Clawson (1951: 148).

We have already seen how federal acquisition activities on this scale were a culmination of post-Civil War trends rather than a radical departure from some previous course. However, during the Depression, the goal of conservation acquisitions shifted almost exclusively toward economic recovery. Government analysts attributed the economic crisis in the agricultural and forestry industries to overproduction. Buying land to take it out of production therefore became a major policy tool. Indeed, based on the Depression experience, one could argue that conservation acquisitions are more likely to occur not in richness but in poorness, as landowners needing a bailout become politically active.

The federal government used relief money to purchase an amazing variety of sites under equally diverse programs. This is not to say that acquisition for park and scenery purposes suddenly passed constitutional muster. Rather, land acquired for economic relief was transferred to the land management agencies with little fanfare. Nor was all of the land acquired high on the wish list of preservationists and other agency supporters. Federal attention focused on submarginal lands, low-productivity tracts on which farming was not profitable, rather than on high-value forests, habitat, or recreation areas.

The government's growing power to interfere with private land and livelihoods reflects New Deal assumptions about both the nature of government and the meaning of ownership. The nation had moved as far as it had ever gone from John Locke; a farmer no longer had near-absolute ownership of his property and in many cases no longer wanted it. Rather, ownership was increasingly viewed as a social construction, serving to protect society at large (Hurt 1985: 248–249). During the 1920s and 1930s, the understanding of "submarginal" reflected a social determination of whether private land was properly serving the general welfare.[1] If it was not, the government moved to alter use, title, or both.

Pushed to the margins by the massive federal mobilization, private and state actors nevertheless continued their own efforts to acquire and protect land, albeit in a manner reflective of hard economic times. Financial and tax pressures motivated even the wealthiest landowners to reduce or reposition their real estate holdings. Private donations nearly doubled the holdings of The Trustees of Reservations, while a new financial arrangement emerged at Fort Ticonderoga: the nonprofit charitable trust, a private form of public ownership. Major philanthropists continued to support NPS expansion in the East, but the Save-the-Redwoods League found itself fending off the NPS involvement that it had sought less than a decade before. Thus, although the Depression marks the peak of public acquisition programs, it also marks the end of a century of relative clarity in the distinction between public and private efforts.

Because most of the land acquisition that occurred during the 1930s was tied to relief programs, this chapter begins by introducing those efforts. It continues by describing how those relief programs affected the four federal agencies: the BBS-Bureau of Sports Fisheries and Wildlife-Fish and Wildlife Service, the NPS, the Forest Service, and the Grazing Service-BLM. The chapter concludes with a shorter look at how private and state efforts coped with the economic calamity of the era.

Agricultural Relief Programs

When farm income fell 70 percent between 1929 and 1932, the crisis was unprecedented and paralyzing.[2] More than one out of four Americans lived on farms at the time, so New Deal programs made extensive efforts to acquire and either retire or rehabilitate submarginal farm lands. We focus on three key programs: the Agricultural Adjustment Act (AAA), the Bankhead-Jones Act, and the statute creating the Civilian Conservation Corps (CCC). By 1946, 11.2 million acres had been acquired under New Deal land utilization programs of this type at a cost of $47.5 million.[3]

The Agricultural Adjustment Act

The Agricultural Adjustment Act was born in a land planning committee established by President Hoover in 1931 to study land utilization and adjustment issues (Wooten 1965: 4; Nixon 1957: 317–318). The committee recommended federal acquisition of a staggering 75 million acres of submarginal land nationwide. Some of the acquired property was to be added to the growing number of state and federal parks and forests (Gray 1936: 260). Other parcels would be used to demonstrate how degraded land could be reclaimed. Former residents would be relocated to land better suited for agriculture, while reclamation projects would provide employment for other displaced workers (Wooten 1965: 5).

The first land acquisition program under the AAA began with $25 million in relief funding.[4] Within a year, it became clear both that the poorest farmers were not benefiting (Wooten 1965: 6–10) and that the Supreme Court was unlikely to protect the program from constitutional challenge.[5] To address both problems, the Department of Agriculture re-cast the AAA in terms of saving soil rather than farmers (Kramer and Batie 1985: 309). Farmers terracing their land, shifting acreage from "soil-depleting" to "soil-conserving" crops, or idling land became eligi-ble for government payments.[6] The ostensible focus on protecting soil gave the program an acceptable federal purpose under the Constitution, but the major objective continued to be raising farm incomes by taking land out of production.[7] Soil conservation thus joined watershed protec-tion and national defense as constitutional justifications for acquiring land, and land "adjustments" continued as a major element of New Deal policy.

The Civilian Conservation Corps

The Civilian Conservation Corps further bolstered New Deal land acqui-sition efforts. Within a month of taking office in 1933, Roosevelt signed the Emergency Conservation Act creating the CCC (Nixon 1957, vol. 1: 143–44). The act granted the president broad authority to put the un-employed to work on conservation projects around the nation. At the program's peak in 1935, more than half a million men were enrolled in over 2,600 CCC camps (Clepper and Meyer 1960: 12).

Because the act required that the CCC "boys" work on public land, the program became a major justification for federal acquisition of land.[8] The difficulty was that most of the unemployed were located in the East, while federal land was concentrated in the West (Kneipp 1936: 446). The solution was to focus land "adjustments" in the eastern United States. The resulting acquisitions added thousands of acres to national forests, parks, and wildlife refuges (Cox et al. 1985: 219). Park purists and wildlife preservationists were concerned about the CCC's frenzy of construction activities and other "improvements," but there was little in-terest in such complaints from the ecologically and aesthetically attuned.

Hundreds of buildings and thousands of miles of roads and trails in national parks and forests were constructed by CCC crews.

The Bankhead-Jones Farm Tenant Act

The Bankhead-Jones Farm Tenant Act[9] authorized acquisitions to retire or rehabilitate land in the drought-stricken Great Plains (Wooten 1965: 12–13). Farmers were not happy with the prices offered during the Dust Bowl years but clamored nevertheless to be included in the program (Hurt 1986: 98; 1985: 251), and many states lobbied to have lands within their jurisdictions acquired. By the time the Bankhead-Jones program was discontinued in 1943, 2.6 million acres had been acquired at a cost of $11.1 million. Fifty percent of the lands purchased were located in the northern plains, and 20 percent in the South (Wooten 1965: 14–20). The Soil Conservation Service (SCS), created in 1935, established local conservation districts to address the soil erosion "menace." The SCS worked primarily through a network of locally elected conservation districts to plan the agency's work. It completed the majority of the acquisitions and managed the lands until it turned most of them over to the USFS in the 1950s.[10]

Economic Relief and the USFS, NPS, FWS, and BLM

These relief programs had an enormous impact on the USFS and the NPS. Although wildlife advocates viewed most Depression programs as destructive of habitat, they too got on board with an unusual set of land acquisition programs. Even the agencies managing the public domain were affected to some degree.

The Forest Service

Among the federal agencies, the Forest Service was the best positioned to take advantage of Depression-era acquisition spending. By the late 1920s, the forestry industry was struggling for economic survival (Steen 1976: 222–224). Government foresters defined the economic crisis in terms of devastation caused by unsound logging practices of financially desperate timber companies. They argued that the cooperation fostered by the 1924 Clarke-McNary Act had failed to improve private forest management[11] and revived their calls for both federal acquisition and regulation of private industry. Federal foresters offered the private sector a quid pro quo: curtailed national forest harvests to reduce government competition with private timber, in return for industry acceptance of more government controls (Steen 1976: 202, 226). Nevertheless, forestry regulation continued to be politically unpopular and constitutionally uncertain.

Acquisition, by contrast, had become an established federal program with clear constitutional authority (U.S. FS 1933a: 16). Not surprisingly, acquisition became the dominant policy for dealing with forest industry problems of the 1930s. The NFRC had already recommended spending $40 million to acquire 9.6 million acres under the terms of the Weeks Act. In 1930 a timber conservation board, appointed at the request of the National Lumber Manufacturers Board, also recommended expanded federal acquisition of forestland (Dana, S. T. 1956: 241; Steen 1976: 224).

The best known of the 1930s USFS forestry reports, *A National Plan for American Forestry* (U.S. FS 1933a), pushed for acquisition at an unprecedented level. The plan concluded rather starkly that "practically all major problems in American forestry center in, or have grown out of, private ownership" (U.S. FS 1933b: v). It flatly rejected regulation, arguing that the Supreme Court was unlikely to approve rules designed to impose high professional standards on private landowners. In addition, the report worried over purely selfish forestland owners (U.S. FS 1933a: 1046–1049, 1343–1349) who might shape any regulations to their own purposes. Arguing that state regulation had also failed throughout the nation (U.S. FS 1933a: 65), the report turned to acquisition as the simplest and surest method (U.S. FS 1933a: 994) for protecting forests (U.S. FS 1933a: 67). The plan proposed a gargantuan twenty-year program in which federal and state governments would purchase 224 million acres of private forestland, more than 1.5 times the size of the existing National Forest system (Swain 1963: 24). In a familiar refrain, it argued that a "fully restored and productive forest resource" would generate ample revenue to offset the $98 million needed for the anticipated purchases (Clapp 1933: 73–74).

The national plan was not adopted, but forest acquisitions did expand more modestly under existing Weeks and Clarke-McNary acts authority.

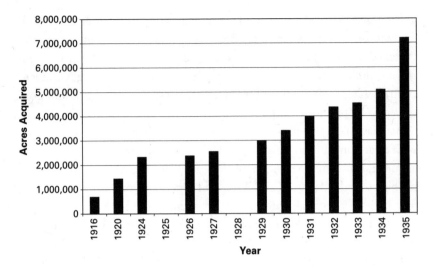

Figure 5.2
Acreage acquired for national forests, 1916–1935. Source: Adapted from U.S. FS (2001a) (no reports available for 1925 or 1928).

The Emergency Relief Act provided $20 million for such acquisitions in 1933 alone (Kneipp 1936: 483). The question of which lands to acquire remained controversial, however, even during a time of economic crisis (Nixon 1957, vol. 1: 191–193). The NFRC wanted to limit acquisition to land within existing purchase areas (Nixon 1957, vol. 1: 182–183), while Roosevelt wanted to show congressional delegations from states where there were no national forests that he was responding to their needs.[12] The president also wanted to keep CCC workers busy during the winter by expanding holdings in the South. A compromise allocated three-quarters of the funding to rounding out existing national forests and one-quarter for acquiring land in new areas, primarily in southern states.[13]

Figure 5.2 shows the trend of acres acquired under the Weeks Act between 1916 and 1935. An initial spurt of post-1911 acquisition appears to have topped off at about 2.5 million acres per year. During the Depression, acquisitions then rose consistently to total more than 7 million acres by 1935.

The same pattern is visible regarding the designation of new national forests shown in figure 5.3. The process moved slowly and focused on

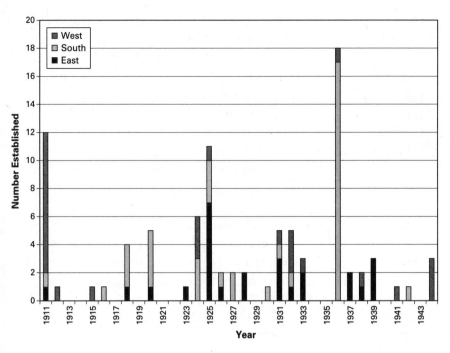

Figure 5.3
Number and location of national forests established from 1911 to 1944. Source:
Adapted from U.S. FS (1997).

the West until the Depression. Then new designations exploded and were
concentrated in the South.

Individuals and corporations were highly motivated sellers of forest
lands. During one particularly frenzied week in 1935, owners who could
not pay their taxes offered the Forest Service 8 million acres (Steen 1976:
229–230). States eager for the economic benefits associated with the
federal forests—new roads, new jobs (Shands 1992: 33), fire protection, and revenue sharing—consented readily to federal purchases. As
acquisitions proceeded, new national forests followed, as figure 5.3
shows.

Still, acquisitions did not go forward quickly enough to please President Roosevelt (Nixon 1957, vol. 2: 172). At one point, it was suggested
that the Weeks Act purchase procedures be bypassed entirely (Nixon
1957, vol. 1: 193). The idea failed, however, and under the willing-seller

terms of the act, the buying spree did not ensure contiguous federal ownership in the new national forests. Even today some acquired forests are actually less than a third federally owned (Shands 1992: 20). In addition, the Forest Service did not consistently acquire subsurface mineral rights. Much federal forestland in the East continues to be divided between federal surface ownership and private subsurface, with the latter reserved by the sellers (Raymond and Fairfax 1999).

Unconcerned by these fragmentary landscapes, the Forest Service pressed ahead with its acquisition agenda. Following widespread flooding in the spring of 1936, the agency devised yet another plan for "Flood Prevention Through Federal Forest Land Acquisition and Management," under which 118 million acres of forestland would be acquired (Nixon 1957, vol. 1: 502). However, as the lumber demands of World War II revived the market, both Congress and potential sellers lost interest in federal land purchases. When the dust settled in 1945, 7.7 million acres had been acquired (Dana, S. T. 1956: 250) for approximately $50 million (Nixon 1957, vol. 2: 319), more than doubling the acreage the USFS had acquired from 1911 to 1930 (see figure 5.2).[14]

Fish and Wildlife Protection

President Roosevelt was not a wildlife enthusiast. The president viewed wildlife as an aesthetic and recreational resource rather than a vital industry, such as forestry, that provided jobs and lumber needed to build houses. Meanwhile, wildlife advocates were alarmed by the habitat destruction accompanying CCC projects as well as New Deal dam and highway construction (Nixon 1957, vol. 2: 67). By the late 1930s, however, wildlife advocates found support in Congress and secured independent funding for federal and state refuge acquisitions, as well as a degree of control over destructive federal water development projects.

Creativity in Wildlife Acquisition Using Economic Relief Funds   Like the USFS, the BBS had also developed administrative expertise in land acquisition. By the time FDR was elected, the agency had surveyed 1.8 million acres and acquired more than 250,000 through purchase, donations from states, gifts, leases, or executive orders (U.S. BBS 1932: 3–18). Nevertheless, wildlife advocates were not adept in turning Depression programs to their advantage and lagged behind the USFS in generating acquisition funds from economic relief.[15]

Wildlife also had friends in Congress (Williamson 1987: 4). In 1930, Peter Norbeck of South Carolina sponsored the creation of the Senate Special Committee on the Conservation of Wild Life Resources (Trefethen 1975: 219), which generated funding for acquiring refuge land (Jahn and Trefethen 1978: 456–470). Belatedly, the BBS began to promote acquisition as economic relief. In 1934, it obtained $6 million in relief funding (U.S. BBS 1934: 2–3). Thereafter the BBS was given up to $4.2 million for land acquisition every year until World War II.[16]

Although acquisition of land did not automatically establish a refuge, a secretarial order from the Department of the Interior, rather than an act of Congress, was enough to authorize the BBS to administer the land as such.[17] That gave the agency the flexibility to develop a consistent program of refuge management (U.S. BBS 1935: 21). Nevertheless, like other agencies, the BBS encountered conflicts with Congress and the president regarding what lands to acquire. The wildlife agency wanted land on major migratory bird flyways, but relief acts like Bankhead-Jones were earmarked for drought-stricken areas in the upper Mississippi Valley and Great Plains. The priorities of willing sellers also drove many acquisitions. That said, the BBS was considerably more selective than the USFS about acquisitions except under special conditions, for example, when the agency required water for migratory birds. Thus, it pursued better lands.[18]

Stretching its limited funds, the BBS became the first major buyer of conservation easements,[19] establishing all-easement refuges in the prairie pothole region of North and South Dakota.[20] Leaving fee title with the original landowner, the easements allowed the agency to impound water, build fences, erect refuge markers, and make the areas habitable and attractive to migratory waterfowl by restoring small breeding areas that had dried up in the drought (Salyer and Gillette 1964: 503). Landowners were desperate for water, and the North Dakota legislature directed counties to exempt all inundated refuge lands from taxation. It also granted the federal government easements over state-owned land for construction and water impoundment (U.S. BBS 1936: 28–29). "Private landowners supported the program enthusiastically, as they granted the

necessary perpetual easements cheerfully" (U.S. BBS 1936: 29). Ultimately, the BBS purchased only 1,039 acres in fee while protecting
57,932 acres with easements. The popular program was extended to
Montana in 1937 and South Dakota in 1938 (U.S. BBS 1937: 36; 1938:
44–45). By 1938, eighty-one easement refuges covered 135,113 acres
(U.S. BBS 1938: 6).[21]

The BBS also began leasing lands with an option to buy, hoping to
have a toe in the door when appropriations increased. In 1933, the
agency acquired options on 10,102 acres, but when no money materialized, it had to allow them to expire (U.S. BBS 1933: 19). In spite of
its creative approach to acquisitions, however, the BBS preferred to own
refuges in full-fee title and without inholders (Nixon 1957, vol. 2: 477,
478). Nor was the agency reluctant to use condemnation, by which it
settled about 15 percent of its early acquisitions.[22]

On a Roll—Major Legislation for the BBS   By the mid-1930s, friends
of the BBS in Congress put together a trio of laws to support wildlife
protection and land acquisition. The Migratory Bird Hunting Stamp Act
of 1934[23] guaranteed future funding for protection of migratory waterfowl. The act adopted a failed 1920s proposal, requiring waterfowl
hunters to acquire a federal hunting stamp (duck stamp) in addition to
any required state license. Stamp revenues were deposited in a U.S. Treasury account known as the Migratory Bird Conservation Fund.

Notably, expenditures from the fund were not subject to congressional
appropriation (U.S. FWS 1992: 48). The BBS could use the money to
survey, acquire, develop, and administer inviolate migratory bird sanctuaries (Wheatley 1970: 158–159). The duck stamp program generated
between $425,000 and $1,111,325 annually between 1935 and 1940
(U.S. BBS 1935: 2; 1936: 3; 1937: 3; 1938: 2; 1939: 5; 1940: 229). This
approach allowed users who benefited from the programs to support
them (Salyer and Gillette 1964: 503), while creating a revenue stream
that wildlife advocates could claim as their own. User fees, long controversial in federal forests and parks, immediately became a major element
of wildlife protection and habitat acquisition.

In 1935, Congress amended the act[24] to authorize the BBS to exchange land. This new authority included restrictions like those on USFS

exchanges—equal value, nonmineral lands—and reflected durable congressional concerns about land exchanges.[25] The same bill addressed the BBS easement program. The secretary of the interior had been authorized to make new rules regarding easement conditions *after* contracts had been signed (Wheatley 1970: 148), a possibility that undercut the program. The amendment provided, reasonably, that the secretary could not change easement conditions unilaterally after the initial transaction. Finally, the amendment brought lands managed by the BBS under a system of revenue sharing nearly identical to the system the Forest Service had been using for some time.

The 1934 Fish and Wildlife Coordination Act[26] acknowledged for the first time that some federal programs destroyed habitat. It directed federal and state agencies to develop a nationwide program of wildlife conservation that took the impacts of government programs into account (Dana, S. T. 1956: 406). The act included BBS authority to acquire land in connection with a project to achieve wildlife benefits in the project area.[27]

Because federal authority over wildlife remained technically limited to protecting migratory birds, wildlife advocates sought funds for acquisition of state refuges via the 1937 Pittman-Robertson Act[28] (Rutherford 1949: 7–8). P-R funds, as they became known, are generated by a federal tax on guns and ammunition. The states involved provide 25 percent of the money for any P-R project and must comply with federal requirements, including developing a state agency to administer the program (Rutherford 1949: 8–10). By 1940, all but five of the forty-three eligible states had passed the legislation necessary to accepting P-R refuges (U.S. BBS 1941: 256; U.S. FWS 1987: 21). Congress specified that P-R funds would be available without appropriation, thus creating the first dedicated fund specifically for acquiring land for conservation purposes. Nevertheless, Congress remained wary of allowing "pork" to accrue automatically. Although it rarely interferes, Congress reviews and approves proposed P-R projects in the annual appropriations process (U.S. FWS 1987: 13).

At the end of the Depression, a series of executive reorganizations reshaped the federal administration of wildlife management. In 1939 the BBS was transferred from the Department of Agriculture to the Department of the Interior. Secretary Ickes merged the NPS Division of Wildlife and the Commerce Department's Bureau of Fisheries with the BBS to create the U.S. Fish and Wildlife Service in 1939 (U.S. BBS 1941: 223, 225).[29] While the moves did not end the chronic institutional instability in the wildlife field, the FWS then enjoyed an unprecedented period of repose.

In sum, at the start of the Depression, federal fish and wildlife protection was spread out over three executive departments and forced to rely on a mixed bag of opportunistic acquisition tools. Nevertheless, the resulting potpourri of Depression-era transactions expanded federal authority, capacity, and tools for wildlife management. The *Geer v. Connecticut* idea that states owned wildlife receded, and federal government programs extended protections far beyond migratory birds.[30] Table 5.2 shows the expansion of acreage in the refuge system between 1929 and 1936. Between 1934 and 1940, 159 new refuges and nearly 7.6 million acres were added, bringing the system total to 263 refuges and more than 13.6 million acres.[31] Nearly all of the acquired lands were obtained using emergency relief funding. In addition, the first ten years of the

Table 5.2
Wildlife Refuge Growth in Acreage, 1929–1941

Year	Alaska	Continental U.S.	Total	% Increase
1929	4,078,482	678,943	4,757,425	—
1930	4,078,483	744,294	4,822,777	1
1931	4,078,482	835,863	4,914,345	2
1932	4,087,402	915,141	5,002,543	2
1933	4,087,402	1,625,619	5,713,021	14
1934	4,087,402	1,762,804	5,850,206	2
1935	4,087,407	2,012,613	6,100,020	4
1936	4,087,408	5,656,615	9,944,023	63
1937	4,287,408	7,144,966	11,432,374	15
1938	4,294,208	7,356,150	11,650,358	2
1939	4,294,208	9,235,952	13,530,160	16
1940	4,294,202	9,341,163	13,635,365	1
1941	4,294,202	9,446,102	13,740,304	1

Source: Gabrielson (1943: 23).

Pittman-Robertson program provided $4.9 million in federal funding to be spent on land acquisition.

The National Park Service

The Depression era is frequently described as a bonanza[32] for the NPS. This is partly true. Through reorganization and executive action, the NPS mission expanded, and the array of NPS units diversified (Swain 1972: 317).[33] The NPS took on important responsibilities for historic preservation and recreation planning. However, to this day, NPS staff remain dismayed by many of the units added during the Depression and continue to regret the perceived "lowering" of park standards that facilitated the growth. Secretary Ickes's[34] combative style sometimes killed promising park opportunities and left inholders in newer units feeling roughly treated and hostile.

Finally, the rapid expansion of NPS management units and areas did not signal acceptance of parks as a legitimate purpose for expenditure of federal funds. Most NPS acquisitions still relied upon state and private donations, and those that did use federal funds were primarily for economic relief rather than scenic or ecological purposes.

Expanding the NPS Notion of What Should Be Conserved   A 1933 executive order transferred all national monuments, memorial parks, historic battlefields, and kindred units managed by the War Department and the Forest Service to the NPS (Swain 1972: 323). That gave the NPS a role in historic preservation and an opportunity to manage resources throughout the nation that were of little interest to other agencies (Foresta 1984: 38). In addition, it provided an enormous boost for park visitation statistics, which had become the yardstick of the agency's popularity in Congress.[35] Reflecting its new responsibilities, the NPS was briefly renamed the Office of National Parks, Buildings, and Reservations. While the agency got its old name back the following year, the new units and subsequent additions added a raft of new and widely varying parks to the system. Before the reorganization, the NPS administered 63 parks and monuments. Afterward, it administered 161 units, including 26 national parks, 82 national monuments, 4 national historical parks, 11 national military parks, 7 national battlefield areas, 5 national historic sites, 1 national recreation area, 9 national memorials, 12 national cemeteries, and 3 national parkways, plus the national capital parks.

The NPS role in protecting historic resources was further expanded in 1935 by the passage of the Historic Sites Act.[36] The bill directed the NPS to survey historic sites, buildings, and objects and, significantly, to acquire the buildings on behalf of the United States. No purchase could be undertaken unless Congress had appropriated money—hence purchases were still approved on a site-specific basis—but the act provides acquisition authority nonetheless.[37] A flood of proposals (Hosmer 1965: 585) followed, leading over the next three decades to the addition of more than 100 historic units to the system (Lee 1972: 47–49).

A year later, the Park, Parkway, and Recreation Area Study Act[38] further expanded the NPS's mandate. The act directed the agency to investigate opportunities to create new parks to meet the recreation needs of the American people. The resulting report, produced in 1941, reflected the NPS's ongoing competition with the USFS by concluding that national forests were too far from population centers to be useful for recreation (Dilsaver 1994: 153).[39] The report envisioned a significant role for states and localities in providing new urban recreation opportunities for citizens, but the idea of partnerships was not yet on the NPS menu. Rather, the NPS saw itself as the coordinator of a national recreation program.

The hostility of NPS employees to historic sites was, and remains, a problem for the agency.[40] The willingness of agency leaders to "dilute" park standards via expansion into historic preservation and urban recreation became a major issue in the 1930s (Miles 1995: 106ff, 113ff). The issue of standards also extended beyond dissent over historic sites. If the unique mission of the NPS was to provide primitive, natural recreation experiences (as distinct from the commodities emphasis of the USFS), then the roads, parkways, and visitor facilities built by the CCC were not in harmony with park purposes. Although the NPS clearly needed some points of access, the "madness of roads" (Edge 1936, in Dilsaver 1994: 138)[41] built to create jobs threatened the purity of "nature as it is," which was ostensibly found in the parks.

Among those alarmed at the dilution of NPS standards was the Save-the-Redwoods League. Although the League's first plan had been to buy groves and donate them to the NPS, by the late 1930s they had decided, along with the Sierra Club, the Wilderness Society, and the National Parks Association, that wilderness was "safer with the federal foresters than with the Park Service" (Schrepfer 1983: 61).[42] League directors concluded that the NPS was degrading the inspirational value of national parks and destroying their primitive character. The redwoods, they believed, "deserved better," and no national park was established by federal purchase or donation in the redwoods for another three decades (Schrepfer 1983: 52–53, 59–64).

Standards also became a central issue in other park acquisitions. Several national groups that were generally supportive of the NPS lobbied against the expansion of Grand Teton National Park on what others considered to be highly technical issues of national park standards (Betts 1978: 206). However, the issue was not technical; it was political.

Mather had taken an ideological position that parks should not be acquired unless they were "pure." Secretary Ickes was more strategic, hoping to outflank the Forest Service by creating less pure units. The secretary reasoned that an NPS unit that allowed hunting and mineral prospecting, for instance, would engender less opposition than a "pure" park (Ickes 1953–1954, vol. 3: 160). To help mollify the purists, Ickes recommended using alternative designations such as "national recreation areas" to distinguish these units from the traditional national parks.

Depression era NPS Directors Horace Albright and Arno Cammerer accepted this impurity, but Cammerer at least wanted it corrected over time. "Because civilization has moved into the choicest areas ... some parks must now be carved out of developed areas." The park ideal, he argued, was something "toward which to work; it should not be something that prohibits us from working" (Righter 1982: 91; see also Albright, quoted in Gilligan 1953: 164). However, Cammerer's argument cuts both ways: purists feared that if the NPS could legitimately acquire an area with a dam, it would be difficult to prevent developers from building a dam in an existing park. The painful memory of the Hetch Hetchy Dam in Yosemite was a bitter precedent in this regard.

New and Diverse NPS Units Under Relief Programs   Land acquisitions funded and authorized under economic relief programs created the appearance that the NPS itself was acquiring land for park purposes. It was not. Except for occasional historic sites, the agency continued to rely on others to expand the park system (Paige 1985). For example, Congress relied upon CCC authorities to appropriate almost $3 million of unemployment relief to supplement state donations in the Great Smokies (Ise 1961: 259). Paradoxically, acquisition authority continued to elude the NPS even as the park system grew rapidly.

Congress did move a few steps closer to funding park acquisitions directly. Borrowing a page from the Save-the-Redwoods League, it authorized a general 50-50 federal-private match to encourage land donations to parks across the country. If a landowner donated half the value of her property, Congress would appropriate funds to purchase the remaining half.[43] Matching funds were used, for example, to expand Yosemite to include 10,000 acres in Wawona Basin. Large amounts of private land (including the still-famous Wawona Hotel) were acquired, starting in 1932 (Runte 1990: 170–172; Sargent 1997: 67–70). Surprisingly, Congress justified this addition as protection for park deer.[44] Numerous small holdings trapped within park boundaries by the expansion became a major problem for the NPS fifty years later. For those landowners not inclined to donate anything (the Rockefellers and Mellons to the contrary notwithstanding), the NPS found that a cooperative appraiser would double the value of the land.[45] The owner would then "donate" half of the doubled value, while the government paid the other half, representing the "real" value of the land. In this way the landowner effectively ended up donating nothing at all (Ickes 1953–1954, vol. 2: 582ff).[46] Government appraisals have been controversial and arguably subject to manipulation ever since, as we will discuss in chapter 8.

Cammerer's idea of "renewable purity" also had consequences for inholders; it implied their removal via fee simple acquisition of their parcels over time. Whereas purity remained the stated NPS preference, agency actions moved rapidly in the opposite direction. To maintain support among locals for park acquisitions, the NPS began to make more generous arrangements for existing landholders who might otherwise oppose designations. Ultimately, as Ickes suggested, the NPS responded to

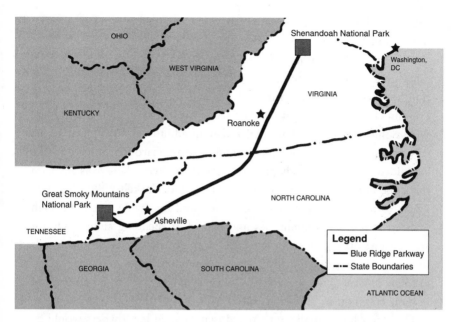

Figure 5.4
Route of the Blue Ridge Parkway. Source: U.S. NPS (1994, Appendix B).

the dual criticism of developers and purists by developing a new vocabulary of park designations. National parkways, seashores, lakeshores, and urban renewal projects were all added to the NPS domain in spite of their sullied status.

The Blue Ridge Parkway   In 1929 Herbert Hoover established a presidential retreat in Shenandoah National Park to boost fund-raising for the park. He also sought to distribute economic relief funds for building scenic highways, including Skyline Drive in the park, and to begin a parkway connecting Shenandoah to the Smokies (Shankland 1970: 298). The resulting Blue Ridge Parkway (BRP) route is shown in figure 5.4. It became the archetype for a series of similar NPS units (Speer and Haskell 2000: 9).

Initial authority for the BRP project came under the 1933 National Industrial Recovery Act (NIRA), which established the Public Works Administration (PWA) to stimulate economic recovery by pumping federal funds into large-scale construction projects.[47] The parkway began in

1933 as a PWA project supported by the CCC, and was taken over by the NPS in 1936.

As in the other southern Appalachian parks, Virginia and North Carolina undertook BRP land acquisitions, using state highway condemnation and acquisition authority.[48] Ickes and the states did not agree on how much land was required. The secretary first requested a 200-foot-wide right-of-way, then later demanded an additional 400 feet of scenic easements on either side of the route. North Carolina agreed to the expanded easements, perhaps because the roadway there was high on the ridge and affected few residents (Speer and Haskell 2000: 32). Virginia resisted the idea of cutting a thousand-foot-wide swath through isolated mountain communities and balked at spending state funds for scenic views during an economic crisis. Virginia also included in its deeds of cession reservations of jurisdiction to maintain state authority to tax gasoline and alcoholic beverages (Jolley 1969: 108–112), a pattern that became common in future cessions.

The states had initially anticipated that isolated landowners would be willing to donate a portion of their land in return for the giving of a paved road into town. However, landowners lost interest when they learned that the BRP was to be a limited-access road with few driveways or points of entry. The result was a rough-and-tumble approach to land transactions that put surveyors on the ground mapping the road before landowners were aware that their land might be included in the project (Jolley 1969: 108–112).

North Carolina's standard method for acquiring highway land was to identify the route and post maps at the county court house. A landowner then had two choices: either accept the road as a benefit that did not require compensation (i.e., a giving), or wait for a year and then sue the state for damages.[49] Neither option was popular with cash-strapped landowners. Nor did the plan meet the long-term needs of the NPS; the state maps did not create clear records of land conveyances, and these inadequate records have confused land title along the BRP in North Carolina ever since. The scenic easements also posed new challenges (Foresta 1984: 242; Williams 1962, chap. 3). The very idea of a scenic easement was unfamiliar at the time, and many landowners were glad to have the cash even if they did not fully understand what they were selling (Jolley 1969: 103–104).

The Eastern Band of Cherokee Indians endured a particularly protracted acquisition process. Planners anticipated that the southern end of the parkway would go through their reservation, on a site where the federal Bureau of Indian Affairs and the state had long contemplated a paved road. The Cherokees agreed to grant a 200-foot right-of-way, but balked at a 1,000-foot swath that would consume much of the tribe's land and force a town to relocate on a floodplain. In 1939 the North Carolina congressional delegation "decided to play hardball" (Speer and Haskell 2000: 40). Congress authorized the secretary of interior to choose land for the parkway with or without Indian cooperation. Finally a new route was selected, and the Cherokees were paid $30 an acre for a 1,338-acre right-of-way.

Virginia proceeded more directly, negotiating with each owner and conveying each deed to the federal government. This process created better records but allowed Virginia landowners to reserve access to the highway from their land. As the farmers sold out to home developers, some of the reserved access rights became major intersections. They have since become a safety hazard and management burden for the NPS, one far more challenging, according to present managers, than the comparatively well-defined easements.

Park Service policy toward inholders also changed during acquisition of the parkway. NPS officials decided that removing inhabitants from Skyline Drive and Shenandoah had been an error; nothing remained of mountain culture for visitors to see. The agency therefore decided to blend inhabitants into exhibits on the BRP (Jolley 1969: 130–131). This is possibly preferable to viewing residents as desecrations (Drury 1946), but it too created problems. The NPS frequently sacrificed historical accuracy to create an idealized vision of mountain life, trapping locals in a marketing scheme that continues to trivialize their lives.

For example, the Park Service used subsidies and leases to sculpt farming practices to meet tourists' expectations. It provided free fence rails to encourage farmers to construct the famous BRP "worm fence" and urged them to stack their cornstalks in scenic shocks along the roadside

(Jolley 1969: 132–133). NPS planners were particularly disappointed with Mabry Mill at milepost 176 (Speer and Haskell 2000, chap. 5). The NPS replaced the kerosene engine that had actually powered the mill with a much-photographed but totally bogus waterwheel, millpond, and flumes. It also tore down an unattractive springhouse, a granary, a chicken house, a woodshed, a washhouse, and a small barn (Speer and Haskell 2000: 96–98). Presto: A monument to pioneer life that met the expectations of urban dwellers and park planners. As elsewhere in the Appalachians, conflicts over acquisition became part of the subsequent management setting; angry locals, who still recall in graphic terms how their grandparents' land was stolen, and problems with imperfect title continue to haunt land protection in the southern Appalachians.

Seashores, Lakeshores, and Urban Units   Parkways were not the only innovative park units. The 1941 NPS *Report on Recreational Use of Land in the United States* recommended acquisition of at least 10 percent of the shoreline of the Atlantic and Pacific Oceans, the Gulf of Mexico, and the Great Lakes (U.S. NPS 1938: 27). Besides meeting new recreation needs, shoreline acquisitions were appealing because they avoided direct confrontation with the rival USFS. Ickes pursued the goal diligently. Although he was successful in having only one coastal unit approved during his time in office, his efforts laid the groundwork for numerous post-World War II acquisitions of shoreline.

Ickes's new unit was the Cape Hatteras National Seashore in North Carolina, authorized in 1937. In a familiar process, the land was again acquired by the state on behalf of the NPS. However, Congress was learning to be supportive of inholders, even when the NPS disapproved, and provided for continuing habitation in the park by excluding towns from acquisition. Beyond those designated areas, however, the seashore was to become a "primitive wilderness" (Ise 1961: 4). Hatteras was the third NPS unit that the state of North Carolina had accepted responsibility for purchasing, underscoring once again the importance of federal investment to states and localities. But cash contributions were slowed by the lingering Depression and then the war. With no relief programs left to fall back on when the war was over, funding from several Mellon family foundations finally filled the gap (Lee 1972: 58–59).

Acquisition of land for urban renewal also became a major NPS growth node. The NPS's first entry in this arena, however, was a debacle. The NPS describes the Jefferson National Expansion Memorial (JNEM)[50] as the first national historic site established under authority of the Historic Sites Act. That is technically correct; the NPS did use the 1936 authority to condemn 47 square blocks of historic waterfront in St. Louis, Missouri. The transaction was the earliest direct NPS purchase and also the first for historic protection (Brown, S. A. 1984: 12).

Yet this ostensibly landmark acquisition is not highlighted in NPS literature, perhaps because the agency soon razed every building on the site, turning it into a gigantic parking lot. This was done at the behest of St. Louis boosters, who wanted federal funding for urban renewal and management of an undeniably local park. At the time, neither the NPS nor the city had any vision of what would replace the old waterfront buildings. They simply destroyed them. The old courthouse and cathedral that today figure so prominently as the historic elements of a scene now dominated by that puzzling aluminum arch are outside the boundaries of the acquired historic district (University of Missouri 2002).

The general pattern of NPS participation in urban redevelopment was not always so destructive. The national park that developed around the Old State House in Philadelphia provides a useful counterpoint. The project was initiated by civic leaders in Philadelphia who were anxious to exploit reverence for the national shrine to buoy their campaign for a "Better Philadelphia" (Riley 1990: 48–49; Greiff 1987: 56–57). Although Philadelphia boosters subsequently dominated the process, the outcome was not a St. Louis-like disaster (Hosmer 1987: ix–x).[51]

The NPS established an early foothold in 1935 by acquiring the nearby Second Bank of the United States from the Treasury Department. The Works Progress Administration funded the acquisition and renovation. The foothold expanded in 1942 when President Roosevelt designated the Gloria Dei (Old Swedes' Church) a national historic site, albeit reluctantly because he believed the project distracted from the war effort (Hosmer 1965: 717–718). Independence Hall and Independence Square were added to the list of historic sites in 1943 after a protracted and contentious NPS effort to develop a cooperative management agreement with the city finally succeeded. Although the NPS manages and interprets Independence Hall, the city still holds title. This mixed ownership arrangement is an early example of the kind of mosaic that dominates early twenty-first century land acquisition for conservation.

Philadelphia boosters then formed the Independence Hall Association to transform the area into a full-fledged national park. The association successfully urged the state legislature to appropriate $4 million to acquire a three-block mall in front of the Hall. At the end of World War II, Congress established the Philadelphia National Shrines Park Commission to make recommendations for a national park (Greiff 1987: 49). Invoking familiar war powers notions, the legislation found

it is proper, fitting, and desirable that the United States of America should properly enshrine these jewels of democracy [in Philadelphia], so that all who visit these hallowed places from the far corners of this glorious democracy and the four corners of the world may be stirred with a feeling of patriotic reverence. [Act of August 9, 1946, U.S. *Statutes at Large* 60 (1946): NPS]

The commission also argued that the task of protecting the area was beyond the resources of the city. "Nor," they concluded, "is it desirable from the point of view of the Nation that the responsibility should be entirely local" (Philadelphia National Shrines Park Commission 1947: xi). Federal legislation passed in 1948 adopted most of the commission's recommendations. The statute rests on the 1935 Historic Sites Act, waives exclusive federal jurisdiction, and authorizes the secretary of the interior to lease out historic buildings. In a most unusual provision, leasing receipts were to be retained in a special account for management of the buildings.[52] Much was at stake for the NPS. This was the first time that the agency had sought and received authority to spend appropriated funds on land for park purposes. When the bell rang on New Year's Eve, 1950, Philadelphia retained title to Independence Hall, but the NPS had acquired a park around it (Greiff 1987: 75).

At about the same time that the Philadelphia transactions were inching forward, acquisition of the George Washington Carver National Monument was authorized shortly after Carver's death in July 1943. Acquisition of his birthplace was delayed, however, by the war and disputes over price, and the government did not receive title until June 1952 (Mackintosh 1969: 33–35). Somewhere between and among the St. Louis, Philadelphia, and Carver transactions, depending on how you date them, the NPS itself acquired land for conservation apart from economic relief programs for the first time.[53]

The NPS emerged from this period conflicted and immersed in controversy. The agency's relationship with local and private groups remained rocky. Although St. Louis and Philadelphia unquestionably sought national park designations, others, such as the Save-the-Redwoods League, fended them off. The agency continued to be anathema to landowners in the southern Appalachians and was only slightly less disliked in the Tetons. Moreover, the NPS took the heat for its state and private acquisition partners (as along the Blue Ridge Parkway) and complicated matters by imposing hunting and similar restrictions on local activities that the USFS did not. Meanwhile, park advocates and employees questioned the new units as deviating too far from the core mission of the agency to protect remote and pristine landscapes. In short, if the Depression was a bonanza for the NPS, it came at a much higher cost than for its sibling agencies. When the war broke out, unneeded nonessential agencies were exiled to Denver or Salt Lake City to make room for more essential services. The NPS boxed up their files, while the USFS stayed put.

No Bonanza at All: The Bureau of Land Management

If the Depression offered a mixed blessing to the NPS, it offered nothing at all to the Bureau of Land Management, which was not created until the late 1940s. The Taylor Grazing Act (TGA) passed in 1934, effectively ending homesteading and creating a new system of federal grazing districts.[54] Despite this ostensible ratification of federal management of the western range, a series of agencies administering the lands were ill-positioned to take advantage of New Deal acquisition programs. The TGA was intended to stabilize the range livestock industry and end competitive and destructive access to the existing public range by allocating exclusive licenses and permits to graze (Raymond 2003, chap. 3; Peffer 1951). Nevertheless, the act maintained the fiction of eventual private ownership of the land, framing all of its regulations as "pending final disposition" of the federal range.

Despite its limited embrace of federal authority, however, the TGA included significant new authorities beyond allowing the CCC to go to work on the western range. It authorized classification and exchange of land, as well as the acceptance of land donations.[55] The new Division of Grazing and its successors interpreted their authority broadly—later characterized as "land manipulation procedures" (Wheatley 1970: S-1)—thereby giving the grazing lands a vital but unanticipated role in other land conservation acquisitions. Many rangeland parcels were transferred to the NPS as parks or monuments, while less suitable properties provided trading stock that allowed the other federal agencies to acquire land without spending money or increasing federal holdings in an area (Wheatley 1970: S-1).

As always, Congress remained wary of exchanges, and the TGA authority was quite narrow, following the model set by the USFS in 1922. Exchanged parcels had to be of equal value, and the secretary of the interior was not authorized to accept or make cash payments to equalize those figures. Moreover, the lands selected by the government had to be in the same state as the lands offered, or not more than 50 miles into an adjacent state (Wheatley 1970: S-2).[56] Finally, the secretary was required to determine that public interests would benefit from the proposed exchange. Thus it was extremely difficult to find tradable parcels under the terms of the act.[57] Under these conditions, the TGA exchange authority was used mainly on small transactions—to block in scattered federal lands and clean up boundaries—and without much discussion for more than forty years.

Despite the TGA's focus on the livestock industry, administrators made some effort to acquire land for recreation through this limited exchange authority. For example, in 1944–1946, the renamed Grazing Service was able to swap public domain land for private parcels to fill in ownership along the North Umpqua River in Oregon for outdoor recreation. The timber industry halted the effort, but the exchanges ultimately constituted 20 percent of the 1990 North Umpqua Area of Critical Environmental Concern (Peterson 1996: 18–19).[58] After the 1946 merger of the General Land Office and the Grazing Service to form the BLM, the new agency also embroidered the edges of the very modest TGA authority to give itself a role in the recreation boom that would follow World War II. Lacking visible public support and bedeviled by commodity interests, concerned staff at the public domain agencies used their shaky "land manipulation" authorities to protect the land as best they could.

State and Private Conservation Acquisitions

Contributions to the national parks absorbed an enormous amount of attention and energy at the state and private level. Large and small donations of land and cash focused on acquiring land for federal parks in already-mentioned places, such as the Redwoods, BRP, and Cape Hatteras. However, not all of the acquisitions wound up in government ownership; private groups also enlarged their holdings during the economic crisis. The Trustees acquired almost as many properties through donations during the 1930s as they had in the four decades since the organization was created (The Trustees of Reservations 2001: 10, 40–41).

The Pell family of Fort Ticonderoga was beset by many of the same issues that confronted less spectacularly endowed landowners: In lean financial times, how does one pay the taxes? In addition, the family continued to struggle with questions regarding how a family allocates access, responsibilities, and costs for managing a historic property among a burgeoning group of cousins and claimants (Fairfax and Guenzler 2001, chaps. 9 and 10). To lighten the tax burden, the heirs established the Pell Family Association in 1931. The association's mission was to preserve the fort, the battlefield, lakeshore, mountains, forests, and farmlands surrounding it; to provide interpretive and educational programs; to manage the fort's library and museum; and to preserve and interpret relevant literature and artifacts.[59] Thus although a private nonprofit group held the assets, the new association was created for exclusively public purposes.

The family ceded title to the fort and much of the surrounding lands to the association in 1943. Thereafter, technically, the Pell family no longer owned the property. However, not unexpectedly, the family continued to manage closely what had officially become a public charitable institution. Although in 1946 the Pell Family Association was renamed the Fort Ticonderoga Association to reduce the appearance of Pell domination, the family continued to occupy the Pavilion as a summer home, and all members of the association board were Pell heirs. Until very near the end of the twentieth century, the fort continued in an odd limbo as a family-dominated public charity. This situation is not unfamiliar to organizations dealing with families that have retained rights in conserved properties. However, public accountability suffered. Continued family stewardship meant that no one challenged the Pells's convenient arrangement.

Conclusions

Success in the economic environment of the Depression sometimes meant not holding onto the farm but persuading the federal government to buy it. Sellers' priorities largely directed land acquisition programs during the Depression. Failing that, landowners reorganized as nonprofits (like the Pells) or donated their land to private conservation organizations like The Trustees for Reservations. The avoidance of significant land use regulations was also a victory for landowners. During this period, the primary goal of acquisition was to provide economic relief, both to the unemployed and to cash-strapped landowners. Although it is rarely discussed today, many of the lands "protected" were simply dumped into the federal lap. Ironically, areas considered too depleted to remain in private ownership at the time are currently administered as wilderness areas.

Before World War II shut down most of the era's acquisition programs, the federal agencies had begun to differentiate. Acquisitions by the USFS and FWS proceeded under general authority, while, with the exception of actions under the Antiquities and Historic Sites acts, individual NPS units required specific congressional action or the help of friendly proxies. The lands that each agency acquired also differed. The USFS tended to purchase industrial holdings, frequently cut over or with logging and mineral rights reserved by sellers. Hence the land was relatively cheap, and, frequently, selling to the USFS was an alternative to abandoning the land. The BBS-FWS had more exacting demands for habitat than the USFS did for forests but was also compelled to compromise them. Nevertheless, the BBS-FWS spread its limited funds across an impressive landscape by experimenting with an equally impressive array of tools: easements, leases, and cooperative management agreements.

It was also the only agency to enjoy a user fee program that provided (and still does today) dedicated funding without appropriations.

The BBS experience with easements in the pothole region of the Dakotas was far more extensive and satisfactory to managers than the more widely discussed NPS experience with easements on the Blue Ridge Parkway. Moreover, an NPS assessment of its easement experience has to be viewed in the context of its intolerance for inholders and preference for exclusive jurisdiction. Even when it could not hold the line politically, the NPS continued to espouse "purity" as a philosophy and to place a high priority on removing inholders and exercising exclusive jurisdiction. The success of the FWS seems more reflective of early experience with conservation easements than these NPS concerns, and current NPS managers have greater problems with the access reservations than the easements. Ironically, because the NPS badly needed to please Congress by attracting visitors and generating local economic benefits, it incurred the dismay of apparently natural allies such as the Save-the-Redwoods-League. Hence the USFS became a more acceptable manager, even for some preserved lands.

6

Roots of Change, 1953–1979

Federal acquisition programs celebrated as an anchor of FDR's economic relief agenda encountered major changes starting in the Eisenhower years (1953–1960) (Rome 2001). Population increases associated with the birth of the "baby boomers" created pressure for increased development of rural lands and timber harvest for housing. Federal policies— tax treatment of mortgage expenses, grants for sewers and similar infrastructure—all encouraged transformation of the landscape. The new interstate highway system literally changed the face of the nation. The Trust for Public Land notes that the net effect of post-World War II highway and housing policies was to "explode the metropolis and scatter it across the countryside" (TPL 2002: 9).

Conflict was inevitable. The relationship between cities and the hinterland was fundamentally altered, as once-remote places from the Adirondacks to Alaska became easily accessible. In the process, new roads directly or indirectly destroyed valleys, watersheds, scenic vistas, communities, and traditional rural livelihoods. The modern environmental movement was shaped in response to those changes (Hays 1987; Rome 2001). On the one hand, activists ardently sought federal regulations to combat air and water pollution and address a host of new issues framed by newly popular ideas about ecosystems. On the other, questions raised by Rachel Carson in *Silent Spring* (1962) and further expressed in debates over clear-cutting and wilderness eroded the legitimacy of Progressive era agencies built on science and centralized decision making.

True, the Progressive era notion of the social obligations inherent in owning property had finally gained significant acceptance as regulation of land use became a major tool of conservation, even at the federal level. However, the regulations did not go uncontested. A new private property rights movement began to develop, as unreasonable expectations about the efficacy of regulatory mechanisms contributed to environmental conflict and further erosion of federal credibility.

Acquisition goals expanded in the wake of these changes. World War II GIs came home to a shortened workweek, paid vacations, and greater disposable income, and the nation headed for the outdoors in an explosion of demand for outdoor recreation (Clawson 1963: 35). In the absence of economic recovery as a justification for acquiring land, federal agencies embraced recreation with a fervor that is, in retrospect, a bit puzzling. Did Americans really believe they faced an outdoor recreation crisis (Dilsaver 1994; Dana, S. T. and Fairfax 1980)? Apparently so, and the NPS mounted an enormous expansion and development program, Mission 66, to respond to growing public demand. Race riots accompanying the Civil Rights movement gave the topic a more urgent spin as "parks for the people" were promoted as an antidote to urban blight. However, environmentalists were soon seeking to protect entire ecosystems, inspired perhaps by the stringent requirements of the Endangered Species Act of 1973. The goals of land acquisition expanded to include these new priorities.

Neither the expansion nor the pursuit of these goals was a wholly federal undertaking. Slightly offstage, private nonprofit conservation groups were forming and revitalizing themselves, largely but not entirely around the identity of land trusts and the tool of conservation easements.[1] As with the federal agencies, land trusts needed time for basic institutional development before they could become dominant participants in land conservation. Indeed, having declared the period between the Weeks Act and the Depression (1911–1932) as a time of consolidation for the USFS and NPS, we find it useful to view the strengthening of private land trusts in this chapter from the same perspective. By the end of the 1970s, the land trusts were primed to become a movement of their own.

Moreover, although it seems that during the 1960s the federal agencies finally achieved a complete set of authorities and programs for acquiring land, the apparent coherence is deceptive. Even the "environmental decade" of the 1970s did not repeat the land acquisition bonanza of the Depression. Newly prosperous landowners resisted sales they had eagerly sought before the war. Moreover, the focus on recreation and habitat significantly altered the kind of land that the federal government acquired. Environmentalists and recreationists were no longer content with worked-over timberland or farmsteads. As a result, the financial costs of acquisition skyrocketed, and a common effect of federal interest in an area was to drive prices even higher (U.S. BOR 1967; Sax 1980a).

We discuss this period in four sections. The first examines the apparent peaking of federal statutory authority for acquisition. The second section traces the mixed impact of those statutory changes on the four federal land management agencies. In the third section we explore the renewed vigor of private conservation, specifically as related to the emergence of the modern land trust movement. Finally, we return in the last section to five familiar stories—The Trustees, Mount Vernon, Fort Ticonderoga, the Redwoods, and Gettysburg—to observe how postwar changes affected private efforts that predated the land trust idea.

Peaking Statutory Authorities for Federal Acquisition

The end of the New Deal forced the land management agencies and their supporters to find a new justification for buying land. This was not difficult; pentup demand for outdoor recreation erupted almost before World War II was over. By the 1950s, a national "crisis" in outdoor recreation was widely discussed. Congress responded in 1958 by establishing yet another commission of distinguished citizens, the Outdoor Recreation Resources Review Commission (ORRRC), whose 1963 report both reflected and anchored a new priority for acquiring land (U.S. ORRRC 1963). Its recommendations focused primarily on providing recreation opportunities in the urbanized East, where people, but not public lands, were concentrated. Thus, acquisition for recreation was a major emphasis.

Five statutes enacted after the release of the ORRRC report appeared to establish a comprehensive federal approach to the acquisition of land for conservation purposes. The statutes provided a coherent set of authorities and funding sources, both especially crucial to the NPS. However, the same laws also suggested that half a century of largely unopposed federal land acquisition was ending. Hostile landowners, property rights advocates, and rival claimants objected to both government and private conservation acquisitions, with increasing political success. This is clear even in the apparent high-water mark of federal acquisition power, the creation of the Land and Water Conservation Fund in 1964.[2]

The Land and Water Conservation Fund

The LWCF provides both authority and funding[3] for the federal government to acquire land for outdoor recreation, a change of particular importance to the NPS and the BLM. The LWCF program has become so popular that it is hard to believe its passage was contentious. However, the LWCF debate occasioned a rare effort by fiscal conservatives to put recreation on the self-supporting basis that nineteenth-century park advocates had promised (Hammond 1969: 92). Despite the argument, Congress never seriously considered fair market value or real cost recovery (Mackintosh 1983, chap. 1), and the LWCF authorized an inconsequential mix of very small fees. Congress has yet to address squarely the issue of federally subsidized recreation programs and user fees.

Passing the LWCF also required balancing federal and state priorities. After considerable wrangling, the LWCF allocated 40 percent of the fund to state and local programs. The state share was critical. The LWCF's most important result was probably that it encouraged the formation of state-level recreation programs, offering federal aid for states in preparing a Statewide Comprehensive Outdoor Recreation Plan (SCORP). An approved SCORP was required for the state to qualify for a 50 percent LWCF match on implementation funding. States could spend their share on both land acquisition and site development, but the federal share was for acquisition only. As can be seen in table 6.1, however, Congress has not consistently funded the states' share.

The LWCF also provided a new source for funding federal acquisitions. Table 6.1 indicates that the NPS generally receives about half the federal funds, while the rest is roughly split between the FWS and the

Table 6.1
Allocation of LWCF Funds, 1964–2000

Agency	Billion $	% of Total	% of Federal share
States	3.2	28	
National Park Service	3.7	32	47
U.S. Forest Service	2.1	18	26
U.S. Fish and Wildlife Service	1.5	13	19
Bureau of Land Management	0.628	5	8
LWCF administration	0.3	3	
Total	11.428	100	
Federal share	7.928	69	100

Source: Zinn (2001).

USFS. Advocates persuaded Congress to raise the cap on LWCF authorizations to its present annual level of $900 million in 1976. The statute has also been amended several times to include a growing suite of conservation goals (Coggins and Glicksman 1984: 147–161).[4] However, the LWCF has disappointed those hoping for a replacement of Depression-era funding for acquisitions; Congress has rarely funded the program fully.

Early land rights advocates were also heard in the LWCF debates. They feared that the LWCF would erode the nation's private property base, shifting too much private land into government ownership. In response, the LWCF confined NPS and USFS purchases to land that is inside established unit boundaries. Furthermore, western representatives, impatient with federal controls emanating from national forests, directed 85 percent of new national forest acreage to areas east of the hundredth meridian.[5]

The Wilderness Act

The 1964 Wilderness Act establishes a special management regime on lands already owned by the federal government and is not usually discussed as an acquisition statute. However, section 5 of the act provides another counter to the growth of federal acquisition. By promising all state and private inholders within wilderness areas adequate access to their property, the act makes public acquisition of those inholdings particularly urgent. Yet it also limits condemnations in wilderness areas, requiring specific authorization from Congress for any transactions with unwilling sellers. Because all federal agencies have had general condemnation authority since 1888, this provision actually withdraws that authority on wilderness lands—a context in which the authority would in fact be most useful. This may sound like a small glitch, but it has become a serious problem because owners of wilderness inholdings rapidly became adept at "greenmailing" management agencies—extracting a high price to become a willing seller (Simon et al. 1998).

Wild and Scenic Rivers and National Trails

Congress was similarly stingy with acquisition authority in the Wild and Scenic Rivers and National Trails acts. The two 1968 statutes authorized the USFS, NPS, FWS, and BLM to identify special management corridors on public land and designed a process for making further designations on state and private land as well. Many advocates did not believe that acquisition was needed for these programs or feared that expansive federal acquisitions would incite opposition. Thus, Congress approved only minimal acquisition authority under the law.

What is more, the authority that exists is poorly designed for protecting corridors (Stevenson 2002). Inside established federal units, acquisition and condemnation are limited to a maximum number of acres per mile. Outside federal units, the relevant agency is authorized to encourage state and local governments to enter into cooperative agreements with landowners, or if that does not happen within two years, to make its own agreements or acquire the lands by purchase or exchange. Condemnation has the same limitation on acreage per mile as it does inside the boundaries of federal units and was prohibited altogether on the Pacific Coast Trail. No land could be condemned within an incorporated village, city, or borough that had adopted zoning to achieve the purposes of the act.[6] And no land could be condemned in an area with more than 50 percent state or federal ownership.

The necessity for condemnation in linear projects such as roads and power lines has long been recognized, but for trails and rivers, which are no less flexible regarding location, Congress limited it (Stevenson 2002). Even willing sellers are thwarted if the agency has acquired more than its allotted acres in a particular segment.

Relocation Assistance Act

The Uniform Relocation Assistance and Land Acquisition Policies Act of 1970 addressed the escalating complaints of landowners displaced by federal acquisitions. The goal was to further protect landowners and reduce hostility to government land purchases—particularly highways and urban renewal projects—without allowing holdouts to gouge the government on price (U.S. Congress, House 1968). It authorizes payments for relocation and cost differentials when finding a "substantially similar" home. Reading the act gives one a feeling of incredulity. *Of course* the agency head is forbidden to require a landowner to vacate a property before being paid for it, or to charge more than fair-market rent if the owner is permitted to remain temporarily on the property as a lessee. That such basic requirements had to be codified at all suggests some of the reasons for growing landowner hostility to federal acquisitions (U.S. Congress, House 1968).

The act also led to uniform federal appraisal standards that began to figure prominently in land acquisition procedures. Appraising real estate, as we saw in Harold Ickes's park acquisitions, is an inexact science subject to manipulation to meet agency or landowner goals. The 1970 statute made an initial attempt at regularizing the process. However, controversy continued and is discussed in chapters 7 and 8 with particular reference to federal land exchanges.

The Payment in Lieu of Taxes Act

As we have noted throughout the preceding chapters, congressional representatives and local boosters regularly bemoan the tax-exempt status of federal lands even while eagerly seeking the benefits that accompany federal facilities. Having relied for decades on compensation via state land cessions required by the enclave clause, landowners and localities struck real paydirt with PILTs. The 1976 act[7] authorized payments nominally in lieu of the taxes that the federal government does not pay on its land. Although the program is never fully funded, it is popular with local officials, and the payments are of some value in softening opposition to federal land acquisitions in many jurisdictions.

Ambiguous Results for Federal Agencies

The federal statutes discussed here suggest that public enthusiasm for federal acquisitions was weakening at the same time that the environment was moving to the top of the public agenda. At the agency level, a similar message emerged. President Kennedy was forced to address personally the destructive NPS and USFS competition of the period. He and the secretaries of agriculture and interior signed an agreement, the "Treaty of the Potomac," which stated that neither agency would plan to appropriate property managed by the other without prior discussion and approval. That did not end behind-the-scenes NPS wangling, but it did dampen the most overt covetousness. The more fundamental problem, however, was that the agencies were under different and conflicting pressures from the administration and Congress.

The Forest Service

The USFS continued to have the most effective federal acquisition program. It entered the postwar period with comprehensive real estate transaction authority. Although the agency soon ran into public hostility regarding wilderness designations and the practice of clear-cutting, its acquisition programs continued to prosper. In 1953, 3.8 million acres that had been acquired under Depression-era land utilization programs were transferred to the USFS. The USFS was expected to manage the areas only until they were sold to private owners, but in 1960 they were renamed "national grasslands," and the agency continues to manage them (Hurt 1985).

More significantly, in 1956 Congress gave the Department of Agriculture general authorization "to acquire land, or interest therein, by purchase, exchange, or otherwise as may be necessary to carry out its authorized work."[8] The legislative debate emphasized research sites (U.S. Congress, House 1956), but the authority also applies to some USFS acquisitions west of the hundredth meridian, on public domain (reserved) forests where Weeks Act and LWCF authorities are nominally restricted.

The Sisk Act[9] of 1967 also added to USFS acquisition power, authorizing the exchange of small parcels of USFS land with states, counties, municipal governments, or public school authorities. Where the exchange partner did not have enough land to offer, the exchange could be completed entirely with cash—indeed, as a purchase. Even better, the statute permitted receipts from those transactions to be held in the Sisk Act Fund, to become available without further appropriation for acquisition of other land. This was a rare opportunity indeed.

The 1976 National Forest Management Act is not generally regarded as minor, but in the land acquisition field, it made only one change, of largely historic interest.[10] In addition to its extensive reformulation of the forest planning process, the new law abolished the National Forest Reservation Commission and transferred its role in evaluating Weeks Act acquisitions to the secretary of agriculture. The secretary is now authorized to create new national forests without consulting Congress, except with regard to obtaining the funding (a large caveat). The secretary has not yet irked Congress by doing so, but the legal process is noticeably less stringent than the legislation that must precede formation of a new NPS unit. As ever, utilitarian forest practices are given greater autonomy and acquisition power than less preeminent recreation purposes.

The Alchemy of BLM Authority

In many ways, the BLM remained the excluded stepchild of new federal land acquisition authority. Its frustrating dance with the range livestock industry (Foss 1960) continued well into the 1970s, and environmentalists failed to consider BLM land when drafting the Wilderness Act. The LWCF also initially ignored the bureau.

Nevertheless, despite these obstacles, the BLM still managed to acquire some land for permanent protection. In 1962, for example, it began efforts to acquire a surplus Coast Guard lighthouse as a part of an effort to protect the King Range, a scenic coastal region in northern California that had been assessed by Park Service planners as being "less than national park caliber" (Peterson 1996: 11). In 1970 Congress authorized the secretary of the interior to acquire King Range land by purchase or exchange. Gradually through such efforts Congress became accustomed to the BLM as something more than just a disposition agency. Soon the bureau was authorized by 1968 amendments to receive LWCF funds and was also included in both the Wild and Scenic Rivers Act and the National Trails Act.

Passed in 1976, the Federal Land Policy and Management Act (FLPMA) finally gave the BLM an authorizing statute twenty-eight years after it was created by executive reorganization.[11] In FLPMA, Congress proclaimed that the remaining public domain would be retained in federal ownership.[12] Congress officially recognized the BLM as a land use planning and management organization with jurisdiction over 470 million acres, and repealed 3,500 old land disposition statutes.[13]

The law also granted the bureau a full range of land transaction authority (Anderson 1979; Rosenthal 1996). The secretary of the interior was authorized to acquire lands or interest in lands by purchase, exchange, donation, or eminent domain. Such acquisitions were limited only by the fact that they had to be consistent with the mission of the department and with applicable departmental land-use plans.[14] At the same time, the unrepealed Taylor Grazing Act limited this power by allowing the BLM to condemn only land needed to access landlocked federal parcels.

Congress also continued to make land exchanges difficult.[15] For instance, the earlier TGA exchange authority is in fact restricted by FLPMA, which requires that both parcels in an exchange must be within a single state.[16] The secretary must also determine that the public interest will be well served[17] by an exchange. The law provides for equal-value exchanges, with up to 25 percent cash equalization. Because the BLM rarely has cash to compensate an owner, the private party normally takes the more valuable parcel and pays the government the difference (Anderson 1979: 665). Federal land use planning must precede all exchanges, and all acquisitions and dispositions must be for fair market value. Incongruously, the agency remains authorized to make below-market transfers to state and local governments under the Recreation Act of 1926 which, like the TGA, was not repealed by FLPMA.[18]

The BLM also continued to serve in this period as a source of land for other agencies, particularly the NPS. BLM lands were exchanged to create park units as disparate as Fire Island in New York and Everglades National Park in Florida. Special acts authorizing the transactions varied slightly, but all were built on TGA exchange authority (Wheatley 1970: 65). More typical was the creation of Canyonlands National Park, in which 90 percent of the relevant lands were simply transferred from BLM administration to the NPS.[19] Thus although the BLM made significant progress toward becoming a full-fledged conservation agency, it started in such disarray that despite its new authority it still functioned primarily as a land disposer.

FWS: Flexible Acquisitions, Weak Management

The FWS fared little better during the 1950s and 1960s. While President Eisenhower was publicly embracing the recreation movement, his secretary of the interior, Douglas McKay, was all but dismantling the refuge system. McKay opened coastal refuges to oil and gas drilling and military use, while cutting the agency's budget so severely that duck stamp acquisition funds were required for basic operations and maintenance (Trefethen 1975: 256–260). Worse, in 1956 the FWS endured yet another reorganization. The commercial fishing industry believed that the post-1940 FWS had gone too far toward a conservation-oriented mission (Clarke and McCool 1996: 114). As a result, the agency was redivided into a Bureau of Commercial Fisheries and a Bureau of Sports Fisheries and Wildlife. In 1970, Commercial Fisheries was returned to the Commerce Department, and the Bureau of Sports Fisheries and Wildlife became the FWS again.

Despite the turmoil (or in part because of it), the agency continued to acquire land under diverse authorities. A 1958 amendment to the Migratory Bird Hunting Stamp Act[20] limited the use of duck stamp funds to acquisition of land. Reflecting growing public concern for wetlands, the act also added small wetlands and prairie potholes to the areas that could be acquired (Environmental Law Institute 1977: 128, n. 11). Because funding was short and the politics of full fee acquisition complex, the FWS again used easements to purchase landowners' rights to drain, fill, or burn wetland areas, thereby preventing those activities (Hester 1981: 4–5). About 20,000 easements covering 1.2 million acres were acquired for $33 million. Congress also loaned the agency $200 million to acquire wetlands, but over time, the loan was forgiven (Hester 1981: 4–5).

When the LWCF was amended in 1968 to allow acquisition of habitat for endangered species, the agency added more than twenty-five new refuges under that authority (U.S. FWS n.d.a). When states complained about the alleged loss of property tax revenue, Congress amended the Refuge Revenue Sharing Act. It offered counties an annual payment of either 25 percent of net revenues from economic uses of the refuge or three-quarters of 1 percent of the adjusted cost of the refuge land, whichever was greater (Fink 1994: 15–16).[21]

However, the FWS was unable to protect its growing system. The 1962 Refuge Recreation Act directed the agency to open its refuges to general recreation. That led to allowing any public uses that were "compatible" with refuge goals. This compatible use concept was carried into the 1966 Refuge Administration Act (Fischman 2003: 45–53; Langston 2003) and has created all kinds of problems with military air and ground exercises, logging, hunting, farming, offroad vehicles, and mining on refuges; many of these conflicting uses have yet to be contained (U.S. GAO 1989: 21).

NPS: Mixed Signals and "Park Barrel" Politics

The NPS enjoyed public affection and apparent support in Congress in this era, and the focus of Mission 66 on expansion combined with LWCF authorities to put the NPS at last into the land acquisition business. However, things began to go badly for the agency just as its long-awaited acquisition authority and funding materialized. Clumsy NPS condemnations caused public outrage and created openings for land rights advocates. Congress promoted NPS expansion in a variety of ways that did not consistently help the service—occasionally approving enormous acquisitions such as the Redwood National Park, and more frequently experimenting with tools for less intrusive and less expensive units: greenbelts, "virtual" parks, and other less-than-fee acquisitions that brought the NPS into conflict with local landowners and exposed the agency's inexperience with acquiring land. Congress also routinely used the NPS to address local land use disputes and fund undistinguished local parks.

The agency was further handicapped by its historic commitment to full fee ownership and exclusive jurisdiction. When it ignored congressional mandates for limited acquisitions, or its own announced policies and guidelines, landowners who had not expected to be in the path of acquisition became hostile.

Expanding NPS Acquisitions: From the Blue Ridge Parkway to Gettysburg   The issue of whether or not an appropriate federal purpose existed for NPS acquisitions was formally resolved in litigation surrounding the BRP.[22] Congress authorized the NPS to acquire land along the parkway, primarily to eliminate the dangerous crossings created by rights-of-way reserved in the 1930s. In 1970, litigation aimed at limiting NPS acquisitions to only those needed for road construction failed. The plaintiffs argued that taking land for recreation was not within the purposes of the statute, but the Fourth Circuit Court of Appeals disagreed. Expectations regarding NPS land acquisition had evolved so distinctly that the court regarded the question of purposes as "frivolous."[23]

Nevertheless, the NPS acquisition authority was far less coherent in practice. Cape Cod National Seashore (established in 1961) is often described as the model for NPS land acquisitions (Sax 1980a: 713, 1976; Wirth 1980: 198). But it is just one of numerous congressional experiments with NPS land acquisition that both the agency and many of its supporters have found difficult to accept. The signature provision of the Cape Cod "model" allows continued private ownership of improved property[24] within the park boundaries. Local governments were required to adopt zoning regulations approved by the secretary of the interior to control the larger impacts of that ownership. If they did not, the secretary was authorized to condemn nonconforming development, using acquisition only as a last resort,[25] and casting the NPS's existing condemnation authority primarily as a threat rather than an effective tool.[26]

The NPS's attempt to achieve control without ownership in Cape Cod has serious weaknesses. First, localities allowed "renovations" in their zoning codes that converted many small seasonal cottages into substantial year-round homes. Second, developers soon discovered that enforcement of regulations required funding for federal condemnations. When the money did not appear, the regulations proved meaningless and development continued (Kornblum 2000: 171).[27]

Congress did not repeat the Cape Cod approach. In a series of acquisitions that followed—Point Reyes National Seashore (in 1962),[28] Sleeping Bear Dunes National Lakeshore (in 1970) (Karamanski 2000), and Buffalo National River (in 1972) (Liles n.d.: 4–5) legislators experimented with scenic easements, protected zones, and other methods of minimizing full fee acquisitions. However, in spite these efforts to limit acquisition in new units, the NPS continued to pursue maximum acres and authority. Once a unit was established and congressional scrutiny reduced, local boosters and the NPS frequently succeeded in expanding the original acquisition goals.

The enthusiasm for new parks also included an emphasis on local rather than national priorities. The agency was hardly a reluctant player in park-barrel politics. In contrast to Mather's worries about park purity, modern NPS Director (1964–1972) George Hartzog openly sought an NPS unit in every congressional district to maximize political support for the agency (Hartzog 1988: 138). In 1976 the NPS began a series of congressionally mandated studies to identify at least twelve new potential parks a year.[29] Congress subsequently ignored many of the recommendations, instead adding units that dumped local redevelopment and recreation costs on federal taxpayers (Ridenour 1994). One statute, the National Parks and Recreation Act of 1978, single-handedly created more than a dozen new park units while increasing funding ceilings, changing boundaries, and authorizing new appropriations for many more.[30]

Despite congressional emphasis on serving constituents' priorities, tension between local residents and the NPS endured. The national park at Gettysburg was a flashpoint. By the 1950s, expanded roads and automobile traffic created both major opportunities for commercial development and an escalated national effort to preserve more of the battlefield. The Associated Press inflamed national preservation sentiments by running photos of historic cannons in front of restaurants, and monuments surrounded by hotel parking lots. At the same time, many in the local community resented the national park and fought new acquisitions. In a weird mutation of the Cape Cod model, Congress made the availability of $650,000 in acquisition funds conditional on the local adoption of zoning to prevent future development (Platt 2001: 51). In Massachusetts,

Congress said "protect the land or we will condemn it." At Gettysburg, the message was "protect the land or we won't either." It is not surprising that no new zoning was enacted.

Congress finally responded to local complaints and established a new park boundary and a 3,874-acre acquisition cap that cut about 11,500 acres out of the previously understood scope of the park described in the Sickles map (see figure 3.2). The new cap exposed the excluded areas to intensive and controversial development over the next twenty years (Unrau 1991: 313–314). Most notoriously, the NPS was unable to stop construction of the Gettysburg Tower, a 307-foot viewing platform that loomed high above the sloping field where Confederate Gen. George Pickett led his ill-fated charge in 1863 (Wilkinson 2000).[31] Lacking authority either to halt the project or to condemn the proposed site, the NPS was reduced to negotiating for a less offensive location.

Not every local resident favored untamed development like the tower. In November 1959, several members of the community formed the Gettysburg Battlefield Preservation Association as a private effort to acquire land for the park. In its first year, the group acquired 173 acres (Platt 2001: 56). With support for development common among the rest of the townspeople, however, it was not until the 1990s that preservation and acquisition conflicts between the NPS and the local community were at least partially resolved.

"Greenline" Parks and Cuyahoga Valley National Park   In spite of the tremendous expansion of the system, and the familiar hosannas of conservation advocates, Congress still did not support the NPS in its preference for full fee ownership. In another step toward mosaics on the land, Congress increasingly favored continued private ownership and extensive NPS cooperation with state and local governments (Smith, J. 1972: 213–236). Many of the new NPS urban and gateway units that reflected the ORRRC emphasis on eastern urban areas therefore took a "greenline" approach.

The greenline idea (Little 1975)[32] comes close to a formal description of why and where full fee acquisition versus easements or other less-than-fee instruments might be appropriate. Where only 5 or 10 percent of a site is intensively used and the rest functions primarily as ambience or a "recreation environment," the greenline idea suggests that government need only acquire the areas with public access, while protecting the surrounding lands with easements or regulation (Little 1975: 17). Congress shared a growing realization that in many cases full fee ownership was neither necessary nor sufficient for an appropriate degree of control. This in turn created a new opportunity for public-private partnerships in modern NPS units, and private conservation groups moved to undertake the less-than-fee transactions that the NPS abjured.

Thus, in a series of these odd new greenline units, the NPS was to play a more avuncular role, providing leadership, expertise, money, or simply the cachet of a national designation. As ever, local elites exploited the new approach, seeking designation as a national park to impose land use controls that they could not achieve through local political processes while avoiding federal condemnations and ownership. The NPS greenline units became a battleground for local pro- and antidevelopment factions, and park boundaries often represented negotiated settlements between the two sides.

In the process, the NPS developed deeply contested and circumscribed land acquisition authorities, and inholders morphed from adversaries into partners. The end result was a landscape dotted with ostensibly federal park units that were not wholly or even significantly federally owned. The mosaics of land holdings confused the public and made it difficult for local landowners to predict what would happen to their property.

Despite its complexity, the greenline model sometimes seemed to work. In the Santa Monica Mountains around Los Angeles, for example, the idea was applied with some success. When the California Department of Parks and Recreation objected to being displaced by the NPS (Little 1975: 7), Congress adopted a cooperative arrangement, and now more than 150,000 acres are administered jointly by the NPS, California State Parks, and the Santa Monica Mountains Conservancy, a private nonprofit group.[33]

Land acquisition at Cuyahoga Valley National Recreation Area (now a national park)[34] began in 1974 as something like a greenline park as well. However, a major acquisition disaster resulted. Prominent citizens in Akron and Cleveland had begun trying to protect the popular tourist area in 1911, forming a Cuyahoga County Park Commission and then a state park. In the 1920s, local boosters sought NPS help for their efforts, but the valley did not meet NPS standards for a national park. The CCC worked in Cuyahoga Valley State Park during the Depression, but after the war, bedroom communities and highways sprouted throughout the area. Local citizens unsuccessfully fought construction of a coliseum, a major utility line, and diverse other developments throughout the 1960s. Finally, in 1966 they succeeded in luring Secretary of the Interior Stewart Udall to the valley, and the process of studying the region for designation as a national recreation area began (Cockrell 1992).

When John Seiberling, the son and grandson of valley residents and conservation advocates, was elected to Congress in 1970, he spearheaded state efforts to establish a national park. President Nixon initially supported the proposal as a part of his emphasis on urban recreation expressed in his Parks for the People initiative. Nevertheless, amid general budgetary concerns, the agency and the National Park System Advisory Board tried earnestly to deflect support from the substandard unit.[35] Partisan politics also played a role; the NPS director noted that "There is no way we are going to make a national park for some rich Democrat from Cleveland!"[36]

In reality, by that time the NPS had very little to say about what would and would not become a national park. In 1974 Congress put together a Christmas tree park package (you vote for mine and I'll vote for yours) that included Cuyahoga. To protect the bucolic scene and meet the concerns of established landowners, Congress specifically directed that private lands should not be acquired in Cuyahoga unless their development threatened the purposes of the park or they were otherwise necessary to fulfill the park's purposes.[37] Congress encouraged the use of scenic easements rather than fee title for improved properties.[38] It set a six-year deadline for substantially completing the land acquisition program at Cuyahoga.

State Republicans all lined up to convince newly elected President Gerald Ford that the political consequences would be dire if he vetoed the bill. Unimpressed, the director of the Bureau of the Budget noted, correctly, that Ohio could stop unwanted local development without federal participation. The president opposed providing federal police and fire services to the area, or reimbursing local agencies for the work (Cockrell 1992). Nonetheless, he signed, and yet another region had successfully foisted local and state park costs onto the federal government.

Since the NPS still had only limited experience in land acquisition, it contracted with Army Corps of Engineers land specialists to implement a professional acquisition program. The Corps was aggressive with private owners. The NPS did not write an acquisition plan, and the park superintendent ignored his congressional mandate and reverted to the NPS acquisition norm, stating, "if you are going to manage it, you have to own it" (Cockrell 1992). Meanwhile, once intense congressional review of the unit's authorization had passed, a local congressman successfully organized support for the NPS to spend $59 million to acquire 11,000 acres. Despite the involvement of the Trust for Public Land, a national land trust that favored a gentler approach, the NPS only protected 153 acres through conservation easements.

Condemning Inholdings in Yosemite   It is surprising that the NPS also encountered enormous hostility in parks we generally think of as reserved, and therefore relatively free from acquisition issues. Yosemite proved to be a major Waterloo for nascent NPS programs. Spurred by its desire to remove all inholders from parks, and by the Mission 66 commitment to expansion, the NPS moved aggressively to rid the Wawona Basin of dozens of small cabin sites and inholders.

Most of the problem properties were, and remain, concentrated in a single section, section 35, in the basin. Ironically, many of the inholders were NPS personnel who could ill afford to relocate. The NPS used a heavy hand, reportedly telling employees to either sell voluntarily or risk losing their jobs.[39] They took a similarly aggressive approach to other residents, many of whose families had owned land in the Wawona area since before the basin had been acquired for the park, and some before the park itself existed. The NPS offered them the opportunity to sell and receive a lease allowing them to remain for ten years, or to face condemnation and immediate removal.

Protesters organized in Yosemite continue to play a major role in opposing land acquisitions throughout the nation. Charles Cushman was among the Wawona inholders who felt abused by the NPS and organized the National Park Inholders' Association to fight removal. As the movement grew, the organization was renamed the National Inholders Association and then the American Land Rights Association. Cushman's aggressive style and organization have sustained extreme hostility toward government land acquisitions for many decades.[40]

NPS Summary   The rapid expansion of the National Park System in the 1960s and 1970s was not a clear benefit to the agency. In many cases, it was stuck with units that it did not want and was not adequately budgeted to manage. Even greenline parks, which do not entail public acquisition of extensive land holdings, are expensive and difficult to coordinate. The NPS tried to regain control of the parks designation process that it had lost to powerful local and congressional boosters. In April 1979, the NPS required each park to prepare a land acquisition plan (later softened to a land protection plan) exploring easements, zoning, cooperative management agreements, and rights-of-way on private property. However, the odd partial and urban acquisitions confused the NPS's self-image as a protector of scenic wonders and natural landscapes. The General Accounting Office (GAO) concluded, succinctly, that the federal drive to acquire lands needed to be reassessed (U.S. GAO 1979).

Laying the Groundwork for Land Trusts and Conservation Easements

Outwardly, land acquisition in the 1950s, 1960s, and 1970s was dominated by federal agencies. However, conservation nonprofits were simultaneously organizing to express their growing discontent with the shortcomings of federal administration. A bitter battle in the 1950s over the Echo Park Dam in Dinosaur National Monument and a similarly acrimonious fight over Redwood National Park in the 1960s and 1970s began a new era in land conservation. Rather than leading the conservation movement as they had in the early twentieth century, federal agencies found themselves being pushed by increasingly aggressive conservation groups. An activist court used the National Environmental Policy Act (NEPA) to make public participation an essential ingredient of administrative decision making (Stewart 1975)[41] and further encouraged environmentalists to pursue their public criticisms of the agencies.

Although many environmental groups embraced litigation as a tool of reform (Sax 1971b), new organizations such as The Nature Conservancy (TNC) and old ones like The Trustees of Reservations headed in a different direction. Rather than suing the government to pursue a desired policy, they organized their own land conservation programs. These groups capitalized on the fact that cumbersome federal acquisition authorities did not always mesh well with the growing complexities of the conservation real estate market; a broker or translator was often needed to entice and assist landowners in selling their lands at maximum economic advantage. Although the idea of private conservation was not new, the name given to these private groups was. As they proliferated and expanded, they began to self-identify as "land trusts."

The Emergence of Land Trusts

Although the term *land trust* has no consistent meaning, the definition favored by the Land Trust Alliance (LTA) is "a nonprofit organization that, as all or part of its mission, actively works to conserve land by undertaking or assisting direct land transactions—primarily the purchase or acceptance of donations of land or conservation easements."[42] Although it is easy to talk about growing numbers of land trusts, one size does not fit all. Land trusts vary enormously within this broad definition. Perhaps the most straightforward way to identify a land trust is to see if it is a member of the LTA. Most of the private organizations discussed in this volume are associated with the LTA, but the MVLA and Fort Ticonderoga, for example, are not. Hence the boundaries are not perfectly drawn.

A small number of land trusts are public—run by federal, state, county, or local governments. Virtually all private land trusts are organized as nonprofits and are frequently called 501(c)(3)s after the section of the federal tax code that describes that specific variety of nonprofit status. The Internal Revenue Service (IRS) prevents private "inurement" (benefit) for those participating in nonprofits.[43] The law also specifies how a group must be organized and do its bookkeeping, as well as establishes expectations regarding the fate of corporate assets should the group fail. The law limits the political activities of nonprofit groups but allows them to pursue unrelated business income. Fort Ticonderoga, for example, owns farms that support its charitable museum activities; the farmland and associated income are taxed, while the museum facilities and income are not (Waite 2002). As charitable organizations, trusts can receive tax-deductible donations, thereby gaining considerable government subsidies for their conservation efforts.

Each land trust has its own style and resources, and each operates in a unique political and legal climate. Some seek government and private grants whereas others rely on donations.[44] These differences result in a wide variety of conservation tools and, it is quite likely, conservation outcomes. Land trusts also differ in the degree to which they engage in political activity. Some argue that because their constituency includes all the landowners within their operating area, they cannot afford to take positions on controversial issues, even proposed local or county land use plans and regulations, or similar issues that will clearly affect their goals. Others believe that land acquisition is only part of their mission, and that ensuring a supportive regulatory climate for protecting land is also an important responsibility. Some land trusts sponsor ballot initiatives and testify at public hearings; others simply "do deals" (Arendt 1999).

It is useful to think of the private land trust community as having three layers. First, local land trusts focus on small and specific geographic areas, a few of which have no paid employees and hold only a handful of easements or properties. Although they are not formally land trusts, in many respects both the MVLA and the Fort Ticonderoga Association would best fit this category. Next, regional groups, including the Society for the Protection of New Hampshire Forests, the Montana Land Reliance (MLR), and The Trustees, play a leadership and coordinating role as well as function as land stewards in their areas. For many years, no group went beyond this regional level. However, the post-World War II era was marked by the emergence of new actors operating at a national (or international) scale. Three organizations dominate this last level of activity: The Nature Conservancy, the Trust for Public Land, and The Conservation Fund (TCF).

National Land Trusts
The national organizations are distinguishable from the regional and local organizations in at least three important dimensions (Rogers 2003).

First, they are more focused on creating and tapping into public funding than managing easements or land. Although TNC holds extensive land in its own preserves, the national groups are more likely to be intermediaries or preacquirers than permanent stewards. Second, they have had sufficient resources to engage in overarching planning to direct an acquisition strategy. Finally, the national groups are the least likely of land trusts to become involved in land regulation issues. They do not confine themselves wholly to the marketplace, but that is their primary arena of operation.

The Nature Conservancy   TNC is the oldest "new" private conservation organization and certainly the largest. Formed as an offshoot of the Ecological Society of America, its mission is to "preserve the plants, animals and natural communities that represent the diversity of life on Earth by protecting the lands and waters they need to survive" (The Nature Conservancy 2004b). Like most land trusts, the TNC began as a small, volunteer-based organization, working in the corner of the American Nature Study Society library (The Nature Conservancy 2003). TNC made its first acquisition in 1955 in New York state with a loan fund established with a grant from the Old Dominion Foundation (a precursor to the Andrew W. Mellon Foundation).

During the 1960s, TNC began a program of expansion and transformation into a "fully professional" organization. It was assisted by grants from major private foundations, most notably the Ford Foundation (Koch and Richards 1977: 749; Endicott 1993). Significant corporate donations and a million individual members also support TNC. It has protected about 116 million acres, 15 million in the United States and the rest internationally, and manages 1,400 preserves. In addition, TNC pioneered the use of biological inventories as a means to establish acquisition strategies. Its Natural Heritage Network Database guides its own programs and is relied upon by governments, universities, and other conservation groups as well (The Nature Conservancy 2004a). The *Washington Post* recently criticized TNC for allowing limited development on its land and for providing services to powerful members of its board. It also recognized TNC as the world's richest environmental group, with assets of $3 billion (Ottaway and Stephens 2003a,b; Stephens and Ottaway 2003a,b,c; Arnold 1999).

The Trust for Public Land   TPL was formed in 1973, partially in response to TNC's emphasis on ecological resources. TPL protects land for use by people and is a major force in urban land conservation, including urban parks, gardens, trails, and watersheds. Like TNC, TPL enjoyed early and continuing support from Ford and other foundations. Unlike TNC, TPL is not a membership organization (although it seeks individual donations) and focuses less on identifying resources to be protected than on helping local groups and state and local governments identify and achieve their own conservation goals. It provides planning and real estate expertise and, most important, advice on generating government and other funding to achieve those goals. When it does acquire land, it typically turns it over to a government agency for management. To date, it has protected 1.4 million acres in forty-five states.

The Conservation Fund   The Conservation Fund was founded in 1985 and is the least familiar of the three national land trusts. It has purposely sought a lower profile and uses major financial resources to build partnerships for conservation transactions. Although it seeks individual contributions, it focuses quite clearly on corporate and foundation support, enjoying a particularly close association with the Richard King Mellon Foundation and the Doris Duke Foundation. TCF claims that it works with "forest and chemical companies, developers, and ranchers to demonstrate sustainable practices that balance economic and environmental goals."[45] As we will see in the discussion of the Northern Forest in chapter 8, TCF is frequently associated with projects that emphasize commercial conservation and ensure sustained wood production on forested lands.[46] It does not hold or manage preserves. TCF has protected about 1 million acres in all fifty states.

The Role of the States in the Development of Land Trusts

Land trusts proliferated rapidly. In the 1950s, there were fewer than fifty (Gustanski and Squires 2000: 15), but by the 1970s, 400 were concentrated in New England and the Middle Atlantic states, and they had already held a first major organizing meeting to form a national alliance. This growth was encouraged by supportive developments at the state and federal levels. Two areas of state activity were particularly important:

statutes permitting private organizations to hold conservation easements and programs supporting protection of agricultural land.

State property law is generally hostile to contracts that limit the market in land (Korngold 1984). Thus it was not well configured to make room for the idea of privately held conservation easements, which imply permanent restrictions on land use. Accordingly, each state had to re-orient its common law of property to define what a conservation easement was, who could hold an easement, and whether or how an easement could be transferred (Mayo 2000). In 1956, Massachusetts became the first state to adopt such legislation. At first the law only allowed government bodies to hold conservation easements (Cheever 1996: 1081). That limitation was lifted in 1969, although Massachusetts law still requires that state and municipal officials approve every privately held conservation easement before it can be recorded with the deed.

Easements as a conservation tool got an enormous boost from The Great River Road in Wisconsin. Mississippi River states tried to promote the River Road as a federal project during the Depression (Ohm 2000: 179–180).[47] The NPS thought it would be too expensive, but Wisconsin continued to pursue the idea and in 1961 allotted $2 million from a cigarette tax toward the acquisition of scenic easements. Early lessons from the Wisconsin program were publicized in William Whyte's pivotal 1968 volume, *The Last Landscape*. Whyte concluded that conservation had reached the limits of regulation and advocated working "with the people who own most of the landscape so that private interest will be coupled with public interest" (Whyte 1968: 101). He preferred simply buying land, but given limited funding, he also proposed tax incentives and conservation easements. However, for those proposals to work, significant changes were needed in both state and federal laws.

In keeping with Whyte's agenda, states took significant action to protect prime farmland from post-World War II suburban sprawl. In 1956, Maryland became the first state to enact an agricultural lands protection program. By the mid-1980s, forty-seven states had some sort of agricultural land conservation program, typically relying on incentives. Some use public funds to buy development rights from large landowners, or authorize local governments to acquire those rights (Hoffman 1986: 1129–1140).

Preferential tax treatment for farmland is also common. The standard way of assessing land to compute a property tax is to evaluate it at its "highest and best" use, which in the case of farmland near expanding urban areas often meant development for residential housing. Preferential assessments and some rural property tax regulations permit agricultural landowners to be taxed instead on the value of the current use of the land. Most programs impose a penalty if a farmer develops land that is preferentially assessed, and many include a contract or similar device that sets a time period during which the land cannot be developed.

Reinventing Old Programs in a New Era

Developments in private land conservation and acquisition were not limited to the new land trust movement. Older, well-established groups made similar and related adjustments in their conservation efforts in order to meet new challenges and respond to new political realities. In some cases, these changes reflected the waxing federal power of the era, as when the Save-the-Redwoods League finally yielded to the idea of a national park in the northern California redwoods. In other instances, however, new innovations (and controversies) in the efforts of seasoned entities such as The Trustees or the MVLA, led to new and more complicated mosaics of conservation and protection on the ground.

The Trustees Pioneer Conservation Easements

As first recreation and then ecosystem protection became conservation priorities, The Trustees' emphasis on stately old homes fell out of step. In addition, by the 1950s The Trustees faced organizational problems. Key officers had been serving as long as twenty-five years, and the first full-time employee, hired in 1929, was still in place. In response, the group gradually began a reorganization that is continuing as of this writing. The group was fortunate to receive a generous endowment just when it was experiencing both a financial pinch and a need to change direction. The infusion of funds allowed The Trustees to hire a new executive director in 1967 to coordinate reform. It established terms of office so that individuals could go on the board and then off it, and volunteer site managers were replaced with professional staff. Finally, the organization became more involved in the life and activities of the communities where it owned property. Trails, new signs, a series of informative booklets and folders, and an expanding calendar of events were developed to increase public use of the properties and, equally important, awareness of the organization and its mission (Abbott 1993: 246).

Inspired by William Whyte's book, The Trustees established a sister organization, The Land Conservation Trust (TLCT), to move flexibly in acquiring easements without compromising The Trustees' donation-based program. Created just as the Massachusetts legislature adopted an agricultural preservation restriction act, the TLCT worked closely with the state to protect prime farmland, acquiring its first easement in 1971. The idea of a preservation restriction (early Massachusetts lingo for a conservation easement) seemed alien and complicated to conservative farmers. In its early years, TLCT played an important role in brokering those transactions for the state.

TLCT also supports limited development of conserved properties to support the preservation of the remaining, more environmentally significant portion (Abbott 1993: 173). A small foundation grant enabled TLCT to establish a revolving loan fund that allowed it to move quickly when open space was threatened. As an affiliate organization, TLCT allowed The Trustees to remain at a safe distance from easements and the subsidy of conserved private land with limited commercial development—ideas that were quite radical at the time. The latter, as evinced by the *Washington Post* critiques of TNC, is still frowned upon in many circles.

The Mount Vernon Public-Private Partnership

Soon after World War II, the area around Mount Vernon faced rapid economic development.[48] In response, residents across the river from Mount Vernon formed the Moyaone Reserve, which allowed only single-family dwellings on minimum 5-acre lots (which was huge at the time in the Washington suburbs) to protect the area. The Moyaone group was an early innovator in scenic easements and farmland conservation and helped establish a separate tax assessment system in the county so that designated open space was not taxed at its development potential.

In 1957 the Moyaone group chartered the Accokeek Foundation to "preserve, protect, and foster for charitable, scientific, and educational uses ... the Maryland shore of the historic Potomac River" (Straus and Straus 1988: 24). The Accokeek Foundation owned parcels along 6 miles of riverfront when the Washington Suburban Sanitary Commission (WSSC) decided to locate a sewage plant across the river from Mount Vernon. Opponents of the project were numerous, and supporters few, but the WSSC had its own taxing and eminent domain authority and consequently posed a serious threat. Other proposals also sprouted, including plans for a golf course directly across the river from Washington's veranda.

Alarmed, the Accokeek Foundation and the MVLA reluctantly approached the NPS for help in 1961 (Straus and Straus 1988: 24–25). Director Conrad Wirth was unresponsive, but Accokeek had contacts in Congress. In October of the same year, President Kennedy signed a bill that authorized a park that was odd even by the creative standards of the era.[49] The bill allowed the secretary of the interior to cooperate with property owners to acquire and administer lands and easements to protect the Mount Vernon viewshed. The statute did not use the word *park*, or any other term suggesting an NPS unit. Undeterred, advocates viewed themselves as "brave" advocates of a "bold experiment": to use scenic easements, not for a viewshed, but as an important element in assembling a park (Straus and Straus 1988: 37). This further threatened the NPS doctrine that full fee ownership was the preferred or exclusive path to effective control.[50]

Not surprisingly, the NPS remained unsupportive.[51] However, under pressure from Accokeek's powerful friends in Congress, in 1963 the Department of the Interior signed an agreement with the foundation in which the group would donate its land to the NPS at no cost after the government had acquired a substantial portion of the remaining lands. In 1967, Accokeek again relied upon its contacts in Congress to secure funding for the project. On Washington's birthday, 1968, Secretary of the Interior Stewart Udall attended a brief ceremony marking the establishment of what was by then known as Piscataway Park (Straus and Straus 1988: 58–61). Figure 6.1 shows the odd combination of

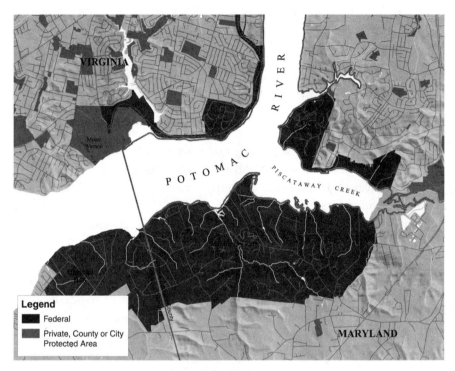

Figure 6.1
Mount Vernon, Piscataway Park, and the George Washington Parkway as a
mosaic of protected land surrounded by encroaching urban development. Source:
Map Courtesy of the National Park Service, National Capital Region, Office of
Lands, Resources and Planning, GIS Division.

residential, diverse NPS,[52] and other state and county conserved lands
that comprise the Mount Vernon mosaic.

Although it still opposed the park idea (Cunningham 1968: 186), the
NPS actually *condemned* a scenic easement, acquiring it from an unwilling seller, to prevent the development of high-rise apartments in the
park. At present, two-thirds of the park's 4,625 acres remain private residential lands subject only to scenic easements. The rest is owned in fee
by the NPS. The result is a new mosaic of public and private rights abutting the original MVLA enclave. As in many greenline parks, local elites
had again used the NPS to impose land use regulations, and the NPS
remains unhappy about it to this day: "Basically we enforce subdivision
ordinances," grumped one old NPS hand.

Fort Ticonderoga Branches Out

Management of Fort Ticonderoga was also being changed by a broadening sense of landscape stewardship, although more slowly than at Mount Vernon. The Pells's charitable foundation completed restoration of the fort by the early 1950s, and the NPS granted the site national historic landmark status in 1962. At the time, the NPS was highlighting stellar sites to demonstrate the need for the pending National Historic Preservation Act (it passed in 1966), and Fort Ticonderoga was an obvious choice. The designation allowed the Pells to apply for federal funds earmarked for renovation and education programs. It also made it difficult to spend federal money in ways that would damage the fort. Soon any "major federal action" with a significant effect on the historic site would require an environmental impact statement under the 1969 National Environmental Policy Act. The new status helped the Pell foundation keep Interstate 87 from cutting right through the fort and stop plans for the East Creek nuclear power plant, proposed near Mt. Independence, right across the lake from Fort Ticonderoga. The fort's growing public profile led the Pells to begin adding non-Pells to the board, which has since stabilized at about two-thirds family members and a third outsiders.

Meanwhile, all around the fort, the recreation boom ignited the Adirondack region with economic activity that outsiders viewed as a threat to the park. As the controversy intensified, Laurance Rockefeller, chair of the New York State Council of Parks, cooked up a scheme for an Adirondack national park (Graham 1978, chap. 24). The proposal pleased no one. Preservationists feared that the NPS's tourist orientation would destroy the state's "forever wild" commitment; Adirondackers simply feared a federal takeover. Laurance's brother Nelson, conveniently the governor of New York, appointed a blue ribbon commission to study the issue. Continuing a long-established pattern for the region, the commission included no local representatives and met in New York City (Graham 1978: 237).

The commission ultimately proposed a new Adirondack Park Agency (APA) to manage the expanding recreation pressures. Established after much legislative wrangling, the APA developed a master plan that designated 96 percent of the 1.2 million acres of state land within the park as

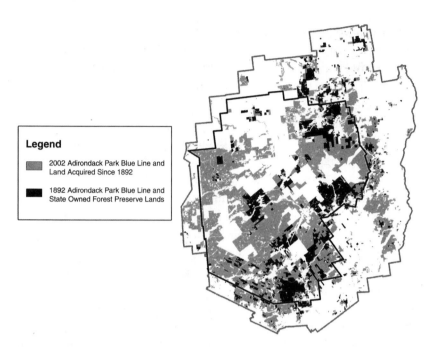

Legend

2002 Adirondack Park Blue Line and
Land Acquired Since 1892

1892 Adirondack Park Blue Line and
State Owned Forest Preserve Lands

Figure 6.2
A comparison of Adirondack Park blue line boundaries and state land ownership
in 1894 and 2002. Source: Adapted from New York State Adirondack Park
Agency. Reproduced with permission.

wilderness and wild forest. On the private land within the "blue line" of
the park boundary—which was expanded to encompass a total of 3.5
million acres—the APA created planning categories, from industrial and
hamlet (village) to low-intensity and rural use (Wuerthner 1988: 75–78;
Liroff and Davis 1981). Figure 6.2 shows both the original and the 2002
blue line, and the acquisitions that have been filling out the expanded
area since 1894.

Unhappy with the APA's combination of early blundering and sancti-
monious assertiveness (Terrie 1997: 53–54), Adirondackers were moved
to frequently theatrical protest. As with the greenline parks, developments in the Northeast spurred a private property rights movement
that far outlasted the better-publicized complaints of the Sagebrush
Rebels, then taking center stage out West (Cawley 1993; Brubaker
1984).

Redwood National Park

By the mid-1950s, development pressure led to renewed controversy over the northern California redwoods. The postwar housing boom tripled the timber harvest in the region, while the state expanded the formerly gentle Redwood Highway into a divided interstate. A disastrous winter of heavy rains in 1954–1955 (and another in 1964) demonstrated that even protected groves were vulnerable when the surrounding watersheds were stripped of cover by timber harvesting. In response, the Sierra Club under David Brower built an aggressive national movement challenging the state-centered approach of the Save-the-Redwoods League. Beginning in 1964 with the publication of its coffee-table polemic, *The Last Redwoods*, the club demanded a national park.

The LWCF made it appear that the NPS had the funds and the authority to make such an acquisition.[53] However, beset by multiple acquisition proposals, the financially strapped agency was unable to pay for even an initial study of the idea and turned to the National Geographic Society for assistance. Private funding for the park's acquisition continued to be a distinct possibility (Dickinson 1974: 221ff). The Save-the-Redwoods League, finally acceding to pressure, supported "minimal well-planned federal involvement based on its traditional program" (Schrepfer 1983: 116). However, the questions of who should do the protecting and what should be protected were closely tied. The League favored federal protection of Mill Creek, a superlative area where the watershed was small enough to be acquired entirely. The Sierra Club favored acquisitions along Redwood Creek, although the area seemed too large to be purchased in its entirety.

The result was a compromise that included a small piece of both sites. A 1968 law created the new national park[54] but limited it to 58,000 acres, including federal acquisition of all three existing state parks.[55] Despite fifty years of state and private conservation of the area, the act provided no future management role for the state. The act also included, at the insistence of then-Governor of California Ronald Reagan, an exchange of BLM and USFS lands for some of the private lands in the park. Reagan was concerned about adding to public ownership in Del Norte County, which was already more than 70 percent federally owned (Schrepfer 1983: 149). Figure 6.3 shows the chronology of land

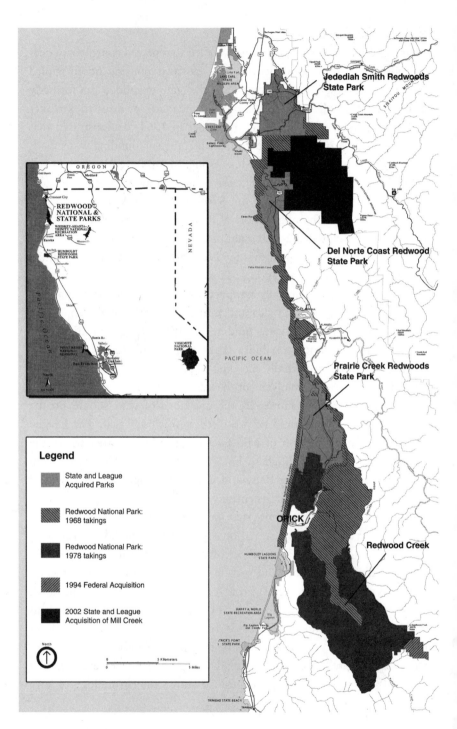

acquisition in the redwoods by the state, the League, and the federal government.

To halt logging and to prevent land prices from escalating during protracted acquisition negotiations, Congress approved a legislative taking. Immediately upon passage of the act, title to 28,800 acres of private land owned primarily by four timber companies became vested with the federal government. The act directed the companies to seek compensation in the United States Court of Claims. The Sierra Club favored this arrangement, arguing that the court of claims would be more sympathetic to environmental concerns than district courts and western juries. That was a costly miscalculation. Most observers agree that the amount the court subsequently awarded the industry was far in excess of the value of the land and timber. The act authorized $92 million from the LWCF to pay for the land. Although this was the largest authorization for land acquisition in the history of the NPS, it was apparently still not enough. By 1997, payments to the four major timber holders had exceeded $180.8 million, and final settlements were still pending with two of them.[56] The final cost was probably closer to $210 million, not including the 13,230 acres of exchanged BLM and USFS land (Schrepfer 1983: 158; Kiester 1993).

If timber companies did very well, localities did not. Concerns about job losses were nominally addressed with assertions about the number of tourists that would arrive to create new jobs. A university study projected that visitors would number over 1.9 million by 1990. The actual number remained below 650,000 throughout the 1990s (U.S. NPS 1991–2000), with each visitor averaging less than an hour in the park (Kiester 1993; Hudson 1979: 805). Moreover, PILTs were eliminated in the final stage of the legislative compromise and did not return. One small town, Orick, was reduced to little more than an inholding by the federal acquisitions (Mathewson 1972).

Aware that the park boundaries were a mess, Congress allowed the secretary of the interior to change them and to enter into agreements

Figure 6.3
Acquisitions by the Save-the-Redwood League and the state and federal governments over time. Source: Adapted base maps from U.S. NPS and California Dept. of Parks and Recreation (2000); U.S. NPS (1978).

with adjoining landowners or acquire property interests from them.[57] However, upstream logging continued in Redwood Creek and threatened park groves. Despite a series of lawsuits by the Sierra Club, the NPS was unable to protect its new properties.[58] Under pressure from the courts, the agency tried a number of approaches, including encouraging state regulation of the abutting lands, but the state's forest practice act had been considerably confused by other litigation. When the NPS proposed harvest restrictions on privately owned land in the Redwood Creek Basin, the state board of forestry declined to act (Hudson 1979: 829–830). Ultimately, the court found that despite the ongoing damage, the NPS had done all that it could without further support from Congress.[59]

Congress tried again to fix the situation. In 1977, the House Government Operations Committee issued a report recommending a familiar three-pronged approach: regulation, acquisition of an additional 21,500 acres, and rehabilitation of many of the cut-over acres (U.S. Congress, House 1977: 5–6). However, Congress accepted President Carter's proposal to add 48,000 acres to the Redwood Creek section of the park, which was more than double the initial proposal. Early versions of both House and Senate expansion bills tried to encourage timber owners to negotiate with the NPS by including authority for the secretary of the interior to regulate harvest on land outside the park. However, in an ever more familiar story, sellers carried the day. The industry preferred acquisition to regulation, and the negotiation language did not make it into the final bill. Instead, the secretary was given authority to acquire, as a "park protection zone," up to 30,000 acres beyond the designated 48,000 (Hudson 1979: 853–855).

Despite industry lobbying for a return to the friendly confines of the court of claims, Congress specified that this time cost recovery would occur in district court (Schrepfer 1983: 219–220). This time, the bill promised generous PILTs to the counties for five years and made extensive authorizations (although limited appropriations followed) to support retraining and employment opportunities for displaced loggers and mill workers. By 1987, the secretary reported expenditures of $363 million for acquisitions under the 1978 act. A decade later, economists calculated the act's total costs at $689.5 million (Berck and Bentley 1997).

A deal of enormous cost and complexity, the Redwoods acquisition is a pinnacle of federal acquisition activity (and expenditures) even as it illustrates many of the limits of that strategy. Clearly, control did not follow from ownership in the region. The state was unable to stop the decimation of the redwoods despite the extensive acquisitions and donations of the Save-the-Redwoods League, and the federal government paid dearly for its acquisitions of private property, not once but twice, because the 1968 condemnation failed to afford adequate protection. The price tag raises questions of equity and the high cost of acquisition. What could we have acquired elsewhere for the same staggering amount of money? Why pour such amounts into the Redwoods, riding roughshod over local values and priorities, while cutting the Gettysburg Battlefield in half?

Finally, in reviewing the Redwoods story, opponents of government acquisition might feel justified in asking whether private conservation really is an alternative to public acquisitions or just the advance team. We do not find in the Redwoods case support for the worry of market economists that government acquisition will preempt private activity. The efforts of the Save-the-Redwoods League show no evidence of being dampened by the federal acquisitions, as figure 6.4 demonstrates. The organization continued to pursue its own acquisition priorities before, during, and after major federal acquisitions, particularly in 1978 and 1994 (cf. Albers and Ando 2003). Rather, the Redwoods narrative suggests a different lesson: that willing sellers run the show. Moreover, it seems that perhaps acquisition programs encourage more acquisition, and nothing is ever enough.

Conclusions

After World War II, federal land acquisition programs reached a peak even as a backlash began. Constitutional concerns vanished entirely as the legitimate goals of public acquisition of land continued to expand. As the objective of economic relief receded, new imperatives to provide recreation and ecosystem protection took its place. All that was lacking was a reliable funding source such as the economic relief funds of the Depression. The LWCF did not entirely solve the problem as aspirations

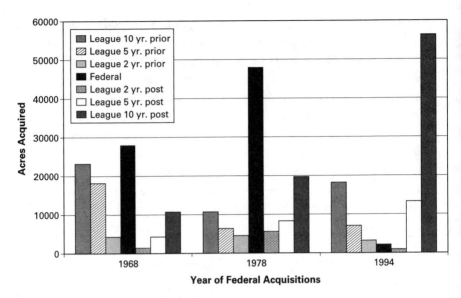

Figure 6.4

A comparison of League acquisitions (number of acres acquired) before and after major federal acquisitions in Redwood National Park. Source: League data courtesy of the Save-the-Redwoods League; they include some land outside the boundary of Redwood National and State Parks (the data provide an excellent estimate, but may contain some errors or omissions). Reproduced with permission. © Permission required for reprint, sale, or commercial use. Contact the Save-the-Redwoods League.

and authorizations continued to outstrip funding. Nevertheless, federal acquisition programs had developed their own momentum, and they proceeded with enthusiasm in the 1950s, 1960s, and 1970s.

The Redwoods case shows how pressure was put on the government to acquire rapidly what was needed before prices rose any further. That proved a vain hope because timber owners obtained vastly more compensation from the court of claims than they would have from their customers. Although the Sierra Club in effect trumped the Save-the-Redwoods League, insisting on a federal takeover of the state-private partnership, that was not a harbinger of the future. Indeed, the high costs and flawed results of the Redwoods deal are a pointed reminder of the limits of acquisition for conservation.

Federal acquisition was in fact losing steam. Congressional reluctance to allow condemnation to protect wilderness, rivers, and trails is a significant indicator of this. Only in the most extreme circumstances, when confronted with a national movement in the Redwoods, did Congress pull out all the stops with not just condemnation but a legislative taking. Condemnation is not, of course, needed for acquisition in circumstances where willing sellers abound and nearly any parcel will do. But as environmentalists and recreationists focused on more commercially valuable parcels, Congress began to balance conservation goals against local preferences and the political cost of forced acquisitions. Part of that balancing can be seen in its efforts to persuade the NPS to buy less than fee title, in greenline parks and elsewhere, and to cooperate more with local supporters.

Even as many private groups like the Sierra Club tried to tell the federal government what to buy and protect, others began developing the tools and policy infrastructure to protect land themselves. State law was revised to make room for conservation easements as a tool of private conservation, and land trusts prepared to direct a new generation of partnered land acquisition programs. Older conservation groups also changed with the times, reinventing themselves and their strategies to deal with new threats and priorities. The result was a dramatic complication of land holdings and protection arrangements, one that would only intensify in the coming decades.

7

Mosaics in the Reagan Revolution

The election of Ronald Reagan in 1980 reflected a rethinking of the priorities of the American political system. Reagan took office amid a serious economic recession, and he argued that the country's "present troubles" resulted from "unnecessary and excessive growth of government."[1] Taking the opposite tack from FDR, he presented a smaller, less expensive government as the key to economic recovery. The "Reagan revolution" espoused a return to the limited, state-centered government favored at our nation's founding. Moreover, Reaganites were highly deferential to private property rights. In the terms of our discussion in chapter 3, after a long period in which Progressive ideas of instrumental property had held sway, one could detect a distinct reassertion of Lockean ideas (Raymond and Fairfax 2002).

Public lands were one of the issues through which Reagan's reconsideration of property and government played out. The administration's view of land as an economic resource was reflected in the growing emphasis on user fees and revenue generation on the public lands (Linowes 1988).[2] Reagan and his Secretary of the Interior James Watt also worked to reduce federal land ownership; Watt's moratorium on federal acquisition of land made him a lightning rod not only for environmental protest but also for congressional ire.[3] On some issues, such as LWCF appropriations, congressional resistance to the Reagan agenda was substantial and effective.

Thus the Reagan era was tailormade for the growing land trust movement. During an administration sympathetic to private landowners who were feeling burdened by environmental regulations, conservation easements provided an appealing alternative. The compensation provided by easements fit well with the Reagan-era preference for a Lockean

understanding of property. Similarly, government officials who were reluctant to take the political heat for passing or enforcing regulations became understandably enthusiastic about using easements instead. Finally,
Reagan's efforts to reduce the size of government led to several serious
rounds of staff reductions in land management agencies.

Land trusts moved to fill the resulting gap in expertise and became essential partners in the acquisition projects that survived. The movement
rapidly grew beyond its eastern seaboard roots while grappling with the
policy changes needed to facilitate the use of conservation easements.
The Land Trust Alliance (neé Land Trust Exchange) was formed to provide coordination among proliferating local organizations.

The expanded role for land trusts further blurred the distinction
between public and private acquisitions and lands. The result on the
ground was no longer federal lands or private preserves, but an enormous extension—in scale, complexity, and frequency—of the mosaics
that had been forming for much of the century. Complex mixtures of
funding sources, participants, land ownership, management tools, institutions, and partnerships became the norm.

We discuss this era's changing ideas about acquisition of land for conservation in three sections. The first provides a brief overview of 1980s
policies that reflect Reagan's approach to government and property. We
pay special attention to the 1985 and subsequent Farm Bills. The second
section discusses the growth of land trusts and the factors that made that
growth possible. We also return to the Blue Ridge Parkway, Mount Vernon, and Fort Ticonderoga to see how mosaics of conservation organizations and tools formed around those long-protected sites. The third
section looks at the efforts of federal agencies to adapt to the renewed
importance of private conservation actors, paying close attention to the
FWS experience with a Montana partnership known as the Blackfoot
Challenge.

New Authorities for Government Acquisition: The LWCF Meets the Farm Bill

The ink was barely dry on the federal government's commitment under
the FLPMA to indefinitely retain the public domain when President Rea-

gan reversed course. Executive Order 12348, issued in 1982, aimed to sell 35 million acres of federal—primarily BLM—land over a period of five years. The proposal was a major break with established assumptions about the scope of government activity and ownership, and it reflected Reagan's enthusiasm for an antienvironmental strain of community activism. Public outcry and FLPMA requirements[4] scotched the proposal, leading some to argue that "nothing remains" of the Reagan emphasis on private rather than bureaucratic decision making (Coggins and Nagle 1990). We argue to the contrary that despite this setback, Reagan's election led to a durable change in federal land acquisition authorities and funding.

Attacking Old Acquisition Tools

Reagan's approach to land conservation started with the presumption that the private owner is both the better land steward and, under our Constitution, the preferred steward. The president brought federal use of condemnation, never more than a last resort, to a dead halt. The administration also imposed a moratorium on all federal land acquisition. Near the end of Reagan's tenure, a 1988 executive order required all federal agencies to assess the takings impact of proposed regulations and actions.[5] Administration efforts were amplified by numerous Supreme Court cases that expanded the range of government actions requiring compensation for private landowners.[6] Those cases raised the political costs and financial risks of enacting or enforcing regulations regarding private use of land.[7]

While Reagan reemphasized the individual parcel owner, a growing cadre of scientists from the new fields of landscape ecology and conservation biology moved in the opposite direction. They conceptualized the protection of enormous landscapes—whole watersheds, mountain ranges, and habitat for endangered species—that required integrated, ecosystem-level management strategies across property lines and political boundaries.[8] Even as the Reaganites were attempting to reunite ownership and control, environmentalists sought new arrangements to regulate land use over broad landscapes and multiple ownership boundaries. Wetlands[9] and wildlife habitat moved to the top of the conservation agenda.

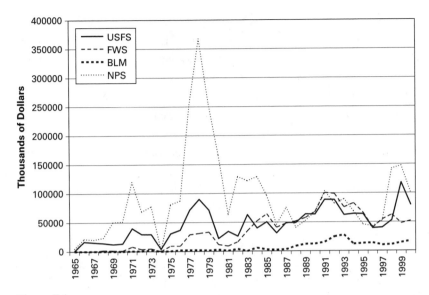

Figure 7.1
Annual LWCF appropriations for federal agencies, 1965–2000. Source: U.S.
NPS (2001).

The results of Reagan's initiatives were mixed. Although federal acquisition activity slowed, it did not stop entirely. Indeed, as figure 7.1 demonstrates, Watt could not scuttle the LWCF; contrary to much discussion, the fund enjoyed fairly steady congressional support throughout the 1980s. A significant boomlet in NPS allocations during the Carter years did not last, but the general pattern is a steady, small increase over time, including during the Reagan years, for all federal agencies. It is surprising that appropriations for the state portion of the LWCF declined over the 1980s and were eliminated in President Bush's 1991 budget (Diamond 1990: 14). Given the Reagan-Bush administrations' stated preference for state and local decision making, the collapse of state funding is perplexing.

Creating New Tools: The 1985 Farm Bill

The 1985 Farm Bill[10] was a benchmark in blending old and new ideas about government and property. Motivations for 1980s changes in a farm policy that had been subsidizing farmers since the Depression were complex. Problems began when a large sale of grain to Russia encouraged farmers to go into debt to buy land at inflated prices. When grain prices crashed, many small farmers lost their land (Church 1986: 2). Evidence that the Department of Agriculture's half-century of investments to prevent soil erosion had failed (Batie 1985: 118–120) and growing environmental pressure to protect wetlands strengthened demands for reform. Finally, liberalization of trade under the General Agreement on Tariffs and Trade (GATT) (and later the North American Free Trade Agreement [NAFTA] and the World Trade Organization [WTO]), put more pressure on agricultural subsidies. If the United States wanted to participate in world agricultural trade, it needed (in theory) to eliminate such subsidies or reframe them as land conservation measures.[11]

It is not surprising that the emphasis has been on the latter. Despite its ostensible fiscal conservativism, the Reagan administration supported farm subsidies. The result was that the Farm Bill became a major element in the growth of land trusts. Land trusts had begun working with states and localities to protect agricultural land in the 1960s. In many areas (particularly in the West), better-watered private lands tend to be more valuable as habitat than public parcels. The trusts had also long recognized that Americans have a deep cultural connection to farms and ranches; the Holstein in Vermont and the cowboy in Wyoming are effective symbols to deploy in promoting land conservation. As a result, when the Farm Bill made billions of dollars available for land conservation on farms, the trusts were ready to take advantage of its programs.[12]

The 1985 bill added myriad new land conservation opportunities. Voluntary conservation was replaced in some instances by quasi-regulation known as cross compliance. Under this system, participation in land conservation programs became a prerequisite for certain forms of federal farm aid. The conditionality of the payment was important because unqualified subsidies were defined by the WTO as a nontariff barrier to free trade (Potter 1998: 80–81).

Because it made agricultural subsidies contingent on good conservation practices, the 1985 Farm Bill was initially regarded as revolutionary. The World Watch Institute declared it to be one of the three greatest environmental policy achievements of the twentieth century (Potter 1998: 61). Perhaps it was. Between 1985 and 2002, Congress added program after program that forced or encouraged land, water, habitat, and soil conservation by ranchers and farmers. Three tools in particular—the Conservation Reserve Program (CRP), the Wetlands Reserve Program (WRP), and the Forest Legacy Program (FLP)—are relevant to land acquisition policy.[13]

The CRP constitutes about 40 percent of the Farm Bill's conservation funding. It authorizes the Farm Services Agency (FSA) in the Department of Agriculture to lease—but not to acquire easements on or title to—ecologically important farmland to take it out of production with the goal of environmental restoration.[14] Farmers who enroll their lands in the CRP develop a restoration plan and receive both an annual rental payment and technical and financial assistance in implementing the plan or in converting sensitive parcels to resource-conserving cover crops (Farm Service Agency 1999).

As temporary leases, however, CRP contracts sometimes look like boondoggles. In Montana, for example, a ten-year CRP contract pays about $300 per acre in total rent on land that would sell in full fee for half to a third of that price. Moreover, research suggests that the bulk of CRP lands are returned to cropping when the leases expire (Potter 1998: 75–76). Thus the CRP can pay an owner two to three times what the land is worth without any assurance of a permanent change in management (although there may be long-term value if the program opens discussion of more permanent or less costly conservation).

Unlike the CRP, the vast majority (85–90 percent in California, for example) of WRP enrollments are permanent.[15] This may seem to be a major improvement over the CRP approach, but the complex partnerships and frequently shifting agency personnel responsible for those easements have also set off alarms. Land trusts are concerned about the stewardship of CRP and WRP easements, which requires both monitoring of compliance and a willingness to enforce easement terms. Government monitoring and record keeping have not been up to land trust expectations. For example, the Natural Resource Conservation Service (neé Soil Conservation Service) monitors its easements annually by remote sensing and "tries to get on the ground" only once every three years. Many land trusts consider annual visits to be essential.

The Forest Legacy Program, added to the Farm Bill in 1990, is a more straightforward land and easement acquisition program. As originally designed, the FLP was intended to facilitate USFS participation in modern land acquisitions. It authorized the agency to move beyond the purchase boundaries of established national forests. However, when two branches of the agency got into an internal snit about which should have the FLP limelight, Congress gave state foresters the power to select sites, complete the transactions, and hold title (Beauvais 1996: 1–3).[16] States commit to participation by preparing an assessment of need (AON) for the program that guides subsequent program activities. The FLP requires a 25 percent nonfederal match of the total project cost, and it allows land and easements held by land trusts to meet that requirement. Forest management activities such as timber harvesting are permitted on FLP lands if the landowner completes an approved stewardship management plan prior to the transaction.

The FLP is also controversial. Environmentalists are concerned that the FLP will perpetuate rather than regulate destructive logging. The property rights movement has been even more vocal in its opposition (Beliveau 1993: 515–519). Although the transactions are initially voluntary, property activists have objected that the FLP gives the federal government too large a role in local land use planning (Beliveau 1993: 517). They also note that because private land trusts are not directly accountable to the public, they should not administer government programs.

In sum, Farm Bill innovations were vital to the expansion of land trusts. Implementation of the programs requires skilled translators and brokers that land trusts have provided. Doubtless their efforts have wrested valuable conservation outcomes from mere farm subsidies. However, the Farm Bill's commitment to land conservation eroded discernibly in the 1996 and 2002 reauthorizations. Farmers' responsibilities under a host of programs were made discretionary again, and county committees were authorized to provide "relief" from conservation requirements in cases of undue economic hardship (U.S. NRCS n.d.b). Moreover, spending priorities have shifted. In 2002, only 18 percent of payments to farmers supported conservation—down a third from 1996. In fact, advocates now fear that the overall environmental effect of the Farm Bill may be negative; Environmental Defense has predicted that "for every acre of wildlife habitat saved as a result of this [2002] Farm Bill, two or more acres of habitat will be destroyed" (Searchinger 2002).

Many persons also conclude that continued subsidies send the wrong messages to both farmers and consumers about the true cost of food. Others would prefer to push industrial agriculture toward more sustainable practices through regulation (Ruhl 2002).

Moreover, despite being a boon to acquisition efforts, the Farm Bill programs shift expectations about ownership in ways we find troubling. Paying landowners for the loss of rights they may not actually own—such as the "right" to spray poison (Pesticide Action Network North America 2004) or destroy wetlands—is effectively compensating them for a diminution of value that is not, even after all of the Reagan-era efforts, a clear legal taking. That seems an unwise strategy, one that risks creating an unsupportable expectation that compensation is required for *any* government control on use of private land. While pandering to landowners in this manner is politically tempting, conservationists should pause "to consider the potential long-term consequences before advocating government purchase of private property rights" (Vandilk 1997: 712).

The Land Trust Movement

The Farm Bill was just one element contributing to the growth of land trusts in the 1980s. Trust organizers worked state-by-state to build the political and legal infrastructure necessary to maintain the movement and become major players in conservation acquisitions. We look at these events in three ways. First, we trace the growth of land trusts from the 1950s to the present. We then look at two major achievements—the gradual development of supportive state laws and the founding of the Land Trust Alliance—that transformed the growing number of land trusts into a national movement. Finally, we look at the continued evolution of tools and ownership arrangements at familiar conservation sites—Mount Vernon, Fort Ticonderoga, the Northern Forest, and the Blue Ridge Parkway. In previous chapters, these sites were discussed as either public or private, or as partnerships. By the late 1980s, they had become something else entirely: complex mosaics of interdependent agents and overlapping tools. The maps of these protected areas show how these complex arrangements form intricate mosaics of ownership and control that can be seen literally on the ground.

Table 7.1
Regional Growth in Number of Land Trusts, 1981–2000

| | Number of land trusts | | | |
Region	2000	1990	1981*	% Increase, 1990–2000
Southwest	57	26	6	119
South Central	25	11	32	127
Southeast	115	62		85
Northwest	69	50	49	38
Pacific	139	79		76
Mid-West	186	119	67	56
Northeast	497	433	155	15
Mid-Atlantic	174	105	59	66
Total	1,262	885	368	

Source: Adapted from Land Trust Alliance (2001a).
*Data for 1981 adapted from Bremer (1984, chap. 2).

Land Trusts—Accelerating Growth
Land trusts achieved tremendous growth in the Reagan years. After modest beginnings in the 1950s, the organizations began to proliferate in the 1970s and exploded in the mid-1980s with the passage of the first Farm Bill. Land trusts were initially a coastal phenomenon, confined largely to New England, where the institutional form first developed, and the West Coast. In the Reagan years, the movement became truly national, and the spread of land trusts continued steadily until 2000. Although most observers expected the increase to level off, the 2003 LTA census included more than 1,500 land trusts (LTA 2004). Nevertheless, a consolidation of smaller trusts has begun. Table 7.1 shows that despite the national growth, land trusts remain concentrated on the coasts, but increases in numbers of organizations and areas protected have been most rapid in the Southwest and south central areas. Land trust activity in terms of acres protected continues to be greatest in the Northeast.

The influence of the Farm Bill is also evident in the stated mission of many of these new groups. While the types of land protected vary, most land trusts focus on themes common to the Farm Bills: wetlands, watersheds, and farmlands are all major targets (see table 7.2). Of course individual land trusts also work to protect habitat, historic and cultural

Table 7.2
Percent of Land Trusts Asserting a Major Interest in Protecting Particular Land Types

Type of land protected	Percent of land trusts working on land type
Wetlands	52
River corridors	51
Watershed/quality	47
Farm/ranch land	46
Nature preserves	45
Open space	43
Threatened or endangered species habitat	42
Scenic views/road	34
Trails	27
Historical or cultural sites	24
Coastal resources	18
Urban open space	10

Source: Land Trust Alliance (2001a).

resources, open space, or a single locally cherished site. Very few, however, work with urban land—a point we revisit in chapter 9.

Building a National Movement

The reasons for the phenomenal growth of land trusts in the last quarter of the twentieth century are complex.[17] Certainly the movement's compensatory, market-friendly approach was well received in the changing political and social environment of the Reagan era. Private foundations that heavily supported land trusts partially displaced Rockefeller-style conservation philanthropy. The threats to special places created by urban sprawl ignited many local groups, and the importance of Farm Bill funding is difficult to overstate. However, some, looking for a simpler explanation of the movement's rise, would point to the gradual stabilization of the tax treatment of donated conservation easements during the 1980s (Small 1979, 1992, 1997a,b, 2000: 55) and the enactment of conservation easement legislation at the state level.

Building on the first state reorientations of the common law of easements described in chapter 6, the National Conference of Commissioners on Uniform State Laws (NCCUSL)[18] proposed a Uniform Conservation

Easement Act (UCEA) in 1981. That model legislation was essentially adopted in twenty-one states and served to focus debate in other jurisdictions. The act addresses the purposes of a conservation easement; the restrictions and obligations that can be contained in one; what organizations can hold such an easement; how long it can or must last; and how it can be modified, terminated, and enforced by third parties.

The commissioners debated the appropriate degree of public scrutiny over both conservation easements and private easement holders. Some, concerned about the potential for groups to frustrate public purposes, advocated strong public oversight; for example, requiring planning agency approval for easements, allowing public agencies to modify or terminate the instruments, or establishing special systems to record them. Others countered that the act was merely "trying to tidy up a ... disorderly corner of the common law" (National Conference of Commissioners on Uniform State Laws 1979: 6) and that public oversight would entangle land trusts in precisely the sort of red tape they sought to avoid. Ultimately, the commissioners decided that the UCEA would not include language mandating public supervision of either land trusts or conservation easements, with the hope that private activity would serve to "supplement and assist in carrying forward public programs of great importance without conflicting with them" (National Conference of Commissioners on Uniform State Laws 1979: 14).

As of this writing, all but one state (Wyoming) has adopted some form of conservation easement law (Eitel 2004). Even those state statutes relying on the UCEA, however, evince considerable variation. For example, although the act includes historic and cultural preservation as a valid purpose of conservation easements, Maine does not. Conservation of agricultural land is not a permitted purpose in Montana, where county commissioners must review each easement. In Massachusetts, by contrast, a state agency does the evaluation.[19] In Virginia, as we discuss later, an organization must have been in existence for five years before it can hold an easement. In Colorado the waiting period is only two years.

The fact that land trusts were not directly involved in the NCCUSL process suggests that, although the land trusts had outgrown their New England roots by 1980, they still lacked national coordination.[20] Many established groups feared that small land trusts were acting with commendable enthusiasm but limited experience. The organizations also feared "rogue" land trusts, unscrupulous operators uninterested in conservation but drawn to the tax relief offered by trust instruments. In light of these worries, early land trusts recognized that a coherent approach was essential to the long-term credibility of easements and land trust professionals.

In the mid-1970s, Boston tax attorney Kingsbury Browne responded to these concerns by developing a newsletter about land trust tax issues. The Lincoln Institute for Land Policy went beyond this initial step by funding one of a series of meetings[21] held in the late 1970s and early 1980s that led to the founding of the Land Trust Exchange (LTE) and provided a staff member to serve as the first director. Incorporated as a nonprofit organization in Massachusetts in February 1982, the LTE published the first edition of *The Exchange: The Journal of the Land Trust Exchange* a month later. According to the journal, the LTE was to be a mutual support system for improved communication among trusts, to "reflect the grassroots nature of the land trust community," and to draw on "the experiences and expertise of those immediately involved in day-to-day land-saving activities" ("Land Trust Exchange" 1982: 1).

These were worthy goals indeed, but the organization faltered in spite of major foundation support (Spader 1983). Concerned land trust leaders met at Feathered Pipe Ranch, Montana, in November 1983, and reconstituted the LTE under Ben Emory, long active in the Maine Coastal Heritage Trust. The LTE remained in Maine long enough to publish two major volumes—*Appraising Easements* in 1984, and *The Federal Tax Law of Conservation Easements* in 1986[22]—and to hold the first Land Trust rally (i.e. annual meeting) in Washington, D.C., in 1985.[23] The publications were crucial in clarifying the controversial issue of appraising partial interests in land for tax purposes.

The Down East sojourn allowed the organization to mature into its twenty-first century plumage. In 1987, the group moved to the Washington, D.C., area, and Jean Hocker moved from the Jackson Hole Land Trust to take over as executive director. High on Hocker's agenda was developing a code of standards and practices for land trust activities. The strength of the land trust community was its local grassroots energy and effectiveness, and no one wanted to impose a top-down set of constraints on the movement. However, rapid growth in the number of land trusts continued to make quality control a concern.[24] National standards, it was thought, could help new, inexperienced organizations get up to speed as rapidly as possible in operating "legally, ethically, and in the public interest and to conduct a sound program of land transactions and stewardship" ("Land Trust Exchange Notes" 1989: 2).

The LTE standards established fourteen basic principles regarding the role of a land trust's board of directors; the basic requirements of legal, ethical, and biologically sound transactions; organizational fund-raising and management; and the relationship between a land trust and landowners, staff, volunteers, and the community. Although many smaller land trusts were horrified by their complexity, more established organizations found the standards valuable in pushing their boards of directors to adopt consistent organizational practices and to evaluate their operations. Funding organizations were also impressed, and many required grantees to adopt the LTE standards as a condition of any financial award.

The organization's tenth anniversary in 1990 signaled the maturation of a new wave of groups into what could legitimately be called a movement. The LTE changed its name to the Land Trust Alliance, moved its offices to downtown Washington, D.C., and initiated a series of training and education programs for land trust professionals. Stephen J. Small produced pivotal guides to further expansion, including *The Federal Tax Law of Conservation Easements* (1997a), which enabled lawyers throughout the country to give their clients detailed information on estate planning and other benefits of the sale or donation of an easement. Rather than remain a clearinghouse, the LTA would henceforth play a leadership role for the rapidly expanding and ever more sophisticated land trust community.

Land Trust Activities and the Emergence of Mosaics

The land trust movement radically altered the landscape around numerous federal and private preserved areas. We return to Mount Vernon, the Blue Ridge Parkway, and the Fort Ticonderoga-Northern Forest area to discuss these changes taking place on the ground.

Mount Vernon   Under intense pressure from surrounding development, the MVLA sought a way to identify areas where development could not be screened (Horstman 1994: 5) from the estate's sightlines. It contracted with the (relatively) new TPL to track development within its viewshed by visually simulating the location and identity of existing or planned structures (Horstman 1994: 4–6). The data showed where existing vegetation and height controls were protecting the view and where more direct controls were necessary.

Armed with that information, the MVLA worked with state and local planners to protect forest cover and limit building heights while supporting Maryland's Chesapeake Bay Critical Area legislation for protection along the shoreline. Cooperation with developers large and small thereby became an important element of the complex Mount Vernon mosaic, which included such minute details as where trees needed to be retained, in common areas and woodlots (Horstman 1994: 4–6). TPL remains involved and has worked on easements and land recently added to Piscataway Park.

Fort Ticonderoga   Things began to change at Fort Ticonderoga when the death of the Pell patriarch raised new issues for the family—including which set of grandchildren would get to occupy the Pavilion—and for the board. The family lowered its profile slightly, moving out of the Pavilion and working with the board to hire the association's first non-Pell director in 1989. At the same time, the Fort Ticonderoga Association (FTA) relinquished its semiprivate status as a membership corporation and was rechartered as an educational public charity.

New leaders at the FTA and in the Champlain Valley began to consider the conservation potential of the fort's extensive land holdings. As at Mount Vernon, the FTA partnered with a private land trust, in this instance the Adirondack Nature Conservancy-Adirondack Land Trust.[25] The trust inventoried the fort's land holdings, finding them to be both diverse and extensive (Folwell 1990: 52). The FTA board resolved to become a better steward of its own lands and to assume a leadership role in the Adirondack region. It also aimed to realize greater income from its parcels and, where possible, to reduce its property taxes (Duffus 1990: 2003).

By 1997 the FTA, the Vermont Land Trust, and the Vermont chapter of the Nature Conservancy, working with local farmers, had obtained agricultural easements on approximately 1,600 acres of viewshed across the lake from the fort. An unusual agreement divides easement monitoring among the groups. The fort does not deal with the agricultural elements of the agreement. It does, however, retain rights, interests, and enforcement responsibilities regarding the archeological resources on the land it formerly owned in fee.

The FTA also worked with TNC, using a large donation from the Mars family (of candy bar fame) to protect a mile of shoreline on a Pell holding on Lake George (where lake frontage sold for $2,000 per linear foot). The FTA board had concluded that holding the land was outside its mission. TNC purchased the fort's property plus one other parcel. The state then purchased both parcels from TNC for $1 million, and the FTA received half of that amount to support its historic preservation programs. This transaction funded a larger TNC effort that has protected more than 2 miles of pristine shoreline on Lake George. Because the properties were within the blue line of the Adirondack Park, they are also included under the "forever wild" provisions of the state's 1894 constitution.

The Changing Timber Industry and the Northern Forest   It is hard to think of a better location for private land conservation efforts than the forests surrounding Fort Ticonderoga. The Northern Forest is nearly 85 percent privately owned. The Northern Forest and major federal land holdings are shown in figure 7.2 along with several of the transactions we discuss here and in chapter 8. Two national forests, purchased under the Weeks Act (Green Mountain in Vermont and White Mountain in New Hampshire); one donated national park (Acadia in Maine); a small complement of wildlife refuges; and several small NPS units (the Appalachian Trail and the Allagash Waterway) add up to only 2.3 percent of the land area (Binkley and Hagenstein 1989: 9–10). While only one million people reside in the 26 million-acre region, it is still vulnerable to urban pressures. More than seventy million people live within a day's drive of the region (Northern Forest Lands Council 1994).

In the 1980s, however, the region was threatened less by sprawl than by the changing economic climate for the timber industry. High inflation

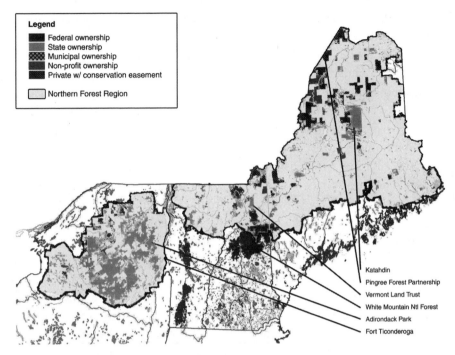

Legend
- Federal ownership
- State ownership
- Municipal ownership
- Non-profit ownership
- Private w/ conservation easement

Northern Forest Region

Katahdin
Pingree Forest Partnership
Vermont Land Trust
White Mountain Ntl Forest
Adirondack Park
Fort Ticonderoga

Figure 7.2
Location of the Northern Forest and mosaic of land ownership. Source: Map courtesy of the Appalachian Mountain Club; Conservation land data provided by the Maine Office of Geographic Information Services, New Hampshire GRANIT database, Vermont Center for Geographic Information, New York Department of Environmental Conservation, Appalachian Mountain Club, and The Nature Conservancy. Reproduced with permission.

and interest rates challenged the timber industry during the Reagan years. Simultaneously, the IRS ended a forty-year practice of granting wood products beneficial capital gains treatment. These factors raised the costs of growing timber and enhanced the perception that long-term investment in forestland was a risky business (U.S. FS 1989: 20).

The Northern Forest debate took place in this new context. For thirty years, a major goal of the timber industry in dust-ups with environmentalists had been to maintain access to raw material, particularly on national forests. The global timber market changed that priority. By the 1980s U.S. timber companies were priced out of the global market in both raw materials and finished goods. The pulp and paper industry in

New England was handicapped by an antiquated infrastructure that could not compete with more efficient Canadian mills. Corporate raiders saw conservatively managed forests as undervalued assets, and takeovers of forest products companies with large land holdings became common. Between 1982 and 1987, more than one-third of the pulp and paper sector's productive capacity nationwide changed hands (U.S. FS 1989: 20–21). Many companies concluded that it was better to buy wood than to own forestland.

As a result of these major land transfers, the loss or fragmentation of the land base in the Northern Forest became a concern for government, industry, and conservationists. NPS supporters continued to suggest a national park designation to address the problem (Docherty 2000), but the states were moving faster. New Hampshire adopted the SPNHF's proposal for a Trust for New Hampshire Lands (Levesque 1989) to make state and private funds available for purchasing land and easements. In New York, voters approved a $250 million bond for acquisition of fee land and easements in the Adirondack Forest Preserve. The Vermont legislature established the Vermont Housing and Conservation Trust Fund, a grant-making entity that supports land conservation and affordable housing (Dennis 1993: 172–194),[26] and the Land for Maine's Future Fund authorized state purchases of fee or less than fee interest in land.

In 1988, following a hostile takeover, Diamond International Corporation put about 1 million acres of Northern Forest land on the market (figure 7.3). Timber interests purchased 790,000 acres in Maine, and about 45,000 acres in New Hampshire were acquired by the state under the Forest Legacy Program, with the USFS holding an easement. The sale attracted regionwide attention and moved the governors of Maine, New Hampshire, New York, and Vermont to establish the Governors' Task Force on Northern Forest Lands to analyze and publicize important Northern Forest resources and the challenges to effective management.

As repositioning in the industry continued, in 1990 the Governors' Task Force recommended forming a second group, the Northern Forest Lands Council (NFLC) (Governors' Task Force Report on the Northern Forests 1990: 8–9; Beliveau 1993: 507–508). The NFLC was active from 1990 to 1994. It worked with the USFS and received federal

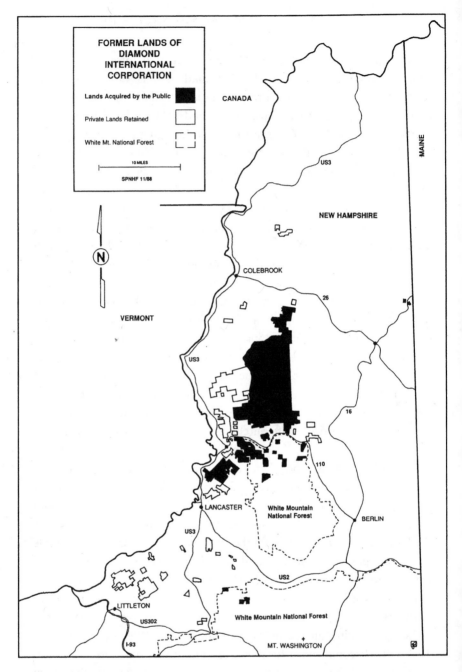

Figure 7.3
Diamond International Lands in New Hampshire in 1988. Source: Blackmer (1989: 15). Reproduced with permission of the Land Trust Alliance.

funding to produce yet another study, *Finding Common Ground: Conserving the Northern Forest*. This long public process bore fruit. When another round of industry land sales hit in the 1990s, an unprecedented alliance of state and federal organizations, timberland owners and investors, and land trusts were ready with recommendations for action (Chan 2004).

The Blue Ridge Parkway   Another diverse group worked to protect the BRP in an era of smaller and leaner federal programs (Brown, W. 1993: 104–145). Although the parkway is a federal park, it is a long and skinny one—about 400 miles long and about a thousand feet wide. For its size, it has many, many neighbors. The problems confronting the BRP therefore vary enormously along its route, depending on the surrounding land uses, land market pressures, and state and local regulatory and conservation programs. The result is a rather daunting array of public and private organizations, each with different constraints, priorities, and resources, working to protect land around the parkway.

The first BRP land protection plan, mandated under 1979 regulations, was completed in 1986 and revised in 1994. The plan contains boilerplate regarding the NPS's willingness to work cooperatively with local government, landowners, and developers to ensure conservation of vital parkway interests, but says nothing about the land trusts that surround it. (U.S. NPS 1986, 1988, 1994: 33, C-1). Nor does the NPS have adequate staff to work with those organizations. Many of the private trusts supporting BRP protection do not even consult with NPS administrators before entering into transactions adjacent to parkway boundaries.

The array of acquisition organizations and procedures is different in each state. In 1966, Virginia established a state agency, the Virginia Outdoors Foundation (VOF), to coordinate the state's land trust activities. Despite being a public entity, the VOF looks and acts very much like a private land trust, promoting land conservation largely by acquiring easements. Because, as indicated earlier, Virginia law prohibits any land trust less than five years old from holding an easement, the VOF coholds many easements with startup groups. In addition, in 1977 the state adopted the Agricultural and Forestal Districts Act, a current-use approach to taxation of farm- and forestland.[27] Finally, in 1997 the legislature created the Open Space Lands Preservation Trust Fund to fund acquisition of easements. These easements are held by VOF, but local co-holders are also required.

State efforts in Virginia are supplemented by numerous private land trusts working on BRP issues. The Valley Conservation Council has protected 27,000 acres of farm and forest in the Shenandoah Valley with easements. The Western Virginia Land Trust (WVLT) works among the small and relatively poor farms in twenty-three counties south and west of rapidly growing Roanoke. It is an unpromising area for donated easements because landowners do not have high enough incomes to benefit from tax breaks. The WVLT is hoping that a new tax credit exchange will help. In 1999, the Virginia legislature granted donors of land and easements a credit against state income taxes of one half of the value that they contribute. The credit is simply subtracted from the amount of income tax the donor owes for the year. And, since 2002, the donor can sell unused portions of the credits to third parties who can use them to reduce their own state tax obligations.[28]

The state of North Carolina has been less active. It has adopted a program under which an easement donor may credit 25 percent of the fair market value of the gift against state taxes.[29] Most of the coordinating of land trust activity is undertaken, however, by the private Conservation Trust for North Carolina (CTNC). Organized in 1991, it is the major player in the state's BRP segment. In 1996, the NPS requested that the CTNC assume a leadership role in protecting the BRP scenic and natural corridor. During the state's official "Year of the Mountains," the CTNC worked with the state to raise $1.3 million to purchase land and easements. In addition, the state's congressional delegation procured $750,000 for easements, and the state legislature and the state Department of Transportation committed $2 million for land acquisition (Roe 2000).

Numerous other North Carolina land trusts also support the BRP. In 1977, the Southern Appalachian Highlands Conservancy was founded. To date it has protected about a thousand acres in the mountain region, including areas bordering both Great Smoky Mountains National Park and the BRP. The Friends of the BRP was established in 1989, and the Blue Ridge Parkway Foundation in 1997. The latter operates under a cooperative agreement with the NPS. Both seek private support to protect the viewsheds, historical buildings, and natural areas associated with the parkway, while also assisting in public education, interpretation, and visitor information programs.

These diverse programs in two states do not add up to a coherent or even predictable acquisition program. The NPS lacks even a map to suggest the dimensions of the evolving BRP mosaic. And it is confined to working within established purchase boundaries. The NPS has a limited ability to deal flexibly with the wide range of situations inherent to a linear park that is all edge and no center. The proliferation of land trusts may be just what is required to work effectively in such a setting. However, their density raises important issues about whether the public is best served by a large number of small organizations all doing slightly different things in slightly different areas without much coordination. Whether there are sufficient resources to sustain the programs and the boards of so many organizations is also not clear. The land trusts appear more successful at acquisitions than the NPS, but the long-term results are not assured.[30]

New Models of Federal Acquisition

The land trusts sustained federal land acquisition efforts during a hostile administration. Under Reagan, it became politically impossible for federal agencies to seek acquisition funding from Congress. Private land trusts could, and did, and the transactions they supported became the surviving elements of the LWCF. Furthermore, in the ever more complex transactions that emerged in the 1980s, land trusts were better positioned than the federal agencies to sculpt deals to the sellers' advantage, fully exploiting federal and state incentive programs, lobbying for changes in tax laws, and adjusting to rapidly shifting real estate markets. As one Forest Service wag explained, it soon became the norm that if a forest supervisor wanted to acquire land, she would call TNC or TPL rather than the regional forester.

In fact, land trusts become so central in preacquiring land for federal agencies that Reaganites soon objected even to this more private form of conservation. They complained first that land trusts were fleecing the government, using all manner of tax breaks and other inducements to buy land on the cheap and then resell it to the government at a premium. In addition, the administration argued that land trusts were using preacquisitions to effectively determine government acquisition priorities.[31] Ironically, the high priests of privatization on the Reagan team were raising important issues of public accountability brought about by the ascendance of private land trusts within government acquisition efforts.

With surprisingly little controversy, Secretary Watt issued regulations in 1983 that addressed these concerns by clarifying the role of land trusts in federal acquisitions under the LWCF.[32] The rules state plainly that a land trust cannot act as the government's agent; that is, the trust cannot commit a federal agency to any particular transaction. The new policy also mandated that agencies sign a letter of intent whenever a nonprofit assisted them in acquiring land (U.S. DOI 1983). Finally, the regulations required full disclosure of appraisal data, the price of any options,[33] and the actual sale price of the land.

The practical impact of these requirements depends on who is participating. Some land trusts will buy an important property without federal guarantees, reselling it with an easement to a conservation buyer[34] if the government fails to consummate the deal. Similarly, some federal land managers simply ignore the fine print and proceed in a manner most likely to get the job done. In this context, the BLM and FWS's flexible authorities have worked to their advantage. Both the NPS and the USFS are bound by a tradition of acquiring units within designated boundaries. The FWS, as the successor to numerous agencies with diverse roles and authorities, is not so constrained, and the BLM, as the manager of the residual public domain, has few boundary limits at all. Given their checkered histories, both agencies are also far more comfortable embroidering at the margins of their authority.

The National Park Service
The Park Service was particularly limited in the land trust era by the congressional emphasis on greenline and other creative park units, combined with inflexible acquisition authorities. As park boundaries became fuzzier, the agency faced two distinct yet sometimes incompatible acquisi-

tion priorities. First, advocates emphasized the "backlog" in authorized park acquisitions in an effort to demonstrate a need for enhanced LWCF appropriations for "completing the parks." The National Parks and Conservation Association (NPCA) pointed to the 2 million acres of privately owned land and 3,000 mining claims that threatened the "integrity of our national parks" (NPCA 1988: v). It is difficult to imagine advocates mounting a parallel effort to "complete" the national forests.

At the same time that many park advocates were pointing with alarm to external threats that also required new acquisitions to expand park boundaries, that discussion was confounded by a series of law review articles asserting that the NPS had the authority to regulate land uses beyond park boundaries to protect federal resources (Sax 1976; Lockhart 1997). Although the legal arguments seem convincing, neither the NPS nor Congress was eager to further antagonize local communities already anxious about the NPS presence (Fairfax 1988: 391–394). The result has been equivocation on the agency's regulatory strategy and more ambiguity in the relationship between ownership and control. Formally, the position is that the NPS will not and cannot regulate land use outside the park units, except where it is specifically authorized to do so (as in the Cape Cod example). In practice, the agency uses moral suasion, incentives, subsidies for conservation initiatives, and its reputation to create pressure and expectations that an external area should be conserved.[35]

The Bureau of Land Management Post-FLPMA

Newly validated by the FLPMA, the BLM became active in the land acquisition field with the passage of two Reagan-era land exchange statutes. The 1980 Santini-Burton Act and the 1988 Federal Land Exchange Facilitation Act (FLEFA) indicate that after more than a century of wariness, Congress was eager to do some deals.

The Santini-Burton Act authorized the sale of federal land near Las Vegas, Nevada, to fund acquisitions to protect the Lake Tahoe Basin. It was a variant on the familiar BLM-as-marketbasket theme, but with careful limitations. Revenues generated by the sale of 700 acres a year in rapidly developing Clark County, Nevada, were not to be returned to the federal treasury but could only be used to acquire private land within three Lake Tahoe national forests.[36] The act also directed the Forest

Service to make payments in lieu of taxes to the local governments where federal land was acquired. The limited program worked. By 2001, 3,490 parcels of Tahoe land totaling 11,345 acres valued at $94.8 million had been acquired by the USFS (Bama 1999).

Emboldened, Congress, land developers, and land acquisition advocates soon turned to land exchanges beyond Lake Tahoe. The number of BLM exchanges doubled between 1982 and 1985 (Bama 1999), and Congress passed the FLEFA in 1988 to further expedite the process (Beaudoin 2000). FLEFA regulations, like FLPMA's, require that any exchange serve the public interest. As a sign of the increasing eagerness to conduct exchanges, however, FLEFA regulations created a laundry-list definition of valid public interests, including an all-encompassing "meets public needs" standard (Bama 1999). In another sign of the times, Congress encouraged agencies to use nonfederal entities in preparing transaction studies and appraisal documents, and to "work cooperatively with private landowners."[37] Finally, the regulations allowed either party to pay expenses or conduct studies that would normally be funded or pursued by the other. Soon after, BLM's private exchange partners were effectively running the transactions in ways that would create mischief in the 1990s.

Turning Necessity into Opportunity: The Fish and Wildlife Service

In a perfect example of turning necessity into opportunity, the FWS began to brag about its flexible acquisition program. During one Watt-era Senate hearing, the agency claimed to have the "greatest experience in the utilization of alternatives to fee of any agency" (Hester 1981: 65). Its deputy director noted that the national refuge system included more than 2 million acres covered by easement, lease, or other agreement with landowners for wildlife protection; and in addition, the agency managed about 1.7 million acres of wildlife habitat on lands held primarily by other federal agencies (Hester 1981: 65).[38]

This flexibility carried over into post-Reagan FWS initiatives to expand acquisition efforts under the Endangered Species Act.[39] Starting in 1997, the service began offering modest grants to state agencies to acquire habitat for listed species as part of an established Habitat Conservation Plan (HCP). While the numbers were tiny at first, in 2001 the service expanded the program and added a second grant to fund state acquisitions that were not related specifically to an HCP. Together, these two sources now offer $60 million per year for habitat acquisition by state agencies. This is modest compared with Farm Bill funding, of course, but it marks a significant movement away from the regulatory approach in the ever-controversial area of protection of endangered species. The allocation of acquisition funds to the states is also consistent with the service's continued emphasis on adapting to local conditions.

FWS flexibility, as we have seen, is the culmination of over a century of loosely accumulated authorities, limited funding, and a generally informal and ad hoc approach to establishing refuges. Whether acquired by easement or by fee purchase (or more typically by a combination of a fee core area and a larger area protected by easements), refuges were generally selected and approved in FWS field offices. A refuge is officially established when the first purchase or donation is acquired. In 1978 and 1980, Congress took a few small steps to rein in this process. At first it required that the agency consult with the state before recommending an area for federal purchase or rental. Later, consultation turned into approval by the governor or relevant state agency (Alvarez, 2002). Even those modest controls, however, leave the FWS with extremely flexible acquisition authority, especially compared with its sister agencies.

The New Federal Model in Action: The Blackfoot Challenge

The flexibility of the FWS is on full display in efforts to conserve the Blackfoot Valley of Montana, home of the Blackfoot River.[40] The river is short, but its watershed is spectacular; Norman Maclean's 1972 best seller, *A River Runs Through It*, made both the glory and decline of the area familiar. The Blackfoot Challenge, as the conservation effort is known, unfolds outside Missoula, as shown in figure 7.4, a place some might consider unlikely for a collaborative effort anchored by the FWS. Yet here the land of private property advocates and third- and fourth-generation ranchers is home to a partnership that has created a mosaic wildlife refuge.

The partnership has evolved over thirty years, beginning in the 1970s, when ranchers became alarmed by a proposed Wild and Scenic River

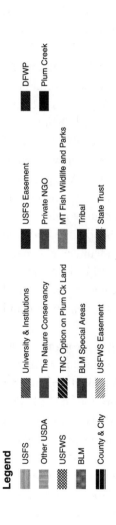

Legend

USFS	University & Institutions	USFS Easement	DFWP
Other USDA	The Nature Conservancy	Private NGO	Plum Creek
USFWS	TNC Option on Plum Ck Land	MT Fish Wildlife and Parks	
BLM	BLM Special Areas	Tribal	
County & City	USFWS Easement	State Trust	

Figure 7.4
Blackfoot watershed location and ownership map showing land ownership and tools of land protection. Source: Courtesy of the U.S. Fish and Wildlife Service, Benton Lake National Wildlife Refuge.

designation. Under pressure to find additions to the system, Interior officials hit upon the Blackfoot River. Local stockmen were horrified at the possibility of federal recreation in their backyard and, convened by local resident Land Lindbergh,[41] quickly organized to preempt the proposal. Establishing the Blackfoot River Recreation Corridor, the landowners designated parking and access points on their own land to limit public access and manage recreational use of the river. The Montana Department of Fish, Wildlife and Parks (MDFWP) and Missoula County joined the effort. The MDFWP decided to regulate recreation on private lands, and the county assumed the liability exposure and took charge of sanitation and garbage collection.

To protect a 10-mile river corridor, the partners invited TNC to acquire easements. More interested in biodiversity than recreation, TNC was unenthusiastic about the project but allowed a single staff member to work out the funding for a suite of land transactions. Before that could happen, the group pushed for state legislation to enable the use of conservation easements, as discussed in chapter 6. The result was Montana's Voluntary Open Space and Conservation Easement Act, passed in 1975. The legislation ignored the UCEA model and included two twists reflective of the political climate in the state. First, a county must review and comment on every easement within its jurisdiction. Second, the statute prohibited local property tax breaks on land under easement. Local governments would not pay for land conservation in Montana. For restoration work, the group turned to the FWS, which already held one 300-acre valley parcel in fee as an anchor for other easements and cooperative agreements.

The loose collaboration worked until a prolonged drought in the 1980s led the group to seek a broader mandate. With the native fisheries near collapse, the Big Blackfoot chapter of Trout Unlimited organized a stakeholder symposium. That resulted in the incorporation of the Blackfoot Challenge as a 501(c) (3) nonprofit corporation. The organization has no members, just an executive director and a goal to raise funds to restore the river.[42]

At present, more than 70,000 of the 300,000 acres of private land in the valley are under easement, and the division of labor is interesting. The FWS blends Farm Bill, LWCF, and Waterfowl Production Area funds (duck stamp money) with its own Partners for Wildlife Program (PFW)[43] to provide financial assistance to landowners. TNC's map of key ecological sites includes the Blackfoot Valley, and so the Conservancy is the major rainmaker for most other federal funds. TNC also works closely with Plum Creek Timber Company, the dominant private timberland manager.

The Montana Land Reliance (MLR) is the regional land trust working in the Blackfoot area. The statewide group grew out of efforts to limit land subdivisions in the 1970s. After some initial reluctance, the MLR now works almost exclusively with donated easements.[44] It does not seek government funds or participate in local political activity. There are enough people in Montana who would rather donate to the MLR than sell to either the federal or state government to make the group one of the largest land trusts in the country; statewide, it holds easements over 487,000 acres in 485 parcels, involving about 460 owners.[45] In the Blackfoot Valley, the MLR works primarily by locating conservation buyers for threatened parcels.

Specific transactions illustrate the remarkably complex workings of this partnership. TNC bought the Potts Nevada Spring Creek Ranch in 2001 after Trout Unlimited identified the site as its number one restoration priority. In the future, the FWS and the MDFWP will work to restore the stream course. TNC may then sell the land back to a rancher with a conservation easement. In another transaction, Ducks Unlimited (DU) purchased 70 very expensive acres near Upsata Lake that had already been subdivided. To reimburse DU, the FWS and the MDFWP both bought easements on the property. TNC raised the money for the federal purchase. The MDFWP was involved in both projects but not as a titleholder. MDFWP policies—most notably a tradition of allowing public access—make many in the state reluctant to deal with them. Figure 7.4 can only hint at the protection tools and land ownerships that make up the Blackfoot mosaic.

Although the land acquisitions get most of the attention, the cooperative restoration efforts of the Blackfoot Challenge are also impressive. The coalition has restored 350 stream miles and more than 2,500 wetland-riparian acres. Conservation-oriented grazing systems have been implemented on more than 45,000 acres. By its fourteenth year the

Challenge had raised more than $5 million for on-the-ground restoration projects (U.S. FWS n.d.c).

All this cooperation can become confusing. Each landowner chooses not only whether to sell or donate an easement to the partnership, but also which specific organization to work with. The FWS is most popular, perhaps because it can start by paying for restoration through Partners for Wildlife funds and then, having built a relationship, do an easement. By 2004, the FWS held 28,000 acres under twenty-nine easements and is negotiating for more. A nice bonus of FWS involvement is that Waterfowl Production Area projects (see chapter 5) are included in the agency's Refuge Revenue Sharing Act and provide some cash for local governments.

The Blackfoot Challenge has focused far more intensely on land acquisition following Plum Creek's announcement that it wanted to log its 89,000 acres, sell them off as residential lots, and leave the area. TNC agreed to play banker, while the Challenge took the lead with planning and community involvement. These acquisitions have caused some problems. TNC does not want to hold the land it purchases, but through a process of public involvement in local communities, led by the coalition, it is trying to identify appropriate permanent landholders, typically the BLM, the USFS, and some private buyers, based on the wishes of each community. However, the three counties involved are very different. Protection of traditional hunting and recreational uses becomes an emotional issue when new conservation owners want to exclude the public and gate their land. "Burdens" created by tax-exempt federal lands are a more familiar problem. Incredibly, perhaps, the Challenge and TNC are attempting to raise an endowment that would pay PILTs to the counties involved.

The partnership has other problems as well. Some in Montana fear that land trusts will erode support for zoning, land use planning, and the regulatory side of conservation by establishing a precedent of paying people not to do bad things. And because the Blackfoot Challenge enjoys so much visibility and support, conservationists working in neighboring valleys are feeling overlooked by funders. Someday the complex mosaic of owners and priorities may also cause difficulties in easement management. Currently, each easement holder monitors and stewards its own interests; an effort to have a single shared easement monitor never caught on. This diffusion of easement enforcement could become problematic in terms of funding and local support, as we discuss further in chapter 9. For now, however, the Blackfoot is a promising mosaic of modern land acquisition strategies, one that includes a vital new role for a federal agency within a much more complicated set of public-private relationships.

Conclusion

President Reagan's hostility to both regulation and government land ownership accelerated the decline of federal preeminence in acquiring land for conservation. By the close of the decade it was almost impossible to imagine the federal agencies acquiring land without the support of private conservation organizations. Public and private actors became deeply entangled and integrated in one another's projects. Beset by budget deficits and resurgent ideas about limited government, public land management agencies downsized and lost personnel in land appraisal and realty departments. Private organizations moved in to take over much of the leg work on acquisitions, moving adroitly in a rapidly changing real estate market to meet the financial planning needs of landowners and to lobby Congress for continued funding. Although it was an effective response to the imperatives of the era, this increasingly public role for private groups also began to raise new concerns about accountability.

It is also important to note the era's new understanding of land and landscapes. While Reagan emphasized parcels with specific owners, conservation biologists emphasized systems defined not by property lines but by ecological services and habitat. Meanwhile, mosaics of tools and owners blurred the distinction between private and public lands. Places we think of as national parks or forests had steadily become mixtures of public, private, and partnership lands. Similarly, land that appeared on the map and even on the tax rolls as private was increasingly dedicated to public benefits for which the owner was compensated.

By the 1980s, the land trust community was no longer wholly private. Volunteers remained important in the smaller land trusts, and donations of private money and land were important to all of them. But as the tax credit situation stabilized and the subsidies in the 1985 Farm Bill poured in, many land trusts became less or more government-funded. Meanwhile, most of the land acquisition programs that had gradually evolved into government undertakings were now all but formally shared with nonprofit groups.

It is often overlooked that in adapting to this new style of operations, some federal agencies exhibited unexpected flexibility. Accordingly, the 1980s may signal an important shift in the agency pecking order. The NPS still lacks sufficient flexibility for the era of mosaics, as the BRP story suggests. The USFS has more resources but lost control of the Forest Legacy Program to the states. In general, the old Progressive era agencies strike most observers as too tradition bound and tied to institutional arrangements of the late nineteenth century to function in this relatively free-wheeling era of new tools and expectations.

Perhaps surprisingly, the BLM and the FWS emerged as extremely adaptable players in the 1980s. These former laggards in acquisition policy were faster to adapt to the tools and practices of the land trust community than other agencies. The FWS had been using easements since the Depression, and the BLM was equally accustomed to dealing with intermixed federal and private lands and land managers. Even in the hostile climate of the Reagan era, the Blackfoot Challenge demonstrates what can be accomplished by a federal agency when it is teamed creatively with diverse state and private organizations focused on a well-defined conservation project.

8

Megadeals and Management Mosaics in the 1990s

In 1994, when Republicans won control of both houses of Congress for the first time in almost half a century, the maturation of an antiregulation, promarket, decentralization-oriented political process was unmistakable. Debate about the nature of ownership and the appropriate extent of government acquisition intensified, and property rights advocates gained ground. The philosophy of limited government was reinforced by concerns about economic conditions as expanding budget deficits led to a downsizing of federal, state, and local governments. The resulting budget cuts, early retirements, and curtailing of many programs made partnerships even more of a necessity for financially strapped public agencies.

In the newly conservative political climate, local groups of multiple stakeholders proliferated amid renewed respectability. Indeed, social scientists were obliged to coin a new term: *civic environmentalism* (John 1994). The push for community control was both inspired and complicated by the increasingly globalized economy (Kemmis 2001; Harvey 2003). Some forms of localism became literally dangerous when rural counties passed ordinances "outlawing" federal land management. Although far removed from such extreme sentiments and actions, land trusts also benefited from this renewal of interest in localism. Advocates touted the grassroots, voluntary elements of the land trust movement, even as it became more professional and less local.

The land trust movement's emphasis on private, entrepreneurial conservation tools also continued to match the times. In pursuit of two increasingly important conservation goals—protecting large landscapes for habitat and containing urban sprawl—the movement focused on easements that would restrict residential development while allowing established land uses to continue. However, as the economy faltered at the start of the 1990s, the trusts experienced many of the same financial constraints that afflicted government.

Meanwhile, conservation funding began to accompany highway bills as well as farm subsidies, in an effort to reduce environmentalist opposition to road construction. Similarly, a century of congressional reluctance to support land exchanges melted away, and conservationists supported enormous land swaps that enabled both conservation and land development. Thus land acquisition continued, not simply as a partnered activity between government and private actors, but as an explicit partner of economic development as well (Sokolove 2003).

In this environment, "commercial conservation" went beyond the tourism of Fort Ticonderoga and the limited development strategies of early land trusts to become a major component of conservation efforts. For example, in 1995 TNC created the Center for Compatible Economic Development to create "new businesses, land uses, and products that would help achieve conservation goals" (TNC 1999). Controversy soon followed. TNC has been roundly thumped, for example, for oil development that allegedly undercut the effectiveness of a Texas preserve intended to protect the endangered Attwater's prairie chicken (Stephens and Ottoway 2003b). Indeed, a growing problem in private conservation is that developers and industry groups are increasingly likely to use tools developed by land trusts to enhance the profitability of their own projects.

We discuss this growing complexity of the 1990s under four headings. The first section reviews important changes in federal acquisition funding and land trust priorities. The second section focuses on a series of very large transactions, including federal purchases, land trust deals, and partnered land exchanges that resulted in mosaics on a grand scale. The third section turns to a series of transactions that have the look of normal conservation acquisitions but in reality are not. Relatively simple checkerboards of mixed land ownership are confounded by arrangements in which diverse governments and land trusts share not just the acquisition efforts but also continuing management responsibilities. The final section returns to the idea of limits, even in an era of mega-acquisitions, by relating the failure of a spectacular federal acquisition funding scheme, the Conservation and Reinvestment Act (CARA).[1]

Developments in Acquisition Funding and the Land Trust Movement

This section explores two elements of the increasingly businesslike business of acquiring land: funding for acquisition and changes in the land trust movement. Federal support of economic development with conservation acquisitions in this era is old news. Government acquisitions and reservations dating back to the nation's capital have buttressed economic growth. That private conservation groups would move in the same direction, however, is noteworthy. Indeed, one could argue that the nature of federal funding has drawn the nonprofit community off target; or one could argue that the sellers' priorities continue to control acquisitions. The land trust community has been clear that its style of conservation fits well with both working landscapes and maintaining a local tax base. Nevertheless, in the 1990s the scale of such operations exploded.

Funding

Funding for land acquisition has been erratic over the past fifteen years. Private money flowed during the economic boom of the mid-1990s and then slowed following the end-of-decade stock market crash. Private foundations and individual donors have drawn back considerably since then, and the LTA experienced a renewed financial pinch, as have many nonprofits. Government support has also soared and crashed: first a deficit and downsizing, then a surplus, now an even worse deficit.

New revenues and fees have again become part of the debate. In 1996, Congress approved fee demonstration projects to support recreation investment on federal lands. The new program allowed designated federal units to retain fees generated by local recreation projects and to reinvest them on-site, but as usual, congressional commitment to cost recovery has been half-hearted (Wohlberg 2000). Although the resulting funds are significant at the margins, they remain small potatoes in the overall picture.

Largely through the intervention of the national land trusts—TPL, TNC, and TCF—the LWCF gradually expanded in this period, although not to Carter-era levels and not for state and local projects. Land trusts also helped to generate local enthusiasm for particular acquisitions and organized congressional support for the necessary appropriations. With the federal agencies suffering from budget cuts, program reductions, and the loss of critical institutional memory and experienced personnel, the land trust movement—and especially TNC, TPL, and TCF—was pivotal in more than 90 percent[2] of the routine acquisitions by all four land management agencies.

Although discussions of acquisition funding continue to focus on LWCF programs, Farm Bill resources have eclipsed the LWCF. Figure 8.1 illustrates this dramatic difference in the two funding pots in 2003. Conservation Reserve Program funds outstripped LWCF appropriations by nearly four to one, and LWCF funding dipped to less than 11 percent of total Farm Bill conservation funds. The wedding of conservation and acquisitions to agricultural subsidies and economic development is plain in these numbers.

The new face of funding has implications for how conservation acquisitions have proceeded. The NPS, for example, relies almost exclusively on the LWCF. The USFS does not, but it has fewer opportunities than either the BLM or the FWS to work with farmers. The dominance of Farm Bill funding favors acquisitions by the BLM and FWS and limits the NPS. Similarly, Farm Bill programs continue to be difficult to administer. Their complexity invites the land trusts to continue to play a central role in making them work.

The Changing Land Trust Movement

In terms of acres acquired, the 1990s were a banner decade for land trusts. Table 8.1 shows the dramatic increase in acres protected by the three national land trusts as well as by LTA members, whose figures are reported separately. By the end of the decade, the groups protected nearly 22 million acres—numbers that are not far out of line with the total acres acquired historically by the federal agencies. Table 8.2 shows that local land trust activity increased most in easements, although the number of acres preacquired for public owners, as well as those held in fee by the land trusts, also grew extensively.

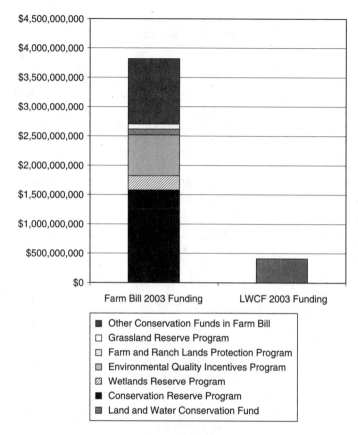

Figure 8.1
LWCF appropriations relative to funding levels for Farm Bill conservation and acquisition programs. Source: Personal Communication, Russ Shay, Land Trust Alliance, August 13, 2003.

As the acres piled up, however, the number of new land trusts began to level off. The drop in new startups may reflect financial constraints at the close of the century or it may simply represent a saturated market. Regardless, few land trusts remained purely volunteer organizations, and even small groups increasingly relied on professional staff with deep experience and valuable skills in real estate and financial transactions, fund-raising, and public relations (Hocker 2001). Professionals had become a routine part of the land conservation "business" and appeared

Table 8.1
Acres Protected by Private Conservation Organizations by Decade

Decade	LTA	TNC	TCF	TPL	Total
1980	680,103	1,729,853	—	29,603	2,439,559
1990	1,903,297	5,670,683	158,264	473,000	8,205,244
2000	6,217,810	12,190,294	2,324,282	1,204,587	21,936,973
2003	NA	14,903,164	3,563,312	1,400,000	19,866,476

Notes: The table includes protection by a variety of conservation methods that include acquisition, conservation easements, management agreements, leases, and acquiring other legal interests (such as mineral rights). The calculation of total acres protected by all groups double counts parcels in which multiple private groups may have been involved. However, it seems worth it to juxtapose the LTA data, which do not include the nationals, with the data from the larger groups. LTA 1980 data are for 1982. Note also that the 2003 total acreage appears to drop only because the LTA 2003 data were not available. NA = not available.
Sources: 1980 LTA data from Bremer (1984); 1990 and 2000 LTA data from Land Trust Alliance (2001a). TNC, TCF, and TPL data were provided by staff at each organization in personal communications.

Table 8.2
Land Protected by Local and Regional Land Trusts (Acres)

Form of protection	1980	1990	2000	Percent increase (1990–2000)
Easements	129,639	450,385	2,589,619	475
Preserves	550,464	435,522	1,237,342	186
Preacquisitions		1,022,640	2,388,264	129
Total	680,103	1,908,547	6,225,225	226

Source: Land Trust Alliance (2001a). The 1980 data are adapted from Bremer (1984).

to be shifting the trusts away from the grass roots that had made them so attractive at the outset.

Facing this reality, the LTA stopped focusing on "growing" the movement. Indeed, a shakeout was clearly evident by the end of the 1990s. In his first Rally address, the new LTA president, Rand Wentworth, welcomed the change, declaring that the group would never again "brag about the number of new land trusts created in a year" (Wentworth 2002). Confronting a 10 percent budget reduction in 2003, the LTA reorganized, downsized, and hired a development director. The LTA no longer relies solely on support from land trusts but now seeks donations and grant support from the same pool as its members.

As acquisitions mounted, the expanding popularity of easements caused concern within the land trust community. At the early 1980s meetings establishing the Land Trust Exchange, the participants were keenly aware that easements are not the best tools for all land conservation. In particular, they are poor vehicles for specifying management prescriptions.

Agricultural land trusts generally resist making such prescriptions. Despite the obvious social and environmental costs of industrial agriculture,[3] they assert that the farmer is the best steward. Similarly, as sustaining forestry has become a priority, flexible land management plans are now an important adjunct to many easement transactions. Perhaps these contractually obligated plans will prove to be effective. However, the public is largely cut out of many easement-defined processes because the relevant documents are defined as proprietary in the easement.

Defense of easements remains a major concern of land trusts. Litigation to enforce easements has given some cause for optimism. Legal challenges remain infrequent, and most courts have supported the easement tool (Gustanski and Squires 2000). The LTA has coordinated strenuous efforts to improve easement drafting, recording, monitoring, and stewardship. Many observers believe easement vulnerability will increase as the original participants in the transactions transfer the underlying fee to subsequent owners. Those less aware of and less enthusiastic about an easement's provisions may move more readily, by inadvertence or outright hostility, to violate its provisions.

The land trust community has also long been concerned about what they call rogue land trusts: developers who use easements to lower their tax costs without creating any clear public benefit. Because the tax benefits of easements are defined largely between the claimant and the claimant's accountant and lawyer, this is a real threat. "Land Trust Approves Bogus Easement Claim" is a much-feared headline in the community. So far, the LTA has done fairly well by setting informal boundaries and standards, although there have been minor scandals and exposés of shady deals.[4] Certification programs—involving audits of land trusts by an independent, third-party organization, for example—are still very much under discussion (Wentworth 2004).

It is also not clear what will happen to easements if land trusts merge or go out of business. The IRS code specifies that the assets of a failing nonprofit are passed to a similarly situated nonprofit. However, it seems reasonable that an organization inheriting another's assets might be less interested than the original negotiator in investing the funds necessary to monitor an easement or defend it in court. Despite these worries, it is evident that easements and land trusts are no longer the new kids on the block. They are the heart of conservation land acquisitions in the United States and appropriately subject to increased scrutiny.

Increasing Scale and Commercialism in Land Acquisitions

Changing economic conditions combined with the new political climate in the 1990s to create a diverse range of acquisitions that were larger, costlier, and more complicated than anything previously seen. The federal government experienced an acquisition spasm, pouring millions of dollars from a fleeting budget "surplus" into the forests of northern California and the mountains of New Mexico. A federal land exchange program also took off and became a well-used (and sometimes abused) method of acquiring land in lean budgetary times. Meanwhile, the Northern Forest transactions reflected the tumult in the private timber industry. A variety of actors and tools combined to protect these lands while allowing continued commercial development. In many of these efforts, the results were mosaics of unprecedented complexity, representing new institutional structures, conservation tools, and ownership regimes.

Land Exchanges

Although they involve government acquisition of private conservation land, modern federal exchanges occupy an ambiguous position in our narrative.[5] The exchanges of the 1990s bespeak a renewed commitment to commercial development. They are almost nothing like the Taylor Grazing Act transactions that cleaned up boundaries or eliminated inholder problems. Instead, they are more like the exchange that produced Mount Rainier National Park in the 1890s: enormous, controversial, and driven as much by the desire to free land for development as by conservation.

Nevertheless, we discuss land exchanges for three reasons. First, in a period when the government cannot or will not fund land purchases, exchanges are appropriately viewed as an off-budget source of funding. Second, the players in these transactions—an odd mix of commodity and land developers and their congressional allies are frequently lined up with land trusts and conservation interests—portray these deals as victories for the environment. Because we are by now accustomed to all kinds of chicanery in the name of land conservation, however, the transactions require a closer look. Third, it appears that we are well past the start of an extensive repositioning of federal land that is being neither analyzed nor debated as such.[6] It is important to explore—and pay more attention to—the new exchanges in that light.

Land Exchanges: Expanding Acres and Controversy   In the period 1989–1999, the USFS and the BLM traded away 1.97 million acres and acquired 2.93 million in return (U.S. GAO 2000: 14).[7] The value of the acres exchanged also increased dramatically. In 1985, the typical land exchange involved parcels worth between $400,000 and $1 million. Ten years later, the average exchange was worth more than $15 million (Draffan and Blaeloch 2000: 83). That is a phenomenal number, given the barriers to completing an exchange. And because the transactions were not always clearly aboveboard and in the public interest, the Forest

Service and the BLM's growing reliance on exchanges created controversy. Twelve different federal audits between 1996 and 2000 intensely criticized land exchanges (Blaeloch 2000).

The primary concern is that exchanges occur outside the competitive market; there are no rival bidders to help define an appropriate price. Fair appraisals are therefore crucial. Yet investigations have regularly identified a pattern of apparently undervalued public resources and inflated appraisals of private parcels (Draffan and Blaeloch 2000; U.S. GAO 2000). A General Accounting Office review of one Tahoe Basin exchange revealed, for example, that a private party acquired 70 acres of federal land appraised at $763,000 and sold it the same day for $4.6 million (U.S. GAO 2000: 19). Fair appraisals are particularly difficult when the transactions involve habitat or other amenity values that are poorly defined and difficult to estimate.

Nevertheless, FLPMA and FLEFA requirements that exchanges involve parcels of nearly equal value tempt participants to jiggle the numbers to make a deal (U.S. GAO 2000: 18). In the Utah Red Cliffs Desert Reserve, which was created to protect the endangered Mojave Desert tortoise, BLM appraisers confronted intense landowner hostility. At issue was whether the land should be assessed at a lower value that reflected the development controls occasioned by the species listing. In this instance, the BLM actually negotiated the appraised value (not the purchase price) with the landowners. The Department of the Interior's Inspector General challenged the transaction, but the proud specialists cited the process as exemplary of FLEFA's mandate to work cooperatively with landowners (U.S. GAO 2000: 5; Cavanaugh 1999; U.S. OIG 1996: 8).

Chicanery extends beyond the agencies; congressional meddling on behalf of corporate owners is routine. In one hotly contested deal, Washington's Senator Slade Gorton expedited a stalled exchange with a rider to an appropriations bill (Brown, S. 2000: 256–258). When the timber company involved began logging its newly acquired parcel, the transaction became an issue in the senator's reelection battle against an environmental activist. Without skipping a beat, Gorton then pushed Congress to appropriate LWCF funds to reacquire the land (Brown, S. 2000: 256).

When things come unstuck, congressional vilification of agencies is also common. Legislators push the agencies hard to facilitate questionable transactions and then denounce them if the public gets wind of a sour deal. One notorious case involved a land developer who began helicoptering building supplies to his inholding on a prominent Colorado wilderness ridgeline. When asked to consider changing his mind, the owner offered to trade his plot for 105 acres outside Telluride, Colorado. Unable to condemn the land or otherwise stop this kind of "greenmail," the USFS appraised both parcels at $640,000, swallowed hard, and completed the much-publicized transaction.[8] Shortly thereafter, the developer sold his Telluride parcel for $4.2 million (see Hearn 1998 and "Trading Away the West" 1998; part II). They may be "off-budget," but these exchanges look increasingly costly for the federal agencies all the same.

Opponents of land exchanges complain of irregularities, biases, and bad outcomes. They observe that by the time a proposed exchange is clear enough to evaluate, it has so much momentum that public opinion has little impact. Moreover, the lack of public participation is exacerbated by FLEFA's efforts to encourage the agencies' trading partners to take over much of the work of the transaction. This gives private landowners enormous leverage in defining the deal. The Forest Service and NPS (but not the BLM) also treat appraisals as proprietary information and do not make them public until after the transaction is complete.[9]

Assembled Exchanges   Assembled exchanges are even more complex and controversial. Agency efforts to acquire environmentally sensitive lands by exchange sometimes founder because the owner of the desired land does not want any readily available federal property. Conversely, the agency may have available land desired by a potential trading partner who has nothing that the agency needs. Assembled exchanges allow outside dealmakers to construct packages of land that will meet the traders' priorities and FLPMA's equal-value requirements.

To illustrate, assume that the BLM wants to acquire important wildlife habitat on a private ranch valued at $30 million. Investors and/or state and local officials are anxious to obtain a smaller but more valuable (say $50 million) BLM parcel near Las Vegas, Nevada, for residential development. A third-party assembler will balance the transaction, acquiring options on $20 million worth of private land attractive to the BLM and offering it in trade along with the coveted ranch in return for BLM's $50 million Las Vegas parcel (see "Trading Away the West" 1998, part III).

Unavoidably, when making commitments of that scale, the assembler works closely with the BLM and is frequently using a line of credit provided by the agency. Such privileged access to public resources strikes many as unfair. Moreover, holding a package of potential transactions together is a delicate process and creates suspicions that one or both parties have manipulated appraisals. Nevertheless, where exchanges are important to different segments of the public, and Congress is unwilling to fund acquisition directly, these seemingly impossible transactions occur with surprising regularity.

Adding to the controversy is the fact that the assembler almost always makes a profit, typically a significant one ("Trading Away the West" 1998). Some assemblers are well-connected land developers or conservation-oriented real estate agents. However, many deals are assembled by land trusts. The trusts justify their profits by using the income for other conservation projects. Nevertheless, the deals are frequently so complex, large, and hidden from public review that the organizations undertaking them are vulnerable to criticism. Often it is difficult to distinguish the land trusts from the real estate moguls as observers assert that private wheeler-dealers are bamboozling the federal agencies. That impression is intensified by the continuing decline in the number of federal appraisers and "landsmen" on the ground.

Steps toward Exchange Reform   Congress enacted bills in 1998 and 2000 that were intended to solve the appraisal problem by turning exchanges into auctions in which bidders would compete to establish the market price. The 1998 Southern Nevada Public Land Management Act (SNPLMA) is very similar in structure to the Santini-Burton Act of 1980. The BLM is authorized to dispose of land in a congressionally designated area of the Las Vegas Valley. The state receives a generous share of the revenue from those sales, but 85 percent is dedicated to federal acquisition of environmentally sensitive lands in the state. Although the BLM, NPS, FWS, and USFS can acquire lands with the money, the BLM manages the receipts. Unlike many other funds discussed in this volume, SNPLMA funds are kept in a dedicated, interest-bearing fund established by the act.[10]

SNPLMA also aimed to enhance public participation in planning the exchanges. A 2001 SNPLMA implementing agreement provides for extensive consultation with local and state governments and local committees established by the BLM (U.S. BLM 2003). The general public and a broad spectrum of participating interest groups are authorized to nominate parcels for sale or acquisition. Those provisions may enhance public accountability in the exchange process.

The 2000 Federal Land Transaction Facilitation Act (FLTFA—not to be confused with FLEFA or FLPMA) uses a similar arrangement for exchange deals nationwide. The program was added as a sweetener to attract acquisition opponents to the bill that authorized the Valles Caldera acquisition, discussed later. Also modeled on the Santini-Burton Act, FLTFA is not confined to Nevada. It authorizes the BLM to auction parcels anywhere that are identified in BLM land use plans as suitable for disposal. Receipts can be used by any of the four agencies to acquire land.

Congress limited FLTFA's potential for creating new federal units, however, by dedicating 80 percent of the receipts to acquisition of inholdings. To balance both the tax implications and the benefits, 80 percent of the revenues from a given auction must be spent in the state where the revenues were generated. Unlike the SNPLMA fund, the FLTFA kitty terminates ten years after passage of the act. The cash-strapped NPS had hoped that FLTFA would direct the BLM to sell lands to fund NPS acquisitions, but the final bill makes auctions discretionary. To date, the BLM director has moved slowly, making it an open question whether the bill will have any impact at all.

The Northern Forest

Federal budget woes were not the only financial constraint shaping land acquisitions. The timber industry's economic problems discussed in chapter 8 ripened into a cascade of transactions in the 1990s. The Northern Forest deals added new layers of complexity to conservation mosaics that have been under creation for almost a century. The resulting maps reveal mosaics of tools, goals, and funding sources as well as of acquisition agents. The relationships are intricate, and the funding is difficult to follow. We tarry on some of the details because they are so emblematic of how land acquisition for conservation both has and has not changed from its nineteenth-century origins.

Many of the deals involved lands held by the Champion International Corporation. Early in the decade, Champion hired the Adirondack Mountain Club (ADK) to conduct a detailed inventory of the recreational and scenic resources on Champion's lands in New York state. The ADK delivered the report in 1993, and a coalition of land conservation, recreation, and forestry organizations formed the Northern Forest Alliance (NFA) to protect forest lands and the timber economy during anticipated sales of Champion land.

In October 1997, Champion announced the sale of 294,000 acres of Northern Forest. In December 1998, The Conservation Fund announced that it had signed a contract to purchase 144,300 acres in New York, 18,000 in New Hampshire, and 132,000 in Vermont, for a total of $76.2 million. TCF relied on government and conservation buyers in each state to acquire and arrange management of the lands. The process was different in each jurisdiction.

Champion in New York   In New York, TCF served as the state's representative. The 144,300-acre transaction was the largest in state history at the time, and it combined government, timber industry, and land trust funds (New York State Department of Environmental Conservation n.d.). In the end, the state kept 29,000 acres in fee, which were added to the Adirondack Forest Preserve. It also retained a working forest easement on 110,000 acres bought by The Forestland Group (TFG), a Chapel Hill, North Carolina, timberland investment management firm. State funding for the purchase totaled $24.9 million and came from 1996 Clean Water-Clean Air Bond Act funds. The private timber share of the land included an additional 4,300 acres outside the park boundary in which the state holds no interest. In response to local concerns about the tax base, New York agreed to pay property taxes on the conservation easement it holds on the 110,000 acres inside the park while TFG will pay its share of taxes on the underlying fee.

Unlike the other Northern Forest states, where private timberland has traditionally been open to the public, the New York acquisition and easements opened lands that had been closed to the public for more than a hundred years (Pataki 1999). To provide a transition period, private hunting clubs that held exclusive camp leases from Champion will retain them until 2013.

The state's working forest easement requires TFG to manage the land for long-term production of high-quality hardwood timber and to make the land available for recreation activities that are compatible with sustainable forestry. TFG will develop a management plan to be approved by the state's department of environmental conservation (New York State Department of Environmental Conservation 1999).

Although the controversy was greater in other states, private property groups did protest the New York deal. Their concerns centered on the increase in state land ownership, the lack of local involvement in the deal, and TCF's role as a land acquisition agent for the state. The Property Rights Foundation of America in Stony Brook, New York, sued but failed to halt the transaction. The decision turned on statute of limitations problems (LaGrasse 2001), but issues of public accountability in this kind of land trust transaction remain controversial. In this case, there is not even a plan that would tell concerned citizens what might happen on the land.

Champion in Vermont   In Vermont, the Champion deal initially went smoothly, with funding provided by the state, the federal government, and numerous private foundations. However, the concerns of local stakeholders and property rights advocates were inadequately addressed in the first phase of the process, and the transaction became quite contentious.

The general location of the affected land in Vermont is shown in figure 7.2. The transaction split Champion's 132,000 acres into three pieces; figure 8.2 shows the resulting land ownership and easements in the transaction. The Vermont Agency of Natural Resources (VANR) acquired 22,000 acres. The land was subject to easements originally held by the Vermont Land Trust but rapidly transferred to TNC as the parcel became known as the West Mountain Wildlife Management

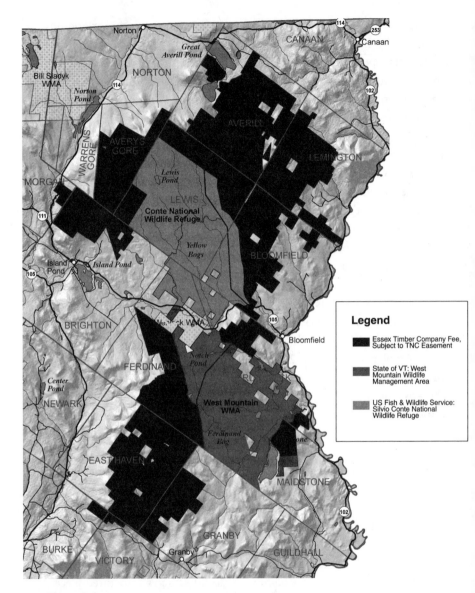

Figure 8.2
Disposition of Champion International lands in Vermont. Source: Courtesy of
the Vermont Land Trust. Reproduced with permission.

Area (WMA). The Essex Timber Company, a private investor, acquired 84,000 acres subject to conservation easements co-held by the Vermont Land Trust and the Vermont Housing and Conservation Board. Finally, the FWS purchased 26,000 acres to become a part of the Silvio Conte National Wildlife Refuge.

The state legislature appropriated funds for its share of the deal, $4.5 million, in March 1999. The state funds secured conservation and public access easements on the private timberlands portions of the West Mountain WMA (Vermont Land Trust 2001). The state also used $4 million from the Freeman Foundation to purchase working forest easements on the Essex Timber lands, and a grant from the Mellon Foundation helped acquire part of the West Mountain WMA in fee.

Intense controversy arose over existing camp leases scattered throughout the acquired property. Leaseholders protested on behalf of their "camp culture," in spite of the fact that their leases were to expire in 2000. To calm the waters, both the Vermont Land Trust and the state agreed to extend the leases for the life of current leaseholders, plus twenty years.[11] Nevertheless, vocal minorities of timber and sporting interests, and some in the legislature, have fiercely fought the planning process for the lands and tried hard to undo the acquisition.

A 12,500-acre ecological reserve within the West Mountain WMA was also controversial. Less than 10 percent of the entire 132,000-acre transaction, the parcel is the only place where logging will be halted and biodiversity will take priority over timber and game management (Northern Forest Alliance 2002). Yet hostility to making any formerly open lands off limits to hunting finally led the governor and other parties to "clarify" the easement. They issued a new contract stating that the easement allowed hunting, fishing, and trapping throughout the WMA.[12]

The Vermont Land Trust's transfer of its easements in the West Mountain area to TNC also angered reserve opponents. Local land trusts provide local experience and a trusted face for large and potentially disruptive transactions. When the home team transferred the easement to a national group viewed by many locals as extreme in its orientation toward natural values and against human ones, the change seemed threatening.

Environmentalists' doubts about the project never reached such a fevered pitch, but many groups continue to fear that allowing working forestry does not afford sufficient conservation on valuable lands and is therefore a sham and a waste of conservation dollars. The Essex Timber easement, for example, is criticized because it actually requires harvesting a set amount of timber annually.

New Hampshire: One Big Deal Follows Another   The New Hampshire transactions are referred to as the "IP Lands deals" because International Paper (IP) purchased Champion International Corporation shortly after TCF's acquisition in New Hampshire was announced. In the first round, TNC agreed to purchase the 18,000 acres in New Hampshire from TCF. TNC then sold about half the land to a conservation buyer and retained the remaining acreage as the Bunnell Mountain Preserve. While that process was under way, IP's acquisition of Champion precipitated a second, larger land deal. TPL persuaded IP to retire its debt from buying the smaller company by selling another 171,500 acres in the headwaters of the Connecticut River.

The Society for the Protection of New Hampshire Forests worked with the local TPL office to organize political support and funding for the larger land deal. State and federal officials immediately organized: Senator Judd Gregg and Governor Jeanne Shaheen established a task force to coordinate decision making within the state. The group conducted extensive public hearings and in December 2001 produced a strategy for funding the purchase and managing the area (Connecticut Lake Headwaters Partnership Task Force 2001).

The strategy was complex. TPL initially borrowed from the Wainwright Bank and Trust Company, a frequent land conservation lender, to fund the $32.7 million purchase (Trust for Public Land 2002b). To recover some of its cost, TPL then sold 146,400 acres to Lyme Timber, a private company interested in ecologically friendly forest practices. TPL also sold 25,000 acres of sensitive habitat to TNC. Ultimately TNC will resell that land yet again to the New Hampshire Department of Fish and Game but will continue to hold an easement. The state used Forest Legacy Program (Farm Bill) money to acquire a working forest management easement on the Lyme Timber holdings to encourage a sustainable timber harvest while providing for public access. It also used a conservation bond and a $2 million grant from the New Hampshire Land and Community Heritage Investment Program (a state entity that funds conservation efforts). When all the bills are paid, the cost of the transaction will have been spread more or less evenly among federal, state, and private sources.

The New Hampshire Northern Forest acquisitions provide an occasion to assess the economists' concerns that if the private sector lies low, it can pursuade the public sector to overproduce conservation, or that an overactive federal program will crowd out private effort. For most of the last century, one of the nation's oldest private conservation groups, the SPNHF, has worked side-by-side with the USFS in New Hampshire as the federal government acquired the White Mountain National Forest (WMNF). The two purchase programs are compared in figure 8.3.

The figure provides heartening confirmation (on a single national forest) for the summary data in figure 5.1. Most of the land acquired by the

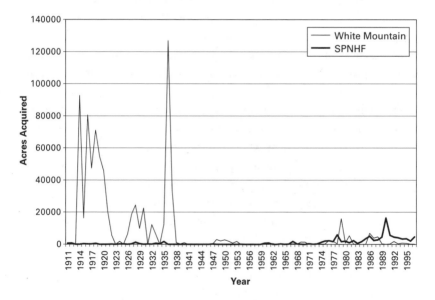

Figure 8.3
A comparison of acres acquired for the White Mountain National Forest with all SPNHF acres acquired in New Hampshire, 1911–1997. Source: Base data courtesy of SPNHF and White Mountain National Forest.

federal government was acquired during the Depression. The figure also confirms that federal acquisition activity for conservation was revived after a World War II slump by funding from the LWCF and the National Trails System Act. More important here, we see no sign of federal activity crowding out private. Even as the LWCF revived federal programs, the land trust movement picked up steam, and SPNHF activities actually dwarfed federal acquisitions. Between 1970 and 1997, the federal government acquired 49,000[13] acres for the WMNF while the SPNHF acquired 86,000 acres throughout the state.

Beyond Champion: Acquisitions in Maine   The Northern Forest transactions in Maine were not a part of the Champion deal. The state had bigger fish to fry. About half of Maine's North Woods (4.8 million acres) changed hands in just eighteen months starting in June 1998 (Docherty 2000: 557).[14] In those unsettled times, the Pingree family, a major forest owner in Maine, announced its intention to sell a conservation easement on 754,673 acres of family-held timberland. The Pingree family has owned and managed considerable portions of the state for almost 160 years. The family was an early adopter of "green certification" of forestry practices and has been a long-time participant in Maine's culture of keeping private woodlands open for public hunting, camping, fishing, and recreation.[15]

The family worked with tax attorney Stephen J. Small, a familiar figure in land trust circles, to construct an easement that would protect the land from development while maintaining timber management. The family then had the easement appraised and granted the New England Forestry Foundation (NEFF) a two-year option to raise money to buy it. The appraised value was $37.10 per acre or about $28 million (New England Forestry Foundation n.d.). The general location of the transaction is shown in figure 7.2 and the mosaic produced in one element of the sale, the St. John region, is shown in figure 8.4.

The Pingrees' solid reputation as land stewards did not protect the deal from considerable complaints. Environmentalists worried that the land was inadequately protected. Their concerns are unsurprising given that NEFF was known not as a conservation or preservation group, but as a nonprofit established to support small woodlot owners. More

Pingree Forest Partnership

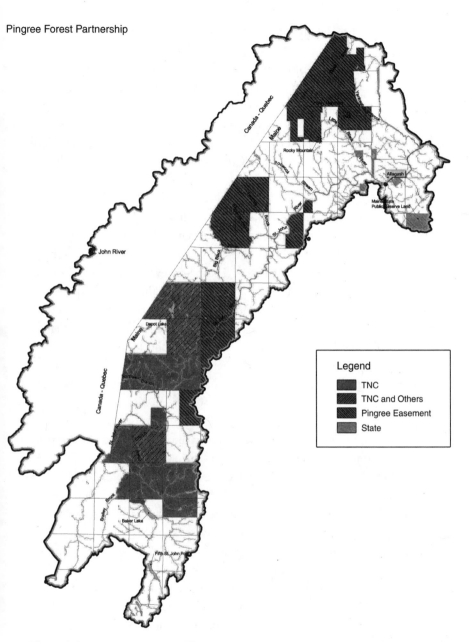

Figure 8.4
The St. John portion of the Pingree sale and resulting mosaic of NEFF easements and TNC and state land. Source: Courtesy of the New England Forestry Foundation. Reproduced with permission.

expected is the fact that the deal continues to be criticized by private property rights groups. Beyond the usual hysteria about United Nations takeovers,[16] activists complained about the perpetuity of the easement, noting that while the Pingree heirs can continue to log, the easement prevents anyone "from ever developing the land, lakes, or rivers for any other purpose other than forestry and open space." They concluded correctly that "for $28 million [the Pingrees] denied all future generations any options of what to do with the land" ("The plan from hell" ... 2001).

Despite the protests, the deal closed in March 2001. Federal and state governments, more than a thousand individuals, and forty-five different foundations had contributed money for what ended up being the largest conservation easement in history. Despite this wide array of actors, however, public comment was limited. The plan developed by the Pingrees for future management of the area is described in the easement as proprietary information. Only NEFF and the landowners will have access to it, and the public will not be invited to comment on its provisions. Yet the impact of these ostensibly private transactions on local economies and expectations is enormous; hence achieving transparency and public accountability has become a major challenge for land trusts and their supporters.

Still More Northern Forest News   The cycle of timber industry restructuring continued. In January 2001, the Adirondack chapter of TNC and the Adirondack Land Trust announced another purchase of 26,562 acres in New York for $10.5 million. In what is becoming routine practice, the purchases preserve opportunities for future logging in the area, while the state's department of environmental conservation will work with TNC to include parts of the tract that protect major lakes and key ecological resources in the Adirondack Forest Preserve.

More interesting is a "debt-for-nature" swap between TNC and the Great Northern Paper Company in Maine. Under the deal, TNC acquired 41,000 acres in fee and a conservation easement on an additional 200,000 acres of land in the Katahdin area of Maine. As shown in figure 8.5, the fee land will connect Baxter State Park to the state Nahmakanta Ecological Reserve and four other conservation areas, and

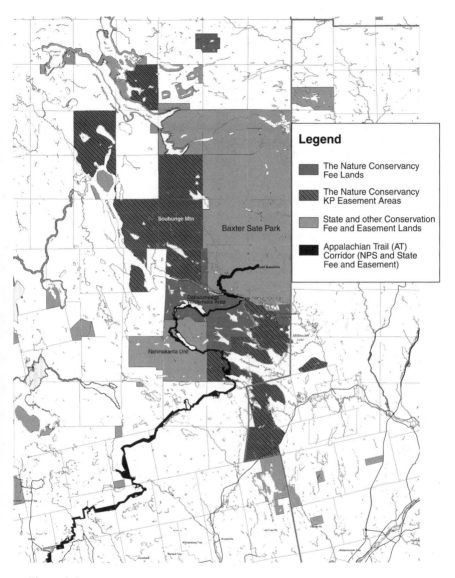

Figure 8.5
Land ownership and tools around Baxter State Park and Mt. Katahdin in Maine.
Source: Map courtesy of The Nature Conservancy. Reproduced with permission.

the easement will ensure both continued sustainable forestry and access for traditional recreational use of the area.

To fund the transaction, TNC purchased $50 million worth of the struggling paper company's existing loans, in order to maintain Great Northern's role in the local economy. TNC then retired $14 million of the loans and refinanced the remainder at less than half the going interest rate. John Hancock Financial Services, which sold the discounted mortgage to TNC, also contributed to the deal. Great Northern filed for bankruptcy nonetheless, but the easement continues to protect the lands involved.

Northern Forest Summary   In the Northern Forest, vast industrial timber holdings suddenly became available for purchase. The conservation response was to acquire them with as little subdivision or change of use as possible. But the area was so vast that doing so required the cooperation of many constituencies: those wanting to protect working forests and jobs, as well as those concerned about watersheds, species habitat, and "traditional" life styles and recreation opportunities. The many goals, jurisdictions, and partners involved required a different kind of subdivision and a protracted dance through a complex political terrain to an even more complex landscape mosaic.

In the process, conservation buyers became a significant element of the industrial timberland market. Timberland owners are clearly using easements to make their land holdings a less attractive target for corporate takeovers of the Headwaters type (discussed later). The resulting mosaics of ownership interests and management restrictions should make it difficult to liquidate timber rapidly in order to retire any debt incurred in a takeover.

Whether Northern Forest easements and the accompanying plans will provide sufficient protection to achieve habitat and biodiversity goals is not clear. In many cases, moreover, the public will never even know what is in the plans, and hence what the easements permit and restrict. Monitoring, therefore, will present extreme challenges. If preventing residential subdivisions was the only goal, then perhaps the deals are indeed "win-win." However, if more was hoped for, or paid for, in terms of ecological protection or civic involvement, the outcomes may be difficult to assess. Sustaining the traditional economic base of Northern Forest communities was a major prerequisite for state and local support for the transactions. Without allowances for continued timber harvest, these transactions would not be happening at all. The Northern Forest deals therefore look more like Weeks Act acquisitions than those that have been associated with the land trust movement.

A Federal Buying Spree at the Close of the Decade

While states and land trusts were having a field day in the Northeast, the federal government leapt back into the acquisition business out west. Powered by a putative federal budget surplus and eager to reduce controversy over public lands management, the government made some stunning acquisitions. The results were mixed, to say the least, and it now appears that the spurt of federal buying was but a brief aberration.

Headwaters   Federal purchase of the Headwaters Forest in Humboldt County, California, is the most contentious and inconclusive conservation acquisition we have studied. Many years of environmental activism on the north coast of California culminated in a "Redwood Summer" of protest and police violence in 1990. The listing of the northern spotted owl (1990) and marbled murrelet (1992) as endangered species strengthened the environmentalists' legal justifications for restricting industrial logging in the area.

The issue was joined in the Headwaters issue following yet another restructuring in the timber industry. In 1985 Charles Hurwitz's company MAXXAM financed the purchase of approximately 211,000 acres of redwood forest with $900 million in high-interest junk bonds. To retire that expensive debt, MAXXAM abandoned the legendary sustained-yield stewardship of the previous owner, Pacific Lumber, and began liquidating what came to be known as the Headwaters or the Ancient Forest. Environmental activists were outraged, and a new front immediately opened in the Northwest's "timber wars."

Once again, federal acquisition emerged as the solution. In 1996, California Senator Dianne Feinstein brokered an agreement with MAXXAM that committed the state and federal governments to acquiring a core virgin grove of about 3,000 acres and another 4,000-plus acres as a buffer. In March 1997, Congress appropriated the federal share of the purchase price—$250 million—in legislation that allowed two years to work out the final details. As negotiations dragged on, Julia "Butterfly" Hill set up housekeeping in a redwood tree named Luna and remained there to dramatize public commitment to saving the trees.

The final contract was signed half an hour before the federal funding commitment expired. The total cost of the transaction to the state and federal governments was about $490 million. As part of the deal, MAX-XAM was required to file a habitat conservation plan in order to acquire a permit to "take" endangered species (i.e., altering their habitat in a harmful manner) on about 200,000 acres (Bundy 1999: 361–364). Unfortunately, both the HCP and a sustained yield plan required under the state's forest management act were still incomplete four years later.

Nevertheless, MAXAAM had sold about 7,000 acres of the 211,000 acquired for about half of what it paid for the entire area, while obtaining a free pass to harvest the rest. Some have argued that even at that price the acquired Headwaters preserve was a bargain—that MAXXAM all but gave them away in order to get the permit to harvest the remaining 204,000 acres.

Others have observed that it would have been cheaper to buy out the whole corporation than the 7,000 acres. The logic of that position is that without the legal permission to take an endangered species, the corporation's land was largely worthless and MAXXAM was in trouble. Clearly, enforcing the regulations would have been a cheaper option. Whether these Endangered Species Act restrictions would have held up legally or politically, however, is an open question. In short, it is not clear what to think.

One could argue that if protecting the land was the priority, the deal did not work. MAXXAM has harvested intensely, but it has yet to prepare the documents required for the incidental "take" permit (Bustillo 2003: A11). Moreover, activists complain that an additional thousand-acre parcel, being advertised as the "Hole in the Headwaters" (Trees Foundation 2000), still must be acquired to protect deeply sloped valleys critical to salmon habitat.

This new advocacy underscores the limits to what land acquisition can achieve. How much is enough is never clear, and apparently there will always be calls for more. Obviously, the same money spent elsewhere would have protected far more land and resources. Perhaps the preservation of civic order made the deal worthwhile—the dispute was persistent and dangerous, and the acquisition does appear to have cooled the political heat somewhat. But when all the facts are known, we wager that Headwaters will be another example of bailing out a powerful landowner, echoing many of the Weeks Act acquisitions of eighty years earlier.

The Valles Caldera   Acquisition of the 100,000-acre Baca Ranch in the Jemez Mountains of north-central New Mexico also raised the issue of how much is enough. Most of the Jemez range has been in public ownership as part of the Santa Fe Forest Reserve/National Forest since the late nineteenth century. The NPS has spent seventy years, however, trying to expand Bandelier National Monument, its "foothold" in the region (see Rothman 1988, esp. chap. 3). Ironically, when nearby owners of the Baca Ranch decided at last to sell, the conservative New Mexico congressional delegation rejected the NPS's restrictive management policies. Instead, Congress added a special $200 million supplement to Land and Water Conservation Fund appropriations available for the purchase.

A Valles Caldera Preserve was established in 2000 as a peculiar adjunct to the national forest.[17] Congress established a wholly owned government corporation, the Valles Caldera Trust, to manage the new federal property. The trust's board consists of seven individuals experienced in local customs and conditions. Moreover, the trust is to manage the reserve as a working ranch that benefits local communities and small businesses. Thus although the form of the acquisition is very different from the Northern Forest transactions, the priority of local economic development is similar in both.

The results, however, may differ significantly. The Valles Caldera statute contemplates that the trust will become self-supporting within thirteen years. Although cost recovery is an oft-broken promise in the acquisition and management of public land, the Valles Caldera may achieve that goal. If the trust fails to bring in adequate revenues, the property may simply be added to the Santa Fe National Forest (Fairfax et al. 2004).

Mosaics of Management: Expanding Roles of Land Trusts

As the land trust movement matured, the mission of many groups continued to expand. Working with public land managers on issues beyond simple acquisition was an important growth area. At Gettysburg and Cuyahoga, for example, private groups played an active role in helping to define, protect, and manage the park on a day-to-day basis. The result has been an integration that makes the labels of public or private increasingly obsolete. Nor has there been any sign that government acquisition efforts are in any way crowding out continued private acquisition activity. Nevertheless, while land trusts made great strides in expanding their collective mission in the 1990s, they neglected a vital element of the conservation agenda: the need for attention to urban areas. This oversight is a worrisome exception to what was otherwise an encouraging decade for the movement.

Gettysburg: Local Land Trusts and Local Management

Events at Gettysburg National Military Park suggest that private groups have become central, not only in federal acquisition programs, but also in day-to-day park management. Land trusts now form the core of a supportive community that has played a major role in defusing enduring NPS tensions with locals.

A donation from the Gettysburg Battlefield Preservation Association (GPBA) broke the existing deadlock. A "nasty, unseemly little skirmish" arose when the land trust tried to give 31 acres to the park (*Philadelphia Inquirer*, June 17, 1986, quoted in Platt 2001: 93).[18] The local congressman complained that the park was "about to take another bite of land and make it 'difficult for real estate people, [and] for builders'" (*Philadelphia Enquirer*, June 17, 1986, quoted in Platt 2001: 93). Congress approved adding the parcel, but to meet concerns about indeterminate park borders, it also initiated a study to recommend formal boundaries for the park. In 1990, a mere 125 years after the Civil War battle, the government finally settled the boundary issue by adding 2,050 acres to the existing park. Congress also created a 5,250-acre historic district around the park, and established a citizens' advisory commission to work with the NPS on park issues, including acquisitions. The NPS was authorized to acquire land in fee within the park and to accept donated easements in the historic district.

The provision regarding donated easements gives the local land trusts an important role in brokering park protection. With the belated clarity of the 1990 bill and the completion of a mandatory land protection plan (LPP) three years later, a collection of land trusts sprang into action. Until the late 1980s, the NPS had no maps of land ownership at Gettysburg and no funds to make them. Lacking a land specialist, it struggled even to determine which parcels in the park were owned in fee and which were under easement. Eventually, local land trusts supplied the maps, and their support for NPS land acquisition became essential.

The Friends of the National Parks at Gettysburg (FNPG) was formed in 1989 to acquire land and easements and turn them over to the NPS. The organization is extremely focused. It holds no property and works only within the formal park boundaries. Starting with 100 members, the Friends now number more than 20,000. The group has been particularly effective in creating partnerships with other land trusts and in working with TCF and TCF funders at the Mellon Foundation to acquire a site critical to interpreting Pickett's Charge. The $1.2 million transaction enabled the Friends to hold the property until the NPS could purchase it—a classic preacquisition.[19]

The Friends' specific focus on the park led to the 1995 formation of the Land Conservancy of Adams County. The Conservancy works to protect farms and historic properties throughout the county and holds easements on 1,200 acres, all donated. Conservancy programs rely on the state's farmland protection plan, which is partially funded by the Conservation Reserve Program. The state program pays the full cost of establishing permanent grass cover on former cropland. At Gettysburg, the program has also been used to reestablish historic field patterns and wetlands destroyed by the NPS in the 1960s (U.S. NPS 2002a,b).

The Civil War Preservation Trust, an amalgamation of the Association for the Preservation of Civil War Sites and the Civil War Trust,[20] also works in Gettysburg and has protected 183 acres. In addition, a private group called Park Watch supports park management; 125 volunteers patrol the park, freeing rangers for other assignments. Finally, the park initiated a program that enlists individual volunteers or groups to care for portions of the battlefield. Members of the general public maintain more than 360 acres of the park (Platt 2001: 125ff). ·

The resulting mosaic at Gettysburg Battlefield is shown in figure 8.6. The map allows one to compare roughly the original Sickles concept with the smaller purchase boundaries authorized in 1990. It also indicates private lands that are a priority for NPS acquisition, NPS easement and fee holdings, and the larger historic district. Finally, it shows the roles played by the FNPG, the Gettysburg National Battlefield Museum Foundation, the Eisenhower National Historic Site, and conservation and agricultural easements held by the Land Conservancy of Adams County and the Adams County Agricultural Land Preservation Board.

What makes this map particularly informative is that it shows vividly the consequences of different institutional approaches to acquisition. Federal reluctance to use condemnation authority to acquire land threatened with development is clear. Much of the area deemed essential in 1895—particularly to the northwest and southwest of the town—is now developed. Even subsequent federal designations, although they may add to the ambience of the area and achieve other goals, do not address that problem. The Eisenhower historic site is not within the 1895 understanding of the park. Similarly, many of the land trust easements and acquisitions are not within the essential park area. Again, they meet other goals, but many central historic properties identified in 1895 remain unprotected.

It may be disturbing to those raised on a Progressive era ideology of federal ownership and management that the federal government cannot protect a national shrine like Gettysburg without all this private and local help. Nevertheless, Gettysburg suggests that some of those Progressive era assumptions are being called into question. While NPS involvement remains central, partnered tools for both land acquisition and land management are at work in even the most important national shrines, apparently with some success.

An NPS Land Trust to Manage Farming in Cuyahoga

An even more surprising collection of management tools has emerged in Ohio at what is now called Cuyahoga Valley National Park.[21] When the NPS initially applied its preferred "natural areas" management regime to

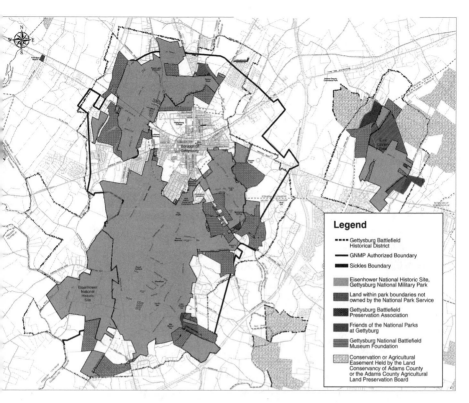

Figure 8.6
A comparison of current land ownership in Gettysburg National Military Park and approximate location of original Sickles map line. Source: Current map, Gettysburg National Military Park. The land's status was compiled from the current set of NPS segment maps. Property lines are based upon a combination of sources, the most reliable of which are GPS (global positioning system) measurements made at existing boundary monuments. The road edges were digitized by the NPS based upon Adams County digital ortho-photographs acquired in 1996. The Pennsylvania Agricultural Land Preservation Office provided digital files of easements held by them and the Land Conservancy of Adams County. Landprot111203.mxd was prepared by the U.S. NPS GNMP RPD GIS on November 12, 2003. Sickles map, National Park Service Technical Information Center Collection.

Cuyahoga, the result was to accelerate the decline of the very agricultural landscape the federal designation was intended to protect. By 2000, the CVNP encompassed 33,000 acres. The NPS owned 19,000 acres, of which only 450 acres were devoted to agricultural purposes. However, the land that the agency purchased with such controversy during the 1970s had turned into a mess of neglected fields and farm buildings (Kelsey 2002).

In response, the NPS developed a new plan to restore agricultural enterprise to the CVNP. The resulting "countryside initiative" was based on a CVNP study of British national parks, where active agriculture is integral to park management (Cuyahoga Valley National Park 2001; see also Gwin and Fairfax 2004). The initiative relies on a private, nonprofit land trust—The Cuyahoga Valley Countryside Conservancy (CVCC)—to exercise the agricultural expertise that the NPS lacks. The goal of the initiative is to rehabilitate and revitalize 30–35 farmsteads, resulting in some 1,500 acres of land in sustainable agriculture within the park boundaries.

The CVCC is funded, not by the NPS, but by private foundations and individuals interested in maintaining sustainable agricultural landscapes in parks. As an outsider, the Conservancy provides technical information on sustainable agriculture to both farmers and the Park Service. It is also a player in determining the park's management regime. The group helps the NPS prioritize rehabilitations of farm properties, recruit and evaluate prospective farm lessees, evaluate and monitor each farm's annual operating plan, and coordinate marketing strategies for the initiative. Without the land trust's expertise in sustainable agriculture and its aid to farmers trying to navigate the NPS bureaucracy, the Cuyahoga countryside initiative would be unimaginable.

A vital CVCC innovation has been long-term (up to fifty years) farm leases with the NPS in order to secure tenure for farmers and the possibility for them to build limited equity. The leases are transferable, subject to approval by park administrators. The rent includes a 50 percent discount on residences because of the loss of privacy inherent in living in a national park. Farmers also pay below-market rent on agricultural lands because they must comply with additional NPS requirements and approved sustainable production practices. An additional rent reduction is available for certified organic producers. Because the sustainable practices will require the farmers to create new retail markets for their products, rent is also discounted during the first ten years of a farm's operation.

The farms, ranging in size from 12 to 61 acres, are suitable for intensive fruit and vegetable production, intensively managed grazing operations, and integrated livestock enterprises. Although certified organic production is favored, it is not required, and noncertified organic production systems are also expected to operate using the same sustainable farming concepts. It is expected that countryside initiative farms will produce high-quality specialty products for local retail sale. Marketing options include pick-your-own crops, community-supported agriculture, local farmers' markets, and direct sales to individuals and restaurants.

The project requires the NPS to rethink its management of resources that are simultaneously natural and cultural (Watt 2001), and it will be a challenge to integrate the initiative into the agency's bureaucracy. Nevertheless, in the most optimistic scenario, the initiative could restore 10 percent of the federal lands within the park to farming. The model may also be transferable to other park units, such as Sleeping Bear Dunes (Michigan), the Delaware Water Gap (Pennsylvania), Point Reyes National Seashore (California), and the Buffalo National River (Arkansas), which include large, formerly agricultural landscapes. Moreover, the experiment may provide a model for moving land trust objectives in preserving agricultural land toward the promotion of sustainable farming.

Redwood National and State Parks

Management arrangements at Redwood National Park took off in an equally innovative direction, even as public and private acquisitions continued. Both the 1968 and 1978 park bills contemplated that the NPS would ultimately take over the existing state parks. Subsequent negotiations got so close to an agreement in the mid-1980s that state park employees actually bought NPS uniforms, and the NPS director arrived for a transfer ceremony. However, at the last minute, the NPS rejected the transfer for reasons that are not known (to us). Thereafter, the relationship between state and federal managers ebbed and flowed, depending on the personnel involved.

In 1994, the state and federal governments signed a memorandum of understanding (MOU) establishing joint management of what is now officially called Redwood National and State Parks. The agreement was unpopular with many oldtimers and resulted in a number of resignations and retirements. However, after a rocky start, the two agencies have adopted a common logo, put both state and federal names on the park map (which nonetheless reflects the familiar NPS "unigrid" format), moved into shared office space, and, perhaps most notably, comingled management funds.

The Save-the-Redwoods League continues to work with the state under this new arrangement. And in spite of the apparent federal take-over of acquisitions in the area (the Headwaters Forest is only a few miles south), the League has steadily continued to buy land in the area. In 2003 the group and the state met a long-standing goal by procuring 25,000 acres in the Mill Creek area, including two complete watersheds, for which the League put up $15 million and the state paid the rest. As part of the acquisition, the state (rather than Congress) agreed to a one-time $5 million PILT payment for Del Norte County (half what the county asked for), which went from 75 percent publicly owned land before the transaction to 78 percent afterward.

We have already noted economists' concerns that public purchases will "crowd out" private efforts at resource protection, squelching them when private groups could do the job better at a lower cost. However, the Redwoods story provides an important counter to the assertion that federal acquisition discourages private efforts. Figure 8.7 shows that the steady accumulation of acres acquired with the participation of the League was not dampened by large federal condemnations in 1968 and 1978, or by a smaller TCF-to-federal preacquisition in 1994. Nor does the federal government dominate the League's program in total acres acquired. Both the League and the state fought NPS involvement in the area, but even after large federal acquisitions in 1968 and 1978, they have held the line against a federal takeover. Instead, they continue to help build the mosaic of conservation in the redwoods that they began assembling more than eighty years ago.

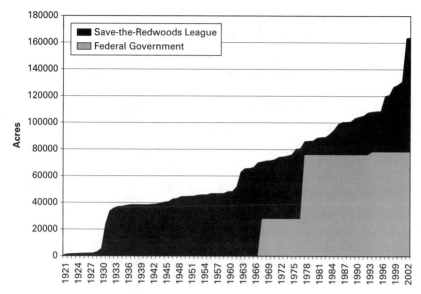

Figure 8.7
Cumulative federal and League acquisitions of land in the Redwoods. The data include land initially purchased by the League and now in state ownership. They also include some lands outside the boundaries of the parks. Source: Data courtesy of the Save-the-Redwoods League. Reproduced with permission. © Permission required for reprint, sale, or commercial use. Contact the Save-the-Redwoods League.

Needed: Funding and Attention to Small Urban Parcels

Land protection in urban areas and for urban people has not attracted such durable attention. Since the LWCF state program collapsed, neither the federal government nor the land trust movement has focused on urban acquisitions. In a movement that emphasizes the number of acres protected, urban plots do not show well in LTA statistics. A citywide effort of decades might protect less than 50 or 100 acres. And the low income and minority communities served by such deals are conspicuously absent from the land trust movement. As a result, urban land conservation is not at present a major part of the story of acquisitions for conservation.

Nevertheless, a quarter of an acre can be a precious space in a dense urban setting, and there are a few exceptional programs that recognize this fact. Some are quite venerable. The Pennsylvania Horticultural

Society (PHS, founded 1827) began to establish neighborhood gardens in Philadelphia in the 1940s by investing returns from its annual flower show in Philadelphia's inner city. There is little problem here with the high costs of acquisition; more than 50,000 vacant parcels are available in the city for next to nothing. Paradoxically, the gardens improve neighborhoods and make them more attractive for development, which can then threaten the original conservation effort. In response, the Neighborhood Gardens Association (a project of Philadelphia Green, itself a project of the PHS) incorporated in 1986 to protect many of those gardens and open spaces as they later became threatened by rising property values in the immediate neighborhood.

Similarly, in 1978 TPL began working with neighborhood groups and a city government program, Green Thumb, to establish and protect urban gardens in New York City. The total acreage is again small; more than 1,000 gardens occupy less than 125 acres of vacant land owned by the city. Many of the same groups have worked with Green Thumb to train local gardeners and to provide tools, plants, and equipment, as well as labor to build growing beds, picnic tables, gazebos, and grape arbors (Trust for Public Land 2001: 5).

The program came under attack in 1998 when Mayor Rudy Giuliani decided to sell off 114 of the city-owned garden sites. In response, TPL purchased sixty-two plots, and a group founded by singer Bette Midler acquired the rest. TPL remains part of a continuing alliance of local groups working to protect the gardens and developing borough-wide land trusts to manage them. TPL will continue to own the sites until those organizations are up and running, and it provides guidance on issues such as payment of taxes, maintenance and liability insurance, and dealing with neighboring landowners and the city.

A small and equally challenging effort in Madison, Wisconsin, provides another example of how land trusts could play a more active role in urban areas. In the Troy Gardens project, the Madison Area Community Land Trust (MACLT) teamed with local residents to protect an urban garden threatened by a residential subdivision. Unable to fund the purchase and protection of the land any other way, the mostly Hmong gardeners working the site reluctantly agreed to work with a community land trust, which implies that one element of the project would be to develop affordable housing (Davis, J. E. and Demetrozitz 2003). The MACLT is now developing affordable housing on a 5-acre portion of the gardens while leaving approximately three-quarters of the parcel in open space that contains a community garden, prairie restoration, recreation space, and an organic community farm (Rosenberg 2004).

Some believe that the relationship between conservation land trusts and community land trusts like MACLT is merely semantic, but organizations like the newly constituted Black Family Land Trust (BFLT) link the two. It helps African-American families in the southern United States hold on to land on which title has been confused by generations of intestate inheritance. This requires establishing clear title for the heirs without forcing them to accept full market control over the land. Like conservation land trusts, the BFLT aims to help the heirs to enjoy the economic advantages of ownership without necessarily having to sell the land. Land trust tools could assist in that process, and professionals interested in diversifying the movement should find ways to collaborate with organizations like the BFLT.

However, it is not clear that the LTA is at present configured to support urban and minority efforts. For example, many in the urban garden and community land trust movements note that LTA rallies offer little that is of use to them. Meanwhile, the land trust movement continues to be predominantly white and explicitly antiurban, which seems neither laudable nor politically prudent. Nonetheless, it is heartening that a few organizations have moved beyond these unfortunate boundaries. We believe their work is critical to the future of the land trust movement.

Reality Check: The CARA Experience at the Century's End

During the brief and heady days of the federal budget surplus, Congress considered, and the House passed by an impressive majority, an astounding package of financial support for land conservation and acquisition. The Conservation and Reinvestment Act was initially aimed at ensuring reliable funding for the LWCF, particularly for the state and local side of the program. Over time the bill grew to authorize an appropriation of $3.1 billion in acquisition funds every year for fifteen years.

The idea took off when the LWCF refurbishment idea was united with long-standing state efforts to share in revenue from the outer continental shelf oil program, which was bulging with cash at the time.[22] In short, the "CARA coalition" represented an impressive alliance of wildlife advocates, county and state officials, land trusts, and environmental groups. The bill looked unstoppable.

CARA represented a potential revolution in federal land acquisition and a repudiation of the Farm Bill approach of tying acquisition funds to commercial subsidies. It would have established the LWCF as a special fund exempt from the annual appropriation process; allowed federal agencies to address a $10 billion backlog of authorized but unfunded acquisitions; permitted LWCF funds to be spent on reducing a $15 billion backlog of maintenance and restoration projects on federally owned lands; expanded funding for resource protection programs; and supplemented the Pittman-Robertson fund with a reliable source of support for state nongame wildlife programs.

What, one might wonder, would induce the House of Representatives to support such huge spending exempt from annual congressional oversight? "Sweeteners" were crucial. First, CARA proposed funding for mitigating onshore impacts of offshore oil development. Second, it would have increased federal payments to local governments, promising permanent appropriations for the PILTs program. Finally, some versions of CARA would have required that an environmental impact statement accompany every federal land purchase, thereby slowing the pace of acquisitions.[23]

Those juicy enticements were enough to convince the House, but despite its broad coalition of supporters, CARA never even got to the Senate floor. A compromise, frequently called "CARA Light," was passed in its place. CARA Light talked big—about $12 billion in acquisition funding over six years—but did not tie the authorizations to actual appropriations beyond the first year. A brief effort to revive the initial CARA proposal died in the new Bush administration. While property rights activists are frequently credited with the defeat of CARA, the bill's failure also illustrates the continuing reluctance of Congress to give up control over annual appropriations.

Table 8.3
State and Local Elections Supporting Land Acquisition and Amounts Authorized, 2000–2003

| Year | Conservation Ballot Measures | | Total (billion $) |
	No. Passed	% Passed	
2000	174 of 207	84	$4.3
2001	137 of 196	70	$1.6
2002	141 of 190	74	$5.4
2003	100 of 134	75	$1.3

Source: Trust for Public Land and Land Trust Alliance (2000–2003).

The story does not end there, however. As CARA went down to defeat, and federal acquisition funds became more and more tied to Farm Bill programs, voters in the states moved to replace the divots. Despite their success opposing CARA, property rights advocates have failed to stop state and local funding measures. In fact, wide, deep, and reliable support for conservation acquisition programs exists at the local level. As table 8.3 shows, year after year, states and localities pass referenda to support acquisition and conservation of open space, wetlands, watersheds, recreation areas, and wildlife habitat by approving bond issues, sales, property, and excise taxes, and authorizations for specific land purchases (Land Trust Alliance 2001b; see also Trust for Public Land and Land Trust Alliance 2000–2003).

This disconnect between regional and national outcomes underscores the fact that the federal government has been most supportive of land acquisition for conservation in the context of subsidizing agriculture. States and localities apparently have a different perspective. The disconnect also confirms the dramatic rebalancing and sharing of responsibilities between government agencies and nonprofits; many of the state and local funds will flow through local land trusts on their way to buying new parcels and easements. What this blending of public funds and private transactions means for future developments is less clear, and a reading of available tea leaves has been blurred by the second Bush administration's clear hostility to environmental issues of all stripes. However, the enduring popularity of these local measures makes it seem likely that conservation acquisitions will avoid becoming an adjunct to the policy of agricultural price supports.

Summary

The 1990s marked the maturation of the land trust movement and the full flowering of mosaics on protected lands. In the Northern Forest, massive acquisition deals led to complicated new arrangements of ownership and control on conservation properties. Similar mosaics helped resolve conflicts in more traditional settings such as Gettysburg Battlefield, where advocates had been arguing about acquisition issues for more than a hundred years. Similarly, land trusts were increasingly integrated into the management of acquired lands, even helping to run NPS programs in Cuyahoga Valley National Park. Everywhere one looks, it seems, record-breaking acquisitions of unprecedented complexity are taking place. We have come a long way indeed from Ann Pamela Cunningham's purchase of George Washington's home.

Peaking at more than 1,200 groups, the land trust movement finally stopped growing in numbers during the 1990s, even as trusts continued to acquire a record number of acres. Taken collectively, national, regional, and local land trusts are now operating at approximately the same scale as the federal government in the area of conservation acquisitions. Indeed, the Northern Forest transactions resemble in many ways the Weeks Act acquisitions of the early twentieth century, except that the lands acquired and protected contain fewer inholdings.

But the federal government has not disappeared from the scene. Congress undertook some of the most expensive purchases in history in the late 1990s, and agencies exploited its increasing tolerance of exchanges to acquire huge tracts of land "off the books." This type of federal funding for acquisition remains bountiful, CARA's demise in 2000 notwithstanding.

Much federal land acquisition is now tied directly—if less explicitly than during the Depression—to economic development via the Farm Bill and similar statues. The federal land exchange program and the growing link between land conservation and support for industrial agriculture is not as odd as it sounds given our history, but it is disquieting to many in the field.

Looking at both federal and private acquisitions in this period, we find no evidence that private efforts are being crowded out by public ones. A more accurate picture is that as Congress becomes ever more enamored of acquisition through exchanges and farm subsidies, the land trusts are holding onto the coattails of the federal agencies, trying to keep them active in actual conservation. Failing that, private groups are proving to be quite effective at using the federal dollars that are indirectly available, through tax benefits and similar incentives, to achieve their preferred conservation purposes. In all these efforts, the work of public and private actors has become ever more interwoven, leading to a steady blurring of the distinction between public and private.

The losers in all this are the urban poor, who historically have enjoyed considerable federal support for parks, trails, and recreation facilities. Congress has cut those programs, and the states and localities have not replaced them. Nor have land trusts moved aggressively to take up the slack. This is deeply unfortunate and poses a significant challenge to land acquisition advocates in the twenty-first century.

9

Conclusions

If Mount Vernon was the right place to start our story, the Cosumnes Preserve in northern California seems an ideal place to end it. Complex mosaics are the signature feature of modern land acquisition, and Cosumnes is state of the art. Many miles from the nearest BLM enclave, a full-time BLM employee manages the preserve for an extraordinary array of conservation landowners (Graziano 1993: 89–90; Eaton and Cooper 1997). Using Farm Bill funds, BLM land exchanges, and almost every other land acquisition fund and tool we have discussed, the partners have protected approximately 40,000 acres of threatened wetlands south of Sacramento in California's Central Valley.[1]

The preserve is home to the largest valley oak riparian forest in the world and is one of the few protected wetland habitats in the state. Its grasslands, vernal pools, and marshes make it a critical stop on the Pacific flyway for migrating and wintering waterfowl. More than 200 species of birds have been sighted on or near the preserve, including Swainson's hawks, sandhill cranes, and white-fronted geese (U.S. BLM 2004).

It was the water, however, that first attracted the federal government's interest. In the 1950s and 1960s, the Bureau of Reclamation eyed the Upper Cosumnes River as a site for thirteen dams, with intensive wildlife management and recreation on the waterway's lower reaches (now included in the preserve) proposed as mitigation. Somewhat surprisingly, the mitigation plan rather than the dams aroused public opposition and derailed the project. Consequently, the Cosumnes is the only free-flowing river remaining in the Central Valley.

The California Department of Parks and Recreation fared little better with a 1970s proposal to create a state park. Although funding for the necessary acquisitions was already available under a state bond measure, locals again protested. Aggrieved by the lack of advance notice that their land was about to be included in the new park, property owners threatened to clear their impressive stands of valley oaks before the plans could come to fruition. In the face of such resistance, State Parks followed the Bureau of Reclamation and backed off.

When TNC showed up in the mid-1980s to work with willing sellers on just a few small acquisitions, the reception was somewhat warmer. The group soon recognized the Cosumnes as a major biodiversity resource and expanded its acquisition program in the area. The BLM became involved in 1987, as part of its participation in the North American Waterfowl Management Plan, to acquire and restore habitat for waterfowl populations. Initially the agency exchanged scattered BLM parcels in the Sierra foothills for land near existing TNC holdings in Cosumnes. The BLM then directly acquired several parcels using LWCF funds and became more actively involved in the growing partnership.

Farm Bill programs have been an important source of acquisition dollars at Cosumnes. Both the BLM and TNC have used money from the Wetlands Reserve Program to acquire farmland easements. The county became involved as a landowner when TNC helped it apply for Farm Bill grants for habitat acquisition. As local farmers became accustomed to the idea that bird habitat was compatible with profitable farming (the migratory waterfowl move on just when it becomes possible to farm on the floodplain), they became receptive to restoration projects. TNC easements lowered land prices and allowed both established and new farmers to acquire farmland in the preserve (Eaton and Cooper 1997).

The BLM manager collects and distributes revenues for all the other preserve owners. TNC pays $10,000 of the BLM manager's salary and shares the cost of a site coordinator with Ducks Unlimited, while the county parks department provides ranger patrols and interpretation. Thus as figure 9.1 shows, the Cosumnes is an excellent example of the postmodern approach to land conservation: a mosaic of protected lands assembled by diverse partners using a complex array of tools, agreements, and funding sources.[2]

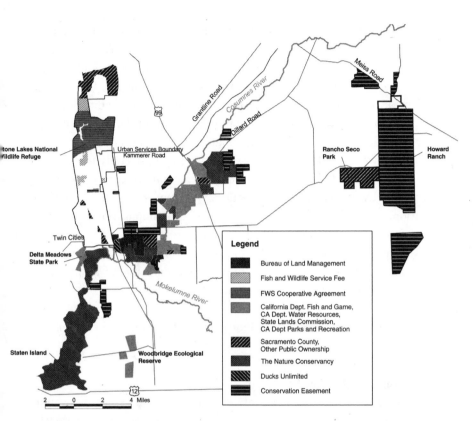

Figure 9.1
Location and mosaic of land protection in the Cosumnes River project area.
Source: Created with the assistance of the Nature Conservancy. Reproduced
with permission.

Although both Cosumnes and Mount Vernon are prominent examples
of successful acquisitions, neither supports the idea that ownership is
an easy or reliable approach to land conservation. "Just buying it" was
difficult for the MVLA in 1856 and did not fully protect Washington's
estate over the long haul. Since then, conservation acquisitions have only
become more complex, as the mosaic of ownership and control arrangements at Cosumnes suggests.[3] Landowners and resource users regularly
contest conservation acquisitions, irrespective of who does the buying.
And just like much-disparaged regulatory tools, both full fee and easement acquisitions raise significant enforcement and management issues.

Partnerships like the Cosumnes are not without precedent. We think here of the long and productive cooperation between The Trustees of Reservations and the state and localities in Massachusetts, and between the Save-the-Redwoods League and the state in California. But management of contemporary mosaics continues to become more intricate.

Our conclusions are therefore complex as well. In the next section we summarize the story we have told, highlighting connections between the changes we have described—in who acquires what lands using which tools—and the drivers of those changes: changing economic conditions combined with evolving ideas about government, property, and conservation. In the third section we reflect upon the implications of our account for persistent myths in conservation policy and for assessing the effectiveness of land acquisition for conservation. Finally, we offer some concluding thoughts about how to transcend the limits of a bucks-and-acres approach to land conservation.

Creating Mosaics: Land Acquisition for Conservation in the United States

Acquisition Before the Civil War

Contrary to the idea that private conservation is a recent innovation, antebellum groups of citizens regularly pursued what are now considered public goals of honoring national heroes and completing historic memorials. The federal government demurred on buying Mount Vernon in part because its authorities over land at that time were weak. Indeed, Congress originally intended to transfer nearly all public lands into private ownership as rapidly as possible. Early federal acquisitions were limited to transactions under the enclave clause for "needful buildings" and the capital, or under the war powers for defense and expressions of nationhood. Trying to imagine a private group buying and preserving Washington's estate today or building a monument in his honor on the National Mall demonstrates how perceptions of the government's proper role in such activities have changed. However, in our first century, public acquisitions for conservation were rare.

The few early conservation efforts by the government were linked to nation building. Acquisition or reservation of historic sites designed to inspire national pride and patriotism were common, as well as acquisition of other properties with military value, such as the naval reserves. Acquisition for scenery or outdoor recreation was rarely discussed, and the notion of conservation as an ecological priority awaited future developments. Nevertheless, in the earliest acquisitions and reservations for naval timber and for medicinal benefits (at Hot Springs, Arkansas), we observe a durable pattern. Federal conservation for utilitarian goals such as timber production proceeds under general authorities whereas efforts to protect scenery and ecological values face greater scrutiny and require unit-by-unit authorization.

Willing sellers were a necessary precondition for nearly all conservation acquisitions in this period. Mount Vernon only came on the market when Washington's heir fell on hard times, and the federal power of eminent domain was still forty to fifty years from being ratified by the Supreme Court. Hence this era exhibits a strong reliance on private acquisitions of land, combined with public reservations of property that never left the public domain.

That said, although Lockean ideas that give preference to private ownership dominated the political and economic landscape, assertions of public land ownership frequently were not "persuasive," to paraphrase Carol Rose. Land and timber speculators plundered New York state, taking title only to strip the land and abandon it to state ownership. Similar stories were played out on federal lands. Easements and partial estates were also rare, awaiting the bundle-of-sticks metaphor of the late nineteenth century. Nevertheless, although mosaics were as yet relatively simple, Bunker Hill, Mount Vernon, and the Washington Monument were all conserved by a mix of public and private actors.

Expanding Federal Authorities and Programs, 1865–1952

After the Civil War, rapid industrial expansion and the development of a more powerful national identity gave new direction and momentum to public reservations and acquisitions. Conservation efforts were marked by an expanding federal role, leading first to broad reservations of land in the West and then outright purchases in the East. New interpretations of the Constitution underwrote this change, giving the federal government authorities over land that had been previously exercised only by states. Private efforts did not disappear, however, even in this era of federal ascension. Private philanthropy was vital to the expansion of the national park system in the East, often with the support of new private conservation groups. The Trustees organized in Massachusetts, for example, the same year (1891) that Congress authorized the president to reserve forests from the public domain.

In fact, private individuals and states continued to make many key nineteenth-century acquisitions, including many Civil War battlefields. Eventually the national government became involved, acquiring land at Gettysburg in a transaction that led the Supreme Court to confirm the federal power of eminent domain under the war powers. Conservation of Civil War sites remains a public-private partnership to this day, neither exclusively nor even primarily a federal project. Commissions of private citizens who had fought in the war were central to managing the acquired lands, a pattern of private oversight of public acquisition efforts that continues in the present.

Federal acquisitions truly picked up steam under the direction of Teddy Roosevelt and Gifford Pinchot in the early twentieth century. New initiatives were undertaken by federal agencies that were initially established to manage reserved public domain land. An expanding concept of valid conservation goals justified many of the purchases. Rather than national pride and historic preservation, Pinchot's philosophy favoring public, scientific management of natural resources paved the way for new acquisitions of forests and watersheds rather than battlefields and presidential estates. The Supreme Court supported this Progressive doctrine in a key series of decisions ratifying federal power over public land (*Camfield, Light,* and *Grimaud*). In the process, restrictions on federal acquisition authorities described in the enclave clause largely faded. However, residual effects remained, including jurisdictional bargaining between state and federal governments over acquired lands that allowed the states to retain many of the benefits of ownership while passing the burdens to the national government.

Despite the expanding federal powers, many nominally public lands remained substantially beyond the government's control. In some cases, local residents simply ignored unpersuasive public claims of ownership. California's protection of Yosemite was so expensive and yet inadequate that the state ceded it back to the federal government (Runte 1979: 57), while destructive timber harvesting in the Adirondacks continued well after the state's "forever wild" constitutional amendment. The army was the only organization available to protect Yellowstone from depredations intensified by its protected status. In general, states and private users made sure to retain key sticks in the bundle of property rights, such as taxation, exclusion, and use, on land legally owned by the federal government.

Nevertheless, many conservation advocates continued to seek public ownership, in part because government regulatory authorities over the use of private land remained largely undefined. The Weeks Act in 1911 was a key moment in this process, authorizing the USFS to acquire private land for watershed protection. Between 1911 and 1929, more than 3 million acres of largely industrial holdings were purchased under the statute. Again, a separate, independent commission oversaw the selection of parcels; Congress did not wholly trust the agency to do so itself. The program avoided condemnation, giving landowners control over what property wound up in federal ownership, and the terms of the act were extraordinarily generous to the seller. Consequently, the eastern national forests constitute a patchwork of public and private lands, averaging only about 50 percent federal ownership.

Our "seller controls" assertion is less clearly applicable to the southeastern national parks that emerged in the 1920s. Again, an external commission supervised the acquisitions. The purchases involved removing many Appalachian smallholders, whose land was usually condemned by the states under highway construction authority before the farmers knew that a park was headed their way. The resulting conflict put park management under a cloud of local resentment that remains an issue to this day. Moreover, the NPS quest for exclusive jurisdiction over its properties and the removal of all inholders created enduring conflict with surrounding communities. By the 1970s, even park boosters had reconsidered their enthusiasm for park units in light of these difficulties.

If willing sellers were rare in the southeastern parks, they were ubiquitous in other Depression-era acquisitions. Federal acquisitions peaked during the 1930s; almost half of all federally acquired lands were purchased during this period of economic crisis. Conservation priorities were secondary; much of the land was purchased mainly to take it out of production or to provide employment for CCC crews. Most of it was in the East and South and wound up in national forests. During this period, the federal government simply could not buy land fast enough to meet the demands of desperate landowners. More than 25 million acres were purchased between the stock market crash of 1929 and the end of World War II.

Nor were private acquisition efforts crowded out by this federal buying spree. Private conservation, particularly of historic homes, intensified with donations to The Trustees of Reservations being a prominent example. Many private owners, large and small alike, could not pay their taxes and gave up their land to conservation organizations either in foreclosures or by donation. Even the Pells were financially strapped and established a public charity to own and manage Fort Ticonderoga.

Depression-era acquisitions reflected new ideas about property. Lockean ideas of ownership were nearing their low point. However, expanded federal ownership continued to encompass varying degrees of effective control. Although the days of widespread trespass and squatting were over, federal agencies did not retain full control over "their" land. Within western grazing districts in particular, federal control was highly compromised by the substantial private claims of ranchers and mineral developers. Split estates and other partial ownership interests in land increased the complexity. Although conservation easements were not yet common, the FWS used them to create refuges in the upper Midwest without dislodging local farmers, and the NPS developed the Blue Ridge Parkway by acquiring scenic easements as well, again complicating the nature of ownership on public lands. A pattern of mosaics was beginning to become clear, particularly on lands in formal public ownership.

The Environmental Era and the Modern Land Trust Movement, 1953–2004

In the economic boom that followed World War II, federal purchases continued, for new purposes but without the urgency of the Depression. The federal government moved to meet the outdoor recreation demands of newly prosperous Americans enjoying unprecedented amounts of leisure time and disposable income. In 1964, the Land and Water Conservation Fund Act codified land acquisition for scenery and recreation as a legitimate federal purpose. At the same time, Congress began to authorize NPS acquisition of diverse new units, even by condemnation. Ironically, the consensus supporting federal acquisition began to erode just as its legal and funding authority was clearly established.

As the "parks for the people" program took root during the Civil Rights era, many new federal units were created in urban areas. Some of these urban experiments—notably in St. Louis and the much-contested acquisitions in the Cuyahoga Valley—were initially fiascos. Others were positive examples of how federal/local partnerships and mixed ownership regimes can result in promising forms of land conservation. Nevertheless, many traditional NPS supporters and employees questioned the wisdom of expanding the agency's mission into suburban and urban areas. Almost inevitably, as the NPS moved into residential areas, relying heavily on condemnations, a backlash resulted. By the late-1970s that option was once again largely off the table.

The NPS was not the only government agency getting into hot water. Despite the multiple-use mandates of the era, the BLM and the USFS were widely viewed as being "in bed" with commodity interests. At the same time, more public rights were exercised on private property. A major suite of federal land use regulations—particularly the Endangered Species Act and the Clean Air and Clean Water acts—weakened the effective control of many private property owners. Media coverage of the Sagebrush Rebellion briefly obscured the quiet emergence of land trusts (as well as a rival property rights movement), and anger against federal authority boiled over.

When Ronald Reagan was elected on an antigovernment, antiregulatory agenda in 1980, both acquisition of public land and regulation on private land took a major hit. Indeed, in a remarkable reversal, land disposition reappeared on the policy agenda while several Supreme Court decisions appeared to reassert traditional Lockean notions of strong private ownership rights. As federal acquisition lost steam, land trusts multiplied and began filling the gap. Despite the setbacks to federal efforts, however, Reagan's attempts to sell off the federal estate failed, and Congress continued to devote significant resources to acquiring land under the LWCF and under new sources like the 1985 Farm Bill.

The Reagan years thrust private land trusts into the spotlight. This was not only because of growing hostility to all things federal; emerging science and advocacy now argued that conservation efforts limited to publicly owned parcels were inadequate. As it became apparent that private lands provided many vital ecological services, including critical habitat for many endangered species, the policy emphasis gradually moved toward preserving entire ecosystems of public and private property. Land trusts emerged as partners who could work more effectively than federal agencies on the private land part of the equation.

Thus, federal managers began calling on TNC, TPL, and TCF when they wanted to acquire a key parcel. Changes in federal tax law and state property law regarding conservation easements, combined with Farm Bill funds, provided essential government support for acquisitions by land trusts. Without such changes, the rapid growth of the land trust movement is unimaginable. By 2003, regional and local conservation groups had used their diverse tools, including conservation easements, to protect more than 16 million acres through voluntary donations or sales.

The result? The strong links between formal ownership and effective control are eroding on private lands even as they did on the public estate a hundred years ago. Many conserved landscapes are now a hodgepodge of public and private claims. On the one hand, willing seller acquisitions dot the landscape with parcels under varying ownership arrangements and degrees of environmental protection. On the other, federal and local land use regulations continue to impose conservation restrictions on private properties. This has produced mosaics of breathtaking complexity, bred substantially by acquisition strategies reputed to offer a "simpler" answer to conservation concerns.

The national land trusts—TNC, TPL, and TCF—have provided the framework in which many of these transactions have occurred. Yet, as the second Bush administration's hostility to environmental protection has taken hold, the local roots of the movement are proving vital. It is of more than symbolic importance that as the phenomenal CARA funding proposals died in Congress, states and localities continued to support funding for conservation acquisitions.

Land Acquisition: Myths, Realities, and Limits

A major goal of this volume has been to examine a neglected and misunderstood aspect of U.S. environmental policy: the use of land acquisition as a conservation strategy. In doing so, we have encountered persistent myths regarding that history. These misunderstandings have contributed to expectations that acquisition is an innovative and much-to-be preferred approach to conservation. Our story suggests, on the contrary, that there are significant limits to what acquisition can accomplish. We revisit and summarize these myths and limits here.

First, we urge dispensing with a pair of overarching misconceptions. It is well past time to abandon the assumptions and vocabulary of the familiar "acquire, dispose, retain" triptych regarding public lands. Besides obscuring the wide range of actual government control over nominally retained lands, the idea also ignores the public acquisition of millions of acres of land that continues today. At the same time, we also see a need to discard a newer, parallel idea: that acquisition of private land for conservation is a late twentieth-century innovation. It is not, as the managers of Mount Vernon, Fort Ticonderoga, and other national treasures would gladly explain. While private conservation groups clearly expanded in scope and strength in the decades following World War II, their actions were not unprecedented. Indeed, some of the most durable private conservation organizations predate both modern land trusts and the federal conservation agencies by half a century or more.

Second, the steady blurring of boundaries between public and private conservation programs is too frequently neglected. The myth of a clean and simple division between public and private makes it easy to leap to familiar conclusions: Public lands provide communal goods and belong to every citizen equally, while private lands are largely exempt from public control. In fact, neither public nor private modern conservation efforts fit cleanly in either category, and it is not clear that they ever did. A protected landscape like the Cosumnes is neither public (BLM) nor private (TNC). It is a mosaic of private, working farmland mixed with state and municipal properties, all supported by a number of voluntary non-profit groups. Split estates in the form of easements create multiple owners even on many individual parcels.

The misapplication of the terms *public* and *private* is not just a semantic problem. The myth that private acquisition transactions are located outside the public sphere creates serious barriers to public accountability. We therefore regret the wilder rhetoric of the property rights movement because we find their complaints regarding inadequate public discussion of private acquisitions to be right on target. The proliferation and fragmentation of such transactions among more than 1,600 land trusts nationally only exacerbates the issue. Assuredly, when federal agencies are major players, the deals are subject to at least nominal public review and sometimes even intense congressional scrutiny. When state funds are appropriated for a transaction, as in the Northern Forest acquisitions, citizens are also generally able to make themselves heard, however formulaically, through hearings and other traditional channels. Nevertheless, in transactions that are presented as private, expectations regarding public comment are unclear and frequently sacrificed to the momentum of the deal.

Third, the history of public and private acquisition "victories" needs to be reassessed in light of our assertion that sellers have driven much of the process. Doing this underscores our conclusion that government programs do not generally crowd out private acquisition efforts. More typically, federal agencies serve as buyers of convenience where the private sector, frequently for good reason, does not act. There is a consolation prize of sorts. Many federally acquired properties were initially uninspiring, yet have been converted by careful management and evolving public expectations into productive and deeply cherished lands. Eastern national forests and the national grasslands are good examples of this. However, we should not deceive ourselves into thinking that the government controls the public acquisition agenda.

Fourth, even if we could move beyond the dominance of willing sellers, it is quite apparent that we neither can nor should "buy" our way out of all or even most of our conservation problems. That we cannot do so is evident from recent, expensive acquisitions of old-growth redwoods in California and prime real estate in New Mexico. At prices close to $100,000 per acre, deals like the Headwaters are going to be few and far between. The demise of CARA only emphasizes the point that federal funds for such acquisitions are likely to remain limited.

Perhaps more important, even if we could print enough money, it would be an error to do so. An undue reliance on acquisition, particularly to avoid the messy and unpopular process of enforcing regulations, is a grave error. Land ownership entails both rights and responsibilities, and it includes at a minimum the duty to avoid harming one's neighbors. The more society compensates landowners for conservation, the more landowners will sensibly conclude that in the absence of such payments, they are entitled to develop their parcels to the detriment of society.

This strengthening of ownership "rights" is similar to the problem of moral hazard in insurance and risk analysis. If we lower the personal costs of engaging in environmentally risky or damaging behavior, we will be sure to get more of exactly the behavior we do not want. This is why deductibles make sense in insurance policies, and why at least some risk of uncompensated regulation is essential in conserving land (Sax 1971a; 1993).

Finally, we return to the most fundamental limit of all: Ownership does not ensure control. The relevant myth here suggests that if you own land, you can protect it. The reality, repeated throughout our story, is that formal ownership frequently provides little control or resource protection at all. This is particularly true on federally owned land, despite federal ownership being commonly portrayed as the preferred tenure arrangement for conservation. In this volume we have described public reservations and acquisitions that allowed looting of naval stores and required the army to restore order in Yosemite and Yellowstone. Lest we dismiss this all as ancient history, current examples include an uncoordinated response to multiple threats in Gettysburg and along the Blue Ridge Parkway, not to mention farms left to fall in ruins within Cuyahoga Valley National Park. Moreover, states and private interests have been quite effective in skimming off the benefits of land ownership while leaving federal owners (and taxpayers) with many of the burdens.

Private conservation owners may control their property more successfully than the government, but Mount Vernon and Fort Ticonderoga demonstrate how difficult it is to maintain even a small estate in the face of encroaching urban forces. In short, there is a growing divide between legal title and effective control on both public and private lands, and rapidly fragmenting mosaics of public and private claims have only widened the gap. In this age of mosaics, acquisition is simply not "the answer" to the conservation question, if indeed it ever was. Many resources, we conclude, are better protected at less cost and with less difficulty through regulation or other options besides purchase.

Expanding the Limits: Going Beyond "Buying Nature"

Having spent considerable effort describing the limits, myths, and generally checkered history of acquisition policy, it seems only fair to spend a few pages reflecting on how we might move beyond the alluring simplicity of just buying it. In doing so, we are acutely aware of the risks. Far too many studies do an admirable job deconstructing existing policy options only to promulgate even more lamentable alternatives as an afterthought. In many cases, we think, it would be better to leave the recommendations out entirely. Yet we resist doing so here, partly out of hubris no doubt, but also because we have benefited from so many worthwhile ideas and suggestions from people working in the field. While we recognize the limits of our own expertise, failing to bring those ideas together would be unfair to the practitioners who take the time to educate academics.

We begin then by reiterating a basic point of our analysis: Holding formal title to land is less important to its conservation than is frequently supposed. Thus, the critical question is not whether to acquire land; it is how to identify the most effective tools for encouraging, limiting, conditioning, or prohibiting particular land uses. Sometimes the answer is acquisition, but more often, we conclude, it is not. A host of regulatory options are available to direct land use without transferring title.

Even if we are correct in our assertion that ownership is not the sine qua non of land conservation success, we must think about when, where, and how acquisition *is* a good idea. Cynical readers might conclude that the major benefits are pecuniary and narrowly distributed— greater cash flow for well-connected (or lucky) private landowners— but that is too glib. Targeted and partial acquisition can make new controls over private land politically palatable. This is not a trivial outcome; during eras of Lockean ascendance such as our own, it may be essential.

In addition, while ownership does not lead to undisputed control, it may strengthen it. Land acquisitions have protected numerous parcels, large and small, public and private, that would likely have been degraded if conservationists had waited for development of local land use plans and regulations. In Gettysburg, a clear government acquisition plan in concert with local land trusts and related support groups has allowed the nation to impose its preferences on a community of largely reluctant local, small landowners. And the Save-the-Redwoods League has pushed for comprehensive state planning and management.

But palatable or not, acquisition is simply too expensive to be more than a minor player in land conservation. Thus, we must consider carefully where and when to spend our scarce acquisition dollars. We organize our thoughts on this matter around the three questions structuring our discussion: who should acquire, what should be acquired, and what tools of acquisition should be used (Merenlender et al. 2003)?

Agents: Who Should Acquire?

The rise of the modern land trust movement has been an undisputed benefit to conservation efforts in the United States. The simplicity of the core idea—local actors organizing to protect their environmental interests through voluntary market transactions—is fundamentally appealing. Indeed, it is so appealing it has served conservation interests well for almost 200 years. We are heartened by this combination of hard-headed economics and diligent local organizing in the service of important conservation goals.

Furthermore, recent experience suggests that land trusts are simply better than the U.S. government at brokering deals. Isolated problems like those discussed in the *Washington Post* are distressing, but they do not erode our confidence in the movement's impressive competence overall. Tools such as tax subsidies that facilitate private acquisitions between willing sellers and buyers strike us as appropriate public expenditures. They are cheaper and more likely to enjoy broad support than full fee purchase and management by public agencies.

We have already observed, however, that the mingling of public and private efforts in land trust activities makes us concerned about ensuring responsiveness to the larger citizenry. Thus, a crucial step in acquiring private land is addressing accountability issues. Fortunately, we see some encouraging signs in this regard on the present landscape, as well as some relatively easy innovations that might improve the situation further.

First, public funding of private acquisitions already passes through a fragmentary but potentially useful filter of oversight. Constraints on non-profits imposed by the IRS are indirect but important. If tax code-based funding is notoriously beyond the control of Congress (Salamon 2002), Farm Bill money is not. Its distribution is presided over by state and regional evaluators, experts, and committees. Finally, the frequency with which acquisition advocates turn to state and local voters for funding support is another form of accountability—voters could shut down many of these programs quite easily. They continue to give them overwhelming support.

Second, since purchasing land for the capital, Congress has consistently put the public acquisition of land under the close scrutiny of external commissions, generally made up of citizens. It is not a very big stretch to view land trusts, particularly the national and regional ones—such as TNC, TPL, TCF, SPNHF, and The Trustees—as acting in a similar capacity. We do not view the current partnership between land trusts and public acquisition funds as a great break with past practice.

Third, both states and the trusts themselves already exercise considerable effort toward ensuring accountability. Conservation easements are defined in state law and subject to extensive state oversight. As noted in chapter 7, the Massachusetts government approves every easement written within its borders. In Montana, county commissions are consulted. In Virginia, the VOF co-holds most easements, and in New Hampshire, the SPNHF guarantees to defend every easement in the state. A recent court of appeals decision in Tennessee held that every resident of the state, as a beneficiary of conservation easements, has standing to enforce them.[4] The LTA, through its education programs and its Standards and Practices, is crucial to the movement's accountability at a national level.

Fourth and finally, many land trust participants believe they are accountable to the community where they live and work. Indeed, many land trusts rely on local funding and, more important, on local volunteers to staff their education centers, serve on their committees and boards, and become dues-paying members. The national organizations partner with state and local land trusts when undertaking transactions. These not-always-compatible bedfellows keep a keen eye on each other.

Such informal checks go only so far, however. Working in a community and responding to its needs is one of the most attractive elements of land trust activity. But the enterprise is typically most responsive to the landowners who might sell or donate land or easements. Accountability in that context often exacerbates the preferential treatment that acquisition tools have long offered to the landed and well to do.

At bottom, the web of formal and informal accountability mechanisms presented in this section suggests that land acquisition for conservation is about as accountable to the general public as any other example of government activity. However, the shortcomings described require that land trust advocates and government officials pay more attention to openness. By openness, we mean first that land trusts must be more forthcoming about the quasi-public character of their programs. Perhaps the only thing worse than private control of public resources and authority, in terms of accountability, is reducing scrutiny of substantially public programs by declaring them private.

Tracking a proliferating set of decisions and acquisition deals undertaken by land trusts with little public notice is a daunting task. Add the fact that there are more than 1,600 groups "doing deals" and holding easements, and the problem only gets worse. A crucial first step, therefore, is for all parties involved to be far clearer that these transactions are not fully private, nor are they entirely philanthropic. Furthermore, land trusts must invite and facilitate public involvement, however challenging that might be.

We are as weary as anyone of the turgid and ritualistic public involvement programs that have accompanied federal agency planning since the 1970s. Nevertheless, ostensibly private acquirers rarely do even that much. A first step is to recognize that land trusts must involve diverse communities in their activities. Indeed, they must do better than the federal agency programs that have all but given democratic participation a bad name. Our story has been, in part, about land trust flexibility in the face of similar government rigidity regarding acquisitions. Surely these organizations, rooted as they claim to be in real communities, can be as nimble and creative about involving their neighbors in planning as they are in structuring preacquisitions.

At a minimum, land trusts could enlarge their range of local contacts by expanding the pool from which they select their boards and employees. They could also work with county and local land use planning programs to ensure that their conservation priorities support local aspirations. We are impressed by TNC's efforts in the Blackfoot to involve local communities in identifying ultimate owners for its Plum Creek acquisitions, but we believe that more creativity is both possible and necessary. The government agencies should be seeking to enhance public accountability through innovative land trust ideas, rather than how to avoid it.

Public accountability would also benefit from some form of public certification of land trusts. The idea is not new. More than twenty years ago, the members of the National Conference of Commissioners on Uniform State Laws debated oversight issues. Their suggestions included restrictions on the types of organizations eligible to hold conservation easements, local or state agency review of easement transactions, and special recording requirements for these unique instruments. Ultimately, such language was not incorporated into the Uniform Conservation Easement Act, but a number of state statutes have adopted more stringent provisions. These include, notably, waiting periods in Virginia and Colorado and state approval in Massachusetts. The examples strike us as useful reminders that public oversight of land trusts is not unprecedented. Further analyses may reveal whether such requirements actually discourage rogue activity and increase public accountability.

The same issues are heating up in Washington. The IRS announced plans to intensify scrutiny of deductions for conservation easements (Small 2004; U.S. IRS 2004),[5] and Congress began reviewing a full range of charitable deductions (Wentworth 2004). The Joint Committee of Taxation (JCT), established to advise members of Congress on revenue matters, added its weight to the discussion. Its lengthy report recommended imposing severe limits on the deductions landowners can take for donating a conservation easement. It proposed that such deductions be limited to 33 percent of the easement's appraised value, and that no deduction be allowed for an easement on a property used by the tax-payer as his or her personal residence.

Where and when *public* acquisition should occur is a stickier question. It should be evident by now that we are far less concerned that government programs might preempt or displace private efforts than are some of our colleagues. Indeed, our primary fear is the opposite: that the sterling reputation of private acquisition efforts will give public land managers and politicians the sense that *all* acquisitions are best left to the private sector. A reverse "crowding out" of public acquisition efforts by private ones would be a terrible mistake.

Yet that appears to be exactly what is happening; the public sector is currently unwilling to acquire land even in situations where it really should. Two points stand out. First, the controversial tool of condemnation is underutilized. Ironically, Congress often withdraws condemnation authority from the agencies in exactly the limited situations (wilderness areas or wild and scenic river corridors) where it makes the most sense. We find this frustrating, particularly since eminent domain is used routinely in highway construction, power line rights-of-way, and similar public projects.

In urging greater use of eminent domain, we are sensitive to past abuses and problems. The NPS' dismal record removing smallholders in Appalachia, Cuyahoga, and even Yosemite is not a big selling point for the procedure. However, condemnation is too important a tool to reject completely simply because some agency programs have been poorly implemented. The key again is transparency and accountability. It is a rare individual who will appreciate the mandatory sale of the family farm, home, or summer cabin. Stronger public leadership must clarify the importance of equitable and environmental priorities, and the fact that land ownership is not an unqualified right but includes duties to society. In exceptional cases, those duties may involve giving up one's property in exchange for fair compensation. Coercion is never pleasant, but the government uses it in many other contexts without major disruption; it should be able to do the same for conservation.

The courts could help in making eminent domain a less odious tool. At present, judicial review of condemnations is minimal. Courts typically ask whether the agency is authorized to condemn land, and if the answer is yes, they look no further (Plater and Norine 1989). Condemnees ought to have a better opportunity to challenge the reasonableness of specific applications of the tool. To that end, we propose that the LTA work with government agencies to identify circumstances when a NEPA-style review of condemnations is in order. This was part of some versions of the CARA. Ritualistic though it may be, it would provide an opportunity for public comment on transactions that have heretofore not enjoyed such transparency.

Second, we see public acquisition (voluntary or not) as essential for those parcels that private conservation buyers are unlikely to acquire. In some cases, these are inholdings or other unique properties that provide a monopoly of sorts to the seller. In others, however, they are areas of minimal interest to private buyers, or at least private buyers wealthy enough to be in the market. In particular, the public sector must focus on acquisitions in areas that land trusts do not serve well: urban areas and poor communities lacking the resources to organize and buy properties themselves. Willing sellers and private acquisition efforts have left clear gaps in the conservation landscape, and public purchase is one of the few ways we can imagine filling those holes. We urge public agencies to do so.

Targets: What Should We Acquire?

Once again, we are generally supportive of the broadening notion of what lands are worth conserving. We especially welcome the expansion of the debate beyond the wilderness absolutism of the early post-World War II decades. However, conservation of working landscapes requires more thought than it has so far enjoyed (Cronon 1995; Fairfax 1996). When agricultural land is "conserved" in ways that facilitate or perpetuate reliance on pesticides or the erosion of topsoil, for example, we begin to get uncomfortable. Moreover, the expansion of conservation goals only makes the identification of specific working landscapes to be protected particularly important.

So what lands should we acquire? We begin with the obvious: Acquisition should appeal in direct proportion to price. Like any other buyer, conservation purchasers should be savvy about a good deal. This sounds absurdly elementary, but the experience of the federal government in

Mount Rainier at the start of the twentieth century and in the Redwoods at its close suggests that the point remains a salient one for public acquisition efforts.[6]

We have little to say, however, about selecting properties of ecological importance. This is partly because we are not biologists and partly because even those who are have only just begun to identify standards for designing nature preserves, determining habitat requirements for protected species, and estimating the impacts of different human uses on ecological sustainability. To the extent that identifying the right lands for conservation requires more knowledge than is presently available, we are hard pressed to answer the question even partially.

We do think it is important to question one principle, common among conservation advocates, that what is not conserved now is lost forever. The idea may justify the tendency, particularly apparent during the Watt years in Interior, for conservationists to prefer new acquisitions to investment in management of existing properties. We have spoken to enough biologists to understand that some resources are not renewable for many ecological purposes. Nor are we sanguine about using easements to "mitigate" the loss of vital habitat (Owley 2005).

Having emphasized the changing nature of conservation priorities over time, we point out once more that almost everything we protect seems to end up being valued, regardless of its initial ecological status. Americans seem enormously accepting of both architectural and natural restorations. We have called the Valles Caldera undisturbed, and we have designated wilderness on national grasslands that had been acquired specifically because they were degraded farms and pastures. Even such obvious political chicanery as the St. Louis waterfront park has become a valuable economic resource and a cherished local landscape. In short, acquiring exactly the right land may not always be as important as one might think, particularly when the supply of relatively unsullied sites is diminishing rapidly. In this respect, conservation often seems to be its own reward.

We also find it troubling that ecological goals, however poorly defined or understood, are the first line of rhetorical defense on many acquisitions. This worries us because we fear that current ecological enthusiasms will push land conservation efforts farther and farther from equity considerations. Acquisition for conservation must be conducted in a more equitable manner. Despite the elitist reputation that has dogged the conservation movement from its beginning, this idea is not without precedent. Public conservation acquisitions have frequently been defined by goals of fairness and social justice. In the Depression, economic relief for the poor was a primary purpose of land acquisition programs. Clearly, well-to-do landowners were among the most obvious beneficiaries of the programs, but the economic needs of the poor and unemployed were a major factor. In the 1960s, bringing recreation access closer to the urban, eastern, underserved population was again a clearly stated goal that did not fully disappear until the Reagan era. In sum, as a nation we have considerable experience in defining conservation goals with reference to social justice.

The emergence of land trusts is, as we have noted, very much a part of the Reagan era. Perhaps it is no coincidence, then, that although early land trust advocates were seriously concerned with equity, the concept has all but disappeared as a movement priority. We see evidence of the problem in land trust priorities and in the faces at LTA gatherings. The movement's clear emphasis is on protecting ecological values and controlling urban sprawl. Those are worthy goals, but they are not enough. In the future, equity must take a more prominent role, not only for its own sake, but also because it is necessary to maintain both the rights acquired, particularly in easements, and the movement's political sustainability.

Equity is a key part of embedding land trust tools and programs in the community, of persuading local people of the importance and validity of the trust's title arrangements. Title, we have repeatedly observed, is not enforceable when the citizenry does not find the asserted rights persuasive. If easements are not seen as valuable to a community, community structures (including courts) that are necessary to sustain them will not operate effectively in their defense. Moreover, local credibility is ethically and politically crucial to the continued use of public funds.

To us, equity means two things in particular for acquisition efforts. First, it means acquiring or otherwise protecting land in all communities, not just rural and wealthy ones. Precisely because land trusts are now substantially running federal land acquisition programs as well as their own, they must pay far more attention to underserved citizens and landscapes. As a practical matter, until urban areas are experienced as pleasant places to live, urban residents will continue to seek clean air and water, aesthetic benefits, and open space in the hinterland, threatening ecological values there with further development.

In other words, even if protecting ecological resources were the only goal, enhancing the cities is still essential. The urban gardens programs of TPL, the Neighborhood Gardens Association, and the Madison Area Community Land Trust, and the efforts of the Black Family Land Trust, all discussed in chapter 8, provide provocative examples of the equity-driven application of land trust tools that we think needs to be far more common.

In this respect, the land trust movement could learn something from a parallel movement: community land trusts (CLTs). CLTs are much like the conservation land trusts we have discussed at length in this volume, using many similar tools to lower the cost of land ownership, albeit for different goals. The typical CLT works on providing affordable housing; some pair this with sustainable rural development. Although much smaller than the conservation trust movement (there are about 100 CLTs in operation in the United States today), CLTs provide useful insights for conservation land trusts trying to develop a more diverse constituency.[7] However, at present, the two types of land trusts do not overlap greatly in their work. Most CLTs are not members of the LTA, and relatively few attend the annual LTA Rally. Nor have land trusts shown much interest, with a few important exceptions, in the urban issues addressed by CLTs. We think more cross-fertilization could be a step forward for both movements.

Finally, acquiring more lands with public access is critical. We recognize that unfettered recreation is not appropriate on all conservation lands. We are also aware that easements complicate the access issue, particularly when an organization relies on donations. Nevertheless, access for the select few is difficult to defend, and that is what many easements, limited development, and conservation buyer acquisitions seem to provide. But this is not an unavoidable outcome. Recall, for example, that The Trustees' land, even its donated parcels, must be open to the public or the organization is subject to property taxes. In New Hampshire, *all*

SPNHF lands are open to the public. Yet according to one study, less than 10 percent of all conservation easements allow access for general recreation (Guenzler 1999: 13). Such outcomes are unacceptable when so many public resources are involved.

Tools: What Instruments Should We Use (and When)?

In terms of acquisition tools, our concerns and suggestions begin with the issue of longevity. The land trust movement has proven that it is highly capable of motivating and organizing local groups to protect small sites of local significance as well as of brokering far larger and more complex transactions. Civic life is enriched by these efforts. The land trust movement has yet to demonstrate, however, that it is capable of stewarding the rights obtained over the long term. Nor is it entirely obvious to us that all such conservation rights should be in perpetuity, as is the general practice, even if there is adequate infrastructure within the movement to defend them (Mahoney 2002).

To begin with, we share the worries of many observers about the future of conservation easements. Setting aside the important questions of durability and enforcement, we are even more concerned about the issue of motive and reputation. Particularly because the boundaries between private and public conservation are fuzzy, and Congress is watching more closely as worries about rogue land trust actions grow, it is essential that the land trust community not allow itself or its credibility to be drawn into dubious transactions.

In addition, we worry about easements held by the large number of land trusts formed since 1985. Those organizations have no real track record and frequently have only limited resources for stewarding and defending easements. Moreover, it is not clear what will happen to these easements in the continuing shakeout among small land trusts. The issue has concerned many in the movement. The main focus of concern is on how easements will fare over time as the original enthusiasm for the tool and the organizations involved fade, and second and third owners buy the underlying fee title. The fate of these easements as various small land trusts merge, go under, or simply atrophy is another major concern.

We wonder as well what will happen when the time for "doing deals" winds down. Numerous island- and county-based land trusts have just about reached the limits of what they can buy, and others are not far from the saturation point. When a land trust's primary tasks are maintaining the achievements of the past rather than extending them, will there still be volunteers, board members, and money for monitoring and stewardship? Experience with public land holdings gives reason for worry—both Congress and the public prefer to create new park units rather than fund the management of existing ones.

Finally, research suggests that land trusts are not monitoring their easements adequately, or even keeping basic records. In a recent study of nine San Francisco Bay Area counties, the authors found that about half of the land protected from 1979 to 1999 (about 800,000 acres) relied upon easements. Yet few of the organizations studied had reserves to cover the costs of enforcement. Worse, the baseline studies essential to both monitoring and enforcing compliance were available for only 40 percent of the easements. Of those, 14 percent were seriously deficient (Guenzler and Douthit 2002; Dana, A. and Dana 2002).

Government easement holders, FWS and NPS experience notwithstanding, are potentially even more troubling. Several studies have found that easements accepted as mitigation for development or as part of planning and permitting processes (Guenzler and Douthit 2002; Owley 2005) have been lost, not recorded, or not monitored. This is especially problematic since once an easement appears to have been abandoned, it becomes extremely difficult to resurrect and enforce, assuming it can be eventually located. Even when the government is actively pursuing and monitoring easements, as under many Farm Bill and Forest Legacy programs, the work remains underfunded and hit-or-miss (Guenzler and Douthit 2002).

We also share some concerns about the longevity and unchanging nature of conservation easements. IRS rules state that any conservation easement must be "in perpetuity" in order to qualify for a tax deduction. This means, however, that a single owner of a parcel can effectively strip that land of specified uses forever. No one, in theory, can repurchase those rights from the land trust in the future. This again raises troubling issues of equity. Allowing a current individual to define the use of land for the next few centuries or longer is granting a lot. Who can even imagine what land use issues will arise in 2020, let alone 2120? A conservation easement that makes excellent sense today may become either useless or ridiculous over time. And as we have seen, conservation goals have changed considerably over the past 200 years.

State laws and common law have been generally hostile to such "perpetuities" in property for just this reason.[8] Thus, we wonder whether there is a place for tax-deductible, renewable ninety-nine-year easements, or some other lengthy but time-limited instrument to protect a given parcel.[9] Alternatively, we could imagine a process by which easements could eventually be transferred, allowing at least a theoretical option for a trust to reposition conservation programs after a lengthy period of time. Of course, such changes would be controversial and would require careful safeguards to prevent abuse. However, the current system invites abuse as well because wealthy landowners take advantage of tax breaks to guarantee the viewshed around their home literally forever. Nor do the obvious concerns seem insurmountable. Resale could be limited to easements more than fifty years old, for instance, and require a unanimous or super-majority vote of the trust's board. Regardless of the specifics, the issue of avoiding the perpetual determination of a land use by a private individual is something that should be considered seriously by land trust activists and policymakers.

It is important not to overstate these issues. The longevity of groups such as the MVLA, which focused only briefly on one deal, is a useful counterpoint. In fact, the few examples we do have of long-standing easements—FWS refuges, the BRP, and Wisconsin's Great River Road—are, contrary to many anecdotal references in the literature, quite positive. And the results of early private conservation—the MVLA, The Trustees, the Fort Ticonderoga Association, and the Save-the-Redwoods League—are nothing less than inspiring.

The main source of funding for public acquisition efforts raises a related longevity issue. Congressional enthusiasm for acquisition via agricultural subsidies is well established; more than half of federally acquired land was purchased during the Depression. Now, even in the absence of an equivalent crisis, Farm Bill money provides the major portion of federal spending in this area. However, there is a real difference between New Deal and Farm Bill programs. During the Depression, the federal government acquired land and managed it in a generally restorative way. Today the bulk of Farm Bill money is not used for restoration and durable protection; it is used for leases.

We have several reservations about this change. First, some of these leases under the Conservation Reserve Program violate our first principle of seeking a good bargain; payments over the life of the lease sometimes approach or surpass the full value of the land itself. Second, as Farm Bill programs return to providing subsidies for industrial agriculture and not much else, they look like a bad bargain. We are particularly concerned when commodity groups such as cattlemen's associations are the easement holder or steward in such programs. These groups must be far more creative in encouraging farm practices that reduce or eliminate pesticides and chemical fertilizers and other unsustainable agricultural practices.

The problem of farm subsidies leads us to reiterate that land trusts must be careful about becoming or being portrayed as advocates of universal compensation for every diminution of property value, or otherwise acting in ways that further ideas about absolute dominion in land ownership. The psychology here seems crucial to us and requires renewed attention to enforcement of basic land use regulations and social expectations about property.

Finally, we think that Congress had it right the first time on exchanges—when they expand beyond limited programs to clean up boundaries and eliminate management problems, they become an invitation to fraud and, almost as damaging, the appearance of fraud. Here the public discussion provided by an environmental impact assessment seems called for, tedious or otherwise. Moreover, we are not convinced that large-scale repositioning of the federal estate is a good idea. At a minimum, it is worth discussing apart from the evaluation of specific deals. Even if this process continues, we conclude that land trusts should not participate. It can only harm the land trust movement if individual organizations allow Congress and developers to imply that these dicey transactions have the approval of the conservation community.

Conclusion

Throughout this volume we have urged readers to take note of the growing mosaics of ownership and control in land conservation today. Yet we have left an obvious question until last: Are mosaics good? Do these intricate webs of ownership and control bode well for land preservation activities?

Our simple answer is yes, mosaics are a positive trend. At their best, they represent a new, collaborative, and sophisticated approach that can approximate the elusive win-win model so frequently touted in conservation circles. Mosaics can mean land trusts helping federal agencies work better with local citizens, acquisitions that conserve key resources while trying to provide local economic stability, and integrated approaches to protecting resources. These are positive outcomes, especially compared with older models of top-down scientific management or unilateral private conservation by wealthy citizens. They also are clearly preferable, in many instances, to waiting for adequate budgetary resources or planning procedures to ensure the protection of threatened sites.

Nevertheless, some acquisition mosaics have not worked as well. The Blue Ridge Parkway is not entirely functional, nor are some of the less savory assembled exchanges. Cuyahoga Valley National Park was a mess until recently and still faces an uncertain future. Complexity, in short, is not a virtue in and of itself and should not be pursued as if it were.

That said, we are inspired by the accomplishments of 225 years of citizen efforts to conserve land. We would be a poorer nation indeed if Mount Vernon were a hotel and all the redwoods were picnic tables. We are gratified that the general public's insistence on participating and being heard has moved The Trustees out of the Harvard Club and into the reach of many, if clearly not most, citizens.

Willing sellers will most likely always define the agenda. Buying nature began as the noticeably clubby concern of elites—both inside the government and out. They have met their own needs and impressed their vision on the landscape in the process. But they have also left a legacy—of land, institutions, and civic participation—that is diverse and dispersed. We have a more than adequate foundation for adding equity and accountability to the architecture and evaluation of conservation mosaics.

Notes

Chapter 1

1. On NPS myths, see O'Toole (1995). On USFS myths, see Fairfax and Tarlock (1979, especially sec. V and n. 106) and Steen (1992: 3–9).

2. The idea is virtually everywhere. See Langford (1972). See also Jackson (1942) and Hampton (1971, esp. chaps. 1 and 2); for a less reverent counter-story, see Runte (1979) and Spence (1999).

3. See "Secretary Lane's Letter on National Park Management," May 13, 1918, reprinted in Dilsaver (1994).

Chapter 2

1. This has been interpreted to mean exclusive jurisdiction. See *United States v. Beavans*, 3 Wheat. 336, 388 (1811); *United States v. Cornell*, 25 F. Cas. 646, No. 14,867 (C.C.D.R.I., 1819).

2. An Act for Establishing the Temporary and Permanent Seat of the Government, U.S. Statutes at Large 1(1790): 130, § 1. On the first Monday of December 1800, the federal government assumed "full and absolute right and exclusive jurisdiction" over the District, its soil, and all persons residing thereon (Tindall 1909: 12).

3. *Kohl et al. v. United States*, 91 U.S. 367; 23 L. Ed. 449 (1875).

4. See the Subscribers Agreement, in Tindall (1909: 85–87) and accompanying proclamations, especially George Washington to Thomas Jefferson, March 31, 1791.

5. The following account based on four major sources: Hough (1878, vol. 1), J. Cameron (1928), Wood (1981), and Snell (1983).

6. *U.S. Constitution*, Art. I. § 8, cl. 13. The standard story is told briefly in S. Dana and Fairfax (1980: 5–6) and Ise (1924: 22).

7. *American State Papers: Naval Affairs* i: 9, as cited in Hough (1878: 10).

8. The same technology shift, as one reviewer notes, also led to establishing petroleum reserves in California, Alaska, and Colorado, again for the navy.

9. *Journals of the Continental Congress* 21 (1781): 1081. See also ⟨http://www.nps.gov/colo/Ythanout/colonhp.html⟩. Our understanding of Yorktown has benefited greatly from a telephone interview (August 20, 1997) and e-mail exchanges with Diane Depew, NPS historian, Colonial National Historical Park, Virginia.

10. We are grateful to Robert Fudge and John Lockewood, NPS staff, Washington, D.C., and Kata Bartoloni for information on the complex Washington situation.

11. Recall the sporadic efforts of anti-immigration activists to dominate the board of the Sierra Club in the 1990s and beyond ("Rock the Vote" 2004).

12. Mackintosh is an updated and partially rewritten version of Lee. Although much of the Mackintosh piece is taken word-for-word from Lee's volume, we have profited from studying both because Lee is seriously out of date. Our understanding of Bunker Hill has benefited from the efforts of Ethan Beelor and Ruth Raphael of the NPS, Jim Gribaudo of the Boston Redevelopment Authority, and Linda McConchie of the Freedom Trail Foundation.

13. All of the above is from Evans and Snell (1982). The volume collates and presents all of the major histories of the Bunker Hill Monument available at the Library of Congress: Frothingham (1849), Packard (1853), Sheldon (1865), Warren (1877), and E. H. Cameron (1952).

14. Preacquisitions are a common tool of contemporary land trusts. They occur when a private group purchases land in advance for a government agency—usually because the agency needs more time to assemble funds and permissions for the transaction than the seller is willing to provide. Preacquisitions are usually undertaken by prearrangement with the agency in question, but occasionally a land trust will preacquire land without any guarantee that an agency will buy it.

15. See Act of the Massachusetts Legislature, February 26, 1825, Appendix six.

16. The association conveyed title of the monument to the state in 1919, and the site was transferred to the NPS in 1974 when the Boston National Historic Park was established. The association continues, in an altered form, to hold an annual meeting in which the NPS participates, and to manage an annual ceremony marking the anniversary of the battle.

17. This account relies heavily on the advice and direction provided by Nick Westbrook, director of the Fort Ticonderoga Association. We have benefited as well from personal interviews with him and with Robert Maguire, long-time association board member; Charles A. Levesque, president of Innovative Natural Resource Solutions; Tom Berry, legislative assistant to Vermont Senator Jim Jeffords; Robert Paquin, legislative assistant to Vermont Senator Patrick Leahy; Louise B. Ransom, founder of the Mt. Independence Coalition; Bill Howland, executive director of the Lake Champlain Basin Program (all in June 2002 in Vermont); Tom Duffus of The Nature Conservancy and a consultant to the Fort

Ticonderoga Association; Chris Maron of the Adirondack Nature Conservancy and Adirondack Land Trust, in New York, at the same time. James Behan's telephone interview with Tom Fox, Fort Ticonderoga curator, in July 1997 preceded his first work on Fort Ticonderoga in 1997. We also enjoy guidance from Jane Difley, president and forester of the Society for the Protection of New Hampshire Forests, who frequently serves as a research assistant-chauffeur-sounding board.

18. Fort Ticonderoga was one of three major visitor attractions in the nation at the time. The other two were Saratoga Springs and Niagara Falls, both relatively close by.

19. This 1856 date has led some to argue that the "first" land trustlike organization was actually the Laurel Hill Association, founded in 1853. However, this association, although it first met on land donated to the town in the 1830s, was primarily concerned with tree planting, street lights, and similar civic improvements (see Cresson 1953).

20. John Washington's reluctance to deal with the state has been normalized; a key element of late twentieth-century land trust success was the continuing reluctance of landowners to deal with government agencies.

21. Johnson (1991: 28–42) is particularly informative on Ms. Tracey's adventures.

22. For example, Ise (1961: 244) views Hot Springs as a health resort rather than a scenic park and therefore not within the scope of his book. Tilden (1970: 124) asserts that this is the "oldest reservation set aside by act of Congress for the perpetual use and enjoyment of the people," which is also incorrect. Congress viewed the action as temporary (Gates 1968). The site was not designated a national park until 1921.

23. An exception is arguably George Catlin, who painted portraits of Native Americans beginning in the 1830s and proposed a national park for their protection (Catlin 1913/1973).

24. O'Toole (1995: 5) notes that "through 1915, more than half the people counted as 'visitors' to the national parks were actually bathers at Hot Springs." Buck (1946: 30–33) discusses the complex path by which Hot Springs officially became a national park.

25. Our discussion of Yosemite National Park has benefited from the comments of and conversations with Jim Snyder, Yosemite National Park historian.

26. *U.S. Statutes at Large* 13 (1864): 325.

Chapter 3

1. *Santa Clara County v. Southern Pacific Railway Company*, 118 U.S. 394 (1886).

2. Recent federal agency public relations campaigns emphasizing "customer service" have occasioned retorts that citizens are not customers but, analogous to

stockholders, are owners. Advocates frequently assert that every American owns *x* acres of land, depending on the population, which defeats key elements of the stockholder notion. Note that a stockholder is very different from a stakeholder, currently defined as a person with a stake in an outcome. Originally, as Gregg Cawley points out, a stakeholder was just the opposite—a disinterested party entrusted with the stakes pending the outcome of a wager or duel. See also former USFS Chief Richard McArdle's early discussion of the multiple use concept: "Every citizen of this country owns a share of stock in the national forests—one share only, no less and no more" (McArdle 1953: 323).

3. Written by that understandably enthusiastic opponent of states' rights, Thurgood Marshall, the decision embraces a previous conclusion: "The power over the public land thus entrusted to Congress is without limitations." Quoting *United States v. San Francisco*, 310 U.S. 29 (1940).

4. This runs in the opposite direction of Appalachian reserves—in which Gifford Pinchot easily hijacked a joint preservationist-utilitarian effort.

5. The organization was called The Trustees of *Public* Reservations until 1953 when they dropped the "Public."

6. Our discussion of The Trustees relies heavily on Abbott (1993). We also have had conversations over several years at Land Trust Alliance "rallies," and in Boston and Nantucket, June 2002, with Wesley T. Ward and Margaret Wheeler, Steve Nicolle, and numerous TTOR field staff.

7. The National Trust and TTOR continue to have cordial relations but are not meaningfully linked. See Gwin and Fairfax (2004).

8. The founders of the National Trust were far more radical politically than the Brahmin Trustees, but the organization did not remain so for long (see Murphy 2002, esp. chap. 3). See Weideger (1994) for a more critical look at the Trust.

9. *U.S. Code*, vol. 16 § 431 (1876). See Torres (1985: 55).

10. *U.S. Code*, vol. 16 § 431 (1876).

11. See Platt (2001: 3), Unrau (1991), and Lee (1972).

12. Our understanding of Gettysburg, past and present, has benefited from frequent visits and e-mails with Terry Burger, journalist; Kathy Harrison, senior historian, National Park Service; John Latscher, superintendent, and Katie Lawhon, public affairs specialist, Gettysburg National Military Park; Vickey Monrean, Friends of Gettysburg National Military Park; Dean Shultz; and Bob Wilburn, Gettysburg Museum Foundation.

13. Confederate veterans from South Carolina and Virginia participated in the Bunker Hill centennial in 1875, the first time former Union and Confederate troops publicly fraternized after the Civil War. The practice of joint reunions later spread to Civil War battlefields, culminating in huge veterans' encampments at Gettysburg in 1888 and Chickamauga in 1889.

14. "Because of its reluctance to arouse the animosity of those who favored the theory of state's rights …" (Nichols, P. 1979: § 1.24[2]: 1–89), the federal gov-

ernment relied on state authorities. See also Meidinger (1980: 18–20) and Hemmat (1986).

15. The law is still in effect: *U.S. Code*, vol. 40 § 257.

16. Brief for the Gettysburg Electric Railway Company in the Supreme Court of the United States, October term, 1894, at 7–8, 30–31, *United States v. Gettysburg Electric Railway Company*, 160 U.S. 668 (1896).

17. Runte (1979: 21) notes the pattern of praising American scenic wonders and "in the same breath deprecating its counterparts abroad."

18. Typically, statutes provided that lease income from concessions would be used for the preservation, improvement, and protection of the property. See, for example, the Yosemite Valley Grant to California, *U.S. Statutes at Large* 13 (1864): 325; *U.S. Code*, vol. 16 § 48.

19. The NPS domination of monuments has weakened over time. President Clinton reserved the Grand Staircase-Escalante National Monument in Utah, as well as other monuments, to be managed by both the Forest Service and the Bureau of Land Management.

20. *Light v. United States*, 220 U.S. 523 (1911).

21. There is little to say about acquisition from native people—who were simply ignored, shoved aside, or exterminated. The literature on NPS treatment of Indians is late in arriving but is growing fast (see Spence 1999). For the Forest Service record regarding indigenous people, see J. Nichols (1976) and DeBuys (1985).

22. The claim was ultimately disallowed by the Supreme Court in *Hutchings v. Low* 82 U.S. 77 (1872).

23. The Mount Rainier Act also permitted prospecting and mining in the park. Single-site reservations for parks are vulnerable to such special provisions. The Rainier grants were subject to enormous litigation and controversy. In the mid-1920s, Congress and the president investigated them extensively.

24. *Hughes v. Oklahoma*, 441 U.S. 322 (1979) overruled the state ownership doctrine, at 338–339. Nevertheless, the institutional structure around wildlife had evolved based on state ownership and has proven durable.

25. *U.S. Statutes at Large*, 16 (1870): 180. Reffalt (1993: 2, as cited in Wong 1997). Aleuts brought to the islands to hunt the seals remained in near-feudal servitude until well into the 1980s (see U.S. Congress. House 1889).

26. President, Proclamation 39, *U.S. Statutes at Large* 27 (1892): 1052, cited in Environmental Law Institute (1977: 127). Also see Reed and Drabelle (1984: 5).

27. Note that the association's contributions are generally presented as salutary, but private contributions are not always so regarded. Observers generally describe ranchers' payments to BLM officials in the 1940s to keep the agency in operation after devastating budget cuts in terms of capture of the Bureau by the livestock interests (Dana, S. T. and Fairfax 1980: 182–183).

28. Individual Indians were allotted 160 acres of land on a reservation. This was ostensibly to their advantage, giving them the diverse benefits of title. However, land not patented was then removed from the tribe and made available for settlement or purchase. Indian land holdings nationwide were reduced by about a third under the Dawes Act. In 1928 the Merriam report (U.S. DOI 1928) described massive fraud in the distribution of Indian lands and funds under the act. The government has yet to rectify the resulting claims, and the current and several previous secretaries of the interior have been held in contempt of court for their inability to address decades of malfeasance. However, 1994 amendments to the Indian Self-Determination Act (P.L. 103–413) allow tribes to "petition" the Department of the Interior "for permission to manage non-Indian properties where tribes have historical, cultural and geographic ties." The Fish and Wildlife Service has identified nineteen refuges where the Indians might take over some management, including the National Bison Range, which now totals 18,541 acres in the heart of the reservation. In April 2003, the FWS announced that a joint management agreement with the Confederated Salish and Kootenai Tribes was in the works (see U.S. FWS 2002b; Matthews 2003).

29. Act of March 1909, *U.S. Statutes at Large*, 35 (1909): 1039, 1051, 1052.

30. The Division of Biological Survey, later the Bureau of Biological Survey, remained in the Department of Agriculture until 1940 (see Reed and Drabelle 1984: 5). The best institutional history is Fischman (2003: chap. 3).

31. Act of March 1, 1911, *U.S. Statutes at Large*, 36 (1911): 961.

32. Until 1924, Weeks Act authority could only be used to acquire lands in the headwaters of navigable rivers and streams.

33. Act of March 1, 1911, *U.S. Statutes at Large* 36 (1911): 961 §§ 10, 11.

34. In 1914, the share of receipts from acquired land was increased to 25 percent of net receipts to match the sharing on reserved forests (see Shands 1992: 34–38).

35. In 1976, the National Forest Management Act abolished the NFRC and redelegated the authority to establish new national forests to the secretary of agriculture.

36. *Griffin v. United States*, 58 F. 2d 674 (1932).

37. No wonder the states were so enthusiastic about the Weeks Act.

38. Buck (1946: 40) cites statements of the entire Oklahoma delegation frankly admitting that they considered the proposed Platt National Park "as one means of securing their share of the federal appropriations."

Chapter 4

1. However, see *Euclid v. Ambler Realty Company*, 272 U.S. 365 (1926).

2. See H.J. Res. 350, 63d Cong., 2d sess. (September 21, 1914).

3. Hosmer (1981, vol. I: 525–526) suggests that the NPS was behind this effort, but we are dubious. We found only one reference to the NPS in the MVLA

archives, in a letter from Lorne W. Barcley, director of the National Parks Association to John M. Evans, chair of the House Public Lands Committee (April 18, 1932) opposing the transfer. However, see Hosmer (1981: 188) as well.

4. Allen Treadway, Member, House Committee on Ways and Means, MVLA Archives, Mount Vernon, Va. to Francis J. Rogers, February 12, 1930.

5. Even the governor of Virginia, while vowing to fight to protect the rights of the state of Virginia in the site should Congress try to take it over, suggested that the ladies should open the grounds "to visitors free of any entrance charges." MVLA Archives, Mount Vernon, Virginia. See Governor Davis to George Bryan, July 21, 1921. Virginia's interest in the property was twofold. First, should the MVLA fail to meet its responsibilities under its charter, Virginia would take title to the land. Second, given the still-operative procedure for acquiring land within a state, it was not clear that the federal government was authorized simply to move in and purchase or condemn the property.

6. Our understanding of the Redwoods has benefited from conversations and communication with Peter Berck; Ruskin Hartley, conservation planner, Save-the-Redwoods League (June 6, 2003 in San Francisco and countless times since); Aida Parkinson, environmental specialist, Redwood National and State Parks; Susan Schrepfer; and Richard Sermon, state park superintendent, Redwood National and State Parks (July 29, 2003 in Crescent City, California).

7. Preacquisitions for states were becoming common at the time. After a long fund-raising effort, the Society for The Protection of New Hampshire Forests acquired Franconia Notch and donated it to New Hampshire in 1927. For an early debate over condemnation, see Schrepfer (1983: 23–33).

8. *U.S. Statutes at Large* 45 (1929): 1083. An enormous fire in 1947 destroyed most of the "cottages" on "Millionaires Row," and significantly changed the nature of visits to the area. However, the park's origin in donations left it without formal boundaries. When an outer limit was established in 1985, after significant rows with local residents, a cap on park acreage was also established. Land outside the boundaries was to be acquired only by easements (Schwartz 1985; U.S. NPS 1988).

9. *U.S. Statutes at Large* 41 (1920): 452–453. Discussed in Ise (1961: 218–221).

10. The Hawaiian land situation is not analogous to that of Native American reservations. See Fairfax and Guenzler (2001, chap. 6 and the references cited there).

11. Referenced in U.S. Southern Appalachian Nat. Park Comm. (1931: 18). A more extensive report was filed in 1926.

12. See *U.S. Statutes at Large* 47 (1932): 37.

13. This still was not enough. In 1938 Congress authorized the use of condemnation authority (citing the 1888 General Act) to acquire lands needed to complete the Great Smoky Mountains National Park in Tennessee. This was, however, during the height of the Depression era, when "anything goes" was the rule on park acquisitions (discussed later).

14. *Cong. Rec.*, 76th Cong., 1st sess., 1939, 84: 10664, 11080, 11172. Discussed in Ise (1961: 263–264).

15. See Schiff (1962) for a reflection on whether the USFS science merited such deference.

16. Compare U.S. NFRC (1920: 3) with Olson (1971). The timber famine was a useful myth for promoting the interests of the scientific forestry community and never had much basis in fact.

17. Recently cut and newly planted areas are especially prone to fires, which could destroy the investment in growing timber, and growing periods of more than a century do not provide an even cash return. The forest industry and scientific foresters used these points to justify subsidies, as opposed to setting timber prices high enough to justify the risks.

18. *U.S. Statutes at Large* 42 (1922): 456.

19. *U.S. Statutes at Large* 43 (1924): 653.

20. *U.S. Statutes at Large* 43 (1928): 1090.

21. A 1925 court case concluded that the General Exchange Act applied only to western reserved forests. Congress acted to extend exchange authority to Weeks Act lands, with the proviso that the NFRC and the state legislature had to approve the exchange (Wheatley 1970: 218).

22. *U.S. Statutes at Large* 43 (1924): 653.

23. The Clarke-McNary Act also authorized the Forest Service to accept gifts of land principally valuable for growing timber (Wheatley 1970: 242). This never became an important element of USFS acquisitions.

24. *U.S. Statutes at Large* 43 (1924): 653, § 6.

25. When they were, the government prevailed. See *Coggeshall v. United States*, 95 F. 2d 986, 989 (4th Cir. 1938) and *Young v. Anderson*, 160 F. 2d 225, 226 (D.C. Cir. 1947), discussed in Wheatley (1970: 237).

26. The Weeks-McLean Bill (cosponsored by the same John W. Weeks of the Weeks Act) was incorporated into the Agriculture Appropriations Act of March 4, 1913, *U.S. Statutes at Large* 37 (1913): 828, 846, 847, 848. Cited in J. Cameron (1929: 95).

27. *United States v. Shauver*, 214 F. 154 (1914), appeal dismissed; 248 U.S. 594 (1919). See Bean and Rowland (1997: 16) and Coggins (1978).

28. Swain (1963: 32–33). Not to be confused with the Migratory Bird Conservation Act of 1928, *U.S. Code*. vol. 16 § 715 (1928).

29. *Missouri v. Holland*, 252 U.S. 416 (1920).

30. Convention of August 16, 1916, *U.S. Statutes at Large* 39 (1916): 1702. We are grateful to intern Anna Rodriguez for her work on the Weeks Act during summer, 1995.

31. Act of August 10, 1912, *U.S. Statutes at Large* 37 (1912): 269, 293.

32. The elk are still a problem. See most recently Chase (1987) and Hess (1993). Today the National Elk Refuge is about 25,000 acres.

33. The Act of June 7, 1924, *U.S. Statutes at Large* 43 (1924): 650, passed two months after the Clarke-McNary Act. See J. Cameron (1929: 109), Gabrielson (1943: 14), Trefethen (1975: 182–184), and U.S. BBS (1925: 23–24).

34. It also led the BBS to lease needed land with the goal of subsequently purchasing it (U.S. BBS 1928: 25–26).

35. Ten thousand acres of the Savanna-Bellevue National Forest were added to the refuge and administered by the BBS, although it formally remained a national forest (J. Cameron 1929: 109–110).

36. *U.S. Statutes at Large* 45 (1929): 1222.

37. The management and administration of the refuges, including the provision for federal wardens, were also supported by direct appropriations. The provision of "inviolate sanctuaries" was a victory for the wildlife "purists" (Swain 1963: 41). However, it proved short lived. In 1949, Congress opened 25 percent of each sanctuary to public hunting, "if compatible with the major purposes" of the area [Act of Aug. 12, 1949, *U.S. Statutes at Large* 63 (1949): 600, ch. 421, § 2, as cited in Environmental Law Institute 1977: 128]; see also Wheatley (1970: 153). In 1958 it increased the allowable hunting area to 40 percent [Act of Aug. 1, 1958, P.L. 85–585, *U.S. Statutes at Large* 72 (1958): 486, at § 2; Environmental Law Institute 1977: 128].

38. Here is more evidence of the constantly receding goal line: In 1941, after 178 refuges had been established, totaling almost 3,500,000 acres, wildlife advocate and scholar Ira N. Gabrielson noted that there was still not enough. "It will require about 75 major units, approximating 4,000,000 acres, to complete the minimum planned program" (see Gabrielson 1941: 231).

39. Wheatley (1970: 147, citing remarks of Representative Andersen, *Cong. Rec.*, 70th Cong., 2nd sess., 1929, 70: 3178).

40. See *United States v. Carmack*, 329 U.S. 230, 241, n. 10 (1946), and *United States v. Montana*, 134 F. 2d 194 (9th Cir. 1943).

41. By continuing to provide appropriations for purchase by condemnation, Congress was said to have "vertically ratified" the use of condemnation (Wheatley 1970: 152). See *United States v. Hunting Rights to Swan Lake Hunting Club*, 237 F. Supp. 290 (N.D. Miss. 1964). See also *Bailey v. Holland*, 126 F. 2d 317 (4th Cir. 1942).

42. Wheatley (1970: 146, citing U.S. Congress. Senate 1935: 3). See also U.S. Congress. House (1935: 3).

43. Given the degree to which Hetch Hetchy shaped conservation advocacy throughout the twentieth century, Mather's subsequent assertion that a hydroelectric power plant in Yosemite "was an absolute necessity in view of the increasing demands for power, light, and heat for the park concessionaires" is stunning (Mather 1916: 17).

44. Our first research on this topic was undertaken by James Behan.

45. The early tendency was to define scenery as mountains (U.S. Congress. House 1916).

46. Many sites that Mather rejected have since been brought into the system at enormous expense.

47. The idea began much earlier, in the 1880s, according to Righter (1982: 22).

48. The act is known at present as the Recreation and Public Purposes Act following amendments made in 1954. It is one of the few disposition statutes not repealed by the Federal Land Policy and Management Act, *U.S. Code*, vol. 43 § 1701.

Chapter 5

1. See Gray (1939, 1936). The definition of submarginal lands is in Gray (1936: 267).

2. Compared with a decrease of less than 2 percent in 2003 (Batie 1985: 107–108; Paarlberg 1982: 1163).

3. More than 37,000 individual properties were acquired. An additional 148,000 acres of public domain were transferred into the land utilization projects (Wooten 1965: 17–18).

4. Although Congress and the Roosevelt administration considered paying with government bonds, all the federal acquisition programs were funded by direct appropriations (see Nixon 1957, vol. 1: 262–263).

5. *United States v. Butler*, 297 U.S. 1, 68–73 (1936).

6. A soil-depleting crop was generally defined as a cash crop that was in surplus. The program is discussed in Kramer and Batie (1985: 307–309; Bowers et al. 1984: 3–10; Benedict 1953: 310).

7. The Supreme Court changed its mind promptly when Roosevelt threatened to add enough additional seats to the Court to gain support for his programs. This judicial response to FDR's "court packing" scheme is appropriately referred to as "the switch in time that saved nine."

8. Roosevelt specifically opposed funding work that was chiefly beneficial to the private landowner. He wrote to Senator Byrnes of South Carolina (May 11, 1933): "[T]he Federal Government cannot properly undertake to reforest privately owned lands without some provision for getting its money back when the timber matures," quoted in Nixon (1957, vol. 1: 144–145, 162).

9. Act of July 22, 1937, *U.S. Statutes at Large 50* (1937): 522. Other titles to the act provided for farm loans and cooperation with state and other public agencies in developing land conservation and utilization programs.

10. U.S. NRCS, n.d.a. President, Executive Order 7908 (1938); *U.S. Statutes at Large 49* (1935): 163; Wooten (1965: 13, 29).

11. See, for example, U.S. FS (1933a: 994) "cooperation which is optional with the forest owners, or public assistance which is not accompanied by the obligation to handle the forest conservatively, has yielded almost negligible results so far as the adoption of good forest practices is concerned."

12. Memorandum from President Roosevelt to the secretaries of interior and agriculture and the director of emergency conservation work, May 3, 1933, in Nixon (1957, vol. 1: 161–162).

13. Excerpt from a presidential press conference, August 11, 1933, quoted in Nixon (1957, vol. 1: 198).

14. As of 1933, 4,727,680 acres had been or were in the process of being purchased (U.S. FS 1933a: 18).

15. See Nancy Langston's story of the Malheur Basin in Oregon (Langston 2003).

16. U.S. BBS (1936: 3; 1937: 4, 5; 1938: 7). We offer these data as suggestive. It is difficult to reconcile the fiscal year allocations reported by the BBS with those reported elsewhere, such as in Nixon (1957, vol. 1: 222, 223, 283, 295, 305, 384, 578–579).

17. Fischman (2003: 32–34) has noted that FWS development is closely tied to executive action. This distinguishes the agency from the NPS, whose units each require a separate act of Congress, and makes it similar to the USFS, which has typically enjoyed general authority and executive control. Fischman's chapter 3 is an excellent place to start.

18. They did not, of course, always obtain them. One oldtimer describes the acquisition of the Hart Mountain Antelope Refuge in Eastern Oregon. A very willing seller owned the top of the mountain, but the relevant habitat was lower down on BLM holdings. In buying the mountaintop, the BBS actually missed the valuable habitat. Aware of this oversight, a group of influentials mainly living in Portland, Oregon, formed an organization called the Order of the Antelope, to "protect the continuation of the area as a national refuge" (Gabrielson 1943: 91–96). Each year the group travels to Hart Mountain to celebrate the questionable acquisition under the stars. The organization also supports wildlife research. Such chicanery did not end with the Depression. See Harrison (1990) for a discussion of a Nature Conservancy-supported FWS acquisition that included no habitat for birds that justified the expenditure. Congress knew that ahead of time and went ahead anyway, apparently helping a constituent unload an undevelopable, hard-to-market parcel.

19. An excellent, underutilized study undertaken for the Outdoor Recreation Resources Review Commission details early federal experience, particularly that of the FWS, with easements (see Williams 1962, chap. 3).

20. In 1936, the Works Progress Administration provided $286,240 for easement refuges in North Dakota (U.S. BBS 1936: 28–29).

21. Many of the properties were scattered, and in 1940 seventy-two of the easement refuges were folded into nearby refuges for administration (U.S. BBS 1941:

227). However, the FWS "likes easements" and less than 5 percent of the original easements have been converted over the years to full fee title (telephone interview, Ron Shupe, refuge supervisor, Mountain-Prairie Region, FWS, June 19, 2003). The easements are difficult to track because they are categorized by the FWS as Waterfowl Production Areas (WPAs) (Fischman 2003: 26–27).

22. U.S. BBS (1935: 21). See also U.S. BBS (1935: 20), which states "approximately 12 percent of lands [were] taken by judicial proceedings because of inability to reach mutual satisfactory price agreements or by reason of incurable defects in title."

23. Act of March 16, 1934, *U.S. Statutes at Large* 48 (1934): 452.

24. Act of June 15, 1935, *U.S. Statutes at Large* 49 (1935): 383.

25. Act of June 15, 1935, discussed in Wheatley (1970: 147–148).

26. Act of March 10, 1934, *U.S. Statutes at Large* 48 (1934): 401.

27. The Tennessee Valley Authority is exempted from the Coordination Act (U.S. FWS 1992: 36).

28. Act of September 2, 1937, *U.S. Statutes at Large* 50 (1937): 917.

29. Fischman (2003: 38–40) chronicles the confusing roots of the FWS.

30. State acceptance of the federal role did not outlast the Depression. The BBS chief wrote to the secretary of agriculture, stating: "I would point out, however, that the various State governments, while accepting the principle of Federal control of migratory game birds have consistently opposed any suggestion that contemplated even a partial control by the Federal government of matters dealing with upland non-migratory game within their borders." Quoted in Nixon (1957, vol. 1: 220).

31. Memorandum from Ira N. Gabrielson, director, Fish and Wildlife Service to Harold L. Ickes, secretary of the interior, September 25, 1940, quoted in Nixon (1957, vol. 2: 476–477).

32. Dilsaver (1994: 165) calls the Depression a "bonanza of development, expansion, and reinterpretation."

33. The best general source on the NPS during the Depression is Unrau and Williss (1983).

34. Richardson (1965) argues that Ickes derailed an Escalante National Monument proposal that resurfaced in great controversy during the Clinton administration.

35. See O'Toole (1995: 11): "Visitation grew rapidly after 1934, mainly due to all the new historic sites and battlefields." See also Foresta (1984: 37, 41).

36. *U.S. Code*, vol. 16 § 461–467.

37. *U.S. Code*, vol. 16 § 462.

38. This act was a consolation prize following Ickes's failure to gain exclusive authority for the NPS to supervise Civilian Conservation Corps recreation projects. The Forest Service successfully removed recreation planning on Department of Agriculture land from the act.

39. In chapter 6 both of those themes return to become the core of the conclusions by the Outdoor Recreations Resources Review Commission.

40. King (1988: 280) asserts that there is no actual "malice in the Park Service's orientation" toward historic preservation. No regional directors or superintendents "burn with the desire to knock down historic buildings or bulldoze archaeological sites," he claims, utilizing a rather minimalist standard. "Rather, it is a matter of thoughtlessness," he concludes.

41. Swain (1972: 319) describes Edge as "an indefatigable park lobbyist."

42. Not that the Forest Service was without cause for worry; the League was also suspicious of a powerful family that was lobbying to sell low-quality redwood lands along the Klamath River. The family succeeded in interesting the USFS in what many considered worthless land (Schrepfer 1983: 59), and a USFS purchase unit was established in the early 1940s. Dickinson (1974: 98–114) discusses the politics of USFS acquisitions in the area.

43. U.S. NRPB (1940, part I: 13).

44. *U.S. Statutes at Large* 45 (1928): 787, ch. 817.

45. An appraisal is a written statement prepared by an independent and impartial qualified appraiser who estimates the value of a property on a specific date and describes the information relied upon in making the estimate. It is an essential element of any land acquisition.

46. Ise (1961: 319) notes that Congress' first appropriation of funds for the acquisition of private lands occurred in 1927, provided it was matched 50/50 from other sources.

47. Before it was replaced by the Works Projects Administration in 1939, the PWA had spent more than $6 billion on job-creating construction projects.

48. About one-third of the necessary land was transferred from the U.S. Forest Service, with some grumbling (discussed in Quin 1997: 63). Some property was acquired by the Area Resettlement Administration; private owners donated some; and some was acquired directly by the Park Service (Speer and Haskell 2000: 30).

49. For a discussion of "givings" and how they relate to takings and compensation, see chapter 1.

50. Our understanding of the Jefferson National Expansion Memorial has benefited from conversations and e-mail exchanges with Thomas Dewey, librarian, Jefferson National Expansion Historical Association.

51. Hosmer (1987: x) puts the Philadelphia experience explicitly into the context of battles between and among the local boosters, NPS architects who emphasized precision in restoration, and the NPS historians who viewed the park as a way to teach the "values of the founding fathers."

52. *U.S. Code*, vol. 16 § 407(s).

53. The standard account of NPS land acquisition authority locates this event in Cape Cod. See W. Brown (1993: 104–105) and Sax (1976). We do not agree.

54. *U.S. Code*, vol. 43 § 315ff (1964). Discussed in Muhn et al. (1988: 37–41).

55. *U.S. Code*, vol. 43 § 315g (1964). See also *U.S. Code*, vol. 43 § 1701 et seq. Discussed in Anderson (1979: 669).

56. Compare this with the exchange authority given to the Northern Pacific Railroad in the Mount Rainier exchange.

57. The 1936 amendments to the act maintained the equal value basis for exchanges with private parties but allowed that exchanges with states could be based upon either equal value or an equal acreage standard. Discussed in Wheatley (1970: 24).

58. This is a special land protection category described in the Federal Land Policy and Management Act, *U.S. Code*, vol. 43 § 1702(a) (1976).

59. Fort Ticonderoga, "Mission," at ⟨http://www.fort-ticonderoga.org/history/mission.htm⟩.

Chapter 6

1. According to the Land Trust Alliance, a conservation easement is "a legal agreement that permanently restricts the development and use of land to ensure protection of its conservation values" (Land Trust Alliance, "What is a Conservation Easement?" at ⟨http://www.lta.org/conserve/easement.htm⟩). A conservation easement is a general term that can include scenic easements, agricultural easements, historic preservation easements, and a host of other goals. Typically, a conservation easement transfers some development and management options (or "sticks in the bundle")—such as the right to subdivide or to cut trees—from the landowner to an organization that holds those rights, called a nonpossessory interest in the land. The fee holder retains all other rights. An easement is distinguishable from the fee, fee simple, or full fee title. All those terms refer to the maximum possible interest one can hold in real property. The fee is of indefinite duration, freely transferable and inheritable. The fee holder is the one who holds the possessory interest in land under a conservation easement; that is, all rights and responsibilities except those identified in the easement. Sometimes the fee holder will reserve particular uses, perhaps to build additional homes, add roads, or plant row crops. Under an easement, the fee holder donates or is compensated for whatever rights are relinquished, and only pays property taxes on the remaining value of the land. The easement holder is responsible for monitoring and enforcing easement terms but, happily, as a nonprofit entity, is not required to pay taxes on the portion of rights that are separated from the fee.

2. Land and Water Conservation Fund Act, *U.S. Code*, vol. 16 §§ 460l-4-11.

3. Although the LWCF is frequently discussed as a trust fund, Congress is too protective of its role in distributing goodies to support automatic funding for such attractive bacon. Congressmen earmark virtually the entire annual appropriation for specific projects in their districts (Zinn 2001). The trust fund idea also incorrectly suggests that acquisitions are to be funded by outside sources.

True, the LWCF is annually "credited" with revenues from recreation user fees, motor boat fuel taxes, and public land sales; a portion of outer continental shelf oil leasing receipts was added later. However, the bookkeeping is a ruse: LWCF money is appropriated annually from the general treasury, and no interest accrues on any theoretical unspent balance.

4. For acquisition of endangered species habitat, see Bean and Rowland (1997: 194, 196); for wetlands, see U.S. NOAA (n.d.).

5. Congress has ignored both agreements. Both agencies can acquire land outside 1964 boundaries with LWCF money because Congress routinely backdates language that adds units to pretend the addition happened on January 3, 1965. Similarly, the 85 percent constraint is not controlling on subsequent congressional acts that specifically contradict it. The USFS is peculiar in that only it regards areas acquired with LWCF funds as wholly subject to agency discretion regarding management. The other three all define the use of LWCF-funded lands solely by LWCF purposes.

6. This is a variant on the Cape Cod model discussed later.

7. *U.S. Code*, vol. 31 § 6901–6907.

8. The legislation is known as "The Department of Agriculture Organic Act," *U.S. Statutes at Large* 70 (1956): 1032.

9. P.L. 90–171, *U.S. Code*, vol. 16 § 484a.

10. National Forest Management Act, *U.S. Statutes at Large* 90 (1976): 2949, passed in 1976 to amend the agency's 1897 organic act [*U.S. Statutes at Large* 30 (1897): 11] after a series of courts had found its timber management program, including clearcutting, unauthorized.

11. *U.S. Code*, vol. 16 § 1600ff. The USFS is included primarily to extend authority to acquire land for access to federally owned land.

12. *U.S. Code*, vol. 43 § 1701(a)(1). The section continues "unless as a result of the land use planning procedure provided for in this Act, it is determined that disposal of a particular parcel will serve the national interest."

13. This figure is Wheatley's estimate (1970: S-1). Like most aggregate figures of federal land ownership, it is potentially misleading. Of the 470.3 million acres administered by the BLM in 1970, 295.4 million were in Alaska.

14. *U.S. Code*, vol. 43 § 1715(a).

15. A BLM land exchange has been called "the most difficult real estate transaction in the world" (Mulford 1984: 23).

16. This has required Congress to pass special legislation to achieve interstate land exchanges (see Rosenthal 1996; Vaskov 2001–2002).

17. *U.S. Code*, vol. 43 § 206(a)(2001).

18. *U.S. Statutes at Large* 44 (1926): 741, as amended, *U.S. Code*, vol. 43 § 869–73. In addition, the transfers of federal land can be made at reduced prices under the Federal Property and Administrative Services Act of 1949, *U.S. Statutes*

at Large 63 (1949): 377, *U.S. Code*, vol. 40 § 484. Under those two acts, federal property can be offered at a discount or free to states and localities for schools, parks, recreational facilities, hospitals, and historic monuments (Mulford 1984: 17).

19. *U.S. Code*, vol. 16 § 459(e)(1964). The remaining 10 percent was acquired from the state of Utah by exchange for other BLM lands.

20. Act of August 1, 1958, *U.S. Statutes at Large* 72 (1958): 486.

21. Revenue sharing on withdrawn refuge lands remained at 25 percent of the net revenues from the land. Counties having refuges on land withdrawn from the public domain also receive payments in lieu of taxes under PILTs (U.S. FWS 1992: 69), but Congress still must appropriate the funds each year. In practice, Congress has generally authorized smaller payments to counties than are authorized in the law.

22. Our discussion of current Blue Ridge Parkway land acquisition programs has benefited from visits, e-mail and telephone conversations with J. David Anderson, Sheila Gasperson, Janet Bachmann, and Greg Johnson, all of the NPS, Blue Ridge Parkway; Chuck Roe, Rusty Painter, and Ed Norwall of the Conservation Trust for North Carolina; Roger Holnback, Western Virginia Land Trust; and Faye Cooper, Virginia Outdoor Foundation.

23. *United States v. 365.0 Acres of Land in Augusta County, Virginia*, 428 F. 2d 459 (4th Cir, Va.) (1970).

24. The statute defines "improved properties" as those consisting of one-family dwellings erected prior to September 1, 1959 (see Foster 1985: 70). The NPS was authorized to condemn commercial and industrial properties inconsistent with the seashore.

25. The legislation also included an advisory commission, with substantial (seven of ten members) local representation, to guide park establishment and management. Cape Cod National Seashore Act, *U.S. Statutes at Large*, 75 (1951): 284.

26. This discussion is based on conversations about Cape Cod with Lauren McKean, NPS planner, fall 1997.

27. Development was so intense that local voters adopted a temporary moratorium on all new construction in 1988 (Colinvaux and Galowitz 1989). In 1990, voters approved a new regional planning and regulatory agency, the Cape Cod Commission, as well as a local land-banking program. See ⟨http:// www.capecodcommission.org⟩. Each of the six towns developed its own local comprehensive plan in the mid-1990s.

28. Point Reyes National Seashore Act, *U.S. Statutes at Large* 76 (1962): 538. Also see Watt (2001: 130–139).

29. *U.S. Statutes at Large* 90 (1976): 1939, P.L. 94–458 § 8.

30. *U.S. Statutes at Large* 92 (1978): 3467.

31. For a wonderful defense of local as opposed to national priorities, see Vowell (2002: 131–140).

32. Little modeled the term *greenline* after the "blue line" boundary of Adirondack Park.

33. The Conservancy is a state-run land trust. It acquires land or interests in land, such as easements (California Environmental Resources Evaluation System 2002).

34. The discussion is based on a series of telephone conversations with Barbara Pollarine of the NPS.

35. Reaction within the NPS to its own first report on Cuyahoga, released in 1971, "was largely 'raised eyebrows and a lot of jokes' about a national park featuring a flammable river" (Cockrell 1992: 80).

36. Cockrell (1992, quoting interview with NPS employee Theodore R. McCann).

37. *U.S. Statutes at Large* 88 (1974): 1784, P.L. 93–555 § 2(b): "The Secretary shall not acquire privately owned lands which are held and used for public recreation uses unless he determines that such lands are essential to carry out the purposes of the Act."

38. *U.S. Statutes at Large* 88 (1974): 1784 § 2(c): "Fee title to such improved properties shall not be acquired unless the Secretary finds such lands are being used, or are threatened with uses, which are detrimental to the purposes of the recreation area, or unless such acquisition is necessary to fulfill the purposes of the Act."

39. See letter, Leslie P. Arnberger, Yosemite superintendent, to Robert A. Bradford, August 23, 1978. Yosemite Research Library Box: Lands-El Portal-General, FS/NPS interchange.

40. See Mariposa County, California, *Weekly Gazette* September 7, 1978, "County Calls for Halt on Inholding Purchases; Cooperation to Insure Compatibility in Wawona," p. 1, 6.

41. Courts have repeatedly held that NEPA does not require an agency to do an environmental impact statement when it is buying property.

42. The Land Trust Alliance, chief coordinating and lobbying organization for the land trust movement, was founded in 1982 and is discussed in chapter 8. See the LTA website: ⟨http://www.lta.org⟩. It operates at a national level but does not acquire or hold land or conservation easements.

43. Charitable institutions such as churches and schools have enjoyed special tax status for centuries. Stacy Dinstell conducted our first research on nonprofits (see Hopkins 1998; Oleck 1977).

44. For a good introduction to land trust activities, see Poole (1993: 62–69).

45. The Conservation Fund, "Mission Statement," at ⟨http://www.conservationfund.org/?article=2401⟩.

46. This emphasis on working landscapes is also reflected in the American Farmland Trust (AFT), founded in 1980 to protect America's best farmland, but with no analogous foot in the movement toward a more sustainable agriculture. The AFT believes that farmers are the best land stewards and that easements should not condition farming practices or tell the farmer how to farm.

47. For an early insight into perceived problems with easements, see Gose (1966).

48. This discussion benefited from conversations with Ann Marie Buckley and Skip Kauffman of the Accokeek Foundation, James Rees of the MVLA, and numerous NPS officials.

49. *U.S. Statutes at Large*, 75 (1961): 780.

50. Hartzog notes that the problem of working in rural areas where there are no zoning codes and a reluctance to promulgate them was first encountered in Piscataway Park. Easements, lease-back and sell-back, and similar tools were first used there and later extended to other areas of the national park system (Hartzog 1988: 257–258).

51. Although the agency was forced into the arrangement, NPS Director George Hartzog devotes three pages of his memoir to the inside story of how the Piscataway Park finally got its crucial appropriation (1988: 149–151). It is still not, however, a "national" park.

52. Fort Washington and Fort Hall were acquired by the NPS during the Depression.

53. Commentators frequently assert that the LWCF was the only or the primary source of funds for land acquisition for the federal land management agencies (Coggins and Glicksman 1984: 155, 161). That is misleading. Although the LWCF is the only consistent source of NPS acquisition funding, Congress often provides special funding, frequently but not always under cover of the LWCF, for special projects such as acquisition of the Valles Caldera in New Mexico (see chapter 9) or the various Redwoods purchases. The 1978 Redwoods acquisitions alone cost more than $689 million, which is about 8.4 percent of all federal LWCF appropriations between 1964 and 2001 combined.

54. An Act to establish a Redwood National Park in the State of California and for other purposes, *U.S. Statutes at Large*, 82 (1968): 931.

55. The Sierra Club had proposed a 91,000-acre park, including all but 100,000 acres of the Redwood Creek Basin; the League, which had made several purchases in the Mill Creek drainage, suggested that the NPS acquire the rest, about 41,834 acres (Hudson 1979: 796–798).

56. The court of claims was problematic because interest on the judgment runs until payment is made; that is, during the proceedings. In the district courts, the government is "required to deposit with the Court their estimated just compensation," which stops accrual of interest (U.S. GAO 1977a: 12–13).

57. *U.S. Code*, vol. 16 § 79(c)(e). Discussed in Hudson (1979: 808–835).

58. *Sierra Club v. Department of the Interior*, 376 F. Supp. 90 (1974), 398 F. Supp. 284 (1975), and *Sierra Club v. Department of the Interior*, 424 F. Supp. 172 (1976).

59. *Sierra Club v. Department of the Interior*, 424 F. Supp. 172 (1976).

Chapter 7

1. Reagan's address is available at ⟨http://www.townhall.com/documents/RR1st.html⟩.

2. When the Office of Management and Budget slashed the NPS budget request, it told the NPS to collect fees instead. Congress responded by freezing entrance fees. However, any politician's embrace of the "user pays" principle is likely to be selective. Reagan defended a grazing fee formula for both BLM and USFS lands that virtually gave away the federal range (Mackintosh 1983).

3. The dispute between Congress and Watt gave rise to numerous General Accounting Office and congressional reports. An early GAO report (U.S. GAO 1979) evinces growing discontent with expansive and expensive federal acquisition programs. Early hearings before the Senate Committee on Energy and Natural Resources (U.S. Congress. Senate 1981) sought alternatives to costly and intrusive federal full fee acquisitions, but, faced with Watt, Congress changed its mind. Hearings before the House Committee on Interior and Insular Affairs (U.S. Congress. House 1984) attacked Watt and were almost hostile to what are consistently referred to in quotation marks as "'alternative' acquisition methods." See also U.S. GAO (1980, 1981). Some assert that the NPS did all it could to discredit easements, paying as close to the full value as possible.

4. The order was announced before the BLM completed any of the land use plans that must precede a sale. Under pressure, the bureau concocted a list of 2.7 million acres that could possibly be sold. Eventually 4.4 million acres were identified (see Coggins and Nagel 1990: 494–496).

5. Ronald Reagan, Executive Order 12630, *Federal Register* 53 (March 15, 1988): 8859. The best general articles on takings are Sax (1964, 1971a, and 1993) and Freyfogel (1995).

6. *Nollan v. California Coastal Commission*, 483 U.S. 825 (1987); *First English Evangelical Lutheran Church of Glendale v. County of Los Angeles*, 482 U.S. 304 (1987); *Dolan v. City of Tigard*, 114 L. Ct. 2319 (1994); and *Lucas v. South Carolina Coastal Council*, 505 U.S. 1003 (1992).

7. The Supreme Court continued to toy with takings law into the next century. More recently, the court's decision in *Tahoe Sierra Preservation Council v. Tahoe Regional Planning Agency*, 122 S. Ct. 1465 (2002) handed the environmental regulators their first clear win in fifteen years, affirming regulations to protect water quality in Lake Tahoe (Georgetown Environmental Law and Policy Institute n.d.).

8. Agencies and advocates coined a number of terms; ecosystem management is probably the most ubiquitous (see U.S. FS 2002).

9. Discussed in Vileisis (1999), the standard reference on the evolution of Americans' thinking about, destroying, and protecting swamps and wetlands.

10. Our understanding of the Farm Bill has benefited from conversations with Alan Forkey, state wetlands biologist, Natural Resources Conservation Service, California Office; Clive Potter, reader in rural policy, Imperial College of Science, Technology and Medicine, London; and Russ Shay, LTA public policy director.

11. Agricultural subsidies were a major agenda item at the Uruguay Round of the General Agreement on Tariffs and Trade negotiations that started in 1986. The negotiations lasted until 1994, but the pressure to reduce subsidies was already apparent in 1985 (discussed in Sheingate 2001).

12. At the LTA's 2002 rally, there were nine panels on farm-related issues. At one panel discussion, attendees were encouraged to "start thinking about this money as part of your cash flow strategy." And indeed, they would be crazy if they did not.

13. The Forest Legacy Program is the only "new news" regarding the USFS in this period. Because it is an element of the Farm Bill, we therefore address the USFS in this section and do not cover it in the discussion of four federal agencies. That may create some awkwardness, but it does underscore the growing importance of Farm Bill funds.

14. Even the "federal" side of the program is a mosaic. The Commodity Credit Corporation administers it through the Farm Services Agency. Support is provided by the Natural Resources Conservation Service, the Cooperative State Research and Education Extension Service, state forestry agencies, and by local Soil and Water Conservation districts (see ⟨http://www.fsa.usda.gov/dafp/cepd/crpinfo.htm⟩).

15. Ten-year contracts are frequently criticized as too short; however, they do permit restoration on land on which other agencies hold easements.

16. The states, however, failed to achieve PILTs for the value of the easement on the land.

17. A. Dana and Susan W. Dana (2002) compare land trusts to the start-up period of the Internet.

18. The NCCUSL has a lengthy, well-defined process for drafting uniform state laws on any topic (Personal communication from Katie Robinson, public communications director, NCCUSL, January 8, 2003); see also King and Fairfax (2004).

19. Massachusetts colleagues praise the requirement and report that easements without clear conservation value have been rejected.

20. Note that while land trusts were proliferating rapidly, they were a bicoastal preoccupation, with blanks in the upper Midwest slowly filling in over the 1990s (see Wright 1993).

21. Key gatherings were held by the French and Pickering Creeks Conservation Trust in Pennsylvania in 1974 and 1979. The Lincoln Institute of Land Policy funded a national consultation on private land conservation in the fall of 1981. A month later, the Montana Land Reliance held a similar meeting in San Francisco. Preparatory papers and much of the discussion from both meetings is captured in Montana Land Reliance and Land Trust Exchange (1982).

22. The first was in cooperation with the National Trust for Historic Preservation and the second with TPL.

23. There were 257 participants. The organization also unveiled a national study of easements (see "Special Issue: Report on 1985 National Survey of Government and Non-Profit Easement Programs" 1985).

24. Some of the larger groups, even those that were working to form the Land Trust Exchange, did not see themselves as land trusts. Perhaps they saw themselves as superior to the groups then sprouting at the rate of about twenty per year. The national organizations recognized the importance of local leadership, enthusiasm, and support. "Fledging" new groups were a major element of TPL programs in the early 1980s.

25. The two organizations are nominally separate, but they have the same staff and board. The Adirondack Nature Conservancy focuses on biodiversity projects and the Adirondack Land Trust on other elements of the landscape.

26. Vermont also passed significant regulation to control clearcutting and aerial application of herbicides and pesticides on timberland.

27. The district also provides protection from nuisance ordinances that would limit customary farming practices, such as manure spreading or prescribed burning (described in Valley Conservation Council 2004).

28. The Virginia transfer program is modeled on a similar program in Colorado. In both states there is a tax credit exchange to match credit holders with parties interested in acquiring them (see Conservation Resource Center 2004).

29. Note that a tax credit is different from a tax deduction. A deduction lowers the income on which taxes must be paid. A credit is subtracted directly from the tax payment due.

30. Lest we create the impression that this inability to work with land trusts is endemic, a brief return to Acadia National Park in Maine is instructive. As in Gettysburg, the donated park continued without a clearly delineated purchase boundary, causing conflict with local communities and landowners. In 1985 Congress established a boundary and an acreage cap for fee acquisitions and also identified land for deletion from the park. However, Acadia, true to its roots, relies most heavily for land protection on donated land and donated conservation easements. Easements do not count toward the fee acquisition cap. Acadia personnel work with many of fourteen land trusts in the area, primarily the Maine Coast Heritage Trust, all of which acquire easements. The park acquired its first easement in 1970, and Acadia officials report that it is not unlikely that the park will some day include more easement than fee lands. At

present, the NPS has 47,448 acres in fee and easement, with another 157 tracts of 1990 acres left to be acquired within the fee boundary. It holds 12,116 acres under 189 easements, all but two of which were donated. Only four or five easements allow public access. However, that provides access to over a third of the eased land because the largest easement, one that was purchased, does allow access. And lest readers conclude that only privately negotiated easements allow special considerations that benefit existing landowners, Congress has written into the Acadia section of the *U.S. Code* numerous detailed provisions for specific properties and landowners affected by the park [see *U.S. Code*, vol. 16 § 341 ff. (2004) and U.S. NPS 1988].

31. This objection seems a bit weak considering the extent to which NPS acquisitions in particular had long depended on donations, but most land trusts make no bones about covering expenses and reinvesting profits in other conservation transactions.

32. Even though the Forest Service was at a safer distance, the Department of the Interior administers the LWCF. It had been the annual practice for the interior undersecretary of Fish, Wildlife and Parks to contact the chief of the Forest Service for that agency's LWCF priorities. During the 1980s, those calls stopped coming.

33. An option to buy entitles the holder to purchase real estate, usually at a stated price. The option holder pays the landowner not to sell the land until a certain date. If the holder does not exercise the option by the agreed-upon date, he or she loses the fee. Frequently in a preacquisition, the land trust will buy an option, not the property itself, for the government. The land trust holds the option until the government acquires the land directly from the landowner. That is useful if hazardous materials are found on the site, so that only parties in the chain of title share liability.

34. Land trusts frequently seek conservation buyers for properties threatened with intensive development. The land trust can act almost as a real estate agent, finding a buyer who agrees to limit development on a property. Perhaps later, the land trust will work with the new owner on an easement. However, until that happens, the land is at a reduced risk of development.

35. Holly Bundock, public affairs officer, Pacific West Region, National Park Service, in a number of letters and e-mails provided our first guidance regarding changes in NPS regulations.

36. The act also directs the Forest Service to restore watersheds and administer erosion control grants to units of local government and to make payments in lieu of taxes to the local governments where federal land was acquired.

37. *U.S. Code*, vol. 43 §§ 2301(12)(A), 2301(14)(B).

38. This should not confuse FWS data; acreage managed or acreage in refuges is not the same as acreage owned or acquired by the FWS. See Fischman (2003) for a fuller discussion of the composition of refuges.

39. We are grateful to Don Morgan of the U.S. Fish and Wildlife Service for these figures and a basic introduction to these section 6 acquisition programs.

40. Our understanding of the Blackfoot has benefited greatly from conversations, visits, and e-mails with Kevin Ertl, Greg Neudecker, and Gary Sullivan of the FWS; Jay Erickson and Rock Ringling of the Montana Land Reliance; Bee Hall of TNC; Allie Duval Jonkel, University of Montana, Missoula; and Bob Kiesling.

41. Son of the famous writer Anne Morrow Lindbergh and her aviator husband Charles.

42. Discussed in U.S. FWS (n.d.b.).

43. The PFW program is another of the Fish and Wildlife Service's odd pockets —a program that provides technical and financial assistance to landowners who are restoring habitat on private lands.

44. Only five of the MLR's easements have been purchased. The landowners involved could not afford to donate, so the land trust worked out a bargain sale—a combination of donation and purchase that minimized taxes and maximized return to the owner.

45. The MLR's largest single easement is 15,000 acres near Great Falls, Montana. Until the Northern Forest transaction discussed in chapters 8 and 9, it was the largest easement in the United States.

Chapter 8

1. Our understanding of the Conservation and Reinvestment Act has benefited from conversations with Jim Beirne and David Brooks, staff, Senate Committee on Energy and Natural Resources; John Doggett, American Farm Bureau Federation; Max Peterson, former chief, USFS, currently with the International Association of State Fish and Wildlife Agencies; Mark Rey, undersecretary, U.S. Department of Agriculture; Margaret Stewart, staff, Senate Budget Committee; and Shawn Whitman, staff to Senator Craig Thomas. Matt Gerhart spoke with all of them July 8–9, 2002, in Washington, D.C.

2. Our understanding of the LWCF in land acquisitions and the role of the land trusts in LWCF transactions has benefited from conversations with Howard Miller of the NPS; Mike Williams, David Sherman, and Dennis Kennedy of the USFS; David Beaver, Dick Todd, Ann Morgan, and Andy Sulti of the BLM; Eric Alvarez of the FWS; and Jim Snow and Mark Rey of the USDA. One story on why the federal funding survived while the state support vanished is related to the notion of acquisition as pork. When the budget ax fell, rather than eliminate federal funds, Congress eliminated the state money, which it viewed as providing ribbon-cutting opportunities for mayors and governors.

3. Examples of land trusts assisting sustainable agriculture are multiplying. For example, we are aware of two land trusts, one in the San Juan Islands of

Washington state and the other in the central coast area of California, which have taken on ownership of mobile processing facilities for small-scale, sustainable livestock producers, in order to make local food production and distribution both possible and affordable.

4. See the *Washington Post* series: Ottaway and Stephens (2003a,b), Stephens and Ottaway (2003a,b,c), and Arnold (1999); and the *Philadelphia Inquirer* series: McCoy and Harris (2002).

5. Start with the *Seattle Times* series "Trading Away the West" (1998). See also Draffan and Blaeloch (2000), U.S. GAO (2000), and U.S. OIG (2001).

6. When combined with the designation of national monuments on BLM lands, the exchanges may appear as an effort to reposition the federal lands. The idea is as follows: New national monuments on BLM land identify the cream of BLM holdings for transfer to the NPS, and the exchanges begin a process of disposing of the rest. President Clinton designated national monuments that for the first time would be managed by the BLM: Agua Fria (Arizona), California Coastal (California), Canyons of the Ancients (Colorado), Carrizo Plain (California), Cascade-Siskiyou (Oregon), Grand Canyon-Parshant (Arizona), Grand Staircase-Escalante (Utah), Ironwood Forest (Arizona), Kasha-Katuwe Tent Rocks (New Mexico), Pompeys Pillar (Montana), Santa Rosa-San Jacinto Mountains (California), Sonoran Desert (Arizona), Upper Missouri River Breaks (Montana), and Vermillion Cliffs (Arizona) and Craters of the Moon (Idaho) (to be comanaged with the Park Service).

7. The BLM only tracks the number of transactions, not the value of land exchanged or acquired.

8. Recall that the federal agencies are prevented from exercising condemnation authority to acquire wilderness inholdings under section 5(A) of the act.

9. BLM appraisals are available to the public before the transaction is complete (see "Trading Away the West" 1998, part II).

10. President Bush's proposed 2006 budget amends SNPLMA to reduce the 85 percent allocated to conservation projects to 15 percent of the fund and allocates the other 70 percent to the U.S. Treasury (Spratt 2005: 57). If this passes, the federal government will be selling land to retire the national debt as Reagan proposed two decades earlier, and the process of federal land disposition, at least in Nevada, will be under full sail.

11. Compare this with a similar dispute in New York, where all private rights to camps expire in 2013.

12. The final plan for the West Mountain Wildlife Management Area is available. See Vermont Agency of Natural Resources 2002. The supplementary agreement is available at ⟨http//www.vlt.org/CIAgreement.html⟩.

13. Those federal acquisitions include 4,216 acres preacquired by TNC and 605 preacquired by TPL, as well as five small SPNHF acquisitions totaling 556.07 acres that are double counted in our data.

14. These sales radically altered the status quo that many traditional land users in Maine were so concerned about protecting. Docherty explains: "Maine is no longer owned by local companies with personal ties to the state. In 1983, when Great Northern Paper was 'one of the most powerful companies in the state,' its chief executive lived in Millinocket [Maine] with his employees. Between 1983 and 1998, Great Northern was sold twice and its workforce dropped from 4200 to 1700. Although many local residents professed relief that the land had been sold to other paper companies instead of the government, the change in ownership and the potential for more sales makes the future of the forest uncertain" (Docherty 2000: 557–558, references omitted).

15. For a brief window into Pingree family participation in Maine conservation, and the "public lots controversy," see Fairfax and Guenzler (2001, chap. 9, esp. pp. 158–159).

16. "How long," the president of the Maine Conservation Rights Institute asked, "before the land suits begin to hit the courts and we can expect to see the U.N. symbol announcing 'ANOTHER WORLD HERITAGE SITE—THE NORTHER[N] FOREST BIO-REGION'" (Joy 2001).

17. In 1990 legislation required to straighten out a previous transaction between the owners and the Department of the Interior, the Forest Service was authorized to study the area for acquisition. Thus the wheels had been greased for a Forest Service-dominated unit.

18. Local opposition was extensive and included other inholders and private landowners and local government officials.

19. Conservation Fund programs reflect the Mellon family's interest in Civil War sites (see The Conservation Fund 2002).

20. The two organizations merged in November 1999. The Association for the Preservation of Civil War Sites was formed in 1989 and the Civil War Trust in 1991.

21. Research on this subject was undertaken by Gerri Unger and benefits from discussion with Darwin Kelsey, CVCC director and John Debo, CVNP superintendent.

22. States do not share outer continental shelf receipts as they do onshore oil and gas revenues derived from public lands. That has never pleased either the coastal states or, more obviously, the noncoastal states. CARA was, in part, a potential hand in the cookie jar.

23. *United States v. Three Tracts of Land . . . in Jackson County Alabama* 377 F. Supp. 631 (1974).

Chapter 9

1. We have benefited from conversations with former BLM director in California Ed Hasty and from an LTA field trip to the area during the 2003 rally in Sacramento.

2. The Stone Lakes National Wildlife Refuge map is available at ⟨http://stonelakes.fws.gov/refugemap.htm⟩. What constitutes a mosaic depends in part on the scale of the map. For example, figure 9.1 includes more than the Cosumnes project. Delta Meadows (state) and Rancho Seco (local utility district) parks, for unclear reasons, are not considered a part of the preserve; neither is the Woodbridge Ecological Reserve, which is managed by the California Department of Fish and Game. Finally, although it is a mosaic all its own, including FWS fee lands and easements, land under cooperative agreement with the FWS, and holdings of a regional sanitary district, the Stone Lakes National Wildlife Refuge (FWS) is also not a part of the Cosumnes project.

3. Other landowners are the California Department of Fish and Game; the California Department of Water Resources; the Sacramento County Department of Regional Parks, Open Space and Recreation; the Wildlife Conservation Board; Ducks Unlimited; and TNC.

4. Tennessee Environmental Council, Inc., et al. v. Bright Par 3 Associates, L.P., et al., No. E2003-01982-COA-R3-CV (Tenn. Ct. App. Mar. 8, 2004).

5. The initial news was worse than it sounds. The IRS targeted several types of deductions that were likely to be questionable and included conservation easements in the same category as deductions for donated automobiles, not a happy place to be. The new IRS Notice [IR-2004-41 (June 30, 2004)] was discussed at a special session of the 2004 LTA Rally in Rhode Island. The JCT report (U.S. JCT 2005) was even worse. It is not clear what the outcome will be, but the future of donated easements is seriously at risk.

6. We note the frequent assertion that timely acquisition can keep costs down (Sax 1980a). In this context, land trust preacquisition activities are particularly important.

7. See Institute for Community Economics, ⟨http://www.iceclt.org/clt/cltlist.html⟩.

8. The law is quite complex (see Dukeminier and Krier 1998: 291 ff).

9. It seems worth noting here that most community land trust leases that limit use of the land run for ninety-nine years.

References

Abbott, Gordon, Jr. 1993. *Saving Special Places, A Centennial History of The Trustees of Reservations: Pioneer of the Land Trust Movement.* Beverly, Mass.: The Trustees of Reservations.

Abernethy, Thomas Perkins. 1937. *Western Lands and the American Revolution.* New York: Appleton-Century.

Adirondack Museum and Adirondack History Network. 2000. "The Great Experiment. A Central Park for the World." ⟨http://www.adirondackhistory.org/newpark/chsix.html⟩.

Albers, Heidi J. and Amy W. Ando. 2003. "Could State-Level Variation in the Number of Land Trusts Make Economic Sense?" *Land Economics* 79(3): 311–327.

Allen, Thomas B. 2000. *The Washington Monument: It Stands for All.* New York: Discovery Books.

Anderson, Frederick. 1979. "Public Land Exchanges, Sales and Purchases Under the Federal Land Policy and Management Act of 1976." *Utah Law Review* 1979(4): 657.

Arendt, Randall. 1999. "Planning for the Better." *Exchange* 18: 1.

Arnold, Ron. 1999. *Undue Influence: Wealthy Foundations, Grant Driven Environmental Groups and Zealous Bureaucrats that Control Your Future.* Bellevue, Wash.: Free Enterprise Press.

Ashburne, Marny, Madeleine Eno, and Katharine Wroth. 2001. "Appalachian Mountain Club. Earnest Seekers: A Journey Through 125 Years of AMC History, Accomplishments, and Personalities." *AMC Outdoors* Jan./Feb. ⟨http://www.outdoors.org/publications/outdoors/2001/2001-125years-main.cfm⟩.

Bama, Lynne. 1999. "Wheeling and Dealing." *High Country News* March 29. ⟨http://www.hcn.org/servlets/hcn.URLRemapper/1999/mar29/dir/Feature_Wheeling_a.html⟩.

Batie, Sandra S. 1985. "Soil Conservation in the 1980s: A Historical Perspective." *Agricultural History* 59: 107.

Bean, Michael J. and Melanie J. Rowland. 1997. *The Evolution of National Wildlife Law.* 3d ed. Westport, Conn.: Praeger.

Beaudoin, Ryan M. 2000. "Federal Ownership and Management of America's Public Lands Through Land Exchanges." *Great Plains Natural Resources Journal* 4: 229.

Beauvais, Ted. 1996. "Legacy Law Changes with 1996 Farm Bill." *Forest Legacy* 1: 1.

Beliveau, Laura S. 1993. "The Forest Legacy Program: Using Conservation Easements to Preserve the Northern Forest." *Boston College Environmental Affairs Law Review* 20: 507–531.

Benedict, Murray R. 1953. *Farm Policies of the United States, 1790–1950: A Study of Their Origins and Development.* New York: Twentieth Century Fund.

Berck, Peter and William R. Bentley. 1997. "Hotelling's Theory, Enhancement and the Taking of the Redwood National Park." *American Journal of Agricultural Economics* 79(2): 287–299.

Betts, Robert B. 1978. *Along the Ramparts of the Tetons: The Saga of Jackson Hole, Wyoming.* Boulder, Col.: Colorado Associated University Press.

Binkley, Clark and Perry Hagenstein, eds. 1989. *Conserving the North Woods: Issues in Public and Private Ownership of Forested Lands in Northern New England and New York.* New Haven, Conn.: Yale School of Forestry and Environmental Studies.

Blackmer, Stephen D. 1989. "Conserving the Diamond Lands." *Exchange* 8(1): 14–16.

Blaeloch, Janine. 2000. "Land Trades Fraught With Problems." *Seattle Post-Intelligencer* July 25, p. B5. ⟨http://seattlepi.nwsource.com/opinion/land25.shtml⟩.

Bowers, Douglas E., Wayne D. Rasmussen, and Gladys L. Baker. 1984. *History of Agricultural Price-Support and Adjustment Programs, 1933–1984.* Agricultural Information Bulletin No. 485. Washington, D.C.: U.S. Department of Agriculture, Economic Research Service.

Bowers, Edward A., B. E. Fernow, and Frederick Law Olmstead. 1895. "A Plan to Save the Forests: Forest Preservation by Military Control." *Century Magazine* 49(4): 626–634.

Boyd, William C. 2002. "New South, New Nature: Regional Industrialization and Environmental Change in the Post-New Deal American South." Ph.D. diss., University of California, Berkeley.

Bremer, Terry. 1984. "Portrait of a Land Trust." In Russell L. Brenneman and Sarah M. Bates, eds., *Land-Saving Action: A Written Symposium by 29 Experts on Private Land Conservation in the 1980s.* Covelo, Calif.: Island Press.

Brewer, Richard. 2003. *Conservancy: The Land Trust Movement in America.* Lebanon, N.H.: Dartmouth College, published by the University Press of New England.

Brockway, Lucinda A. 2001. *A Favorite Place of Resort for Strangers: The King's Garden at Fort Ticonderoga.* Ticonderoga, N.Y.: Fort Ticonderoga.

Brown, Margaret Lynn. 2000. *The Wild East: A Biography of the Great Smoky Mountains.* Gainesville: University Press of Florida.

Brown, Sharon A. 1984. *Administrative History: Jefferson National Expansion Memorial, 1935–1980.* n.p.: National Park Service.

Brown, Susan Jane M. 2000. "David and Goliath: Reformulating the Definition of 'The Public Interest' and the Future of Land Swaps After the Interstate 90 Land Exchange." *Journal of Environmental Law and Litigation* 15(2): 235–293.

Brown, Warren. 1993. "Public/Private Land Conservation Partnerships in and Around National Parks." In Eve Endicott, ed., *Land Conservation Through Public/Private Partnerships.* Washington, D.C.: Island Press, pp. 104–128.

Brubaker, Sterling, ed. 1984. *Rethinking the Federal Lands.* Washington, D.C.: Resources for the Future. Distributed by Johns Hopkins University Press, Baltimore, Md.

Buck, Paul Herman. 1946. *The Evolution of the National Park System of the United States.* Washington, D.C.: U.S. Government Printing Office.

Bundy, Kevin. 1999. "The Headwaters Agreement: A History, Summary and Critique." *Hastings West-Northwest Journal of Environmental Law and Policy* 5(3): 361–365.

Bustillo, Miguel. 2003. "Ruling Could Stymie Loggers." *San Francisco Chronicle* May 21, p. A11.

California Environmental Resources Evaluation System. 2002. "Santa Monica Mountains Conservancy Programs." ⟨http://ceres.ca.gov/wetlands/introduction/santa_monica.html⟩.

Cameron, E. H. 1952. *Of Yankee Granite, An Account of the Bunker Hill Monument.* Boston: Bunker Hill Monument Association.

Cameron, Jenks. 1928. *The Development of Governmental Forest Control in the United States.* Baltimore, Md.: Johns Hopkins University Press.

———. 1929. *The Bureau of Biological Survey: Its History, Activities, and Organization.* Baltimore, Md.: Johns Hopkins University Press.

Campbell, Carlos. 1960. *Birth of a National Park in the Great Smoky Mountains: An Unprecedented Crusade Which Created, as a Gift of the People, the Nation's Most Popular Park.* Knoxville, Tenn.: University of Tennessee Press.

Carson, Rachel. 1962. *Silent Spring.* Cambridge, Mass.: Riverside Press of Houghton Mifflin.

Catlin, George. 1973. *Letters and Notes on the Manners, Customs and Conditions of North American Indians.* Reprint of 1913 edition. New York: Dover.

Catton, Theodore. 1996. *Wonderland: An Administrative History of Mount Rainier National Park.* Seattle, Wash.: National Park Service, Cultural Resources Program.

Cavanaugh, David. 1999. "A Successful Approach to Voluntary Acquisitions." *Right of Way Magazine* May/June: 8–13.

Cawley, R. McGreggor. 1993. *Federal Land, Western Anger: The Sagebrush Rebellion and Environmental Politics*. Lawrence: University Press of Kansas.

Chan, Emily C. 2004. Northern Forest Conservation Easements: An Analysis. Honors Thesis. College of Natural Resources. University of California, Berkeley, Draft on file with authors.

Chandler, Alfred D., Jr. 1977. *The Visible Hand: The Managerial Revolution in American Business*. Cambridge, Mass.: Belknap Press.

Chase, Alston. 1987. *Playing God in Yellowstone*. San Diego: Harcourt Brace Jovanovich.

Cheever, Federico. 1996. "Public Good and Private Magic in the Law of Land Trusts and Conservation Easements: A Happy Present and a Troubled Future." *Denver University Law Review* 73(4): 1077–1102.

Church, William L. 1986. "Farmland Conversion: The View from 1986." *University of Illinois Law Review* 1986(2): 521–561.

Clapp, Earle H. 1933. *Major Problems and the Next Big Step in American Forestry*. Summary of a report prepared in response to Senate resolution 175. Washington, D.C.: U.S. Government Printing Office.

Clarke, Jeanne Nienaber and Daniel McCool. 1996. *Staking Out the Terrain: Power and Performance Among Natural Resource Agencies*. 2d ed. Albany: State University of New York Press.

Clawson, Marion. 1951. *Uncle Sam's Acres*. New York: Dodd, Mead.

———. 1963. *Land and Water for Recreation: Opportunities, Problems and Policies*. Chicago: Rand McNally.

Clawson, Marion and Burnell Held. 1957. *The Federal Lands: Their Use and Management*. Baltimore, Md.: Published for Resources for the Future by Johns Hopkins University Press.

Clepper, Henry and Arthur B. Meyer, eds. 1960. *American Forestry: Six Decades of Growth*. Washington, D.C.: Society of American Foresters.

Cockrell, Ron. 1992. *A Green Shrouded Miracle: The Administrative History of Cuyahoga Valley National Recreation Area, Ohio*. Omaha, Nebr.: National Park Service, Midwest Regional Office, Office of Planning and Resource Preservation, Cultural Resources Management. ⟨http://www.cr.nps.gov/history/online_books/Cuyahoga/⟩.

Coggins, George Cameron. 1978. "Federal Wildlife Law Achieves Adolescence: Developments in the 1970s." *Duke Law Journal* 3: 753.

———. 1998. "Regulating Federal Natural Resources: A Summary Case Against Devolved Collaboration." *Ecology Law Quarterly* 25(4): 602.

Coggins, George Cameron and Robert L. Glicksman. 1984. "Federal Recreational Land Policy: The Rise and Decline of the Land and Water Conservation Fund." *Columbia Journal of Environmental Law* 9(2): 125–236.

Coggins, George Cameron and Doris K. Nagel. 1990. "'Nothing Beside Remains': The Legal Legacy of James G. Watt's Tenure as Secretary of the Interior on Federal Land Law and Policy." *Boston College Environmental Affairs Law Review* 17: 473–550.

Colinvaux, Catherine M. and Stephen D. Galowitz. 1989. "A Modest Proposal: The Cape Cod Referendum for a Moratorium on New Development." *Harvard Environmental Law Review* 13: 559–584.

Connecticut Lakes Headwaters Partnership Task Force. 2001. "IP Lands Chronology." ⟨http://www.nhdfl.org/ct%20lakes%20task%20force/taskforce_chronology.htm⟩.

Conservation Resource Center. 2004. Tax Credit Exchange Program. ⟨taxcreditexchange.com⟩. Last visited Nov. 19, 2004.

Cowart, Richard H. and Sally K. Fairfax. 1988. "Public Lands Federalism: Judicial Theory and Administrative Reality." *Ecology Law Quarterly* 15(3): 375–476.

Cox, Thomas R., Robert S. Maxwell, Phillip Drennon Thomas, and Joseph J. Malone. 1985. *This Well-Wooded Land: Americans and Their Forests from Colonial Times to the Present*. Lincoln: University of Nebraska Press.

Cresson, Margaret French. 1953. *The Laurel Hill Association 1853–1953*. n.p.: Eagle Printing and Binding.

Cronon, William. 1995. "The Trouble with Wilderness; or, Getting Back to the Wrong Nature." In William Cronon, ed., *Uncommon Ground: Toward Reinventing Nature*. New York: W. W. Norton.

Cunningham, Roger A. 1968. "Scenic Easements in the Highway Beautification Program." *Denver Law Journal* 45: 167.

Cuyahoga Valley National Park. 2001. "Countryside Initiative Request for Proposals: Leasing Opportunities for 2001." ⟨http://www.nps.gov/cuva/management/countryside/countrysiderfp.pdf⟩.

Dana, Andrew C. and Susan W. Dana. 2002. "Rogue Land Trusts, Abused Conservation Easements, and Regulation of the Private Land Trust Movement." Draft on file with authors.

Dana, Samuel T. 1956. *Forest and Range Policy: Its Development in the United States*. New York: McGraw-Hill.

Dana, Samuel T. and Sally K. Fairfax. 1980. *Forest and Range Policy: Its Development in the United States*. Rev. ed. New York: McGraw-Hill.

Davis, John Emmeus and Amy Demetrozitz. 2003. *Permanently Affordable Homeownership: Does the Community Land Trust Deliver on its Promises?* Burlington, Vt.: Burlington Community Land Trust.

DeBuys, William. 1985. *Enchantment and Exploitation: the Life and Hard Times of a New Mexico Mountain Range*. Albuquerque: University of New Mexico Press.

Dennis, Pamela M. 1993. "A State Program to Preserve Land and Provide Housing: Vermont's Housing and Conservation Trust Fund." In Eve Endicott, ed., *Land Conservation Through Public/Private Partnerships*. Washington, D.C.: Island Press, pp. 172–194.

Diamond, Henry. 1990. "Reflections on the Past, Perspectives on the Future." In *America's Heritage: Proceedings of a Symposium on the 25th Anniversary of the Land and Water Conservation Fund*. National Recreation and Park Association: Arlington, Va. pp. 14–16.

Dickinson, Joel Ray. 1974. "The Creation of Redwood National Park: A Case Study in the Politics of Conservation." Ph.D. diss., University of Missouri.

Dilsaver, Lary M., ed. 1994. *America's National Park System: The Critical Documents*. Lanham, Md.: Rowman & Littlefield.

Dilsaver, Lary M. and Douglas H. Strong. 1993. "Sequoia and Kings Canyon National Parks: One Hundred Years of Preservation and Resources Management." In Richard J. Orsi, Alfred Runte, and Marlene Smith-Baranzini, eds., *Yosemite and Sequoia: A Century of California National Parks*. Berkeley: University of California Press; San Francisco: California Historical Society.

Docherty, Bonnie. 2000. "Maine's North Woods: Environmental Justice and the National Park Proposal." *Harvard Environmental Law Review* 24(2): 537–561.

Donnelly, Charles. 1924. "The Facts About the Northern Pacific Grant." St. Paul, Minn.: Northern Pacific Railway Co. Mimeograph.

Draffan, George and Janine Blaeloch. 2000. *Commons or Commodity? The Dilemma of Federal Land Exchanges*. Seattle, Wash.: Western Land Exchange Project.

Drury, Newton B. 1946. "Private In-Holdings in National Park System." *Land Policy Review* 9: 3.

Duffus, Tom. 1990. *Fort Ticonderoga: Natural Resources Inventory and Action Plan*. Keeseville, N.Y.: The Adirondack Nature Conservancy/Adirondack Land Trust.

Dukeminier, Jesse and James E. Krier. 1998. *Property*. 4th ed. New York: Aspen Law & Business.

Dunn, Durwood. 1988. *Cades Cove: The Life and Death of A Southern Appalachian Community, 1818–1937*. Knoxville: University of Tennessee Press.

Eaton, Mike and Rick Cooper. 1997. "Building a Public-Private Partnership to Protect the Consumnes River." March 13. Videocassette. On file with authors.

Edge, Rosalie. 1936. "Roads and More Roads in the National Parks and National Forests." Pamphlet no. 54. New York: Emergency Conservation Committee.

Eitel, Michael R. 2004. "Wyoming's Trepidation Toward Conservation Easement Legislation: A Look at Two Issues Troubling the Wyoming State Legislature." *Wyoming Law Review* 4: 57–111.

Endicott, Eve. 1993. "Preserving Natural Areas: The Nature Conservancy and Its Partners." In Eve Endicott, ed., *Land Conservation through Public/Private Partnerships*. Washington, D.C.: Island Press.

Environmental Law Institute. 1977. *The Evolution of National Wildlife Law*. Washington, D.C.: Environmental Law Institute.

Evans, G. Rodger and Charles W. Snell. 1982. *Historic Structure Report, Bunker Hill Monument: 1818–1916, Historical Data and Architectural Data Sections, Boston National Historical Park, Massachusetts*. Denver, Col.: National Park Service, Denver Service Center, Branch of Historic Preservation, Mid-Atlantic/North Atlantic Team.

Fairfax, Sally K. 1987. "Interstate Bargaining over Revenue Sharing and Payments in Lieu of Taxes: Federalism as if States Mattered." In Phillip O. Foss, ed., *Federal Lands Policy*. Westport, Conn.: Greenwood Press.

———. 1988. "The Essential Legacy of a Sustaining Civilization: Professor Sax on the National Parks." *Ecology Law Quarterly* 25: 385–410.

———. 1996. "The Gentle Use of Working Landscapes." *Different Drummer* 3(3): 16–19.

Fairfax, Sally K. and Darla Guenzler. 2001. *Conservation Trusts*. Lawrence: University Press of Kansas.

Fairfax, Sally K., Lauren Gwin and Lynn Huntsinger. 2004. "Presidio and Valles Caldera: A Preliminary Assessment of Their Meaning for Public Resources Management." *Natural Resources Journal* 44(2): 445–474.

Fairfax, Sally K. and A. Dan Tarlock. 1979. "No Water for the Woods: A Critical Analysis of United States v. New Mexico." *Idaho Law Review* 15: 509–554.

Farm Service Agency. 1999. "Fact Sheet: Conservation Reserve Program." ⟨http://www.fsa.usda.gov/pas/publications/facts/html/crp99.htm⟩.

Feldman, Martha S. and Anne M. Khademian. 2001. "Principles for Public Management Practice: From Dichotomies to Interdependence." *Governance: An International Journal of Policy and Administration* 14(3): 339–361.

———. 2002. "To Manage is to Govern." *Public Administration Review* 62(5): 541–554.

Fink, Richard J. 1994. "The National Wildlife Refuges: Theory, Practice and Prospect." *Harvard Environmental Law Review* 18(1): 1–135.

Fischman, Robert. 2003. *The National Wildlife Refuges: Coordinating a Conservation System Through Law*. Washington, D.C: Island Press.

Folwell, Elizabeth. 1990. "The Green Keepers." *Adirondack Life* 21(Nov./Dec.): 48.

Foresta, Ronald. 1984. *America's National Parks and Their Keepers*. Washington, D.C.: Resources for the Future. Distributed by Johns Hopkins University Press, Baltimore, Md.

Fort Ticonderoga. 2003. "Mission." Fort Ticonderoga National Historic Landmark. ⟨http://www.fort-ticonderoga.org/history/mission.htm⟩, last visited Nov. 19, 2004.

Foss, Phillip O. 1960. *Politics and Grass: The Administration of the Taylor Grazing Act.* New York: Greenwood Press.

Foster, Charles H. W. 1985. *The Cape Cod National Seashore: A Landmark Alliance.* Hanover, N.H.: University Press of New England.

Freidel, Frank and Lonelle Aikman. 1988. *George Washington: Man and Monument.* 3d ed. Washington, D.C.: Washington National Monument Association with the cooperation of the National Geographic Society.

Freyfogle, Eric T. 1995. "The Owning and Taking of Sensitive Lands." *UCLA Law Review* 43(1): 77–138.

Friedman, Lawrence M. 1973. *A History of American Law.* 2d ed. Birmingham, Ala.: Gryphon Editions.

Frothingham, Richard. 1849. *History of the siege of Boston, and of the battles of Lexington, Concord, and Bunker Hill.: Also an account of the Bunker Hill Monument.* Boston: C.C. Little J. Brown.

Gabrielson, Ira N. 1941. *Wildlife Conservation.* New York: Macmillan.

———. 1943. *Wildlife Refuges.* New York: Macmillan.

Gates, Paul W. 1968. *History of Public Land Law Development.* Written for the Public Land Law Review Commission. Washington, D.C.: Zenger Publishing.

Georgetown Environmental Law and Policy Institute. n.d. "GELPI Library of Recent & Noteworthy Taking Decisions." ⟨http://www.law.georgetown.edu/gelpi/takings/courts/decisions.htm⟩.

Gilligan, James P. 1953. "The Development of Policy and Administration of Forest Service Primitive and Wilderness Areas in the Western United States." vol. I. Ph.D. diss., University of Michigan.

Gose, Thomas. 1966. *Scenic Easements in Action: Manual for Conference Workshops on Planning, Administration, Non-Governmental Program, Legal Aspects.* Presented by the State Highway Commission of Wisconsin [and others], December 16–17, 1966. Madison, Wis.: University of Wisconsin.

Governors' Task Force on the Northern Forests. 1990. *Northern Forest Lands Study.* On file with authors. Distributed by US Forest Service.

Graham, Frank. 1978. *The Adirondack Park: A Political History.* New York: Knopf.

Gray, L. C. 1936. "The Social and Economic Implications of the National Land Program." *Journal of Farm Economics* 18: 257.

———. 1939. "Federal Purchase and Administration of Submarginal Land in the Great Plains." *Journal of Farm Economics* 21: 123.

Graziano, Angela. 1993. "Preserving Wildlife Habitat: The US Fish and Wildlife Service and the North American Waterfowl Management Plan." In Eve Endicott, ed., *Land Conservation Through Public/Private Partnerships*. Washington, D.C.: Island Press, pp. 85–103.

Greeley, William B. 1951. *Forests and Men*. Garden City, N.Y.: Doubleday.

———. 1953. *Forest Policy*. New York: McGraw-Hill.

Greiff, Constance M. 1987. *Independence: The Creation of a National Park*. Philadelphia: University of Pennsylvania Press.

Grossman, Gene M. and Alan B. Krueger. 1995. "Economic Growth and the Environment." *Quarterly Journal of Economics* 101(2): 353.

Guenzler, Darla. 1999. *Ensuring the Promise of Conservation Easements*. San Francisco: Bay Area Open Space Council.

Guenzler, Darla and Shelton Douthit. 2002. *Workshop: Creating and Maintaining A High Quality Easement Stewardship Program*. Pacific Land Trust Conference. South Lake Tahoe, California, 25 April.

Gustanski, Julie Ann and Roderick H. Squires, eds. 2000. *Protecting the Land: Conservation Easements Past, Present, and Future*. Washington, D.C.: Island Press.

Gwin, Lauren and Sally K. Fairfax. 2004. "England's National Trust: What Can It Teach U.S. Land Trusts." Paper presented at Land Trust Alliance Rally, October 29–31, Providence, Rhode Island.

Hamilton, Edward Pierce. 1964. *Fort Ticonderoga: A Key to A Continent*. Boston: Little, Brown.

Hammond, Kenneth A. 1969. "The Land and Water Conservation Fund Act: Development and Impact." Ph.D. diss., University of Michigan.

Hampton, H. Duane. 1971. *How the U.S. Cavalry Saved Our National Parks*. Bloomington: Indiana University Press.

Harrison, Craig S. 1990. "The Oahu Forest Bird National Wildlife Refuge: A Case Study in Why the U.S. Fish and Wildlife Service Should Improve Its Procedures for Acquiring New Wildlife Refuges." Mimeograph on file with authors.

Hartzog, George B. 1988. *Battling for the National Parks*. Mt. Kisco, N.Y.: Moyer Bell.

Harvey, Rachel. 2003. "The Jarbidge Shovel Brigade: Backlash in the Global Hinterland." Paper presented at the Fifth Annual Globalization Conference: Decentering Globalization, University of Chicago.

Hays, Samuel P. 1959. *Conservation and the Gospel of Efficiency: The Progressive Conservation Movement, 1890–1920*. Cambridge, Mass.: Harvard University Press.

———. 1987. *Beauty, Health, and Permanence: Environmental Politics in the United States, 1955–1985*. New York: Cambridge University Press.

Hearn, Kelly. 1998. "On the Offensive: Developer Tom Chapman." *High Country News* February 16. ⟨http://www.hcn.org/servlets/hcn.Article?article_id=394⟩.

Hemmat, Steven A. 1986. "Parks, People and Private Property: The National Park Service and Eminent Domain." *Environmental Law* 16(4): 935–961.

Hess, Karl, Jr. 1993. *Rocky Times in Rocky Mountain National Park: An Unnatural History.* Niwot: University Press of Colorado.

Hester, F. Eugene. 1981. *Statement to the Workshop on Public Land Acquisition and Alternatives, Senate Committee on Energy and Natural Resources, July 9.* Publication 97-34. Washington, D.C.: U.S. Government Printing Office.

Hocker, Jean. 2001. Address at Society for the Protection of New Hampshire Forests 100th Anniversary Convention. Mt. Washington, New Hampshire.

Hoffman, Sandra H. 1986. "Farmland and Open Space Preservation in Michigan: An Empirical Analysis." *University of Michigan Journal of Law Reform* 19: 1107.

Hopkins, Bruce R. 1998. *The Law of Tax Exempt Organizations.* 7th ed. New York: Wiley.

Horstman, Neil W. 1994. "Protecting the Viewshed of Mount Vernon." *Exchange* Fall: 4–6.

Horwitz, Morton J. 1977. *The Transformation of American Law: 1780–1860.* Cambridge, Mass.: Harvard University Press.

Hosmer, Charles B., Jr. 1965. *Presence of the Past: A History of the Preservation Movement in the United States Before Williamsburg.* New York: Putnam.

———. 1981. *Preservation Comes of Age: From Williamsburg to the National Trust, 1926–1949.* 2 vols. Charlottesville: University Press of Virginia.

———. 1987. Foreword to *Independence: The Creation of a National Park,* by Constance M. Greiff. Philadelphia: University of Pennsylvania Press.

Hough, Franklyn. 1878. *Report upon Forestry from the Committee Appointed to Memorialize Congress and the State Legislatures, Regarding the Cultivation of Timber and the Preservation of Forests.* vol 1. Microbook Library of American Civilization Series. Salem, Ore.: Salem Press.

Hudson, Dale A. 1979. "Sierra Club v. Department of Interior: The Fight to Preserve Redwood National Park." *Ecology Law Quarterly* 7(3): 781–860.

Hurt, R. Douglas. 1985. "The National Grasslands: Origin and Development in the Dustbowl." *Agricultural History* 59 (April): 246.

———. 1986. "Federal Land Reclamation in the Dust Bowl." *Great Plains Quarterly* 6: 94–106.

Ickes, Harold L. 1954–1955. *The Inside Struggle, 1936–1939,* vol. 2. *Secret Diary of Harold L. Ickes.* New York: Simon and Schuster.

———. 1954–1955. *The Lowering Clouds, 1939–1941,* vol. 3. *Secret Diary of Harold L. Ickes.* New York: Simon and Schuster.

Ise, John. 1924. *The United States Forest Policy.* New Haven, Conn.: Yale University Press.

————. 1961. *Our National Park Policy: A Critical History*. Baltimore, Md.: Johns Hopkins University Press.

Jackson, Turrentine. 1942. "The Creation of Yellowstone National Park." *Mississippi Valley Historical Review* 29 (September): 187.

Jahn, Laurence R. and James B. Trefethen. 1978. "Funding Wildlife Conservation Programs." In Howard P. Brokaw, ed., *Wildlife in America, Contributions to an Understanding of American Wildlife and Its Conservation*. Washington, D.C.: Council on Environmental Quality.

John, DeWitt. 1994. *Civic Environmentalism: Alternatives to Regulation in States and Communities*. Washington, D.C.: CQ Press.

Johns, Joshua Scott. 1996. "All Aboard: The Role of the Railroads in Protecting, Promoting and Selling Yellowstone and Yosemite National Parks." Master's thesis, ⟨http:/xroads.virginia.edu/~MA96/RAILROAD/home.html⟩.

Johnson, Gerald W. 1991. *Mount Vernon, The Story of a Shrine an Account of the Rescue and Continuing Restoration of George Washington's Home*. Rev. ed. Mount Vernon, Va.: Mount Vernon Ladies' Association.

Jolley, Harley E. 1969. *The Blue Ridge Parkway*. Knoxville, Tenn.: University of Tennessee Press.

Journals of the Continental Congress, 1774–1789, Worthington C. Ford et al., eds. Washington, D.C. ⟨http://memory.loc.gov/ammem/amlaw/lwjc.html⟩.

Joy, Henry L. 2001. "Maine's Death Knell." In *All Maine Matters: News and Comment for/by the People of Maine*. On file with authors.

Kangas, Steve. 1997. "Timelines of the Great Depression." *The Great Depression: Its Causes and Cure: Liberalism Resurgent.* ⟨http://mirrors.korpios.org/resurgent/Timeline.htm⟩.

Karamanski, Theodore J. 2000. *A National Lakeshore: The Creation and Administration of Sleeping Bear Dunes National Lakeshore*. Washington D.C.: National Park Service, U.S. Department of the Interior.

Kelsey, Darwin. 2002. "The Countryside Initiative at the Cuyahoga Valley National Park." *Forum Journal* 16(4): 35–40.

Kemmis, Daniel. 2001. *This Sovereign Land: A New Vision for Governing the West*. Washington, D.C.: Island Press.

Kettl, Donald F. 1988. *Government by Proxy: (Mis?)Managing Federal Programs*. Washington, D.C.: CQ Press.

Key, V. O. 1968. *The Responsible Electorate: Rationality in Presidential Voting, 1936–1960*. New York: Vintage Books.

Kiester, Edwin, Jr. 1993. "A New Park Saved the Tall Trees, But at a High Cost to the Community." *Smithsonian* 24(7): 42–63.

King, Mary Ann and Sally K. Fairfax. 2004. "The UCEA and Accountability for Conservation Easements: Learning from the NCCUSL Process." Paper presented at Land Trust Alliance Rally. October 29–31, Providence, Rhode Island.

King, Thomas F. 1988. "Park Planning, Historic Resources and the National Historic Preservation Act." In David J. Simon, ed., *Our Common Lands, Defending the National Parks*. Washington, D.C.: Island Press.

Kneipp, Leon F. 1936. "Uncle Sam Buys Some Forests: How the Weeks Law of Twenty-Five Years Ago is Building up a Great System of National Forests in the East." *American Forests* 42(10): 443–445, 483–484.

Koch, Janet and Thomas W. Richards. 1977. "The Role of Philanthropy in the Environmental Field: Preservation of National Lands and Historic Properties." In *Research Papers Sponsored by the Commission on Private Philanthropy and Public Needs*. Vol. II. Washington D.C.: U.S. Department of the Treasury, p. 735–752.

Kornblum, William. 2000. "Cape Cod: Challenges of Managed Urbanization." In Gary Machlis and Donald Field, eds., *National Parks and Rural Development: Practice and Policy in the United States*. Washington, D.C.: Island Press, pp. 165–180.

Korngold, Gerald. 1984. "Privately Held Conservation Servitudes: A Policy Analysis in the Context of in Gross Real Covenants and Easements." *Texas Law Review* 63(3): 433–495.

Kramer, Randall A. and Sandra S. Batie. 1985. "Cross Compliance Concepts in Agricultural Programs: The New Deal to the Present." *Agricultural History* 59 (April): 307.

LaGrasse, Carol W. 2001. "Update on Adirondack Litigation." Speech to Adirondack Park Agency Local Government Review Board, Baxter Mountain Lodge. Keene, N.Y., May 30. ⟨http://prfamerica.org/Update-5-30-01.html⟩.

Lambert, Darwin. 1989. *The Undying Past of Shenandoah National Park*. Boulder, Col.: Roberts Rinehart.

Land Trust Alliance. 2001a. "Summary Data from the National Land Trust Census." ⟨http://www.lta.org/newsroom/census_summary_data.htm⟩.

———. 2001b. "Voters Invest in Open Space: 2000 Referenda Results." Washington, D.C: Land Trust Alliance.

———. 2004. "About Land Trusts: National Land Trust Census." ⟨http://www.lta.org/aboutlt/census.shtml⟩.

"Land Trust Exchange." *Exchange* March 1982. p. 1.

"Land Trust Exchange Notes." 1989. *Exchange* 8(1): 2.

Langford, Nathaniel Pitt. 1972. *The Discovery of Yellowstone Park: Journal of the Washburn Expedition to the Yellowstone and Firehole Rivers in the Year 1870*. Rev. ed. Lincoln: University of Nebraska Press.

Langston, Nancy. 2003. *Where Land and Water Meet: A Western Landscape Transformed*. Seattle: University of Washington Press.

Lee, Ronald F. 1972. *Family Tree of the National Park System*. Philadelphia, Pa.: Eastern National Park & Monument Association.

————. 1973. *The Origin and Evolution of the National Military Park.* Washington, D.C.: National Park Service, Office of Historic Preservation.

Leopold, Aldo. 1949. *A Sand County Almanac.* New York: Oxford University Press.

Levesque, Charles. 1989. "Public/Private Cooperation: The Trust for New Hampshire Lands." *Exchange* 8(2): 10–12.

Liles, James. n.d. "Buffalo National River Draft Administrative History." Obtained from author. Unpublished.

Limerick, Patricia Nelson. 1987. *The Legacy of Conquest: The Unbroken Past of the American West.* New York: Norton.

Linowes, David F. 1988. *Privatization: Toward More Effective Government, Report of the President's Commission on Privatization.* Urbana: University of Illinois Press.

Liroff, Richard A. and G. Gordon Davis. 1981. *Protecting Open Space: Land Use Control in the Adirondack Park.* Cambridge, Mass.: Ballinger.

Little, Charles E. 1975. *Green-line Parks: An Approach to Preserving Recreational Landscapes in Urban Areas.* Washington, D.C.: U.S. Government Printing Office.

Locke, John. 1960. *Two Treatises of Government* [1689], ed. Peter Laslett. Cambridge: Cambridge University Press.

Lockhart, William J. 1997. "External Threats to our National Parks: An Argument for Substantive Protection." *Stanford Environmental Law Journal* 16: 3–74.

Lustig, R. Jeffrey. 1982. *Corporate Liberalism: The Origins of Modern Political Theory, 1890–1920.* Berkeley, Calif.: University of California Press.

Mackintosh, Barry. 1969. *Booker T. Washington National Monument: An Administrative History.* Washington, D.C.: National Park Service, Division of History, Office of Archeology and Historic Preservation.

————. 1983. *Visitor Fees in the National Park System: A Legislative And Administrative History.* Washington, D.C.: National Park Service, History Division. ⟨http://www.cr.nps.gov/history/online_books/mackintosh3/index.htm⟩.

————. 1990. *The National Parks: Shaping the System.* Washington, D.C.: U.S. Dept. of the Interior.

Maguire, J. Robert., ed. 1995. *Tour to the Northern Lakes of James Madison & Thomas Jefferson, May–June 1791.* Ticonderoga, N.Y.: Fort Ticonderoga.

Mahoney, Julia. 2002. "Perpetual Restrictions on Land and the Problem of the Future." *Virginia Law Review* 88(4): 739–787.

Marsh, George Perkins. 1864. *Man and Nature; Or, Physical Geography as Modified by Human Action.* New York: Scribners.

Mather, Stephen T. 1916. *Progress in the Development of the National Parks.* Washington, D.C.: U.S. Government Printing Office.

Mathewson, Kathryn Jane. 1972. "Planning Around National Parks Case Study: The Redwood National Park." Master's thesis, University of California, Berkeley.

Matthews, Mark. 2003. "Back on the Range?" *High Country News* July 7: 4.

Mayo, Todd D. 2000. "A Holistic Examination of the Law of Conservation." In Julie Ann Gustanski and Ronald H. Squires, eds., *Protecting the Land: Conservation Easements Past, Present, and Future.* Washington, D.C.: Island Press, pp. 22–54.

McArdle, Richard. 1953. "Multiple Use—Multiple Benefits." *Journal of Forestry* 51(5): 323.

McCoy, Craig R. and Linda K. Harris. 2002. "Preservation Easements: A Guide." *Philadelphia Inquirer* February 24–27. ⟨http://inquirer.philly.com/specials/2002/preservation/⟩.

Meidinger, Errol E. 1980. "The 'Public Uses' of Eminent Domain: History and Policy." *Environmental Law* 11(1): 1–66.

Merenlender, Adina, Lynn Huntsinger, Greig Guthey, and Sally K. Fairfax. 2004. "Land Trusts and Conservation Easements: Who Is Conserving What for Whom?" *Conservation Biology* 18(1): 65–76.

Merriam, John C. 1934. *The Tasks Ahead of the Save-the-Redwoods League.* Berkeley, Calif.: Save-the-Redwoods League.

Miles, John C. 1995. *Guardians of the Parks: A History of the National Parks and Conservation Association.* Washington, D.C.: Taylor & Francis in Cooperation with National Parks and Conservation Association.

Millard, James P. 1997. "Forts Carillon and Ticonderoga." America's Historic Lakes. ⟨http://www.historiclakes.org/Ticonderoga/Ticonderoga.html⟩.

Miller, Joseph. 1973. "Congress and the Origins of Conservation: Natural Resource Policies, 1865–1900." Ph.D. diss., University of Minnesota.

Milward, H. Brinton and Keith G. Provan. 2000. "Governing the Hollow State." *Journal of Public Administration Research and Theory* 10(2): 359–379.

Montana Land Reliance and Land Trust Exchange. 1982. *Private Options: Tools and Concepts for Land Conservation.* Covelo, Calif.: Island Press.

Muhn, James, Hanson R. Stuart, and Peter D. Doran. 1988. *Opportunity and Challenge: The Story of the BLM.* Washington, D.C.: U.S. Dept. of the Interior, Bureau of Land Management.

Muir, John. 1909. *Our National Parks.* Rev. ed. Boston: Houghton Mifflin.

Mulford, Jon K. 1984. "Federal Land Sales and Exchanges." In University of Colorado, Boulder, Natural Resources Law Center, *The Federal Land Policy and Management Act.* Boulder: Natural Resources Law Center.

Murphy, Graham. 2002. *Founders of the National Trust.* London: National Trust.

National Conference of Commissioners on Uniform State Laws. 1979. *Proceedings in Committee of the Whole: Uniform Conservation and Historic Preservation Agreements Act.* August 10. On file with the National Conference of Commissions on Uniform State Laws.

————. 1980. *Second Proceedings in Committee of the Whole: Uniform Conservation and Preservation Easements Act.* July 27. On file with the National Conference of Commissioners on Uniform State Laws.

National Parks and Conservation Association. 1988. *Land Acquisition: Completing the Parks.* Washington, D.C.: National Parks and Conservation Association.

National Research Council. 1993. *Setting Priorities for Land Conservation.* Washington, D.C.: National Academy Press.

Nedelsky, Jennifer. 1990. *Private Property and the Limits of American Constitutionalism: The Madisonian Framework and its Legacy.* Chicago: University of Chicago Press.

New England Forestry Foundation. n.d. "Pingree Forest Partnership: The Pingree Forest Easement." ⟨http://www.newenglandforestry.org/downloads/Pingree %20CE%20final.pdf⟩.

New York State. Department of Environmental Conservation. 1999. "Governor Announces Largest Land Conservation Deal Ever." Press release Dec. 9. ⟨http://www.dec.state.ny.us/website/dpae/pubs/winenv99.html#Governor%20 Announces%20Largest%20Land%20Conservation%20Deal%20Ever⟩.

————. Department of Environmental Conservation. n.d. "Questions and Answers About Champion Land Agreement." On file with authors.

Newburn, David. 2002. "Spatial Economic Models of Land Use Change and Conservation Targeting Strategies." Ph.D. diss., University of California, Berkeley.

Nichols, John. 1976. *The Milagro Beanfield War.* Rev. ed. New York: Ballantine Books.

Nichols, Philip. 1979. *The Law of Eminent Domain.* 3d ed. New York: M. Bender.

Nixon, Edgar B., ed. 1957. *Franklin D. Roosevelt & Conservation 1911–1945.* 2 vols. New York: Arno Press.

Noll, Roger. 1971. *Reforming Regulation: An Evaluation of the Ash Council Proposals.* Washington, D.C.: Brookings Institution.

Northern Forest Alliance. 2002. "West Mountain WMA ... It's Still Not Over." ⟨www.northernforestalliance.org/petition/westmt/westmountainACT2.htm⟩.

Northern Forest Lands Council. 1994. *Finding Common Ground: Conserving the Northern Forest.* Concord, N.H.: Northern Forest Lands Council; New Hampshire Division of Forests and Lands. ⟨http://www.northernforestlands.org/ fcg.htm⟩.

Ogden, Gerald Rupert. 1980. "Forestry for a Nation: The Making of a National Forest Policy under the Weeks and Clarke-McNary Acts, 1900–1924." Ph.D. diss., University of New Mexico.

Ohm, Brian W. 2000. "The Purchase of Scenic Easements and Wisconsin's Great River Road: A Progress Report on Perpetuity." *Journal of the American Planning Association* 66 (Spring): 177.

Oleck, Howard. 1977. *Trends in Nonprofit Organizations Law: A Wake Forest University Law Seminar*. Philadelphia, Pa.: American Law Institute-American Bar Association Committee on Continuing Professional Education.

Olson, Sherry H. 1971. *The Depletion Myth: A History of Railroad Use of Timber*. Cambridge, Mass.: Harvard University Press.

Olszewski, George O. 1971. *A History of the Washington Monument, 1844–1968*. Washington, D.C.: U.S. Department of the Interior.

Opie, John. 1987. *The Law of the Land: Two Hundred Years of American Farmland Policy*. Lincoln: University of Nebraska Press.

Osborn, Henry Fairfield. 1919. "Sequoia—the Auld Lang Syne of Trees." *Natural History* 19 (Nov.–Dec.): 612.

Osborne, John B. 1901. *The First President's Interest in Washington As Told by Himself*. Washington, D.C.: Columbia Historical Society Records.

O'Toole, Randal. 1995. "Tarnished Jewels: The Case for Reforming the Park Service." *Different Drummer* 2 (Winter).

Ottaway, David B. and Joe Stephens. 2003a. "Nonprofit Land Bank Amasses Billions: Charity Builds Assets on Corporate Partnerships." *Washington Post* May 4, p. A1.

———. 2003b. "Landing a Big One: Preservation, Private Development." *Washington Post* May 6, p. A9.

Owley, Jessica. 2005. "Involuntary Conservation Easements: The Hard Case of Endangered Species Preservation." *Journal of Environmental Law and Litigation* 19 (forthcoming).

Paarlberg, Don. 1982. "Effects of New Deal Farm Programs on the Agricultural Agenda a Half Century Later and Prospect for the Future." *American Journal of Agricultural Economics* 65: 1163.

Packard, Alpheus S. 1853. *History of the Bunker Hill Monument*. Portland, Maine: B. Thurston, Printer.

Paige, John C. 1985. *The Civilian Conservation Corps and the National Park Service, 1933–1942: An Administrative History*. Washington, D.C.: National Park Service.

Pataki, George E. 1999. "Governor Announces Historic Conservation Deal Completed." Press release. July 1. ⟨www.state.ny.us/governor/press/year99/july1_99.htm⟩.

Peffer, E. Louise. 1951. *The Closing of the Public Domain: Disposal and Reservation Policies, 1900–50*. Stanford, Calif.: Stanford University Press.

Pesticide Action Network North America. 2004. *Chemical Trespass: Pesticides in Our Bodies and Corporate Accountability.* San Francisco: Pesticide Action Network North America.

Peterson, Gene. 1996. *Pioneering Outdoor Recreation for the Bureau of Land Management.* McLean, Va.: Public Lands Foundation.

Philadelphia National Shrines Park Commission. 1947. *Report of Philadelphia National Shrines Park Commission to the Congress of the United States.* Philadelphia: The Commission.

Pinchot, Gifford. 1911. *The Fight for Conservation.* New York: Doubleday, Page.

———. 1947. *Breaking New Ground.* New York: Harcourt Brace.

Pisani, Donald J. 1987. "Promotion and Regulation: Constitutionalism and the American Economy." *Journal of American History* 74: 740.

Plater, Zygmunt J. B. and William Lund Norine. 1989. "Through the Looking Glass of Eminent Domain: Exploring the 'Arbitrary and Capricious' Test and Substantive Rationality Review of Governmental Decisions." *Boston College Environmental Affairs Law Review* 16 (Summer): 661–752.

Platt, Barbara L. 2001. *"This Is Holy Ground": A History of the Gettysburg Battlefield.* Harrisburg, Pa.: Huggins Printing.

Pollock, George Freeman. 1960. *Skyland, The Heart of Shenandoah National Park.* n.p.: Virginia Book Co.

Poole, William. 1993. "Preserving Urban and Suburban Gardens and Parks: The Trust for Public Land and Its Partners." In Eve Endicott, ed., *Land Conservation through Public/Private Partnerships.* Washington, D.C.: Island Press, pp. 61–82.

Posner, Paul L. 2002. "Accountability Challenges of Third-Party Government." In Lester M. Salamon, ed., *The Tools of Government: A Guide to the New Governance.* New York: Oxford University Press.

Potter, Clive. 1998. *Against the Grain: Agri-Environmental Reform in the United States and the European Union.* Oxon, UK: CAB International.

Pratt, Joseph Hyde. 1936. "Twelve Years of Preparation for the Passage of the Weeks Law." *Journal of Forestry* 34: 1028.

Public Broadcasting Service. n.d. "Great Depression Indicators." *The First Measured Century.* ⟨http://www.pbs.org/fmc/timeline/ddepression.htm⟩.

Puter, Stephen A. Douglas. 1908. *Looters of the Public Domain.* Portland, Ore.: The Portland Printing House.

Quin, Richard. 1997. *Blue Ridge Parkway.* NPS-HAER Report No. VA-NC-42. n.p.: National Park Service.

Raymond, Leigh. 2003. *Private Rights in Public Resources: Equity and Property Allocation in Market-Based Environmental Policy.* Washington, D.C.: Resources for the Future Press.

———. 2004. "Economic Growth as Environmental Policy? Reconsidering the Environmental Kuznets Curve." *Journal of Public Policy* 24(3): (in press).

Raymond, Leigh and Sally K. Fairfax. 1999. "Fragmentation of Public Domain Law and Policy: An Alternative to the 'Shift-to-Retention' Thesis." *Natural Resources Journal* 39(4): 649–753.

———. 2002. "The 'Shift to Privatization' in Land Conservation: A Cautionary Essay." *Natural Resources Journal* 42: 599–639.

Reed, Nathaniel P. and Dennis Drabelle. 1984. *The United States Fish and Wildlife Service.* Boulder, Col.: Westview Press.

Reffalt, William. 1993. "Historical Chronology: The National Wildlife Refuge System." Historical Perspectives Seminar, Charleston, South Carolina. Shepherdstown, W.Va.: Refuge Management Training Academy.

Richardson, Elmo. 1965. "Federal Park Policy in Utah: The Escalante National Monument Controversy of 1935–1940." Salt Lake City: Utah State Historical Society.

Ridenour, James. 1994. *The National Parks Compromised: Pork Barrel Politics and America's Treasures.* Merrillville, Ind.: ICS Books.

Righter, Robert W. 1982. *Crucible for Conservation: The Struggle for Grand Teton National Park.* Boulder: Colorado Associated University Press.

Riley, Edward M. 1990. *Starting America: The Story of Independence Hall.* Reprint, Gettysburg, Pa.: Thomas Publications.

"Rock the Vote; Sierra Club Elections." 2004. *The Economist* 371 (April): 32.

Rodgers, Andrew Denny, III. 1951. *Bernhard Eduard Fernow: A Story of North American Forestry.* Princeton, N.J.: Princeton University Press.

Roe, Charles E. 2000. "Use of Conservation Easements to Protect the Scenic and Natural Character of the Blue Ridge Parkway: A Case Study." In Julie Ann Gustanski and Ronald H. Squires, eds., *Protecting the Land: Conservation Easements Past, Present, and Future.* Washington, D.C.: Island Press, p. 221–229.

Rogers, William. 2003. "The Nationals." Presentation in panel entitled Past as Prologue at the Land Trust Alliance rally, Sacramento, Calif.

Rome, Adam. 2001. *The Bulldozer in the Countryside: Suburban Sprawl and the Rise of American Environmentalism.* Cambridge, U.K.: Cambridge University Press.

Roosevelt, Nicholas. 1970. *Conservation Now or Never.* New York: Dodd, Mead.

Rose, Carol. 1994. *Property and Persuasion: Essays on the History, Theory, and Rhetoric of Property.* Boulder, Col.: Westview Press.

Rosenberg, Greg. 2004. "Community Land Trusts." Presentation at the Who Owns America IV Conference, Land Tenure Center, University of Madison, Wisconsin.

Rosenthal, Ian. 1996. "The Case for Interstate Land Exchanges." *Virginia Environmental Law Journal* 15(2): 357–401.

Rothman, Hal. 1988. *Bandelier National Monument: An Administrative History.* Professional Papers No. 14. Santa Fe, N.M.: National Park Service, Division of History, Southwest Cultural Resources Center. ⟨http://www.nps.gov/band/adhi/adhi.htm⟩.

———. 1989. *America's National Monuments: The Politics of Preservation.* Lawrence: University Press of Kansas.

Ruhl, J. B. 2000. "Farms, Their Environmental Harms, and Environmental Law." *Ecology Law Quarterly* 27(1): 263.

Runte, Alfred. 1979. *National Parks: The American Experience.* Lincoln: University of Nebraska Press.

———. 1984. *Trains of Discovery: Western Railroads and the National Parks.* Flagstaff, Ariz.: Northland Press.

———. 1990. *Yosemite: The Embattled Wilderness.* Lincoln: University of Nebraska Press.

Rutherford, Robert M. 1949. *Ten Years of Pittman-Robertson Wildlife Restoration.* Washington, D.C.: Wildlife Management Institute.

Salamon, Lester M. 1989. *Beyond Privatization: The Tools of Government Action.* Washington, D.C.: Urban Institute Press.

———, ed. 2002. *The Tools of Government: A Guide to the New Governance.* New York: Oxford University Press.

Salyer, J. C. and F. G. Gillett. 1964. "Federal Refuges." In J. P. Linduska, ed., *Waterfowl Tomorrow.* Washington, D.C.: U.S. Government Printing Office.

Sargent, Shirley. 1997. *Yosemite's Historic Wawona.* Rev. ed. Yosemite, CA: Flying Spur Press.

Sax, Joseph L. 1964. "Takings and the Police Power." *Yale Law Journal* 74: 36.

———. 1971a. "Takings, Private Property and Public Rights." *Yale Law Journal* 81: 149.

———. 1971b. *Defending the Environment: A Strategy for Citizen Action.* New York: Knopf.

———. 1976. "Helpless Giants: The National Parks and the Regulation of Private Lands." *Michigan Law Review* 75(2): 239–274.

———. 1980a. "Buying Scenery: Land Acquisitions for the National Park Service." *Duke Law Journal* 4: 709–740.

———. 1980b. *Mountains Without Handrails, Reflections on the National Parks.* Ann Arbor: University of Michigan Press.

———. 1993. "Property Rights and the Economy of Nature." (Symposium on *Lucas v. South Carolina Coastal Council*). *Stanford Law Review* 45(5): 1433–1455.

Schiff, Ashley L. 1962. *Fire and Water: Scientific Heresy in the Forest Service.* Cambridge, Mass.: Harvard University Press.

Schrepfer, Susan. 1983. *The Fight to Save the Redwoods: A History of Environmental Reform, 1917–1978.* Madison: University of Wisconsin Press.

Schwartz, Kathleen. 1985. "A Case Study: The Federal Government's Use of Conservation Easements." *Exchange* 4(3): 12–13.

Scott, William B. 1977. *In Pursuit of Happiness: American Conceptions of Property from the Seventeenth to the Twentieth Century.* Bloomington: Indiana University Press.

Searchinger, Tim. 2002. "Statement of Environmental Defense on Farm Bill Passage." Press release May 8. 〈http://secure.environmentaldefense.org/pressrelease.cfm?ContentID=2008〉.

Sellars, Richard West. 1997. *Preserving Nature in the National Parks: A History.* New Haven, Conn.: Yale University Press.

Selvin, Molly. 1987. *This Tender and Delicate Business: The Public Trust Doctrine in American Law, 1789–1920.* New York: Garland.

Selznik, Phillip. 1966. *TVA and the Grass Roots: A Study of the Sociology of Formal Organization.* New York: Harper & Row.

Shands, William E. 1992. "The Lands Nobody Wanted: The Legacy of the Eastern National Forests." In Harold K. Steen, ed., *Origins of the National Forests: A Centennial Symposium.* Durham, N.C.: Forest History Society.

Shankland, Robert. 1970. *Steve Mather of the National Parks.* 3d ed. New York: Knopf.

Sheingate, Adam D. 2001. *The Rise of the Agricultural Welfare State: Institutions and Interest Group Power in the United States, France and Japan.* Princeton, N.J.: Princeton University Press.

Sheldon, William W. 1865. *Memoir of Solomon Willard: Architect and Superintendent of the Bunker Hill Monument.* Boston: Bunker Hill Monument Association.

Simon, Jim, Deborah Nelson, Danny Westneat and Eric Nalder. 1998. "Private Owners Play Game of Backcountry Speculation and Win Big Profits, Prime Land from Feds." *Seattle Times* Sept. 28, p. A6.

Small, Stephen J. 1979. "The Tax Benefits of Donating Easements in Scenic and Historic Property." *Real Estate Law Journal* 4: 320.

———. 1992. *Preserving Family Lands: Essential Tax Strategies for the Landowner.* Boston: Landowner Planning Center.

———. 1997a. *The Federal Tax Law of Conservation Easements.* 4th ed. Washington, D.C.: Land Trust Alliance.

———. 1997b. *Preserving Family Lands, Book II: More Planning Strategies for the Future.* Boston: Landowner Planning Center.

———. 2000. "An Obscure Tax Code Provision Takes Private Land Protection into the Twenty-First Century." In Julie Ann Gustanski and Ronald H. Squires, eds., *Protecting the Land: Conservation Easements Past, Present, and Future.* Washington, D.C.: Island Press, pp. 55–66.

———. 2003. "Conservation Easements Today: The Good and the Not-So-Good." Presentation Sess. 4B2 at the Land Trust Alliance Rally, Sacramento, California.

———. 2004. "Tax Analysts-Special Report: Proper- and Improper-Deductions for Conservation Easement Donations, Including Developer Donations." *Tax Notes* 105(2): 217–224.

Smith, Charles D. 1956. "The Movement for Eastern National Forests, 1899–1911." Ph.D. diss., Harvard University.

———. 1960a. "The Appalachian National Park Movement, 1885–1901." *North Carolina Historical Review* 37(1): 38–65.

———. 1960b. "The Mountain Lover Mourns: Origins of the Movement for the White Mountain National Forest, 1880–1903." *New England Quarterly* 33: 37–56.

Smith, James N. 1972. "The Gateways: Parks for Whom?" In Conservation Foundation, *National Parks for the Future: An Appraisal of the National Parks as They Begin Their Second Century in a Changing America*. Washington, D.C.: Conservation Foundation.

Snell, Charles W. 1983. *A History Of The Naval Live Oak Reservation Program, 1794–1880: A Forgotten Chapter in the History of American Conservation—Gulf Islands National Seashore—Florida/Mississippi*. Denver, Col.: National Park Service, Denver Service Center.

Sokolove, Jennifer. 2003. "Doing Good by Doing Well: Entrepreneurial Environmentalism in the American West." Ph.D. diss., University of California, Berkeley.

Spader, Allan D. 1983. "Director's Note." *Exchange* Summer: 2.

"Special Issue: Report on 1985 National Survey of Government and Non-Profit Easement Programs." 1985. *Exchange* 4(3).

Speer, Edward G. and Jean Haskell. 2000. *The Blue Ridge Parkway: An Administrative History*. Johnson City, Tenn.: Center for Appalachian Studies and Services.

Spence, Mark. 1999. *Dispossessing the Wilderness: Indian Removal and the Making of the National Parks*. New York: Oxford University Press.

Spratt, John M., Jr. 2005. *Summary and Analysis of the President's Fiscal Year 2006 Budget*. Washington, D.C.: House Budget Committee, Democratic Caucus.

Steen, Harold K. 1976. *The U.S. Forest Service: A History*. Seattle: University of Washington Press.

———, ed. 1992. *The Origins of the National Forests: A Centennial Symposium*. Durham, N.C.: Forest History Society.

Stegner, Wallace. 1954. *Beyond the Hundredth Meridian; John Wesley Powell and the Second Opening of the West*. Boston, Mass.: Houghton Mifflin.

Stephens, Joe and David B. Ottaway. 2003a. "$420,000 a Year and No-Strings Fund: Conservancy Underreported President's Pay and Perks of Office." *Washington Post* May 4, p. A21.

———. 2003b. "How a Bid to Save a Species Came to Grief." *Washington Post* May 5, p. A1.

———. 2003c. "Nonprofit Sells Scenic Acreage to Allies at a Loss: Buyers Gain Tax Breaks with Few Curbs on Land Use." *Washington Post* May 6, p. A1.

Stevenson, Katherine. 2002. "Statement Before the Senate Energy and Natural Resources Subcommittee on National Parks, Concerning ... Federal Authority Relating to Land Acquisition from Willing Sellers." Mar. 7. ⟨http://www.nps.gov/legal/testimony/107th/willsell.htm⟩.

Stewart, Richard B. 1975. "The Reformation of American Administrative Law." *Harvard Law Review* 88(8): 1667–1813.

Straus, Robert Ware and Eleanor B. Straus. 1988. *The Possible Dream: Saving George Washington's View.* Accokeek, Md.: Accokeek Foundation.

Swain, Donald C. 1963. *Federal Conservation Policy, 1921–1933.* University of California Publications in History Series, v. 76. Berkeley: University of California Press.

———. 1972. "The National Park Service and the New Deal, 1933–1940." *Pacific Historical Review* 16 (Aug.): 312.

Terrie, Phillip G. 1997. *Contested Terrain: A New History of Nature and People in the Adirondacks.* Syracuse, N.Y.: Syracuse University Press.

The Conservation Fund. 2002. "$1.2 Million Purchase Protects Historic Medal of Honor Site at Gettysburg." News release. June 7. On file with authors.

The Nature Conservancy. 1999. "The Forest Bank: Protecting Our Working Forests." ⟨http://nature.org/initiatives/programs/forestbank/⟩.

———. 2003. "Milestones." ⟨http://nature.org/aboutus/history⟩.

———. 2004a. "1970's and 1980's—Natural Heritage Network." ⟨http://nature.org/aboutus/success/success/art5362.html⟩.

———. 2004b. "About Us." ⟨http://nature.org/aboutus⟩.

"The plan from hell—a huge land conservation easement in Maine." 2001. *Discerning the Times: Digest and Newsbytes* 3(4). ⟨http://www.discerningtoday.org/members/Digest/2001digest/apr/plan_from_hell.htm⟩.

Thompson, Barton H., Jr. 2002–2003. "Conservation Options: Toward a Greater Private Role." *Virginia Environmental Law Journal* 21(2): 245–315.

Tilden, Freeman. 1970. *The National Parks.* 2d ed. New York: Knopf.

Tindall, William. 1909. *Origin and Government of the District of Columbia, Printed for the use of the Committee on the District of Columbia, House of Representatives.* Washington, D.C.: U.S. Government Printing Office.

Torres, Louis. 1985. *To the Immortal Name and Memory of George Washington: The United States Army Corps of Engineers and the Construction of the*

Washington Monument. Washington, D.C.: Historical Division, Office of Administrative Services, Office of the Chief of Engineers.

"Trading Away the West." 1998. *Seattle Times* Sept. 27–Oct. 2. ⟨http://seattletimes.nwsource.com/news/special/landswap/⟩.

Treanor, William Michael. 1995. "The Original Understanding of the Takings Clause and the Political Process." *Columbia Law Review* 95(4): 782–887.

Trees Foundation. 2000. "What Is Headwaters Forest?" July 17. ⟨http://www.treesfoundation.org/html/publications_article_39.html⟩.

Trefethen, James B. 1961. *Crusade for Wildlife: Highlights in Conservation Progress*. Harrisburg, Pa.: Stackpole Co.

———. 1975. *An American Crusade for Wildlife*. New York: Winchester Press.

Tribe, Lawrence. 1976. "Intergovernmental Immunities in Litigation, Taxation, and Regulation." *Harvard Law Review* 89: 682.

Trust for Public Land and Land Trust Alliance. 2000–2003. "LandVote Annual Reports." ⟨www.lta.org/newsroom/pr_110602.htm⟩.

———. 2001. "New York's Community Gardens—A Resource At Risk." ⟨http://www.tpl.org/content_documents/nyc_community_gardens.pdf⟩.

———. 2002a. *Taking the High Road: Protecting Open Space Along America's Highways*. San Francisco: The Trust for Public Land.

———. 2002b. "Connecticut Headwaters Campaign (NH)." ⟨http://tpl.org/tier3_cd.cfm?content_item_id=7140&folder_id=258⟩.

Trustees of Reservations. 2001. *Annual Report*.

Udall, Stewart L. 1963. *The Quiet Crisis*. New York: Holt, Rinehart and Winston.

United States. Bureau of Biological Survey (BBS). 1925–1941. *Report of the Chief of the Bureau of Biological Survey*. Washington, D.C.: Dept. of Agriculture.

———. Bureau of Land Management (BLM). 2002. "Public Land Statistics 2002." ⟨http://www.blm.gov/natacq/pls02/⟩.

———. Bureau of Land Management (BLM). 2003. Memorandum of Understanding: Interagency Implementation of the Federal Land Transaction Facilitation Act of 2000. MOU-350-2003-04. May 6.

———. Bureau of Land Management (BLM). Folsom field office. 2004. "Cosumnes River Preserve." ⟨http://www.ca.blm.gov/folsom/cosumpres.html⟩.

———. Bureau of Outdoor Recreation (BOR). 1967. *A Report on Recreation Land Price Escalation*. Washington, D.C.: Department of the Interior.

———. Congress. House. 1889. *Fur Seal Fisheries of Alaska*. H. Rpt. 3883. 50th Cong., 2nd sess.

———. Congress. House. 1916. *To Establish National Park Service*. H. Rpt. 700. 64th Cong., 1st sess.

———. Congress. House. 1935. *To Amend Migratory Bird Hunting Stamp Act of Mar. 16, 1934.* H. Rpt. 886. 74th Cong., 1st sess.

———. Congress. House. 1956. *Committee on Agriculture, Hearings on H.R. 11682 and 11689.* 84th Cong., 2d sess., June 17.

———. Congress. House. 1968. *Committee on Public Works, Uniform Relocation Assistance and Land Policy Act Hearings Before the Committee on Public Works on H.R. 386.* 90th Cong., 2d. sess., 11, 12, 17–19, Sept. 24.

———. Congress. House. 1977. *Report 95–106.* 95th Cong., 1st sess.

———. Congress. House. 1984. *Committee on Interior and Insular Affairs, Land Acquisition Policy and Program of the National Park Service.* Cte. Print No. 7. 98th Cong., 2d sess.

———. Congress. Joint Committee on Taxation (JCT). 2005. *Options to Improve Tax Compliance and Reform Tax Expenditures.* JCS-02-05. Available on the internet: ⟨http://www.house.gov/jct/s-2-05.pdf⟩ (Last visited February 23, 2005).

———. Congress. Senate. 1894. *Memorial from the Geological Society of America Favoring the Establishment of a National Park in the State of Washington.* S. Mis. Doc. 247. 53d Cong., 2d sess.

———. Congress. Senate. 1935. *To Amend Migratory Bird Hunting Stamp Act of Mar. 16, 1934.* S. Rep. 822. 74th Cong., 1st sess.

———. Congress. Senate. 1981. *Workshop on Public Land Acquisition and Alternatives.* Publication 97-34. Washington, D.C.: U.S. Government Printing Office.

———. Department of the Interior (DOI). 1928. Committee on "The Problem of Indian Administration." *Report of Interior Department Committee on "The Problem of Indian Administration."* Washington, D.C.: Department of the Interior, Office of the Secretary.

———. Department of the Interior (DOI). 1983. *Guidelines for Transactions Between Nonprofit Conservation Organizations and Federal Agencies.* Washington, D.C.: U.S. Government Printing Office [codified in *Code of Federal Regulations*, 48(1983): 36342].

———. Fish and Wildlife Service (FWS). 1987. *Restoring America's Wildlife, 1937–1987.* Washington, D.C.: U.S. Government Printing Office.

———. Fish and Wildlife Service (FWS). 1992. *Digest of Federal Resource Laws of Interest to the U.S. Fish and Wildlife Service.* Washington, D.C.: U.S. Government Printing Office.

———. 2002a. *Annual Report of Lands Under Control of the U.S. Fish and Wildlife Service as of September 30, 2001.* Washington, D.C.: U.S. Fish and Wildlife Service, Division of Realty.

———. Fish and Wildlife Service (FWS). 2002b. Tribes and Fish and Wildlife Service Announce Plans to Negotiate Joint Management of Bison Range. News release. ⟨http://mountain-prairie.fws.gov/CSKT-FWS-Negotiation⟩.

————. Fish and Wildlife Service (FWS). n.d.a. History of the National Wildlife Refuge System. ⟨http://refuges.fws.gov/history/index.html⟩.

————. Fish and Wildlife Service (FWS). n.d.b. Montana-Prairie Region, Partners for Fish and Wildlife, "The Blackfoot Challenge," ⟨http://www.re.fws.gov/pfw/montana/mt6.htm⟩.

————. Fish and Wildlife Service (FWS). n.d.c. "Pacific Region. Stone Lakes National Wildlife Refuge." ⟨http://stonelakes.fws.gov/refugemap.htm⟩.

————. Forest Service (FS). 1914. *Purchase of Land under the Weeks Law in the Southern Appalachian and White Mountains.* Washington, D.C.: Government Printing Office.

————. Forest Service (FS). 1933a. *A National Plan for American Forestry: A Report Prepared in Response to S. Res. 175 (22d Congress).* Washington, D.C.: U.S. Government Printing Office.

————. Forest Service (FS). 1933b. *A National Plan for American Forestry. Letter from the secretary of agriculture transmitting in response to S. Res. 175 (Seventy-second Congress) the report of the Forest Service of the Agricultural Department on the forest problem of the United States.* Washington, D.C.: U.S. Government Printing Office.

————. Forest Service (FS). 1961. *The National Forest Reservation Commission: A Report on Progress in Establishing National Forests.* Washington, D.C.: U.S. Department of Agriculture.

————. Forest Service (FS). 1989. *The Northern Forest Lands Study of New England and New York: A Report to the Congress of the United States on the recent changes in landownership and land use in the northern forests of Maine, New Hampshire, New York and Vermont.* Rutland, Vt.: Northern Forest Lands Study, U.S. Department of Agriculture.

————. Forest Service (FS). 1997. *Establishment and Modification of National Forest Boundaries and National Grasslands: A Chronological Record: 1891–1996.* FS-612. Washington, D.C.: Department of Agriculture.

————. Forest Service (FS). 2001a. National Forest Lands Annual Acreage, 1891–2000. "Land Areas Report of the National Forest System as of September 30, 2000." ⟨http://www.fs.fed.us/land/staff/lar/LAR00/table21.htm⟩.

————. Forest Service (FS). 2001b. "Land Areas Report as of September 30, 2000." ⟨http://www.fs.fed.us/land/staff/lar/LAR00/table4_1.htm⟩.

————. Forest Service (FS). 2002. Pacific Northwest Research Station. "Changing the Scale of Our Thinking: Landscape-Level Learning." *Science Findings.* 45(July). ⟨http://www.fs.fed.us/pnw/sciencef/scifi45.pdf⟩.

————. General Accounting Office (GAO). 1977a. *Information on the Acquisition of Lands for Redwood National Park, Department of the Interior, Department of Justice: Report of the Comptroller General of the United States.* CED-77-122. Washington, D.C.: General Accounting Office.

————. General Accounting Office (GAO). 1977b. *To Protect Tomorrow's Food Supply: Soil Conservation Needs Priority Attention: Department of Agriculture, Report to Congress*. Washington, D.C.: General Accounting Office.

————. General Accounting Office (GAO). 1979. *The Federal Drive to Acquire Private Lands Should be Reassessed*. CED-80-14. Washington, D.C.: General Accounting Office.

————. General Accounting Office (GAO). 1980. *Federal Land Acquisitions by Condemnation—Opportunities to Reduce Delays and Costs*. CED-80-54. Washington, D.C.: General Accounting Office.

————. General Accounting Office (GAO). 1981. *Federal Land Acquisition and Management Practices: Report to Senator Ted Stevens*. CED-81-135. Washington, D.C.: General Accounting Office.

————. General Accounting Office (GAO). 1989. *National Wildlife Refuges: Continuing Problems with Incompatible Uses Call for Bold Action*. CED-89-196. Washington, D.C.: General Accounting Office.

————. General Accounting Office (GAO). 2000a. *BLM and the Forest Service: Land Exchanges Need to Reflect Appropriate Value and Serve the Public Interest*. GAO/RCED-00-73. Washington, D.C.: General Accounting Office.

————. General Services Administration (GSA). 1957–2002. *Summary Report of Real Property Owned by the United States Throughout the World*. Washington, D.C.: General Services Administration, Office of Administration.

————. Interdepartmental Committee for the Study of Jurisdiction Over Federal Areas within the States. 1956–1957. *Jurisdiction over Federal Areas within the States: Report*. vols. 1–2. Washington, D.C.: U.S. Government Printing Office.

————. Internal Revenue Service (IRS). 2004. Treasury and IRS Issue Notice Regarding Improper Deductions for Conservation Easement Donations. IR-2004-86. June 30. ⟨http://www.irs.gov/newsroom/article/0,,id=124485,00.html⟩.

————. National Forest Reservation Commission (NFRC). 1920. *Progress of purchase of eastern national forests under Act of March 1, 1911 (the Weeks law)*. Washington, D.C.: U.S. Government Printing Office.

————. National Forest Reservation Commission (NFRC). 1933. *Review of the Work of the National Forest Reservation Commission, 1911–33*. Washington, D.C.: U.S. Government Printing Office.

————. National Forest Reservation Commission (NFRC). 1961. *A Report on the Progress in Establishing National Forests*. Washington, D.C.: Department of Agriculture, Forest Service.

————. National Oceanic and Atmospheric Administration (NOAA). n.d. "Legislative Summary LWCF." ⟨http://www.csc.noaa.gov/opis/html/summary/lwcf.htm⟩.

————. National Park Service (NPS). 1938. *Recreational Use of Land in the United States: Part XI of the Report on Land Planning*. Washington, D.C.: U.S. Government Printing Office.

———. National Park Service (NPS). 1986, 1988, 1994. *Land Protection Plan, Blue Ridge Parkway: Virginia and North Carolina.* n.p.: Washington, D.C.: Department of the Interior.

———. National Park Service (NPS). 1988. *Land Protection Plan, Acadia National Park. Bar Harbor Maine.* Washington, D.C.: Department of the Interior.

———. National Park Service (NPS). 1991. *Acadia National Park: General Management Plan and Environmental Assessment.* Denver, Col.: Department of the Interior.

———. National Park Service (NPS). 1991–2000. Public Use Statistics Office. "National Park Service Statistical Abstract." ⟨http://www2.nature.nps.gov/stats/⟩ and ⟨http://www2.nature.nps.gov/stats/abstractmain.htm⟩.

———. National Park Service (NPS). 1993. *Independence National Historical Park Statement for Management. S.l.* Washington, D.C.: Department of the Interior.

———. National Park Service (NPS). 2001. "Appropriations from the Land & Water Conservation Fund." On file with authors.

———. National Park Service (NPS). 2002a. "Gettysburg Replants Battlefield Thicket." *Gettysburg Quarterly: The Official Newsletter of Gettysburg National Military Park* 9(3): 1.

———. National Park Service (NPS). 2002b. "Return to 1863 Field Sizes Funded by New Farm Program." *Gettysburg Quarterly: The Official Newsletter of Gettysburg National Military Park* 9(3): 2.

———. National Park Service (NPS). 2002c. Public Use Statistics Office. "List of Acreages by Park 9/30/02." ⟨http://www2.nature.nps.gov/stats/acrebypark02fy.pdf⟩.

———. National Park Service (NPS). n.d. "St. Louis Revisited 1930-present." Jefferson National Expansion Memorial. ⟨http://www.nps.gov/jeff/lmore4.htm⟩.

———. National Park Service (NPS) and California Department of Parks and Recreation. 2000. *Redwood National and State Parks, Humboldt and Del Norte Counties, California: General Management Plan/General Plan.* Denver, Col.: Department of the Interior; Sacramento: California Department of Parks and Recreation.

———. National Park Service (NPS) and California Department of Forestry. 1978. Additional Lands, Redwood National Park: Humboldt County, California. Map 167-80,005-D. Washington, D.C.: U.S. National Park Service.

———. National Resources Planning Board (NRPB). 1940. Land Committee. *Public Land Acquisition in a National Land-Use Program: Report of the Land Committee to the National Resources Planning Board.* Washington, D.C.: U.S. Government Printing Office.

———. Natural Resources Conservation Service (NRCS). n.d.a. A Story of Land and People. ⟨http://www.nrcs.usda.gov/about/history/story.html⟩, last visited Nov. 22, 2004.

————. Natural Resources Conservation Service (NRCS). n.d.b. Highly Erodable Land Conservation Fact Sheet. ⟨http://www.nrcs.usda.gov/programs/helc/HELCfact3.html⟩.

————. Office of the Inspector General (OIG). 1996. *Nevada Land Exchange Activities*. 96-I-1025. Sacramento, Calif.: Office of the Inspector General, Western Region.

————. Office of the Inspector General (OIG). 2001. *Land Exchanges and Acquisitions, Bureau of Land Management, Utah State Office*. Report No. 2001-I-413. Sacramento, Calif.: Office of the Inspector General, Western Region.

————. Outdoor Recreation Resources Review Commission (ORRRC). 1963. *Report: Recreation in America*. Washington, D.C.: Government Printing Office.

————. Public Land Law Review Commission. 1970. *One Third of the Nation's Land: A Report to the President and to the Congress*. Washington, D.C.: U.S. Government Printing Office.

————. Southern Appalachian National Park Commission and Henry Willson Temple. 1931. *Final Report of the Southern Appalachian National Park Commission to the Secretary of the Interior, June 30, 1931*. Washington, D.C.: U.S. Government Printing Office.

University of Missouri, St. Louis. 2002. "Jefferson National Expansion Memorial." St. Louis Virtual City Project. May 17. ⟨http://www.umsl.edu/~virtualstl/phase2/1950/buildings/jeffersonexpansion.html⟩.

Unrau, Harlan D. 1991. *Gettysburg National Military Park and National Cemetery Pennsylvania: Administrative History*. Denver, Col.: National Park Service.

Unrau, Harlan D. and G. Frank Williss. 1983. *Administrative History: Expansion of the National Park Service in the 1930s*. Denver, Col.: National Park Service, Denver Service Center. ⟨http://www.cr.nps.gov/history/online_books/unrau-williss/adhi.htm⟩.

Valley Conservation Council. 2004. Agricultural/Forestal Districts Fact Sheet. ⟨http://www.valleyconservation.org/agforfacts.html⟩, last visited Nov. 16, 2004.

Vandilk, John M. 1997. "Waiting for Uncle Sam to Buy the Farm . . . Forest, or Wetland? A Call for New Emphasis on State and Local Land Use Controls in Natural Resource Protection." *Fordham Environmental Law Journal* 8(3): 691–712.

Vermont Agency of Natural Resources. 2002. "Final Management Plan for the West Mountain Wildlife Management Area (WMA)." ⟨http://www.state.vt.us/anr/fpr/lands/champion/westmt/final.pdf⟩.

Vermont Land Trust. 2001. "Champion Lands Project: Press Release on Easement Clarification—West Mountain WMA Partners Announce Clarifications to Easement." Nov. 31. ⟨http://www.vlt.org/CIpressrelease.html⟩.

Vaskov, Nicholas G. 2001–2002. "Continued Cartographic Chaos, Or a New Paradigm in Public Land Reconfiguration? The Effect of New Laws Authorizing

Limited Sales of Public Land." *UCLA Journal of Environmental Law and Policy* 20: 79–108.

Vileisis, Ann. 1999. *Discovering the Unknown Landscape: A History of America's Wetlands*. Washington, D.C.: Island Press.

Vowell, Sarah. 2002. *The Partly Cloudy Patriot*. New York: Simon & Schuster.

Warren, George Washington. 1877. *The History of the Bunker Hill Monument Association During the First Century of the United States of America*. Boston: J. R. Osgood.

Waterson, Merlin. 1994. *The National Trust: The First One Hundred Years*. London: BBC Books; The National Trust.

Watt, Laura A. 2001. "Managing Cultural Landscapes: Reconciling Local Preservation and Institutional Ideology in the National Park Service." Ph.D. diss., University of California, Berkeley.

Weideger, Paula. 1994. *Gilding the Acorn: Behind the Façade of the National Trust*. London: Simon & Schuster.

Wentworth, Rand. 2002. "President's Address." Land Trust Alliance Rally, Austin, Texas.

———. 2004. "Senate Finance Committee Pushes Reforms—LTA Proposes New Ethical *Standards and Practices*." *Exchange* 23(2): 3.

Westbrook, Nick, n.d. "Chain of Title to the Garrison Grounds at Ticonderoga." On file with authors.

Westbrook, Virginia. 2001. *Relishing Our Resources: Along Lake Champlain in Essex County, New York*. Crown Point, N.Y.: Champlain Valley Heritage Network.

Wheatley, Charles F. 1970. *Study of Land Acquisition and Exchanges Related to Retention and Management or Disposition of Federal Public Lands*. Prepared for the Public Land Law Review Commission. Washington, D.C.: Public Land Law Review Commission.

Whyte, William. 1968. *The Last Landscape*. Garden City, N.Y.: Doubleday.

Wilkinson, Todd. 2000. "Battlefields' New Enemy: Strip Malls." *Christian Science Monitor* July 11, p. 1. ⟨http://www.csmonitor.com/durable/2000/07/11/fp1s3-csm.shtml⟩.

Williams, Norman, Jr. 1962. *Land Acquisition for Outdoor Recreation—Analysis of Selected Legal Problems*. Report to the ORRRC, Study Report 16. Washington, D.C.: U.S. Government Printing Office.

Williamson, Lonnie L. 1987. "Evolution of a Landmark Law." In Harmon Kallman, ed., *Restoring America's Wildlife, 1937–1987: The First 50 Years of the Federal Aid in Wildlife Restoration (Pittman-Robertson) Act*. Washington, D.C.: Fish and Wildlife Service.

Wilson, James Q. 1975. "The Rise of the Bureaucratic State." *The Public Interest* 41: 77–103.

Wirth, Conrad. 1980. *Parks, Politics, and the People.* Norman: University of Oklahoma Press.

Wohlberg, Beth. 2000. "No recreation fees—for now." *High Country News* August 14. ⟨http://www.hcn.org/servlets/hcn.Article?article_id=5936⟩.

Wong, Jennifer M. 1997. "A Forgotten History: The Virtual Slavery of the Alaskan Aleutians and the Initial Cluster of United States Wildlife Refuges." Paper on file with the authors.

Wood, Virginia Steele. 1981. *Live Oaking: Southern Timber for Tall Ships.* Boston: Northeastern University Press.

Wooten, H. H. 1965. *The Land Utilization Program 1934 to 1964: Origin, Development, and Present Status.* Agricultural Economic Report No. 85. Washington, D.C.: U.S. Department of Agriculture, Economic Research Service.

Wright, John B. 1993. *Rocky Mountain Divide: Selling and Saving the West.* Austin: University of Texas Press.

Wuerthner, George. 1988. *The Adirondacks: Forever Wild.* Helena, Mont.: American Geographic Publishers.

Yard, Robert Sterling. 1928. *Our Federal Lands: A Romance of American Development.* New York: Scribner.

Zinn, Jeffrey. 2001. *Land and Water Conservation Fund: Current Status and Issues.* CRS Report 97-792. National Library for the Environment, March 16. Washington, D.C.: Congressional Research Service, Library of Congress. ⟨http://cnie.org/NLE/CRSreports/Public/pub-1.cfm⟩.

Cases Cited

Bailey v. Holland, 126 F. 2d 317 (4th Cir. 1942).

Buskirk v. Adirondack Park Agency, no. 401-91 (N.Y. Sup Ct., Essex Cty, filed Aug. 13, 1991).

Camfield v. United States, 167 U.S. 518 (1897).

Coggeshall v. United States, 95 F.2d 986, 989 (4th Cir. 1938).

County of Santa Clara v. Southern Pac. Ry. Co., 118 U.S. 394 (1886).

Dolan v. City of Tigard, 114 L. Ct. 2319 (1994).

Euclid v. Ambler Realty Co., 272 U.S. 365 (1926).

First English Evangelical Lutheran Church of Glendale v. County of Los Angeles, 482 U.S. 304 (1987).

Fort Leavenworth R. Co. v. Lowe, 114 U.S. 525 (1885).

Geer v. Connecticut, 161 U.S. 519 (1896).

Griffin v. United States, 58 F.2d 674 (1932).

Hughes v. Oklahoma, 441 U.S. 322 (1979).

Hutchings v. Low, 82 U.S. 77 (1872).

Kleppe v. New Mexico, 426 U.S. 529 (1976).

Kohl et al. v. United States, 91 U.S. 367; 23 L. Ed. 449 (1875).

Light v. United States, 220 U.S. 523 (1911).

Lochner v. New York, 198 U.S. 45 (1905).

Lucas v. South Carolina Coastal Council, 505 U.S. 1003 (1992).

Missouri v. Holland, 252 U.S. 346 (1920).

Munn v. Illinois, 94 U.S. 113 (1877).

Nollan v. California Coastal Commission, 483 U.S. 825 (1987).

Pennsylvania Coal Co. v. Mahon, 260 U.S. 393 (1922).

Sierra Club v. Department of the Interior, 376 F.Supp 90 (1974).

Sierra Club v. Department of the Interior, 398 F.Supp 284 (1975).

Sierra Club v. Department of the Interior, 424 F.Supp 172 (1976).

Tahoe Sierra Preservation Council v. Tahoe Regional Planning Agency, 122 S.Ct. 1465 (2002).

Trombley v. Humphrey, 23 Mich. 471 (1871).

Tennessee Environmental Council, Inc., et al. v. Bright Par 3 Associates, L. P., et al., No. E2003-01982-COA-R3-CV (Tenn. Ct. App. Mar. 8, 2004).

United States. v. 365.0 Acres of Land in Augusta County, Virginia, 428 F.2d 459 (4th Cir, Va 1970).

United States v. Beavans, 16 U.S. 336 (1811).

United States v. Butler, 297 U.S. 1 (1936).

United States v. Carmack, 329 U.S. 230 (1946).

United States v. Cornell, 25 F. Cas. 646, No. 14,867 (C.C.D.R.I., 1819).

United States v. Gettysburg Elec. R. Co., 160 U.S. 668 (1896).

United States v. Grimaud, 220 U.S. 506 (1911).

United States v. Hunting Rights to Swan Lake Hunting Club, 237 F. Supp. 290 (N.D. Miss. 1964).

United States v. Montana, 134 F.2d 194 (9th Cir. 1943).

United States v. San Francisco, 310 U.S. 16 (1940).

United States v. Shauver, 214 F. 154 (1914).

United States v. Shauver, 248 U.S. 594 (1919).

United States v. Three Tracts of Land Containing a Total of 1,174 Acres More or Less, in Jackson County Alabama, 377 F.Supp 631 (1974).

West Coast Hotel Co. v. Parrish et al., 300 U.S. 379, 57 S. Ct. 578 (1937).

Whitman v. American Trucking Association, 121 S.Ct. 903 (2001).

Young v. Anderson, 160 F.2d 225 (D.C. Cir. 1947).

Index

0